THE CHICAGO

NAACP

AND THE

RISE OF BLACK

PROFESSIONAL

LEADERSHIP,

1910–1966

BLACKS IN THE DIASPORA

Darlene Clark Hine, John McCluskey, Jr., and David Barry Gaspar
GENERAL EDITORS

THE CHICAGO

NAACP

AND THE
RISE OF BLACK
PROFESSIONAL
LEADERSHIP,
1910–1966

Christopher Robert Reed

INDIANA UNIVERSITY PRESS / BLOOMINGTON & INDIANAPOLIS

The paper used in this publication meets the minimum requirements of American National Standard for Information Sciences—Permanence of Paper for Printed Library Materials, ANSI Z39.48–1984.
(∞)™

Manufactured in the United States of America

Reed, Christopher Robert.
The Chicago NAACP and the rise of black professional leadership, 1910–1966 / Christopher Robert Reed.
p.   cm. — (Blacks in the diaspora)
Includes index.
ISBN 0–253–33313–X (cloth : alk. paper)
1. National Association for the Advancement of Colored People. Chicago Branch—History.
2. Afro-Americans—Civil rights—Illinois—Chicago—History—20th century.
3. Afro-American leadership—Illinois—Chicago—History—20th century.
4. Chicago (Ill.)—Race relations.
I. Title   II. Series.
F548.9.N4R44   1997
305.896´073077311—dc21   97–9017

1 2 3 4 5   02 01 00 99 98 97

CONTENTS

Contents

PREFACE

FADED MEMORY AND THE OUTCOME of intellectual curiosity intersected in 1987 to stimulate my interest in writing this book. Viscerally, I have vivid childhood memories of Chicago's legendary and influential Bronzeville, the African American South Side enclave recognized nationally for decades because of its politics, businesses, churches, and various entertainments. One indelible recollection involves the sight and sounds of civil rights activists, marching near our longtime family home at 3159 South Parkway, and their determined, rhythmic chants: "Jim Crow must go! Jim Crow must go!" I tucked this recollection away for almost four decades until cognitively I connected it, almost in a revelatory manner, with the substance of a 1987 article I completed on the professional origins of local black civic leadership.

This piece, titled "Black Chicago Civic Organization before 1935," challenged the contention that black Chicagoans lacked a socially differentiated class structure and the necessary will to support a civic infrastructure before the Civil Rights Revolution of the 1960s.[1] Assuming that the evidence I presented proved the case to the contrary, the article allowed me to link the type of civil rights advocacy I remembered from the 1940s with its earliest roots as established through scholarship. While I cannot accurately recall which of the South Side's many protest organizations initiated the particular action that is embedded in my memory, one certainty emerged; the one organization that had achieved primacy in the city as *the* agency of African American protest between 1933 and 1957 was the Chicago branch of the National Association for the Advancement of Colored People (NAACP). So, perhaps it was the branch. However, the exact identity of the group was and is not as important as the makeup of its leadership, its rootedness in the protest tradition, and the character of its activities and the consequences that resulted.

Significantly, what I could now clearly reminisce about and understand represented a major part of the essence of a perpetually evolving African American urban history. A discernible black professional class emerged around the time of the first World War and tested its mettle in confronting and surmounting racial obstacles, balancing disparate working-class and

Preface

middle-class agendas, and seeking harmony among the various kinds of relationships possible in Chicago's highly charged political arena.[2] With the emergence of the Chicago NAACP in 1910 an ideal channel, or vehicle, through which to express the professional class's agenda of attaining the American Dream appeared. As a professional-led organization, the Chicago NAACP reached its fruition during the 1920s and 1930s, experienced its maturation during the 1940s and 1950s, and faced its near dislodgement by the incipient militant working-class (Black Power) thrust of the 1960s.

Once it assumed vanguard status, the Chicago NAACP contributed substantially to civic improvement and the political awakening that black Chicagoans experienced in succeeding decades. As the branch positioned itself to become an effective vehicle for social change, it inevitably threatened groups and organizations heavily vested in the protection of the racial status quo. It planted, therefore, the seeds of its own possible demise at some point in the future. Yet, as part of the burgeoning network of vigilance committees (which were quickly transformed into branches), the Chicago NAACP early and easily secured its place in history. Its programmatic thrust either opened or contributed to opening the doors of equal opportunity in housing, employment, education, and public accommodations. By the 1930s, its leadership style provided a model of constrained, mainstream militancy (during a decade of provocative rhetoric) that was emulated by other branches nationwide as well as by local civil rights groups. Its unswerving commitment to racial equality shaped a new mindset, particularly among African Americans; from this base a perpetual resistance to second-class status grew. By 1959, the branch boasted of having the largest membership within the NAACP based on its proven service. Even the election of Harold Washington in 1983 as the city's first black mayor tapped obliquely into this legacy of fomenting anti-Establishment protest and endorsing bedrock democracy.

In less than a generation after reaching its apogee, the saga of the Chicago branch and its professional leadership faded into obscurity, even in the minds of many who participated in its making. Several factors contributed to its fall into historical oblivion, beginning with the destruction of local branch records by fire. Meanwhile, an organizational history, proposed by branch leader Archie L. Weaver in the early 1950s, was never completed; so, posterity was further deprived of essential knowledge about the Chicago NAACP. Moreover, the branch's growing programmatic effectiveness and formidableness represented a challenge to the hegemony of Congressman William L. Dawson's political machine in the mid–1950s, making a subsequent confrontation inevitable, along with the branch's slide from civil rights leadership. This clash was especially pivotal because in its aftermath other civil rights advocates grew to distrust the branch's motivations, so they facilely dismissed the Chicago NAACP's contemporary as well as its past accomplishments.[3]

Preface

Late in the decade of the 1960s, timely and favorable circumstances brought the official opening of *The Papers of the NAACP* at the Library of Congress in Washington, D.C., facilitating research into the dynamics of the national organization and most of its branches. Scholarship dealing with national office activities was soon forthcoming in massive volume.[4] Fortunately, the opportunity existed for a full-length study of the Association's first affiliate, which was organized in Chicago in 1910. Beyond the extensive holdings that comprised the *NAACP Papers*, additional archival materials, housed at the Library of Congress and elsewhere in Washington, and also in Madison and Chicago, provided a virtual treasure trove of information on what the branch and its leadership did, how it operated, and why it was either passive or active at any particular point in its history. This book represents, largely, a work that is heavily archives-driven. However, information obtained from major secondary sources also contributed significantly to the substance of this study, especially that resulting from studies conducted under the auspices of the various academic departments at the University of Chicago, which analyzed the entire city as though it was its urban laboratory. The works of Charles S. Johnson, E. Franklin Frazier, and St. Clair Drake, all trained at the University of Chicago, formed the bases from which Chicago in the 1920s through the 1960s was better understood. Finally, direct interviews with some of the leading professional and nonprofessional participants and observers in this saga of urban class and institutional development lent an especially authentic tone to life as it was interpreted.

Interpreting African American life and thought in Chicago in depth rested on considering several major factors. First, the character of the city's African American population during the first two-thirds of the twentieth century lacked a presumed homogeneity. An indisputable heterogeneity, sometimes deliberately overlooked, endured despite the obvious expectations evident in the writings of outside observers. Changing conditions within the global, national, and local political economies, as well as internal group differences, all intersected: These elements included socioeconomic class, gender, pigmentation, education, occupation and professional attainment, and, appropriately for a city of migrants, provenance. Beyond transformations in space, temporal conditions produced an urban, sometimes cosmopolitan, population that better supported both the NAACP movement and the concept of racial equality by World War II than it had in previous decades.

Scholarly analyses of black Chicago society and culture before the prosperity of the 1920s concluded that African Americans lacked a class structure based on clearly defined economic criteria. Sociologist St. Clair Drake's 1940 description of turn-of-the-century social stratification provided a glimpse of a society that included refined persons, respectables, and undesirables, different because of cultural attributes rather than levels and modes of economic acquisition.[5] In contrast, historian Allen Spear wrote in 1967 of a black community led by an upper-class elite grounded in one variant of a racial ideology that yielded its hegemony sometime around 1905 to a rising middle-class business group firmly rooted in a competing ideological variant that had an economic mooring. Both groups, amazingly, were so small as Spear depicted them as to be barely discernible among the 30,000 African Americans in the city.[6] In contrast, what historian Kenneth M. Kusmer found for Cleveland at the same period appeared more applicable for Chicago because his framework explained the presence within the branch's leadership of such a universally influential person as African American Dr. Charles E. Bentley, an incomparable professional. Bentley, whose role is examined closely in this text, represented an elite leader with an influence far beyond the limits of a 1905 pivot.[7]

When historian Robert H. Wiebe encountered this problem of identifying class strata in his study of the roots of progressivism, he explained it as follows: "[I]n part, the new middle class was a class only by courtesy of the historian's afterthought."[8] This explanation aptly applied to Bronzeville. Whatever the truth of the matter, the Great Migration of 1915–1918 contributed significantly to the emergence of a discernible middle class by the 1920s. As part of the phenomenon of global war, black class formation and restructuring were replicated in the post–World War II period, affecting the Chicago NAACP in a most salutary manner. The emergence of the middle class confirmed the existence of a social group previously overlooked and needed to provide indigenous, professional leadership in the cause of civil rights. And, with this group's constantly rising expectations, racial advocacy in the twin spheres of civics and politics served as major channels through which it sought egalitarian attainment.

When sociologists St. Clair Drake and Horace R. Cayton broached the subject of interracial relationships, they encountered sundry contradictions. While the lifestyles of the Caucasian elite and middle-class reformers were unique to a privileged white world, these close observers of the South Side postulated that, in contrast, "Bronzeville's upper class [was] a well-trained but only moderately well-to-do group [which had] more leisure time than the rank and file, but nevertheless [had to] work for a living."[9] This latter group, in reality a middle class, along with the growing clusters of working-class blacks dispersed throughout South Side and West Side neighborhoods, was determined to achieve racial equality so that one day there would be a black leisure class to enjoy the full fruits of American citizenship. Just how the middle class and working class resolved their inherent differences and interacted to promote racial advancement demonstrated the overwhelming, pervasive strength of racial pride, consciousness, and solidarity in African American life.

A second factor was the recognition of organizational strength. The Chicago NAACP demanded treatment as a powerful, influential entity in its own right. More than ample documentation affirmed its ability to sustain a locus of power despite its relationship with a much more powerful central office in New York. As the branch demonstrated organizational vitality, it was clearly a case in which an administrative hierarchy composed of black professionals shaped its operations to meet the needs and aspirations of a rapidly urbanizing population moving toward cosmopolitanism.[10] As I searched for this locus of power, I located the impetus for decision-making and organizational direction as originating within the presidency. The process of identifying from among the professional cadre those qualified to lead the branch drew upon two groups and employed two methods. The Executive Committee, which was the governing body, and the black community at large acted as reservoirs of potential leadership. Presidents were selected by power brokers from 1913 until 1946 and elected through contentious, democratic means from 1948 through 1960 and beyond. The former method contributed to the sometimes oligarchic rule that marked early branch history; the latter provided evidence of its maturation. Despite the constancy of internecine struggle about which person or group would control its internal locus of power, this was never a case of village infighting for its own sake. Rather, *real* power shifts and the growing accessibility to positions of influence by black Chicagoans motivated these actions.

The third factor embraced a recognition that no Chicagoan or any onlooker seeking the source of the city's vitality in the twentieth century could ever overlook the importance of the Chicago strain of politics (encompassing partisan, machine-dominated Chicago party activities and politicized government). Politics overlapped and interacted with increasing regularity with the Chicago NAACP's organization, programmatic activities, and ideology. The interest of all Chicagoans in the dynamics of politics *was* and *is* of such importance that the activities emanating from this sphere influenced the civic activities of the branch and its professional leadership. Indeed, Chicago's politicized government and political parties formed an integral part of the saga of the Chicago NAACP. Whereas the political machines of Republican William "Big Bill" Thompson and Democrats Anton Cermak, Edward J. Kelly, and Richard J. Daley affected the branch dramatically, so did its black components, led, beginning in 1915, by an indigenous, semi-independent, professional political leadership, which continued through the 1960s.[11]

Under the influence of Edward "The Iron Master" Wright, Oscar De Priest, and William L. Dawson (who once held meetings in the parlor at 3159 South Parkway), blacks within the civic and political spheres progressed through three phases of political development unique to black Chicago. Between 1885 and 1915, the relationship rested on a symbiotic arrangement highlighted by the black-initiated passage of the Illinois Civil Rights Act in 1885. The election of the first black member of the Chicago City Council in 1915 began another phase, one marked with cooperation.

Preface

This cooperation gave way to competition and antagonism with the formation of the Dawson machine by the late 1940s and early 1950s. The neutralization of the Chicago NAACP as the city's primary civil rights organization resulted from this antagonism as Dawson committed black political energies and resources to his "party first, race second" doctrine. The character of this civic-political arrangement depended significantly more often than not on whatever developmental phase the black machine had entered than on any other factors of politics, civics, or civil rights.

An overlooked indigenous leadership of immense talents served as a fourth factor to be considered. This convinced me over time to reject any unconscious reliance on the timeworn "Great Man" theory in history to account for the subtle, definitive, or indeterminate meanings of historical events. Extant data invalidated any extraordinary influence or power wielded by members of either gender—including the likes of Jane Addams, Ida B. Wells-Barnett, and Julius Rosenwald—over the branch during its earliest days. In a similar vein, as the branch reached the mid-century mark, neither U.S. Representative William L. Dawson nor Mayor Richard J. Daley shaped the branch's course of action deliberately and directly. That all five individuals had some influence to varying degrees is acknowledged, but none exercised ultimate power or influence as is popularly assumed. On the other hand, three individuals within the branch distinguished themselves in terms of their contributions to the cause of racial advancement, each serving the organization for over forty years and more, until his or her death. They were Archie L. Weaver (serving from 1910 to 1958), Earl B. Dickerson (c. 1910–1916 to 1986), and Beatrice Hughes Steele (1939 to 1991).

Acknowledgment of the epochal influences of the twentieth century, manifested in two world wars along with global economic depression and superpower ideological conflict, shaped the chronology of this narrative. Chapter divisions embraced three distinct periods: from the Progressive Era through 1916; from the advent of the First to the end of the Second World War (1917 through 1945); and from the post–World War II era to 1958. An epilogue analyzes the branch's place in the modern civil rights movement of the 1960s when Dr. Martin Luther King, Jr. arrived in Chicago to lead civil rights demonstrations (and eventually disposed of the name South Parkway as well as some of its oldest memories).

Significantly, these black Chicagoans who led or served the branch are treated as *subjects* making history rather than as *objects* of policy decisions enacted by others. A revised focus on agency replaces a previous one centering on passivity and victimization. Lastly, it is my hope that as this history contributes to a better understanding of African American history and race reform movements, it also meets the challenge of historians of the last several decades who called for a fuller investigation into the meaning of the urban African American experience in its own right and also contextually.[12]

DEDICATION AND ACKNOWLEDGMENTS

**To the Old Ones who sacrificed.
To the Old Ones who nurtured and directed me—
and who still do so today.**

I wish to thank the archival staffs at the Library of Congress, the Chicago Historical Society, the Historical Society of Wisconsin, the University of Chicago, and the University of Illinois at Chicago for their assistance over the past two decades. Further, my appreciation runs deep for faculty comments and criticisms since 1987. Especially supportive were Elizabeth Balanoff, Brigitte M. Erbe, Lawrence Frank, and Lynn Y. Weiner at Roosevelt University. From the University of Michigan, Hanes Walton, Jr. shared his insight into the pervasive political dimensions of African American thought and behavior, even in ostensibly civic organizations such as the Chicago NAACP. Attorney Chester S. Beattie, Jr. of Austin, Texas proved an especially incisive reader and critic, while Marionette C. Phelps and Theodore Rich plowed through the earliest versions of this work searching for truths and uncovering myths and errors. Patrick Weathersby, Lynnett Moore, and Jearlean Fleming rendered important technical assistance through their word-processing skills at a time when the manuscript was in a totally unmanageable form. The editorial staff at the Indiana University Press, in particular Roberta Diehl and Joan Catapano, proved that humaneness still thrives in academe. Finally, my immediate family, Robert, Malcolm, William, Audrey, Ashley, and Dominique, remained supportive, always oblivious to the calendar. My wife, Marva, another child of the Bronzeville community and former *Chicago Defender* librarian, inspired while remaining constantly supportive. Of course, I alone bear the burden of answering inquiries into the many interpretations offered in this study.

1

Prologue: Making the NAACP Branch "a Necessity" in Chicago

> The most famous initials in America are
> N.A.A.C.P. . . . . The most written-about voluntary
> association in America is the N.A.A.C.P. The
> most damned group of citizens . . . is the
> N.A.A.C.P.
>
> —Langston Hughes, 1962

In 1933, Chicago NAACP president A. Clement MacNeal optimistically presented a strategic plan to his Executive Committee which called on the branch to make itself "a necessity" in the lives of black Chicagoans.[1] What MacNeal envisioned had been accomplished on the national level by James Weldon Johnson during the 1920s. As the Association's first black national secretary, Johnson moved the Association from organizational to institutional status in a process described by historian Joyce Barbara Ross as follows: "An organization is transformed into an institution when it becomes a product of social needs and pressures. The goals it seeks to fulfill and the functions it serves come to be viewed by the larger community as almost indispensable, even vital."[2] By the mid–1950s, after nearly half a century of dedication to the advancement of civil rights, this is the role the Chicago NAACP assumed and the image it merited on the eve of the Civil Rights struggle of the 1960s.

However, achieving institutional status ultimately depended on having the appropriate personnel available and ready to assume leadership positions. This indispensable cadre took on the responsibility of explaining the nature of the challenge facing African Americans as they sought attainment of their contemporary social needs. Further, they devised strategies and adopted tactics aimed at remediation to insure advancement along the axis of race for the emerging middle class and masses. Renowned sociologist E. Franklin Frazier, an acute social observer as well as a participant in Chicago life, analyzed the elements that produced this leadership as early as 1928: "The most significant aspect of this development is the emergence of an intellectual leadership which is not dependent for status upon the Colored group but stands upon the intrinsic worth of its achievements."[3] From the post–World War I years on, a group of professionals—first physicians, later attorneys—led the Chicago NAACP. Their very existence was impressive, given the nation's racial discriminatory practices. Moreover, their occupational attainments represented triumph in a national arena which was urbanizing as an expression of its modernity and had come to rely on specialized, competitively educated personnel to fill its infrastructure.

Achieving institutional status, the ultimate *triumph,* depended on how well the Chicago NAACP advanced through a series of *trials,* or tests and experiments, to prove its right to exist, as well as a host of *tribulations,* or adversities. The abolitionist crusade of the antebellum period inspired activism on behalf of racial equality not only in its own era, which extended through the Reconstruction, but again at the dawn of the twentieth century. This revival of the highest ideals of American society, democratic inclusion and equality of opportunity irrespective of racial origins and skin color, produced the NAACP movement in 1909 and, within the wake of its fervor, a neo-abolitionist crusade for equal rights. The second goal of nineteenth-century abolitionism, the extension of citizenship rights, was revived under the rubric of the "New Abolition" by the children, grandchildren, and intellectual heirs of the original abolitionists.[4] This was the first trial—to overcome a national mindset steeped in racism. Almost as an attestation to the validity of the belief in linear progress, the ideal of racial equality grew and matured until, by the time of global conflagration and superpower ideological conflict at mid-century, it had become part of American public policy everywhere except in the South. Its early, limited ideological acceptance was enhanced by the continuous demographic and economic changes taking place in Chicago which served to increase its relevance. Another trial demanded that whites and blacks develop a mutual sense of *trust,* based on cooperative, altruistic interaction. This relationship was thought to be achievable if the two races could overcome a *distrust* rooted in suspicions emanating from the legacy of slavery along with existing racism. *Mistrust,* by degrees, became less insurmountable once confidence in cross-racial intentions was established and yielded to the best in humanity in the positive milieu following the end of World War II. Finally, an indigenous leadership was needed to direct a programmatic thrust that reflected the aspirations of the African American people.

The Chicago NAACP experienced its share of tribulations in attempting to establish organizational viability and relevance to the needs of its constituents in the way of interracial and intraracial class division, with political challenges as well as civic competition, and with gender differences. Social change in the nation and in Chicago dramatically altered and advantageously favored the branch's chances for success. The elevation in class status among black Chicagoans, along with collaboration across class lines in pursuit of a common goal, was singular. The fortuitous circumstance of encountering a friendly, indigenous political machine (until a mid-century clash changed the relationship) prevented the smothering of the branch during its formative period. The persistence demonstrated by Chicago NAACP and other equal rights advocates never to relinquish their dream of a color-blind America served as exemplary models over decades for the eventual broad popular support that was finally manifested by mid-century. The emerging role of women as branch leaders also proved revolutionary as well as decisive in propelling the branch forward.

At its genesis during the Progressive Era, the branch began its interminable metamorphosis from committee to branch, from patriarchy to democracy, and from organization to institution. In 1910, after its organization as a vigilance committee, its success and power were linked integrally to its ability to attain organizational stability, programmatic relevance, and ideological acceptance. This process evolved through three distinct phases of hegemonic change. The first period covered the initial twenty-three years of the branch's existence, from 1910 through 1932. It featured a biracial patriarchy of men of high socioeconomic status, led by Judge Edward O. Brown, Dr. Charles E. Bentley, and attorney Harold L. Ickes. Their manner of leading the branch strangely conformed to racist expectations of black behavior and disturbed many blacks. Activism was avoided so as not to foment mass dissatisfaction with the status quo. Furthermore, accepted elitist notions as to the need of maintaining both social and physical distance between the hierarchy and the rank and file membership persisted. As a result, the black support that was needed to sustain the branch remained low. This deficiency also stymied fund-raising for both the local and national efforts. Finally, this patriarchy degenerated into an oligarchy which, in turn, contributed to the branch's enervation. For fifteen years, this coterie held sway until 1925 when a black patriarchy under doctors Carl G. Roberts and Herbert Turner's influence replaced it for slightly less than a decade. An experiment in unilateral racial leadership was set in place which generated an insatiable desire to retain it in perpetuity.

A second phase lasted fourteen years, from 1933 through 1946. The previous change to unilateral racial leadership signaled the probability of black middle-class involvement. With the advent of the New Deal period, a solidly black middle-class coterie did, in fact, lead the branch, with the former editor of the militant *Chicago Whip*, A. C. MacNeal, and attorney Irvin C. Mollison in command. The inclusive class composition of the branch throughout its hierarchy and membership, along with the assertiveness of its rising middle-class leadership, allowed democracy to take root. The branch's general membership increased as programmatic appeal broadened, making fund-raising not altogether impossible in spite of the Great Depression. After decades of languishing as an organization, the Chicago NAACP emerged during the Depression as a major force for racial equality. Nevertheless, it was not until the war years that the most important changes contributing to the democratization of the branch occurred. Economic opportunities, along with the democratizing influence of branch president Oscar C. Brown, Sr., produced a newly configured branch. A host of upwardly mobile blacks belonged; there was a return of white participation; and the representatives of organized labor found a home in which they could combine their economic and racial tenets of egalitarianism.

These *petit bourgeois* and working-class egalitarians assumed control under the leadership of postal organizer and leader Henry W. McGee, who took office in July 1946. This transition began the third phase and cemented democratic traditions within the branch's hierarchy as well as within the membership. With democracy, a new inclination developed. This tendency moved programmatic direction from a moderate strategy to a more militant approach as the expectations of blacks to experience the American Dream went unrealized.[5] Working-class elements joined the leadership and engaged in decision-making for the first time. Labor and left-wing activist participation increased, and the general population more readily accepted the branch as its advocate. As a result of this juncture, the Chicago NAACP achieved institutional status.

The clearest manifestation of what the Chicago NAACP attempted and accomplished appeared in its programmatic activities. Initially legalistic, persuasive, and legislative in form, and aimed at removing the vestiges of slavery as manifested in early twentieth century racism, the branch's plan of action and activities became a major force for racial change. Each decade seemed to bring innovations geared toward greater efficiency. During the Depression era, direct action—boycotting and picketing—enlarged the branch's arsenal of protest weapons, which already included court action, indignation meetings, lobbying, and letter writing. By the 1950s, mass assemblages and street demonstrations, along with quasi-political action, turned the branch into an extraordinarily aggressive pressure group. The scope of its programmatic concerns ranged from eliminating discrimination in employment, to objecting to exclusion in housing, to protesting inequities in education. Significantly, by the 1950s, the branch intensified its support for the efforts of its southern black brethren during the beginning of a third abolitionist crusade.[6] Further, it broadened its activities locally to include supporting blacks who were being prosecuted for felonious criminal acts, when the crime could be linked to the effects of societal racism.

What the branch accomplished organizationally and programmatically also rested on the *raison d'être* of the NAACP's existence and mission as embodied in its ideology. Formally, it is what New York racial egalitarian Joel E. Spingarn referred to as early as 1912 as the "New Abolition." In the folksier jargon of the barbershop, street corner, and social club headquarters, the slogan "the whole loaf or none at all" encapsulated the meaning of the struggle for full realization of equal rights. However, its incorporation into the American way of life depended on the widespread promotion of racial equality as part of a new public policy, along with its voluntary adoption as a personal attitude and pattern of behavior. The struggle to gain ideological acceptance extended from the dawn of the new century into the World War II era, when the nation finally evinced a major shift in its attitudes toward amicable race relations.

Chicago as the locus of this struggle for the "whole loaf" had existed as a hotbed of ideological contention throughout its history. Anti-slavery, or abolitionist, sentiment occupied center stage during the antebellum period, then yielded to pro-labor agitation in the Gilded Age. Early in the twentieth century, a new age dawned and with it came a near total acceptance among whites of the doctrine of Nordic superiority. Although some blacks rejected this notion of Anglo-Saxon supremacy, its pervasive influence convinced many of them to challenge their own worth and potential to compete as equals with whites. Many others chose a belief system that approximated the tenets of Booker T. Washington's accommodationist racial strategy. So, throughout the branch's history, the perceived militancy associated with racial equality met its counterbalance in racial moderation.

A major ideological strain evolving in the twenties (especially among the business class) was referred to as the "Dream of the Black Metropolis." The racially self-contained enclave of which it boasted embodied varying elements of egalitarianism—militant and moderate—along with black nationalism, depending on its adherents' interpretation. In the meantime, the nationalism of Marcus Garvey's Universal Negro Improvement Association grew as a potent force within the various black neighborhoods throughout Chicago.

In the following decade, the attitudes and values of Congressman Arthur W. Mitchell, an Alabaman by birth and a self-professed disciple of Booker T. Washington during his youth, exemplified moderation in race relations. Newly arrived southern migrants in 1915 and subsequent years also often held fatalistic views; consequently, they opposed racial equality with its antithetical promise of a better tomorrow and sought the practical and the immediate. By the late 1940s and into the next decade, Mitchell's successor in the Congress, William L. Dawson, acted as the voice of moderation at a time in the city when circumstances dictated immediate changes in race relations.

Other ideological influences were important and pervasive. From the Right, the influence of Garveyism in the 1920s yielded to the black Islamic revitalization of the Nation of Islam (the Black Muslim movement) in the 1950s. A number of blacks supported this ideology because of their longing for an existence free of American racism, separate if need be. And from the Left, Communism enjoyed its greatest popularity during the 1930s and remained a major force into the 1950s, until the rise of McCarthyism. Socialism emerged during the 1920s as a doctrine of interest and enjoyed a modicum of support through the 1950s as well.

The branch's attainment of institutional status by mid-century represented the culmination of a process of empowerment of one of the two major countervailing forces in Chicago's black community. One force was the race egalitarian or integrationist movement, which always aimed to make the American Dream a reality for black Chicagoans as soon as possible. Its primary vehicle was the Chicago branch of the NAACP. The other power was the black political machine. Led initially by Edward Wright and Oscar De Priest, it was affiliated with Mayor William "Big Bill" Thompson's Republican organization as well as with those at the county and state levels. After 1933, Democratic mayor Edward Kelly and the Cook County Democratic machine induced the black electorate to abandon its allegiance to and leadership within the Republican Party. William L. Dawson led this new Democratic bloc by the late 1940s and early 1950s.

By mid-century, the simultaneous empowerment of the two movements resulted in conflict and, finally, confrontation. Within the branch, the ascension of a professional leadership, albeit one owing its attitudes and values to its base in organized labor, came into power in January 1954. CIO organizer Willoughby Abner became chairman of the Executive Committee with a pliant president as his ally. Within two years, Abner assumed the presidency in his own right. His election placed a militant in the tradition of previous branch president A. C. MacNeal (who constantly challenged the Establishment and the status quo) at the head of the branch, which was the most viable and visible civil rights organization in black Chicago. Since Abner promoted a programmatic thrust that called for the organization of all blacks in the city on a precinct-to-precinct basis to seek immediate change in the racial status quo, black political leadership had understandably grown wary of NAACP intentions.

In the political sphere, the movement toward black political empowerment had been under way since even before 1915 when Oscar De Priest became the first black alderman on the Chicago City Council. Despite a major shift in party realignment that was two decades in coming, racial consciousness had remained constant and undergirded most black political behavior. So, whether Republican or Democratic, racial advancement remained as a major focus. Around 1955, Congressman Dawson solidified his power over five black wards in the city and strengthened his influence over virtually all black political life. In Dawson's agenda for race advancement, party politics assumed preeminence over all other considerations. As the congressman assumed power and spoke as a major voice in the emerging Daley machine, his tendency toward silence, or, more correctly, the avoidance of public utterances on matters of racial advancement, increased. Once the independent leadership of the branch publicly challenged Dawson's stance on the future of racial advancement, the battle ensued.

2

Progressive-Era Chicago, 1900–1919

The problem of the twentieth century is the problem of the color line—the relation of the darker to the lighter races of men in Asia and Africa, in America and the islands of the sea.

—W. E. B. Du Bois, 1903

We strangely force one race to demand as a right what is given from God.

—Jane Addams, 1911

THE PROGRESSIVE THRUST sweeping the nation maintained its dynamism in Chicago for over two decades while reaching its peak between 1907 and 1911.[1] However, its predominantly White Anglo-Saxon Protestant adherents lacked the vision and will to extend its benefits equally to all of the city's residents. Part of the reason was extant demographics; simultaneously, ideology played an equally important role. In census years 1900 and 1910 the small black population of 30,150 and 44,103, respectively, virtually disappeared among a Chicago citizenry reaching 1.7 and 2.2 million.[2] Yet, in contrast to its limited size, the black presence in the American psyche loomed huge, posing a major problem for those progressives accustomed to ignoring the need for racial justice as well as those committed to challenging and eliminating racism. Generations of entrenched, negative assumptions concerning race converged in early twentieth century American thought to proffer ideas that challenged primarily the necessity and then the character and means of recognizing the African American quest for full citizenship rights.

Relations between the two races conformed to a superordinate-subordinate arrangement disturbingly analogous at times to a caste system.

This racial system rationalized opposition to any demonstration of black racial advancement by denying its possibility, first theoretically, and then through the distorted interpretation of observable conditions and facts. "We must not forget," W. E. B. Du Bois wrote in 1903, "that most Americans answer all queries regarding the Negro *a priori.*"[3]

The preponderance of the nation's progressives thus interpreted the level of existing black material deprivation and social disorganization as an affirmation of what probability foreshadowed. Moreover, they linked it speciously to a mythical black genetic inferiority and a predetermined place for every group in the world's racial pecking order. To these ideologues, impoverishment and crime represented distinct black racial defects. Challenging this perception in its first annual report, the NAACP declared that "it abhor[red] Negro crime, but still more the conditions which bre[d] crime, and most of all the crimes committed by mobs in the mocking of the law, or by individuals in the name of the law."[4] Within this ideological climate, South Carolina's one-eyed, race-baiting senator, Benjamin "Pitchfork Ben" Tillman, visited Chicago during the Progressive Era, sharing with his cohorts instructions on how to maintain racist controls over the black Chicagoans.

When Chicago's white progressives, whose ranks comprised members of the professions and included religious leaders, social workers, educators, and social scientists, embraced morality as a desirable social end, they targeted prostitution, gambling, and alcohol abuse that pervaded the city, but more likely than not misdiagnosed the root causes.[5] Likewise, in pursuit of a civic remedy to the problems evident in inadequate, deteriorating, and exorbitantly priced slum housing, the city's progressive leaders failed miserably. Even Daniel Burnham's *Chicago Plan [of Civic Betterment]* in 1909, his brilliantly conceived plan for a symmetrically designed city, emphasized grand boulevards, parks, and magnificent public buildings and ignored the need for housing for the working men and women who built the "City of the Big Shoulders." The city's social settlement workers and social scientists did no better. They investigated, exposed, but usually disregarded solutions aimed at eliminating the city's slums. Meanwhile, Chicago supported a morally offensive color line that forced African Americans into subservient occupations and segregated pockets of housing.

Chicago's racial milieu degenerated to such an extent in 1910 that renowned black dentist and race equality advocate Dr. Charles E. Bentley became uneasy "in launching any new movement for a cause as unpopular as ours."[6] Moreover, this degeneration alarmed Jane Addams, who observed: "Not only in the South, but everywhere in America, a strong race antagonism is asserting itself, which has modes of lawlessness and insolence. The contemptuous attitude of the so-called superior race toward the inferior results in a social segregation of each race."[7] Her friend, the Rev. Celia Parker Woolley, was equally disturbed, and, on the occasion of the golden anniversary of the issuance of the Emancipation Proclamation, shared her perception that the white race had to "emancipate [it]self from that race arrogance and belief in [its] own inherent superiority and right of rule which is today the greatest obstacle in the Negro's path."[8]

The insidious and pervasive influence of this racism went neither unnoticed nor unchallenged by a minority of progressives who were racial egalitarians. They took the sobriquet that found its expression in "neo-abolitionism." Yet, even they encountered opposition from within the liberal progressive coalition. In 1917, Chicago Urban League supporter L. Hollingsworth Wood regarded the adherents of immediatism on the issue of racial equality as dreamers of the impractical. What he disdained as theoretical was an ideology embracing the ideal of equality between the races that was basically economic and political in character and sometimes even social. Sometimes overtly and, at times, covertly, a dichotomy grew between groups of white and black Chicago progressives. The distinguishing factor between the groups hinged on their support for either an immediatist or a gradualist strategy of racial advancement.

By 1909, the enthusiasm for reform created a milieu in which neo-abolitionists could adopt the theory of racial equality as a working possibility, firm in the belief that this ideology would liberate both whites and blacks from the shackles of racism. The extent to which this ideology gained acceptance was conditioned by the time and place it appeared as much as by the energy expended on its behalf. The time could not have appeared more propitious to progressives of the neo-abolitionist persuasion because the notion of change was becoming pervasive.

Quite often the neo-abolitionists were given to moralistic outbursts and stances that gave their activities the appearance of a crusade. With a moral fervor that bordered on righteousness, this intensity and inclination toward ideological purity became indispensable to the fulfillment of the organization's mission. Given the zealous abolitionist origins of the NAACP ideal, the weight of historical consistency virtually dictated this mode of thought and action. In 1912, at the height of progressivism, Oswald Garrison Villard, a leading spokesman of the NAACP, president of the *New York Evening Post,* and grandson of abolitionist William Lloyd Garrison, addressed the fourth annual conference of the NAACP meeting in Chicago about its mission. At this racially integrated convocation, courageously hosted by Jane Addams, Villard made the following fervent announcement: "Ours . . . is a battle for democracy, pure and undefiled. It is not for us to compromise, however much others feel the necessity for doing so . . . [the NAACP] asks no favors, no privileges, no special advantages for those disadvantaged ones, whose fathers and mothers but fifty years ago were still being sold upon the auction block."[9] Villard rekindled the fervor of neo-abolitionism embodied in the national NAACP's Purpose which sought "to uplift the colored men and women . . . by securing to them the full enjoyment of their rights as citizens, justice in the courts, and equality of opportunity everywhere."[10]

The racial egalitarians of Chicago rarely deviated from this ideological stance, but when they did, it was due to the need to reconcile the pragmatism of American life and thought to the realities of black material deprivation, the existence of a racial caste system, and sometimes their own latent racist inclinations. Judge Edward Osgood Brown needed to see black material advancement firsthand on the outskirts of Tuskegee Institute in rural Alabama to revitalize his sometimes wavering ideological commitment.[11] Chicago Public Schools superintendent Ella Flagg Young also developed deeper appreciation of black people as achievers when she made a trip to Tuskegee as a guest of the renowned Chicago philanthropist Julius Rosenwald, and of Booker T. Washington. It gave her greater resolve when challenging racial discrimination at the Wendell Phillips High School on the South Side, the scene of creeping prejudicial behavior among white students.[12]

Clearly, as a group white racial egalitarians did not completely rise above the entrenched racism of their day. Chicago Urban League historian Arvarh E. Strickland evaluated the social workers who initiated the Urban League movement and found that they "rejected the possibility of eliminating all social ills through sweeping change in either the political or economic system."[13] Chicago housing historian Thomas L. Philpott, in his study of reform between 1890 and 1930, described some of these same middle-class settlement house reformers in the aggregate as decidedly racist to the core, even if they did not realize their biases.[14] Even with their limitations, their response to bettering race relations was nevertheless both courageous and inspiring.

In the eyes of historians two generations removed in time, the triumph of neo-abolitionism in Chicago could be realized only if Booker T. Washington's ideological influence was overcome. Many historians found disagreement among blacks over which strategy should be endorsed for racial advancement. Accordingly, they wrote of the importance of a schism in which a Washington camp competed vigorously for hegemony over the hearts and minds of black Chicagoans with an influential, determined Du Bois faction.[15] The concept, however, of totally divisive ideological warfare in Chicago lacks contemporary evidence to support its existence. While there was disagreement among African Americans in a population of 30,000 in 1900 and 44,000 in 1910, it never reached the heights presumed and presented by historians and other writers.

Disagreement over the best means to use to advance black racial aspirations persisted for three reasons. First, Booker T. Washington's tenets did, at times, complement the new neo-abolitionist ideology. At a Chicago NAACP meeting in 1914 the peripatetic neo-abolitionist Joel E. Spingarn of New York delivered an unusually incisive explanation to his audience: "Idealism . . . it is the function of the [NAACP] to kindle. Mr. Washington is doing a needed work in making a strong and prosperous people from which the Association may recruit strength. But the two sides of the general movement must thus supplement each other, for together they represent the balance of utilitarianism and idealism which is the character- istic gait of American progress."[16] Further, contemporary editorials in the *Chicago Defender* and the *Chicago Broad-Ax* captured the essence of the black community's feelings on the matter when they explained that Washington's strategy "represented a line of thought that was essential to the masses living under the conditions from which he arose," but that when radical and conservative ideologies were evaluated "both were necessary to complete the armament of this oppressed race . . . [, so] why the hysteria from the advocates of either plan for race advancement; surely both have our interest at heart, and both being earnest and zealous, why let the zeal become embittered . . . ?"[17] As to the *Defender's* specific posture on and contribution to the proper course of race advancement, longtime NAACP stalwart Archie L. Weaver recalled that "our objectives and [its] platform were identical—only [it] was five years ahead of us."[18]

Near mid-century when he wrote his autobiography, militant black clergyman Reverdy Ransom remembered that while he was in Chicago there were differences but no such schism. He recalled that "these two theories of Negro progress were not absolutely contradictory."[19] St. Clair Drake's study of Negro churches and voluntary associations, completed in 1940, corroborated this view.[20] Longtime NAACP egalitarian stalwart attorney Earl B. Dickerson, who devoted two-thirds of his ninety-five years in the service of the movement under both the branch and national banners, reflected in 1984 that there never appeared to be any sense of urgency among Chicagoans to choose between the two ideologies.[21] Re- cently, Booker T. Washington biographer Louis R. Harlan assessed the national situation as being one that fell far short of a total ideological split.[22] There was personal animosity in abundance, to be sure, and it was intense, but it existed in Chicago as part of an ideological struggle on how to best assure group racial advancement.

Moreover, blacks in Chicago shared a tradition of viewing economics coupled with racial solidarity and self-help as components of their strat- egy of racial advancement.[23] This arrangement existed before Booker T. Washington made his historic Atlanta Compromise Address in 1895 and established his National Negro Business League in 1900. From the pages of the *Chicago Conservator* and Isaac C. Harris's *Colored Men's Professional and Business Directory* (1885) to those in the *Chicago Defender* and *Broad-Ax* during the Progressive period, continuous pleas supported this strategy.

Second, the bulk of the black civic leadership apparently ignored what- ever furor might have developed from their vantage points at the

Appomattox Club (the professional and businessmen's club organized in 1900 by college-trained New Yorker Edward Wright), the *Chicago Defender*, and within the high-status Baptist, A.M.E., and Episcopal churches (all with college-trained clergy). These blacks saw a complementary rather than competing use for the Du Bois and Washington approaches to attacking racism. Their importance to the cause of racial equality might be assessed from an observation made in 1913: "The colored people often state that the colored professional men, lawyers and physicians, rather than the ministers and social workers, have been the real factor in the social improvement among the Negroes of Chicago."[24] The initial edition of black Chicago magnate Anthony Overton's *Half-Century Magazine*, published in August 1916, further placed the issue in perspective. In all probability, Kathryn M. Johnson, a former NAACP field agent for *The Crisis*, wrote the maiden editorial: "As the Race Problem is ever with us, we shall discuss and shall entertain discussions of the same from time to time. We appreciate that we are now living in a commercial era and that the factors of paramount importance in the solution of this problem are economy, industry—the making and saving of money—and business development. We also appreciate that in the upbuilding of the race, unity, cooperation and race patronage are essential."[25]

Third, heterogeneity, rather than, as often assumed, social undifferentiation categorized the black rank and file. Longtime residents who were "old settlers," short-term residents, attracted by the Columbian Exposition of 1893 and by strikebreaking opportunities at the turn of the century, and newly arrived migrants who came to the city during and after 1915 comprised this mass of ordinary citizens. In the aggregate, the equal rights advocates expected this composite group to constitute its primary base of support in Chicago, which was consistent with New York's plan for a national organization. For the most part, the black masses remained aloof from this new ideological thrust. Their primary desire centered around freedom from white interference in black affairs. With the passage of time in the new century, they found the necessary ingredients for contentment within the city in the fledgling dream of a self-contained racial enclave under their control. In this they resembled some of the European immigrant groups.

It is also important to consider that many blacks accepted voluntary separation as a way of life. Within their all-black churches, social clubs, and fraternal orders, blacks adjusted to a form of racial proscription which continually forced to accept the reality of their powerlessness, lack of choice, and immobility. In the workplace, they were excluded from industry and relegated to service occupations until World War I. In their search for housing, they found themselves restricted to undesirable areas throughout the city. In education, the recurring threat of segregation posed a major problem. Black Chicagoans developed a particular northern brand of racial fatalism over time that originated from both their contemporary experiences in Chicago and the subconscious ones they brought from the plantations, small towns, and cities of the South.

Not unlike the situation that developed among Chicago's immigrants, black isolation in American life shaped the attitudes and worldview of African Americans. If an event did not involve members of their group, they ignored it. Accordingly, an event of international magnitude such as the sinking of the luxury liner *Titanic* in 1912 received almost no coverage in the *Defender* and went unreported in the *Broad-Ax*. What concerned the black working class the most were occurrences most relevant to them. The reaction to pugilist Jack Johnson's pursuit of happiness in his choice of mates, which ran afoul of white sociosexual codes in the city as well as in the nation, assumed importance as a group experience. White racial resistance to Johnson's lifestyle propelled him—this resident of the South Side and denizen of the "Stroll," the promenade of black and tan cabaret life along south State Street—into celebrity. At the same time, the very small black civic leadership, which was church-going and which adhered to high moral standards, disliked many aspects of his lifestyle. But they, too, could sympathize with a fellow citizen's right to choose his own mate and avenue to happiness.[26] The treatment accorded Johnson seemed all too familiar to persons who had lived through the racial hypocrisy practiced in the South and at that time taking root in the North. Certainly consistent with patterns in African American culture, this homage paid Jack Johnson as race hero in the teens would be replicated by another pugilistic hero in the thirties in the person of Joe Louis.[27]

Louis R. Harlan's treatment of Chicago's black working class, described as a population comprised "mostly of the inarticulate, the unskilled working and servant class," revealed only a part of their collective socioeconomic character as well as the saga they experienced while improving their lives.[28] If they were inarticulate, Chicagoan Fannie Barrier Williams found that their activities belied any ignorance associated with this trait. She reported that hundreds of young men availed themselves of the opportunities provided by church-sponsored literary club and other social activities in an effort to improve themselves. Also, when it came time to form associations to work for black betterment, they readily organized for action. Williams observed: "His [the Negro's] love for organization is a sort of racial passion. Suggest to the average man something ought to be, and he immediately proposes an organization. There is scarcely a thing in religion, in politics, in business, in pleasure, in education, in fighting race prejudice, or anything else described that is not the object of organization."[29] If they worked as unskilled workers it was more indicative of a lack of opportunity than of desire or ability. "In the matter of employment," Williams further observed, "the colored people have lost in the last ten years nearly every occupation of which they once had almost a monopoly." She analyzed perceptively that "any group that can be systematically deprived of one occupation after another becomes an easy victim to all kinds of injustice. When they can be reduced to a point to be pitied, they will cease to be respected."[30]

Blacks simply refused to accept parameters set by whites on certain dreams they pursued. While investigating housing conditions on the West Side and the South Side, a University of Chicago researcher found blacks unwilling to settle for substandard living conditions. "Some of this overcrowding would be unnecessary," he observed, "if the colored people were willing to follow the customs of other nationalities and use all of the room in their apartments as sleeping-rooms. . . . unlike the immigrant, even the poor colored people like to keep a kitchen and 'parlor' and occasionally a dining room, distinctly as such and not crowded with beds." The researcher encountered an aversion to anything that stamped the black family as unusual and inferior and went on to conclude that "the Negro, with a weekly wage no larger, and usually smaller, than that of his immigrant neighbor, endeavors to maintain a standard of living more similar to that of the native-born white citizen than does the immigrant."[31]

During the Great Migration of 1915–1918, newly arrived migrants exhibited an assertiveness consistent with the feelings that originally convinced them to leave their homes in the South to settle in Chicago. Described by migration historian James R. Grossman as persons who developed a new strategy of racial advancement as part of a new grassroots social movement, they also ignored the Chicago NAACP. Their immediate needs were met as they pursued economic, political, and educational opportunities. In regard to their dreams of their place in the "open" society that Chicago offered, Grossman wrote: "There is little evidence that black southerners coming to Chicago were especially interested in integrating per se; most of them were concerned about legal protection, political rights, and access to the paths to security or mobility. . . . In some aspects of everyday life, many newcomers looked forward to freedom from whites; they evinced little desire to attend integrated churches or spend leisure time with white people."[32] As for the recruitment efforts of white and black progressives on behalf of the Chicago NAACP, many questioned not only the possibility of race equality (which carried with it the germs of social equality despite protestations even from some leading Chicago movement spokespersons), but also its relevance to their lives.

Whatever the character of life that blacks carved out for themselves, the acceptability of blacks as political and economic equals in the white mind was directly related to black progress in the areas of community betterment and personal discipline. This became a matter of such importance that various Methodist and Baptist churchmen and civic leaders, such as Ida B. Wells-Barnett and Robert S. Abbott, spent a disproportionate amount of their time involved in improving the quality of community life by raising group standards. When Booker T. Washington came to Chicago in 1910 and 1912, he used this theme as part of his appeal to blacks. Blacks were urged to become more competitive, to assume control over the neighborhoods where they predominated numerically, and to prepare to be criticized for any untoward developments within their communities. He encouraged black Chicagoans by appealing to their sense of racial chauvinism. After observing and meeting with some members of southern Europe's working class, he boasted: "The European thinks slow, moves slow and works slow. The Negro can beat him. But the northern [American] white man thinks fast, moves fast[,] and works fast. Prepare yourself to beat him."[33] And, contrary to what Du Bois in *The Crisis* wrote about Washington's 1912 visit, the Tuskegeean was not asking any more from blacks than white progressives in Chicago, such as Jane Addams and the Rev. Celia Parker Woolley, were asking.[34]

Black Chicagoans were also aware that the best of intentions of the city's progressives did not always produce beneficial results for black citizens. The issue of street vice—gambling, prostitution, and petty theft—disturbed them greatly. When the time came in the fall of 1912 for a citywide clean-up inspired by progressives, the question in the minds of blacks was simply where the denizens of the underworld would go. They hoped not into their communities which were already adjacent to vice districts because of a segregated housing pattern. The Rev. Reverdy Ransom complained of this and other forms of white condescension which contributed as much to black distrust of whites as to the latter's outright hostility toward blacks. "When any question arises which affects the public good our white fellow-citizens rarely, if ever, call the colored men into cooperation," Ransom opined, "but we would gladly unite to sustain civic righteousness. We are never consulted except when something happens in the black belt."[35] Interracial mistrust notwithstanding, the future of race relations in Chicago looked brighter as the second decade of the new century dawned.

3

From Vigilance Committee to Branch, 1910–1916

THE GENESIS OF THE NAACP movement came in the aftermath of the infamous Springfield, Illinois, race riot of 1908. Because of where and when it happened, this tragedy particularly disgusted the less than substantial coterie of racial egalitarians found among the massive ranks of northern progressives. The violence occurred in the vicinity of Abraham Lincoln's home and at the start of what appeared to many to be the dawn of an enlightened, progressive century. It included the lynching of an eighty-four-year-old victim whose only offenses were having a black skin and a white wife. In a racial climate that was deteriorating not only regionally in the South but also nationally, two New York City progressives, William English Walling and Oswald Garrison Villard, respectively conceived the idea of, and initiated the call for, a national meeting to discuss ways to protect the endangered rights of America's black citizens.

At the birth of the NAACP movement, Chicago race egalitarians responded to Villard's "call" in the spring of 1909 with both immediacy and enthusiasm. Jane Addams, Ida B. Wells-Barnett, Rabbi Emil G. Hirsch, the

Rev. Jenkin Lloyd Jones, Mary McDowell, Professor William I. Thomas of the University of Chicago, Louis F. Post, and William F. Salter were Chicago's signatories among the sixty progressives nationally[1] who supported Villard's appeal, issued on Abraham Lincoln's birthday. Chicagoans manifested their interest by traveling to New York to a two-day civil rights conference beginning on May 31, 1909.

The events at the conference set the tone for future race relations within the movement for decades to come. After patiently listening to white progressives bare their individual souls over the injustices done to blacks in the aggregate, W. E. B. Du Bois described the scene: "[With exasperation,] the black mass moved forward and stretched out their hands to take charge. It was their problem. They must name the condition. Three great thoughts were manifest: Intense hatred of further compromise and quibbling in stating this problem to the public; wavering uncertainty as to just what practical steps were best; and the last but not least suspicion of the white hands stretched out in brotherhood to help."[2]

The manifestation of such racial suspicion led J. Max Barber, a militant newcomer to Chicago and a victim of the 1906 Atlanta race riot, to exclaim in a prepared speech on the floor of the assembly: "If you are going to solve the race problem, you must have men of the William Lloyd Garrison stripe. You must have men that will be willing to stand up for humanity, and for their convictions on this question."[3] Barber's credentials were appropriate for the challenge he issued. He was a member of the Niagara Movement as well as editor of Atlanta's *The Voice of the Negro* until driven out of that city by terrorists for courageously exposing the roots of the racial massacre of 1906. Although the subjects of organizational purpose and structure assumed an urgency to whites, the outspoken and intrepid crusader against lynching Ida B. Wells-Barnett also rose from the floor to challenge whites on this burning issue of uncompromising commitment to and action in behalf of the cause. As the worst possible scenario began to unfold around her, she exclaimed in frustration: "They are betraying us again—these white friends of ours."[4]

The role of Ida B. Wells-Barnett within the NAACP movement was fixed in the aftermath of this opening chasm between blacks and whites on how deeply ingrained one's commitment was to neo-abolitionism, which in her eyes had to be unwavering. In response to pleas to exercise a cautious approach at this earliest of interracial encounters, Barber and Wells-Barnett appeared oblivious to the possibility that they might offend either white race egalitarians or the black supporters of Booker T. Washington. Wells-Barnett was widely recognized for her outstanding service in the cause of racial advancement over the previous two decades. Early in the 1890s, she had carried the banner against lynching virtually singlehandedly, both throughout the nation and abroad to England.

This civic dynamo, the child of Mississippi slaves, was born into the same condition as her parents just as the "peculiar institution" of slavery was ending. She remained in Mississippi during the post-Reconstruction period, attending Shaw College (now Rust College), and rearing her orphaned siblings. As an early feminist she persistently challenged a male-dominated society. She also made a decision that did not sit well with her white feminist sisters when she chose to marry and seemingly to abandon the cause of gender equality. Wells-Barnett choose widower Ferdinand Barnett, a prominent black Chicago lawyer and newspaper publisher. She took an even more committed step when she started a family in whose presence she enjoyed the responsibilities of homemaker and mother. Notably, the diminutive crusader still found time for her numerous, legendary civil rights activities.

Beyond her initial apprehensions in New York, almost immediately another incident soured her impressions of this radical experiment in race relations. When Du Bois assumed the responsibility of drawing up the list of forty egalitarian stalwarts who comprised the Committee of Forty, or the National Negro Committee (the forerunner of the National Association for the Advancement of Colored People), he omitted Wells-Barnett's name but included the Rev. Celia Parker Woolley's. Membership on the National Negro Committee confirmed leadership in behalf of racial equality as well as the authority to oversee the implementation of the resolutions passed during the two-day conference. Wells-Barnett's exclusion from the locus of organizational power disappointed her also because she had been assured beforehand that her name was to be included. Attempting to appear calm, she nonetheless seethed inwardly over what not only she, but also some of the white racial egalitarians, saw as an affront. When Du Bois belatedly attempted to rectify the error by inserting her name on the committee's roster he was met with her rebuff. Retrospectively, Wells-Barnett regretted having turned down this remedial gesture that resulted from the magnanimity of others. But at that moment, she experienced the uncontrollable sense of outrage and impetuosity that often characterized her demeanor. Consequently, her decision stood.[5]

Du Bois bears additional responsibility for the incident because he initially substituted the name of his close friend and Niagara Movement leader, Dr. Charles E. Bentley, in place of Wells-Barnett's. He no doubt made his decision based on a sense of camaraderie with Bentley coupled with a discomfort related to Wells-Barnett's personality and socio-educational background.[6] Du Bois's defense was that since Wells-Barnett belonged to Rev. Celia Parker Woolley's Frederick Douglass Center the inclusion of both women would have been redundant. As a matter of fact, Bentley was also affiliated with the Center as were most of Chicago's black egalitarians.[7] Du Bois's action served to exacerbate Wells-Barnett's belief that white progressives in general and certain educated, elitist black males in particular could not be trusted to serve an organization that purported to elevate a proscribed race.[8]

Back in Chicago, as egalitarian progressives wrestled with the inherent problems of transforming an ideal considered too theoretical into an organization during the second decade of the century, the active participation of nationally renowned progressive Jane Addams of Hull House appeared to be the major precondition for the early success of the Chicago NAACP movement.[9] Hailed as the logical choice for leadership of the Chicago movement by neo-abolitionists in New York and Chicago because of her public image and persona, she was elevated to the status of "Saint Jane" in the years preceding World War I. As the daughter of an Illinois abolitionist with New England roots, Addams possessed the necessary stature to penetrate the barriers of white racial supremacy, paternalism, and indifference that pervaded Progressive-Era Chicago. Her biographer, Allen F. Davis, made this appraisal: "She did not entirely avoid the racist attitudes of her day, but she came closer to overcoming them than most of the reformers of her day."[10] Addams's feelings were strong enough for her to write in 1911: "We strangely force one race to demand as a right what was given from God."[11]

Despite this aura of civic leadership, Addams's ascendancy as the leader of the Chicago NAACP movement failed to receive total support from within the egalitarian coterie. Ida B. Wells-Barnett questioned Addams's commitment to racial equality based on both personal and indirect observations of Addams's performance as a leader in championing other civic causes. Although Wells-Barnett requested and received Addams's assistance in successfully thwarting an attempt to segregate the city's schools in 1903,[12] she also gained the knowledge that Addams could acquiesce on a principle, as she did in a 1905 school controversy over teaching credentials.[13] In that dispute, much to their dismay, Addams decided with the Establishment against the teachers in one of the cases.

During a moment of introspection, Addams described herself as having a "temperament and habit [that] had kept me rather in the middle of the road [on matters of contention]."[14] This tendency toward neutrality led some white contemporaries to lament their having followed her: "We had made the mistake in Chicago of considering Jane Addams as a moral leader and treated her as such and expected her to do in very difficult positions what a William Lloyd Garrison would do. . . ."[15] Another consideration, however, might have influenced her: the need to raise funds for Hull House from among the city's various elites. Alienating them would have only weakened her efforts.

Philpott found that Addams and other egalitarians hedged on the issue of social equality so as to not cause a social backlash from other white progressives.[16] In the white popular mind, social equality was synonymous at its worst with interracial marriage, or, at its least, close social contact. Yet, Addams and her friend Celia Parker Woolley were, to their credit, promoters, to a certain extent, of the very social equality they disdained publicly.

The other egalitarians in Chicago with direct abolitionist links included Judge Edward Osgood Brown, the son of a Massachusetts abolitionist and sitting magistrate on the Illinois Appellate Court; Unitarian minister Celia Parker Woolley, the daughter of abolitionist parents; and Jenkin Lloyd Jones, another Unitarian minister whose abolitionist commitment had been tested on the battlefields of the Civil War.

Judge Brown, familiarly clad in a waistcoat, eloquently lauded his roots. In 1912, he wrote in *The Crisis:* "I should feel unworthy of the Massachusetts ancestry from which I sprang if I could bring myself to indifference [to segregation and discrimination]."[17] The jurist could also waver in his commitment to egalitarianism, however, when under pressure. He introduced Earl B. Dickerson (an African American destined to become the branch's most influential member after World War II and who was a recent graduate of the University of Chicago's Law School) to his Loop law office colleagues as an aspiring attorney worth employing. When Brown met unexpected opposition from his partners, who feared a loss of clients if Dickerson was associated with the firm, he acquiesced and Dickerson accommodated himself to this humiliating experience.[18]

New England Unitarian minister Woolley sought to ameliorate racial tension in Chicago in the early twentieth century by bringing the culturally refined members of both groups together in close proximity. She believed "that mutual knowledge must precede sympathy and sympathy must precede any attempts to minimize race friction and economics and other handicaps on the Negro."[19] Woolley purposely founded the Frederick Douglass Center in the heart of the Black Belt in 1901 to move racial egalitarianism beyond theory into practice. The Center's letterhead boldly pronounced that its purpose was "to promote a just and amicable relationship between the white and colored people." At the Center, members of the black elite, such as Ferdinand and Ida B. Wells-Barnett, and S. Laing Williams and Fannie Barrier Williams, could interact with members of the city's white civic and academic leadership even though they were barred from the downtown all-white civic clubs.[20] On many occasions, Woolley stood adamantly in behalf of racial equality. She lambasted city school officials about threatened school segregation and public officials about creeping discrimination in publicly funded facilities. In 1912, after learning of discrimination against black nurses at Cook County Hospital, she contacted the head of the nurses and demanded an immediate change in policy.

Woolley faltered occasionally in carrying the burden of promoting racial equality among her fellow whites. Perhaps her actions were a part of a strategy; perhaps they were not. While Woolley promoted social contact at her Frederick Douglass Center at a level that frightened many whites, who frowned on social equality or any extended form of social contact with blacks, in a contradictory stance in 1907, she tried to allay white fears of interracial marriage by attempting to show them that black stoicism and self-respect operated against blacks' developing any interest in interracial unions. In the Center's booklet, this explanation was given: "The dread question of 'social equality' is neither sought nor avoided. . . . The Negro is not pushing himself socially into the company of his white friends and acquaintances. On the contrary, he is practicing very plain, self-respecting reserve in the matter. . . . The best type of Negro feels that he has a work to perform in the loyal justification of his people."[21]

The Rev. Jenkin Lloyd Jones was born in Wales and reared in Michigan during the antebellum period. Unlike Addams and Brown, whose commitment to egalitarianism stemmed from derivative and intellectual roots, his was experiential. A veteran of numerous Civil War battles, he returned north after the conclusion of hostilities and eventually settled in Chicago as a member of the Unitarian clergy. As recognition of his abilities, he was chosen to head All Souls Church in 1882. Throughout the remainder of the nineteenth century he was "tireless and aggressive . . . [as he] sought to promote [humanitarianism]."[22]

By the beginning of the twentieth century, Jones concluded regretfully that "the battle for equality had not ended at Appomattox." Chiding his twentieth-century contemporaries who overlooked the need for a continued militancy to secure justice for blacks, he glorified in "the cleaner ethical vision [that proved] the fathers were more nearly right than their condescending and compromising sons."[23] He was hailed by the *Chicago Defender* and recognized by the colored citizens of Chicago as the venerable "apostle of equal rights." Yet when he found a few words of praise for the work of Washington at Tuskegee, W. E. B. Du Bois, nearly one thousand miles away in New York, criticized him as a threat to the cause of racial equality.[24] Notwithstanding this unfair assault from afar, Jones remained a stalwart in the movement until his death late in the decade.

There were three Kentuckians who had tenuous as well as unusual links to that state's rich abolitionist heritage. One was Robert McMurdy, Judge Brown's colleague on the bench, who spent his youthful years on Chicago's South Side in the Hyde Park community, which housed the University of Chicago. Another was Willoughby Walling, the brother of William English Walling, who "conceived the idea of a national biracial organization of 'fair-minded whites and intelligent blacks' to help right the wrongs of the Negro."[25] The Walling family had once owned slaves but cleansed themselves of this affliction as a matter of conscience. And finally, there was Sophonisba Breckenridge, a professor and dean of women at the School of Civics and Philanthropy, the University of Chicago, and a cousin by marriage of national NAACP leader Oswald Garrison Villard of New York.

Through deed and pen, McMurdy ably demonstrated his commitment to egalitarianism. He revealed his innermost feelings on race relations and justice in his only novel, *The Upas Tree* (1912). While the novel primarily explored the pursuit of justice as an ideal, the characterization of the protagonist's servant, Robert, also represented the Negro in the ideal. Robert sometimes surpassed whites in his attributes of high character, being a paragon of intelligence, dignity, and perseverance.[26] In this case, McMurdy indulged in what historian George Fredrickson described as "romantic racialism," common among neo-abolitionists who endorsed racial equality.[27]

Willoughby Walling served actively in the early Chicago NAACP movement where he pronounced his familial loyalty "to carry out the ideas of my brother."[28] His affiliation with the movement during its committee phase (1910–1913) contributed to its reaching its permanent branch status after three years of building.

Sophonisba Breckenridge, one of the six social workers and settlement house leaders in the organization, distinguished herself for the length of her commitment, which extended into the 1930s. As a close friend of Jane Addams, her presence in the movement lent additional legitimacy to its existence in the eyes of whites.

Other social workers besides Breckenridge and Addams helped found the movement. Among them was Thomas W. Allinson, who headed Henry Booth Settlement House, located less than a mile south of Hull House in the city's impoverished West Side immigrant ghetto. George Arthur, a black man, headed the black Wabash Avenue YMCA, which had been constructed in the heart of the Black Belt. Ida B. Wells-Barnett created her own haven for recently arrived and socially adjusting young colored migrants in 1911 under the banner of the Negro Fellowship League.

The social justice advocates who comprised the ranks of the leadership of the early NAACP movement influenced professional and civic groups as well as others throughout the city. Such notables as heiress Anita McCormick Blaine (Mrs. Emmons Blaine) and philanthropist–merchant prince Julius Rosenwald of Sears, Roebuck fame were among their ranks. Both Blaine and Rosenwald functioned primarily as financial contributors, responsive mainly to the national office's appeals to fill its coffers.

Blaine, a close friend of Jane Addams, lent support to many of the causes that her friend endorsed, but particularly to the NAACP. On one rare occasion, Blaine appeared on the dais at the 1912 convention, along with her mother, immediately bestowing a new legitimacy on the fledgling movement in Chicago. Given Blaine's lack of interracial contacts along with the crush of her other commitments, hers was a limited involvement. Her privileged social status dictated a level of social isolation that is unimaginable in this day of television and other forms of electronic literacy. In fact, she never saw an African American until she visited her father's ancestral Virginia while in her teens.[29] Nonetheless, she developed a respect, albeit slightly patronizing, for the aspirations of black people.

Rosenwald's role and influence in the movement seem to have been misunderstood, and in recent scholarship have been exaggerated beyond the bounds of substantiation.[30] Rosenwald enjoyed a complex relationship with the NAACP movement in that he uncompromisingly endorsed the gradualist strategy associated with Booker T. Washington while openly affiliating with an organization diametrically opposed to anything but an immediatist approach to race relations. At the 1912 Chicago convention, he admonished racial egalitarians to remember that even in Chicago injustice could affect non-blacks.[31] In 1914, he reminded Villard of his other broad-based interests, which included his concerns for Russian and Polish Jews and their adjustment to American life in the Chicago Maxwell Street ghetto and for educationally starved southern blacks. "There is no doubt in my mind that the work the [NAACP] is doing is extremely valuable," he stated, "but other phases of service for individuals of that race are of greater personal interest to me."[32] He did not concern himself with weakening the Chicago NAACP movement, but rather attempted to avoid involvement in a concern of secondary interest.

One incisive assessment of Rosenwald's mindset concluded that he "always seem[ed] to have looked on [the racial prejudice which produced the evils of segregation] as a mental attitude to be [eliminated silently], not a thing to be fought in the open."[33] His wife's comments in a related vein are no doubt illustrative of the core of his conservative thinking. Augusta Rosenwald addressed a racially mixed assemblage in Alabama in 1915 about her observations on a recent trip to Palestine. While in the Middle East, she and her husband sought to ascertain how well Jews and Arabs were adjusting to each other in a hostile environment. She stated that she believed in "solving the problem of harmony between all races, not by breaking down prejudice [through agitation], but by disarming it. Each [the Jew in Palestine and the Negro in America] so radiates the dignity and worth of his work in the world that the defenses of prejudices must fall down before him."[34]

Julius Rosenwald's importance to the Chicago NAACP movement was alleged to have stemmed from an influence or power which he is presumed to have exerted over people, program, and organization, but which remains undocumented to this day. In the wake of a decade of rather unimpressive programmatic victories (in which regard Chicago was no less effective than any other branch within the fledgling NAACP movement), many writers looked for the cause and found it in the idea that Rosenwald used his position in accordance with his ideological leanings to undermine or steer the branch into moderation.

Such action would have been inconsistent with his character. Moreover, on only one occasion did he make any gesture that could be construed to be openly partisan to the Washington program. In 1915, Rosenwald chartered a train to take part of the branch's leadership down to the annual commencement at Tuskegee. Those accompanying him included Judges Brown and McMurdy, Addams, Blaine, and Jones. Dr. Bentley reported on the trip with guarded satisfaction. Writing to Prof. Joel C. Spingarn, by this date a leading national proponent of racial egalitarianism, Bentley gave his diagnosis: "Nearly all—Judge Brown included—have been overwhelmed by what they saw without taking into account what it has cost. . . . I see the need for missionary work among the directory to the end that they see the whole picture. In this I have every hope, for at heart they want to know more of the question." Bentley's confidence in his fellow directors was further buoyed by the knowledge that an accommodationist speaker had visited the branch in Chicago two weeks prior to the Tuskegee sojourn without making converts. Bentley told Spingarn this "dreaded event has come and gone without injury to our policies and ideals."[35]

An imagined threat that Rosenwald used his wealth as a lever to influence black Chicago politics was also unsubstantiated. Rosenwald directed his wealth primarily toward philanthropic ends, and on those occasions when he used it outside that sphere, such as in local progressive politics, he had no influence of note. This inability to affect victory for reform politics, it must be noted, occurred much to his chagrin.[36] Like Mrs. Blaine and other wealthy Chicago donors, Rosenwald usually gave $1,000 per year to the national office and little or nothing to the Chicago branch, where the need was presumably less immediate.[37] He responded to a solitary appeal from the Chicago branch in 1914, contributing $325.27 to its operations, and was not asked to give again until 1920.[38] In his mind, perhaps the price of his support for the branch was his approval of the other members of the governing board, referred to as the Executive Committee.[39] However, there is no evidence that Rosenwald had any influence of any magnitude over the hierarchy as regards its composition. By 1915 or 1916 his interest had faded, and his personal secretary, William C. Graves, stopped attending branch meetings. Graves attributed his departure, however, solely to the irregularity and unproductivity of the meetings.

Within the Chicago NAACP movement, the Tuskegeean's program of gradualism was not seen collectively as a threat to the branch. Rather, to some it appeared to be a complementary strategy which directly attacked the problems of economic deprivation and low social status. Only the ideologically unswerving Wells-Barnett, Bentley, and McMurdy rejected it outright. To these stalwarts, the gradualist ideology placed an inordinate burden on blacks to prove their human, moral, and material worthiness for eventual, rather than immediate, citizenship rights. This undeserved burden was totally unacceptable to them.

Basically, Booker T. Washington's program emphasized duties over rights, the primacy of economics and material advancement over the enjoyment of citizenship's privileges. The branch's racial egalitarians were divided into three groups which, to their advantage, however, did not have divisive allegiances. Those early committee members usually associated with Washington's approach were S. Laing Williams, Dr. George Cleveland Hall, and Julius Rosenwald. Others, such as Addams, Brown, George Packard, and the Revs. Jones and Woolley, exhibited a tendency to listen and observe with impartiality. Then there were those three members who were completely opposed to everything that emanated from Tuskegee.

Deep within the Washington coterie, incredulity grew as to how opposition to Booker T. Washington appeared in the first place. S. Laing Williams, who acted as a major pipeline to Tuskegee, felt legitimate discomfort with the *ad hominem* attacks directed against Washington. His loyalty to Washington was based to a great extent on the Tuskegeean's having helped him gain a U.S. assistant attorneyship. Early in 1910, during the NAACP's incipient stage of development, Williams wrote regularly to Emmett J. Scott, Washington's personal secretary, who willingly accepted disparaging reports on the activities of the egalitarians.[40] At year's end, Williams responded: "The Walling–Du Bois–Trotter combination . . . held several meetings, but I cannot see any evidence of permanent interest in [Chicago for the NAACP]." Williams's concern prompted him to contact the national secretary, Frances Blascoer, to inquire if the movement that was ostensibly anti-racist was, in fact, anti-Washington. He concluded: "At heart they are hostile but they are menaced by the overwhelming sentiment of the country that Dr. Washington is everlastingly right in his doctrine and in his views and work."[41]

Allen H. Spear described the linkage between ideology and leadership to illustrate the source of what he categorized as strong antagonism in Chicago toward Washington and his program. Yet, it appeared to be centered in a segment of the city's black leadership which numbered only perhaps a score or more.[42] That included the Barnetts, Ferdinand and Ida, along with attorney Edward H. Morris. The members of the Niagara Movement (which was defunct by 1909) were expectedly hostile to Washington. Their ranks included Dr. Bentley, James Madden, J. Max Barber (and, possibly again, the ardent anti-Washingtonian Edward H. Morris).

Not surprisingly, Bentley wanted the men of the Niagara Movement to join the Chicago NAACP en masse.[43] At one meeting held in the company of the renowned black surgeon Daniel Hale Williams, the group lambasted both Washington's character and his administrative competence. They also criticized Washington for lacking the intellectual vision to develop a comprehensive program for race advancement.[44]

Several "New Englanders" comprised the movement's other supporters of social justice. Chroniclers of the city's history as well as contemporaries noted the presence of whites from New England in a city which always attracted large numbers of white Southerners. New Englanders were assumed to be more readily supportive of racial egalitarianism.[45] Among their ranks were men such as Arthur Aldis, born in Vermont, educated at Harvard, and successful in real estate. There was Rhode Island–born, Brown-educated George Packard, who was a member of the law firm to which Judge Brown belonged. Norman Waite Harris of Massachusetts founded the bank that carried his name. His son produced a sympathetic history of early abolitionism in Illinois.[46]

Other local civic notables rounded out the ranks of the movement. Charles R. Crane, a native Chicagoan, gained recognition as a leader in the municipal reform movement[47] as well as for being an owner of a huge manufacturing firm. Clarence Darrow began attracting attention during this period as an up-and-coming civil libertarian. Rabbi Emil Hirsch, who earned his reputation as a noted rabbinical scholar, headed the newly constructed Sinai Temple at Forty-Sixth and Grand Boulevard, and became the cause's second major Jewish supporter. And Charles Hallihan, presumably Irish Catholic, served as editor of the *Chicago Evening Post*, one of the city's major dailies and affiliated with Villard's *New York Evening News*.

Progressive-Era Chicago embraced a number of white progressives whose interests in the advancement of blacks ranged from the tenuous to the substantive. Although they might not have joined the movement formally, because of their social standing they shared common social ties with the racial egalitarians and sometimes gave quiet support to their activities. Edward F. Dunne contributed notably to progressivism as an enlightened judge, mayor, and governor. This Irish American reform politician was a dedicated racial egalitarian and spoke in unequivocal terms about the possibility of an improvement in the Negro's status through opportunity: "I believe in Negro progress. I do not believe that he has progressed backward, as the paradox has been put. He has been held back through race prejudice, which has placed every obstacle in his way. . . . You can not argue the race question on reason. It is bound by too much prejudice. But give the colored man the encouragement and assistance to advance, and I believe he is certain to command the respect which must be the aggressive factor in allaying the race prejudice that grips the South. That same aversion is with us here in the North."[48]

Another recently arrived Chicagoan was budding white sociologist Robert E. Park. Ironically, he had been transplanted by mid-decade onto the campus of the University of Chicago from Booker T. Washington's southern influence. Park had observed American race relations at their worst while serving at Tuskegee Institute as Booker T. Washington's personal secretary. In his subsequent works on race relations, written in collaboration with the pioneer in sociology William Isaac Thomas, Park rejected racial gradualism as a paradigm for racial progress. He proceeded further, along with Thomas, to develop the bases in social thought of the "Chicago School" of sociology. His innovative approach was described as follows: "[Park] shifted the emphasis in the study of race relations from the justification of preconceived impressions to a detailed analysis of the social and psychological factors molding race relations. Data from Park's analyses questioned the validity of the usual arguments against school integration, equal employment opportunities, and open housing. His research also challenged the tradition of innate black inferiority. Park theorized that racial alienation was the product of social and psychological insecurity that compelled whites to keep blacks in inferior positions."[49]

Then there was Hobart C. Chatfield-Taylor, offspring of a prominent New England family, with roots deep in that section's soil and politics. He ostensibly identified with the equal rights movement but articulated his true views in his historical sketch of the city, *Chicago* (1917). This document manifested his feelings much more clearly than his attendance at the fourth annual conference of the NAACP, held in Chicago in 1912. His references to blacks as grinning waiters and dusky adventurers as well as support for racial restrictions in housing in the Hyde Park community belie any commitment to racial equality.[50]

Of course, the city's neo-abolitionist coalition received its most basic affirmation from the presence and, most importantly, the participation and support of African Americans within its ranks. Six played important roles in the original leadership of the Chicago NAACP movement and comprised the fourth segment. The best known advocates of equal rights were Dr. Charles E. Bentley and Ida B. Wells-Barnett. Both were persons who earned national reputations in the struggle in behalf of racial egalitarianism, who developed into bitter personal foes of Booker T. Washington, and who were given to obstinacy in their dealings with others. In microcosm, the differences that Wells-Barnett and Bentley exhibited showed the depth to which intraracial tensions pervaded the new century's civil rights movement.

Diminutive in stature, Wells-Barnett was an egalitarian stalwart with an indomitable spirit regardless of obvious dangers. Hers was not and never could be a world of compromise to injustice.[51] If Jane Addams was

Saint Jane before World War I (before her image was eroded by her peace efforts), then Ida B. Wells-Barnett was Joan of Arc. Wells-Barnett's candid disapproval of Jane Addams's expected ascendancy as the "Mother" of the early Chicago NAACP movement motivated her to criticize Addams's leadership in 1910. "I don't expect a great deal to result from [Addams's] activity, for the very good reason that Miss Addams . . . simply has not the time nor the strength even if she had the inclination to lead this new crusade," she wrote to Joel E. Spingarn.[52] What the prophetic Wells-Barnett referred to as inclination, or mental bent, described the commitment each egalitarian had to make in order to sustain "new abolitionism."

In one head-to-head encounter with Addams, Wells-Barnett thought herself an obvious victor. On a vote on whether or not to establish an independent house organ such as *The Crisis*—the eventual choice—or rely on other newspapers and journals to communicate the message of racial equality, Addams's recommendation of the latter course was voted down.[53] The Rev. Celia Parker Woolley had also come within reach of Ida B. Wells-Barnett's scathing pen based on a racial decision Woolley made in deliberately choosing a white woman over her to head the Frederick Douglass Center.

Wells-Barnett considered Mary White Ovington of the national office in New York, another abolitionist's daughter and known as the "Mother of the New Emancipation," as too weak and too ill-informed about the nature of African American life and aspirations to assume a leadership role in the egalitarian struggle. She described Ovington as having "basked in the sunlight of the adoration of the few college-bred Negroes who have surrounded her, but has . . . fallen short of helping a race which has suffered as no white woman has ever been called upon to suffer or to understand."[54] In contrast, Ovington's opinion about black leaders like Wells-Barnett was that they were individuals "whose greatest efficacy lay in personal rather than in highly disciplined, organized activities."[55] In this and other dealings with racial egalitarians, Wells-Barnett felt an isolation due to race. She finally concluded that "our white women friends were not willing to treat us on a plane of equality with themselves."[56]

On the other hand, Edwin C. Bentley reached the apex of his profession—dentistry—despite his race. This factor, among others, helped explain why he was also the opposite of Wells-Barnett in his dealings with and attitude toward whites. Though Wells-Barnett was uncomfortable when working with whites, Bentley was at ease, interacting with amicability. He was a child of antebellum Cincinnati free persons of color, a very light-complexioned African American who was occasionally mistaken for a Caucasian, and a professional man who enjoyed a downtown white clientele as well as high status among whites both inside and outside his professional circles. Having graduated from the very reputable Chicago College of Dental Surgery (later the Loyola University School of Dentistry until its recent closure), he had had the best professional training. His professional accomplishments were many, and he was anointed "the father of the public schools' oral hygiene movement" among American school children.[57] Bentley remained active within the branch's hierarchy until 1926, enjoying a length of service longer than any other egalitarian leader from this period.

The differences among African Americans extended to another circle of activists within the movement's hierarchy. Dr. George Cleveland Hall and attorney S. Laing Williams emphasized the need to fuse egalitarian ideology, which was more theoretical than practical, with gradualist ideology. Hall was a surgeon at the all-black Provident Hospital, personal physician to Booker T. Washington when he visited Chicago, and a promoter of the Chicago chapter of the National Negro Business League. Moreover, he and his wife competed with Bentley and his wife for the top position in refined Black Belt society. Williams held his position of U.S. Assistant Attorney because of Washington's influence. This fact and his seemingly unswerving loyalty to his patron have relegated Williams to an inglorious place in the history of militant black Chicago. While not a complete sycophant, Williams's respect for and fealty to the Tuskegeean caused him to develop an animosity toward those individuals who opposed his patron along personal lines. S. Laing Williams's career within the federal bureaucracy ended abruptly in late 1912, with Woodrow Wilson's victory in the presidential election. Probably for the first time in their relationship, Booker T. Washington was unable to protect him. Shortly thereafter, Williams, who appeared to have extremely high survival instincts, agreed to accept the vice-presidency of the newly formed branch of the Chicago NAACP after Arthur Aldis was unable to fill the position because of national and international travel commitments.

Above all, Williams was a complex individual with diverse interests. His credentials among African Americans were impressive for this period. He was an alumnus of the University of Michigan and Columbian Law School of Washington, D.C., and along with his wife, publicist Fannie Barrier Williams, pursued a path of upward social mobility among the black and white elites. Acknowledged by intellectuals Alexander Crummell and W. E. B. Du Bois of the American Negro Academy as a person with cerebral qualities, Williams was chosen early as a member of that august body.[58] S. Laing Williams joined Dr. Bentley in the Equal Opportunity League in 1903 and by 1913 assumed the vice-presidency of the Chicago NAACP.[59] Questions about his legal abilities were raised by both contemporaries and historians,[60] but they were acceptable to the progressive coterie that ran the branch, since he won appointment as the branch's first legal counsel in 1914.

Turn-of-the-century Chicago had to be duly impressed with both the quality and the diversity of these stalwarts of the NAACP movement. Yet as impressive as this assemblage was in the aggregate, the character of its composition confronted the movement with the very real problems of race, class, organizational experience, occupation, gender, and ideology on a recurring basis. As the city in general focused on the specter proposed by the meshing of the races, the suspicion and latent tension extant between the races within the movement were being obscured. The roots of interracial divisiveness were generated in the 1909 New York meeting and revived quickly once the delegates returned to Chicago. Among the blacks, no one individual's anguish more personified this tension than did Ida B. Wells-Barnett's. Yet, with the optimism so characteristic of progressives, she felt enthusiastic enough about the future likelihood of racial progress in 1911 to declare that the cause of equal rights would produce "the new movement for our emancipation . . . [since it] has the germ of immortality."[61]

A possibility of organizational immortality notwithstanding, from the perspective of some white racial egalitarians it appeared unrealistic to place too much control in the hands of blacks who were their social inferiors along class lines. As the third greatest obstacle to be overcome within the movement's ranks, class differences also appeared glaringly insurmountable. Several of the prominent men of the committee belonged to elite clubs in the Loop, such as the Hamilton, City, and Union League, where blacks were observable only in their capacities as servants. Arthur Aldis, George Packard, and N. W. Harris were all in this category.[62] In addition, class dictated residency. Most of the whites lived far away from blacks, some as far north on the Lake Michigan shoreline as palatial Lake Forest, a distance of twenty miles. Educationally, they received their training at Harvard, Yale, Brown, and Chicago.

Occupationally, the whites held major positions of leadership in the city's political economy. Theirs was a social and civic status that shone in sharp contrast to their black counterparts who were struggling for basic recognition of their humanity and citizenship rights. Of the six blacks who were included within the ranks of the hierarchy, two were doctors: Bentley and George Cleveland Hall, who was a graduate of Bennet College. The generally held view perceived training at this college suspect as to an overall level of excellence. S. Laing Williams was a struggling attorney without exceptional leadership skills. George Arthur was a social worker at all-black institutions on the South Side. Ida B. Wells-Barnett was a housewife, social worker, and sometime municipal employee. Garnetta Tibbs's occupation was unknown. So, blacks carried an obvious disadvantage with regard to organization and networking in a white-dominated society. As a result, only the names of Bentley and Wells-Barnett figured prominently among the neo-abolitionists.

Organizing the "new abolitionism" in the new century proceeded with a balance between energy and deliberation. By 1910, within one-half year of the formation of the National Negro Committee, the movement in Chicago organized itself on a loose, informal basis into a vigilance committee.[63] With this action, the NAACP's first local affiliate evolved, a harbinger of what was to become a national network of branches beginning in 1913.[64] In the course of its development, the scope of the obstacles it had to overcome exceeded anything imaginable in New York in 1909.

What evolved structurally into a vigilance committee was formed around the most notable personages among progressives committed to racial equality—Addams, Bentley, Jones, Wells-Barnett, Woolley, and Willoughby Walling. With their skills as publicists they dominated this committee, employing the progressives' tactic of using publicity and moral suasion to produce change. The group included, in addition to the six aforementioned writers, Judges Edward Osgood Brown and Robert McMurdy, along with Charles T. Hallihan, editor of the *Chicago Evening Post*. Conspicuously missing were the two major black newspaper publishers of the city, Abbott and Taylor. Quite possibly they may not have wanted to join a virtually all-white group even though they all sought the same end—racial equality. Or, it might have been because, in 1910, neither had the socioeconomic status or civic standing which would have made him acceptable to the upper- and middle-class white racial egalitarian leadership if he had desired membership. One factor of strategic importance became evident quite early. If there was to be a truly national organization, a committee had to be established in Chicago. Excluding the eastern-seaboard cities of Washington, Baltimore, Philadelphia, New York, and Boston, Chicago existed as the only other major metropolis sympathetic to the fledgling NAACP ideal and movement. As the movement's linchpin beyond the eastern seaboard, well-populated Chicago was expected to build a financial base in the city for local activities as well as to attract philanthropists, such as Blaine and Rosenwald, whose help was needed for national endeavors.

Reliance on a volunteer group to run the branch in the manner of the national office presented the branch with another of its major organizational problems.[65] Its leaders balanced demanding professional responsibilities with their new civil rights commitment. Brown and McMurdy were sitting judges; Hallinan ran a newspaper; Addams, Woolley, Allison, and Wells-Barnett administered the affairs of settlement houses; Williams was a struggling attorney; Jones, age sixty-seven in 1910, still heeded the call to preach; and Hall and Bentley tended to their medical practices. As for the two philanthropists, Blaine and Rosenwald, neither had the time or the inclination to run the committee and its successor structurally, the branch.

The absence of a paid chief administrative officer, serving in the capacity of an executive secretary, to operate a permanent office from which daily activities were conducted represented another obstacle to both the growth of the organization and the implementation of the NAACP program. In contrast, the national office in New York City resembled a beehive of activity, with a paid staff and volunteers. The age factor also affected the organizational and programmatic growth of the local unit. At a time when the age of New York NAACP leaders averaged thirty-five in 1909, the Chicagoans were almost a generation older, with an average age of fifty-three.[66] The difference in the level of experience and maturity no doubt made the acceptance of centrality, or national office hegemony over branches, problematic. Although Bentley accepted the concept of centrality during the branch's formative years,[67] his future attitude and that of his successors was not guaranteed.

From incipient discussions and meetings in 1910, more formal deliberations followed in 1911 and 1912 centering on structure, the method of operation, and a constitution. Willoughby Walling, whose brother, William, had assumed the mantle of leadership in New York as the chairman of the national executive committee, became a major spokesman for the Chicago movement. As vigilance committee secretary, Walling espoused support for an organization that was structured according to his brother's ideas.[68] Adoption of this approach dictated that activism would precede the establishment of a structure. Further, a broad-based, inclusive membership was envisioned.[69]

The Walling plan differed considerably from that conceived by Bentley, who was affectionately referred to in organizational correspondence as "the doctor." This consummate professional envisioned the formation of an organization that concentrated on raising funds and building a membership that brought together like-minded individuals, and that would garner prestige among all Chicagoans. In this vein, "the doctor" pursued activities that promoted racial equality through the dissemination of information and propaganda as well as through investigations based on extensive research. Bentley's plan duplicated his schema for the Niagara Movement in 1905.[70] As such, it dictated a course leading toward exclusivity and the gradual organizational development of a mass base. Not unexpectedly, his approach appealed to the influential, if not the circumspect, among the committee's white leadership. Subsequently, Bentley's plan was adopted and implemented.

Accordingly, Bentley's status and influence within the organization grew to such an extent that he became the leading spokesman for the Chicago movement. His rise was also attributable to the absence of a continuous, assertive white leadership. By the 1920s, Bentley would be recognized as the branch's kingmaker.[71]

During this early phase of its development, the branch's organizational fabric suffered because of the movement's dependence on a hierarchy under WASP hegemony, its limited influence in both the white and black communities, and an inexhaustible willingness on the part of its members to engage in extensive volunteerism. As the decade progressed, the influence of the First World War reached such intensity and was so pervasive that it produced an erosion of the Progressive Decade's enthusiasm for peaceful domestic change. Just as progressivism generally succumbed to enervation,[72] the egalitarian ranks of the Chicago NAACP experienced the effects of this trend. The quality of the leadership diminished at the same time because of the constant departure of key personnel as the constitutionally prescribed rotation of officers took effect.

Without a viable membership and widespread popular support, Judge Brown was selected, rather than elected, president in 1913. He remained in the presidency for the remainder of the decade. Jane Addams reduced her involvement by 1913 because of her commitment to the international peace movement. She did not revive her interest (except for her call in 1915 while in New York for concerted civic action against the racist motion picture, *Birth of a Nation*) until pressured by Mary White Ovington of the national office in 1922.[73] Ida B. Wells-Barnett cooperated with the branch in 1913 but afterwards never participated actively in any NAACP-related activities. The Rev. Celia Parker Woolley and banker N. W. Harris decided that they could not serve on the Executive Committee and contribute effectively beyond what they had done in the past.[74] Following the same trend, when the two-year tenures of service of heiress Anita McCormick Blaine and Charles T. Hallinan expired in 1915, they declined to renew their ties to the branch. Willoughby Walling also left the branch after his two-year term as treasurer ended in 1915.

The drain on the branch's leadership continued as Dr. George Cleveland Hall and Julius Rosenwald's representative on the Executive Committee, William C. Graves, stopped attending meetings sometime around 1915 or 1916 because of what they perceived to be chronic inactivity from the egalitarians led by Judge Brown. Rosenwald still contributed to the branch's operations as late as 1920, so his representative's departure from the branch was due more to the character of the leadership and ineffectiveness of the program than to some imagined ideological conflict.[75] Perhaps the most debilitating blow came when S. Laing Williams left the organization to devote full time to his law practice in order to provide for his family. Throughout 1914, he served the branch as its legal advisor but with a limited effort at fighting discrimination in the courts.

At this time, the direction and operations of the branch fell by default into the hands of a select few: Bentley, Jones, and McMurdy. All were able, enlightened, but aging. As they closed ranks to perpetuate what they considered their obligation to the egalitarian crusade, they had evolved into an oligarchy. Prisoners of their own class and status, they resolved to serve the cause as best they could.

The branch's constitution mandated large-scale meetings of the membership, but only on a quarterly basis, a limitation that could not have been more pleasing to Brown and Bentley. They wished to minimize mass-level participation in the running of the organization because of their distrust of the judgment of the rank and file among the small, predominantly black membership. Large-scale meetings were called only irregularly during and following the war years. Concomitantly, the meetings of the Executive Committee required only a quorum of five to transact the branch's business, and they became the only assemblages in which decision-making was made. Apparently lost in these maneuverings were the guiding principles of egalitarianism, delaying democracy, or inclusiveness. Full participation did not occur until the national office forced it on the Chicago leadership during the 1920s.

The initial structure of the organization called for working committees to carry out the branch's program. Committees on legislation, grievances, and membership were established in 1913. The legislation committee consisted of four of the most influential members on the Executive Committee: Brown, McMurdy, Hallinan, and George Packard, the replacement in 1913 for manufacturer and municipal reformer Charles R. Crane. The grievance committee included Williams, Bentley, Sophonisba Breckenridge, and Packard. In contrast, the membership committee was composed of four of the least influential persons within the branch's hierarchy: Garnetta Tibbs, a black woman added to the leadership as a replacement for banker N. W. Harris; George R. Arthur, the black secretary of the Wabash Avenue YMCA; Thomas Allinson of the Henry Booth Settlement House; and S. Laing Williams. A fourth committee on education was formed in 1914 to fight a growing public sentiment favoring segregation in the Chicago Public School system.

Before Hallinan left the branch in 1915, he handled its publicity as chairman of the press service. In his able hands, news of the Chicago branch appeared in *The Crisis* as well as locally in the *Tribune, Defender, Broad-Ax,* and *Evening Post.* In all probability Hallinan was largely responsible for the favorable editorials about egalitarianism that appeared from time to time in the white press, such as the one in the *Tribune* in 1914 which read: "After all factors are brought within view, the human paradox appears that whenever the Negro, in spite of the staggering handicaps under which he moves, has forced himself upward he thereby places himself in competition with whites, and immediately becomes the object of opposition. . . . The wisdom of Abraham Lincoln who said 'This government cannot endure permanently half slave and half free' is wisdom today. Our policy toward the Negro most certainly and most profoundly will react upon ourselves. This is a consideration which gives to the movement for the advancement of colored people the force of enlightened self-interest."[76]

Not unexpectedly, the work of the membership committee did not produce satisfactory results. Although the branch's records indicated in both 1912 and 1913 that the organization had "many new members," this unit's failure was evidenced by the branch's small membership of 275 persons in 1916. This figure positioned Chicago in eighth place among all branches nationally, with the leading branch, Washington, having 1,164 members and ninth-place Des Moines having 222.[77] At the time, U.S. census data indicated that the city's overall population had reached 2,185,283 in 1910 with a black component of 44,103. Clearly, by no reasonable standard of measurement had the branch reached a point where it could be considered a dominant force in the city. However, one bright spot existed. It was manifested in the number of NAACP sympathizers (or perhaps Du Bois aficionados) that was larger than the membership total, as judged by the subscriptions to *The Crisis* in 1914. Illinois attracted the largest readership nationally with 3,388 subscribers.[78]

Despite the slow growth in membership, major occupational blocs joined the branch in 1914. The enrollment of the car porters from the Northwestern Railroad evidently came as a positive response to the NAACP's efforts to save their jobs from a racist plot of job elimination inspired by the Brotherhood of Railroad Trainmen in 1913.[79] The enlistment of black U.S. postal workers who belonged to the Phalanx Forum demonstrated that the upwardly mobile portion of the working class could be attracted to the organization's cause if the branch's agenda was inclusive and effectively presented as such. The Phalanx Forum, which had been founded in 1910 and was affiliated with the Appomattox Club, represented a group with a commitment to egalitarianism corresponding to the NAACP's.

The finances of the branch, which were to have come from the membership dues as well as from contributions from wealthy white supporters such as Blaine, Rosenwald, Harris, and Aldis, proved to be limited. Whites contributed to this and other altruistic organizations usually on the condition that the persons being served, if able, also share in the financial burden. Rosenwald was a well-known promoter of this type of contribution. Among the masses of blacks, who demonstrated their impressive abilities at fund-raising in their churches and other racially controlled institutions, there was a shared belief that the responsibility of financing a white-led, racial egalitarian organization rested in the hands of white philanthropists.[80]

Over the years and despite the elitist attitudes of some of its leaders, the branch demonstrated to black working men and women that it existed more for the latter's benefit than it did for some unattainable theoretical goal. As a result, their support grew but slowly. One very creative example of reaching out to the Black Belt community took place during the summer of 1914. A street carnival was held that attracted thousands of participants and counterbalanced the apathy so often shown toward the branch. The event proved successful, raising over $400.[81]

The branch achieved higher visibility within the Black Belt by staffing a permanent office with a paid employee or volunteer board member. By 1914, S. Laing Williams performed legal and administrative services out of this facility; but he required compensation. The arrangement proved expensive, so the branch cooperated with the city's Legal Aid Society to get as many discrimination cases as possible taken to court.[82] With this demonstrated inability to organize and function efficiently, the branch accomplished little during 1915 and 1916. Not surprisingly, organizational inertia resulted eventually in a stagnant program.

As early as 1910, one dramatic event in particular provided evidence that racial equality had reached pragmatic as well as operational levels, both as a crusade and as a living ideal. In its urgency it sparked remedial action from among the ranks of black neo-abolitionists and garnered the nation's attention. Equal rights advocates aided Steve Green, a fugitive Arkansas sharecropper, in obtaining justice while in Chicago. Green had shot and killed his former white landlord in self-defense after being wounded himself in an unprovoked attack. What precipitated the incident was Green's attempt to control his own life by working on land that provided adequate compensation for his labor and subsistence for his family. In doing so, Green had broken a southern taboo by going to work in a place of his choosing. After the shooting, Green fled and successfully reached Chicago, where misplaced trust in a fellow black Arkansan led to his arrest. Extradition to Arkansas loomed, but so did the probability of an appointment with a lynch mob.

At this juncture, Ida B. Wells-Barnett purportedly set the city's protest machinery into motion, which eventually led to Green's being freed.[83] Green was rescued at the southern border of Illinois and returned to Chicago for an extradition hearing that was described vividly by the *Broad-Ax:* "Never before in Chicago was there such a trial, rivalling as it did even the old underground [railroad] scenes of a half century past. The court room was crowded with men and women of both races, but unlike the scenes of the past, the man was ably represented by his own race. . . ."[84] In what amounted to the best of the old as well as the best of the new, this reference conjured up memories of abolitionist days when Chicago proudly wore the epithet "sink hole of abolition" because of its intense support of fugitive slaves.[85] Steve Green won his freedom and pursued his destiny in the city.

Communicating closely with Ida B. Wells-Barnett, whose presence in pursuit of racial justice made her appear ubiquitous, the national office of the NAACP sought publicity to demonstrate to the nation the strength of its commitment to changing a racially hostile environment. This case of a beleaguered sharecropper provided the perfect example as well as conveying a significance beyond the increased standing it gave the national organization. It also seemed to spur the local NAACP movement onward by creating a sentiment for interorganizational cooperation. Disparate elements within the black community acted as one unit as the Negro Fellowship League, the Appomattox Club, the *Chicago Defender,* and political leader and attorney Ed Wright of the Second Ward's black Republican organization coalesced.[86]

Success in the Green case was followed by months of prosaic activities, culminating in the spring of 1912 with the vigilance committee's hosting of the fourth annual conference of the NAACP. After four months of preparations, this landmark meeting convened and symbolized what America could become in realizing its highest ideals, even if only for a three-day period beginning on Sunday, April 30. Differences of race, gender, religion, and politics were subordinated to the goal of making racial equality a reality. The opening addresses of Oswald Garrison Villard and Judge Edward Osgood Brown at the newly opened Sinai Temple on South Parkway at Forty-Sixth Street set the tone for the conclave. Despite a deluge of rain, Villard's appeal for support of the NAACP's objectives stirred an overflow crowd of 1,500. He declared indignantly: "That it [the NAACP] exists at all is in itself an indictment of our American democracy." He noted that "theoretically, all but those most imbued with race prejudice grant the justness of our contentions," and that no special favors were being demanded by blacks while, in fact, the nation owed them for centuries of unremunerated labor and meritorious military service. Villard spoke of how the nation's acquiescence placed a greater set of burdens on the backs of African Americans in contradiction to Natural Law which called for unfettered competition. He scorned a "nation [that] boasts of opportunity . . . [and] then makes a prompt exception to the rule and says that the colored man may rise . . . but only so far as his white fellows will let him." In his peroration Villard argued that "our treatment of the colored people of today tarnishes the country's good name, mocks and flouts our republican institutions and makes a hypocrite of the nation. . . ."[87]

Judge Brown followed Villard on the program. He stressed the need of fair-thinking whites to see their involvement in extending opportunity to all as a matter of duty, rather than as some beneficent gesture to a downtrodden race. Brown declared: "It is a duty every American of the white race owes to himself and his fellow white citizens quite as much as he does to the Negro to see to it . . . that the color of a man's skin shall not subject him to insult, oppression and injustice in a country boasting of its democracy, its liberty and the political equality of its citizens." The jurist concluded that "every advance that the Negro has made[,] has rendered the more brutal and cruel, the meaner and more dishonorable[, the] acts of discrimination and insult against him."[88]

The throngs of supporters who attended the assemblies were no doubt swayed by the Sunday sermons given by cooperating ministers, priests, and rabbis throughout the city entitled "The Lynching Evil in the Country." Two meetings at Hull House also generated interest in and enthusiasm for the conference. A Monday luncheon held at the all-black Provident Hospital on the city's South Side fostered a good feeling among blacks as to the conference's inclusivity. At each meeting, the amiable intermixing of whites and blacks gave visual testimony to the practicality of the egalitarian message.

On the second and third days, meetings catered to an enthusiastic public that overflowed the 700 seats in cavernous Handel Hall at Randolph and Wabash Avenues in the Loop (in what is now the Marshall Field building). On a daily basis (excluding the executive session of Monday morning) hundreds filled the hall while hundreds more were turned away. At the Tuesday night session, the last public meeting of the conference, over 1,000 persons failed to get seats as Ida B. Wells-Barnett and four other speakers informed the crowd of the wickedness of racial discrimination and the virtues of racial equality. This session also featured three of the city's wealthiest citizens on the podium—Mrs. Cyrus McCormick, her heiress daughter, Mrs. Emmons Blaine, and Mr. Julius Rosenwald.

The conclave presented Jane Addams with her finest day as a racial egalitarian as she acted as the NAACP's official hostess. The presence of Abdul Baha'u'llah of Persia, hailed as the apostle of universalism and founder of Baha'i, indicated the global interest being evinced in the fledgling American equal rights movement. Ida B. Wells-Barnett addressed the assemblage, and so did Julius Rosenwald, who struck a cautionary note in reminding the assemblage that there were ethnic Americans whose rights were also endangered.[89] A series of salutary journalistic descriptions of the conference placed it firmly in the abolitionist tradition.[90]

Constitutional empowerment became the next most important step forward for the equal rights crusade in Chicago. In April 1913 the national office issued a charter to Chicago and with it official branch status.[91] However, some of the same internal and external influences of interracial tension and racist opposition that deleteriously affected the Chicago NAACP's organizational development extended to its programmatic activities. The branch's program had a lifespan that was measured in clusters of months and seasons instead of years.[92]

Using the 1913 national guidelines for branches as a basis, a comparison can be made as to what was attempted and what was actually accomplished. Twelve goals had to be met for branches to be considered effective components within the NAACP network. Each branch was given the mandate "to watch for hostile state or municipal legislation as well as injustice in the courts; to work to eliminate discrimination and work to keep it from expanding; to seek legal redress through test cases in the courts; to secure new laws and ordinances to protect the lives and property of citizens where appropriate; to encourage education for all children at all grade levels; to conserve the health and healthful habits of citizens; to oversee occupational opportunities and diversity of work, especially for youth; to cooperate on civic boards and commissions with whites; to monitor the media as well as promote a free flow of information about blacks; to interact with whites of good will; to encourage voting and the maintenance of good government; and, to meet monthly to discuss executive operations as well as quarterly to inform the membership of pertinent matters affecting their civil rights."[93]

Of the twelve guidelines, the Chicago NAACP adhered to only half. Part of the local inertia resulted from Judge Brown's belief that support for the Association's strategy meant that the national office was the trendsetter in protest activities and that the branches fulfilled only a supportive role. Because of this stance, Brown's critics accused him of being too willing to bask in the light of the achievements of the national office while accomplishing little locally.[94] Whatever his perception of what the branch should have been doing, the branch's constitution and guidelines clearly called for a comprehensive local initiative against growing racism in Chicago that never manifested itself in this first decade. Another factor affecting programmatic success merits mention. No program could prove itself successful over time without the cooperation of the dominant white majority and its leadership, which set public policy on race.

Yet there was notable movement toward eliminating racism. As early as March 1913, a group of prominent black egalitarians representing the Appomattox Club and the *Chicago Defender,* who were reluctant to affiliate with the branch, did meet with its biracial leadership in the Loop to discuss ways of fighting the rising tide of racism in the city. Symbolically enough, they gathered at the prestigious all-white City Club.[95] An insightful discussion ensued and agreement was reached to cooperate in sending a delegation to the state capital at Springfield to combat what the *Defender* referred to as an incursion of "Southern Bourbonism" into the city and state. This coalition lobbied in April against a spate of discriminatory bills affecting the right to marry according to choice, to travel without seating restrictions, and to retain employment without fear of racial firing.[96]

Three sets of laws had been introduced into the Illinois General Assembly, with perhaps the worst being the "Full Crew Bill." This progressive legislation called for the removal of 143 black railroad porters on at least ten railroads operating in Illinois, supposedly in the name of efficiency. Charles Hallinan, reading an incisive argument drawn up by Judge Brown, declared, "Industrial openings for the colored man are so rare that it seems to us contrary to the dictates of natural justice as well as opposed to sound public policy to deprive an entire group of colored men of employment which they have carried on to the satisfaction of their employers and the public, unless there is a paramount public necessity."[97] Cognizant of what needed to be done and how, Chicago's neo-abolitionists successfully halted this bill at its introductory phase in the Illinois legislature.

The next assault on social justice came after a representative from southern Illinois, a section of the country which exhibited traits of both racial conservatism and outright racism, attempted to introduce legislation that promoted segregation throughout the state on railroads and other public carriers. This bill clearly violated the Illinois Civil Rights Act. With its obvious legal weakness exposed, its demise was ensured when it was left to languish in a Senate committee.

The last in the set of odious bills sought to prevent marriages between blacks and whites. There were five separate bills that came from both the lower and middle tiers of the state. Robert S. Abbott and other blacks knew that they were aimed at pugilist Jack Johnson, who had gained national notoriety for his courting of white women and subsequent marriage to one of them. Public pressure from whites mounted, so Johnson fled the country into a self-imposed exile in Europe lasting for seven years. Abbott's *Defender* noted the hypocrisy involved and editorialized that the prize-fighter was being "crucified for his race."[98]

Employing a previously used strategy, black State Representative Robert R. Jackson from Chicago's South Side repeatedly maneuvered these bills into committee where they languished by design. The credit for the victories in Springfield was attributed by *The Crisis* to the branch, but once again the concerted and rather effective efforts of the NAACP had formed only a part of a comprehensive, well-coordinated campaign. Much like the branch, Representative Jackson took almost complete credit.[99]

The branch did not act in accordance with either national guidelines or the black community's wishes to encourage greater job opportunities, fuller participation in the academic aspects of education, and heightened involvement in political matters. Throughout this decade and into the next, other groups and agencies such as the Negro Fellowship League, the Appomattox Club, and the *Chicago Defender*, rather than the Chicago NAACP, carried the torch of protest advocacy for civil rights.[100]

The character of Chicago politics posed an inherent threat to organizing for civil rights within the civic sphere. Even before there was a dreaded Chicago political "machine" to loom as the bane of progressives (and later liberals) everywhere, both the direct and indirect influence of political activities in various forms—electoral, governmental (administrative, legislative and judicial), and party- or machine-oriented—extended beyond its normal sphere, and, for the most part, affected the movement for racial equality adversely. Although the altruistic yet self-serving actions of politicians would be treated with suspicion by future generations of Chicagoans because of the city's early history of civics dominating politics in the black community, what occurred at this time was anything but anomalous. Neither political participation nor officeholding precluded an interest in protecting the civil rights that political participation won as early, in fact, as Illinois's first civil rights law in 1885. Between this period and the branch's emergence, relations between the civic and political realms were symbiotic.[101] However, the activities of Jane Addams in 1912 did compromise the relationship between the civic and political spheres, producing negative results immediately and presaging what the future held.

When the Progressive Party convention was held in Chicago in 1912, all of the black delegates from the South were systematically refused their seats. Conversely, all black delegates from the North were seated. If the former maneuver was acceptable on the grounds of rotten elections, the refusal of Roosevelt to adopt a civil rights plank, which had been customary procedure for Republicans, was not. This dastardly move on the part of Roosevelt immediately incurred the ire of many progressives. Jane Addams entered the controversy at two levels. Her high profile at the convention produced controversy based on her politically puritanical persona and subsequent refusal to refute or at least separate herself from Roosevelt's policy of racial exclusion for the sake of political expediency.[102] Since the day of reckoning from black political empowerment was still far in the future, there was no major threat to the egalitarian movement at this time. However, there would come a time when hostile gestures by the NAACP or its leaders would evoke political retaliation.

During this decade, the black political machine was in a phase of incipient development. So, politicians carefully nurtured the mutual interests in racial issues that they shared with their constituents. Oscar De Priest, who was elected in 1915 as the first black member of the Chicago City Council, stood valiantly for equal rights two years later while defending himself from a *Tribune* editorial accusing him of pushing racial equality too far. He was often given to bluster, but this action appeared genuine. De Priest declared, "[I] was a Negro before [I] was an alderman, and . . . if insisting on the rights of a Negro should mean that [I] would never set foot in the [City] Council, [I] would still insist."[103] Black legislators serving in the General Assembly were traditionally elected by fellow blacks who expected them to demonstrate a commitment to civil rights. Because of this expectation, the state-level black politician acted as much as a civil rights advocate as a legislator. Robert R. Jackson was just one in a series of representatives who fulfilled his role with great skill.[104] With this tacit commitment from their state representatives, blacks in Chicago experienced a strong sense of security.

However, beyond individual and black group commitments to the advancement of civil rights in Chicago and Springfield, the major role of the black South Side political organization has to be understood in conjunction with the rise of the Republican machine of Mayor William "Big

Bill" Thompson, which controlled municipal government between 1915 and 1927, and again from 1927 to 1931. The election of "Big Bill" Thompson as mayor in 1915 and the subsequent formation of his Republican machine coincided with, built up, and nurtured the Second Ward's black political organization under Edward "The Iron Master" Wright. Thompson was a New Englander by birth and scion of the abolitionist tradition which treated blacks with a humanity that made him in actuality more of a racial egalitarian than most of his racially progressive fellow whites.[105] Thompson came to be hailed as the second Lincoln by blacks in Chicago.

Ed Wright led an organization that provided the electoral balance of power which put and kept Thompson in office. Yet Wright's Second Ward organization was concomitantly an integral part of a citywide organization of various competing ethnic and religious groups which was "a patron of minority groups and a broker for business."[106] Because of its emphasis primarily on party maintenance and enhancement at the expense of social change, the more it grew, the more it stymied comprehensive black advancement in employment, housing, and education, which was perceived by whites as a threat to the status quo.

The second decade of the twentieth century witnessed a rebirth of interest in the theoretical possibility of achieving full racial equality. The Chicago NAACP, the vehicle for its success, established itself within an environment which nurtured fertile ground for growth. Despite internal and external obstacles related to class, intraracial and interracial tension, ideology, and politics, the branch was slowly emerging as a Chicago fixture, fastened, but not very securely, to the Chicago civic fabric.

4

"The New Negro" in the Black Metropolis, 1917–1924

Since the World War, there has been a revolutionary change in the psychology of the Negro. He now will work with whites or permit them to work with him; but he resents it when they work for him—he being their ward. He wants to control to a large degree his own affairs. . . . His racial conscience has been greatly developed. Our trouble in Chicago has been that this has been taken too much into account.

—*Robert W. Bagnall to Carl G. Roberts, 1925*

In order to serve the newly created as well as old wants of the Negro population a large group of professional men and women were attracted to the city. This group has become large enough to comprise a new leadership as well as a distinct class. . . . This new class of professional and business men is setting the standards of behavior for the rest of the community.

—*E. Franklin Frazier, 1929*

THE ADVENT OF World War I in 1914 and subsequent U.S. involvement by 1917 convinced many white progressives that the domestic struggle against racial inequality assumed less importance than, first, eliminating bellicose authoritarianism in order "to make the world safe for democracy"; second, ending the brutality of war itself, as advocated by Addams, Blaine, Jones, and Hallihan; and, third, assisting the southern migrants who were attracted north by economic opportunities to adjust to urban life. With America's entry into the war in 1917, the national NAACP succumbed to the general pro-war argument as well as, somewhat, to the compromise legacy of Booker T. Washington (who died in 1915). Du Bois and Joel E. Spingarn (who subsequently fought in the war) initially criticized and later reversed themselves on the federal government's proposition that black army officers be trained in racially segregated facilities.[1] The two NAACP leaders accepted the arrangement along with the compromising argument that without the special camps, there would be no black officer corps to provide leadership for black troops as they entered battle. The endorsement of this backward step in race relations placed these racial egalitarians in the sphere of ethical relativism that pervaded the war years. The desired end—victory over German tyranny—was thought to justify belligerence as a suitable means of restoring peace in Europe just as it did this homefront accommodation to racism.

Two generations later, World War I veterans and Chicago NAACP leaders Earl B. Dickerson and Oscar C. Brown, Sr., reflected positively on the arrangement as one that was necessary and that paid long-term dividends. Officers' training produced a cadre of leaders for the Black Belt in postwar decades. Meanwhile, other black Chicagoans held steadfastly to the conviction that racial equality was ideologically inviolate. Both Bentley and Hall rejected the concept of segregated camps altogether at a May 1917 meeting, at which Robert S. Abbott commented, "Something is wrong when patriotic, loyal citizens ready and able to fight, are compelled to petition their government for an unprescribed approval to fight for it."[2] According to Bentley's biographer, when the "doctor" was confronted with the probability of having to examine white and black soldiers in separate dental facilities, he became indignant.[3] Just what form this indignation assumed unfortunately is unknown; but, consistent with Bentley's strict adherence to principles, he could conceivably have refused to participate in military examinations.[4]

The war-induced migration of approximately 50,000 black Southerners increased the city's black population by 148.5 percent as the overall black population climbed from 44,103 in 1910 to 109,458 by the time of the 1920 census. This spectacular demographic increase affected the branch negatively by relegating its crusade firmly to a secondary role in the lives of black and white Chicagoans, who were now demanding services to help migrants adjust to city living. By 1916–1917, Chicago's race egalitarians developed a strong interest in the seven-year-old Urban League movement which emphasized economic and social adjustment to urban life rather than a change in race relations. With so many unassimilated newcomers in the city, even branch president Edward O. Brown considered a smooth transition to city life "of the greatest importance to the Negro."[5] He was joined by Jane Addams, who wrote to Mrs. Emmons Blaine soliciting her support by observing that "the condition of the newly migrated Negro is an especially hopeless one."[6]

The formation of a Chicago Urban League meant that the basic needs of black migrants in the areas of employment, housing, education, and urban etiquette would be met, so Julius Rosenwald quickly lent his support. His personal secretary, William C. Graves, urged persons with whom he corresponded in Rosenwald's behalf not "to confuse the Chicago Urban League with the [Chicago] NAACP [which was burdened by] chronic inactivity [when assistance was needed immediately]."[7] Even the egalitarian *Defender* clamored for an Urban League affiliate to be established as public concern and support grew.

With the formal establishment of the Chicago Urban League by 1917, many of the founding members of the Chicago NAACP movement were found conspicuously among its Board of Directors: Addams, Brown, Rosenwald, Hall, Woolley, Breckenridge, and Blaine. Several paradoxes illustrated the extent of ideological change that was taking place. The first president of the League, Professor Robert E. Park of the University of Chicago's Department of Sociology, served previously as a personal secretary to the late Booker T. Washington and lauded the latter's influence over his thinking on America's race problem. And in 1918 Celia Parker Woolley offered the League the facilities of the Frederick Douglass Center as its headquarters, nearly a decade and a half after its establishment as a testimony to racial egalitarianism in action.

The conditions of the Chicago branch deteriorated to such an extent that Judge Brown felt compelled to write to Dr. Arthur B. Spingarn (brother to Joel) in New York, pleading: "We need inspiration and encouragement for our work such as [only] you can give us."[8] When the East St. Louis, Illinois, riots occurred in the summer of 1917, the branch responded by sending $200 in assistance. Meanwhile, the *Defender* sent money and Ida B. Wells-Barnett to the scene to render whatever assistance was needed.[9]

Partial resolution of the branch's problems came the next year as Dr. Bentley formulated a reorganization of the branch, ambitiously hoping to attract as many as 2,000 members. His reform plan was geared to correct some of its basic organizational deficiencies, and although it overlooked the problem of rule by the few of the few, it did result in the establishment in spring 1919 of a branch office and the employment of a full-time secretary who would report to the board and handle cases involving discrimination.[10]

The office, located at 3125 State Street in the heart of the Black Belt, provided a desperately needed visibility and service outlet. The *Defender* observed that with its opening "the work of the local branch passed into that phase of constructive activity which makes [it] a most desirable and highly valuable asset . . . in the effort to better conditions."[11] It opened under the direction of A. Clement MacNeal, a newcomer to Chicago from Louisiana by way of Yale University, who was destined to become the branch's most activist president before World War II. MacNeal well fit the prototype of the emerging "New Negro." He was educated under competitive circumstances, articulate, future-oriented, courageous when pressed in racially confrontational situations, and determined to make racial equality a reality during his lifetime.

Then occurred what historian William M. Tuttle, Jr., described as one of the most dramatic and tragic events of the "Red Summer of 1919."[12] The infamous Chicago race riot began on Sunday evening, July 27, 1919, on the South Side lakefront, ultimately resulting in 38 fatalities, 520 injuries, and thousands of dollars in property damage. At its bloody conclusion after four days, it afforded the branch an opportunity to bring a modicum of justice to the handling of the whole devastating episode as well as improve the NAACP's image. But apprehension by Brown and Bentley delayed action on behalf of black riot defendants initially because of fear that some of them might be guilty of felonious criminal activities.[13]

While the branch pondered its course of action, the wheels of justice ground to a halt in Chicago. Cook County states attorney MacLay Hoyle reported a list of indictments to the investigating grand jury which contained the names solely of blacks, despite the fact that nearly two-thirds of the fatalities and injured were black. One case involved a black man who, as an occupant of a car attacked by white rioters, fought back and stabbed a rioter to death. He was arrested and thrown into a jail cell where he lay unattended with injuries for a week.[14] Responsible citizens repudiated the states attorney's actions and he was forced to act in an impartial, professional manner which resulted in the indictment of whites along with blacks.

Arthur T. Aldis, an early white progressive supporter, considered the riot the result of smoldering racial prejudice that ultimately manifested itself in a breakdown of democracy. He felt that religious and political justice was overdue and necessary for a true democracy to exist.[15] In A. C. MacNeal's assessment of the riot, the "issues in it were two: lawlessness per se and discrimination because of race." Regarding the latter, he castigated a criminal justice system which proved itself color-conscious: "The courts are alive to the need of meting out punishment and affording protection where discrimination occurs on the part of colored people against white people and ample defense is assured the victims." MacNeal concluded: "Where the discrimination is against the colored people there is not the same certainty of clear justice and able defense of the victims is not assured to the same degree. We feel that it is the duty of this community to know that all colored persons who are guiltless shall have adequate defense . . . fifteen white and twenty-three colored persons were killed in the riot. The arrests attained a ratio of five colored persons to one white person and the indictments show a similar ratio."[16] The national office equated what transpired in the wake of the county indictments with a northern version of a lynching.

Local action began when Chicago Urban League president Robert E. Park organized the Joint Emergency Committee to protect the rights of blacks who had fallen victim to malfeasance in the criminal justice system. On the sidelines, the branch waited for NAACP president Joel E. Spingarn to arrive from New York. Once Spingarn surveyed the riot landscape, he played no small role in energizing branch officers, along with local and state governmental officials, to correct an obvious maladministration of justice. But decisive NAACP action was not forthcoming until October when the Chicago NAACP established a broad-based, biracial group called the Committee to Secure Justice for Colored Riot Defendants. Dr. Bentley assumed the chairmanship and A. C. MacNeal became its secretary.[17]

After scrutinizing the facts of the situation, the Committee appealed for the support of erstwhile branch members Julius Rosenwald, Mrs. Emmons Blaine, Jane Addams, Mary McDowell, and Sophonisba Breckenridge. Noted social settlement worker Dr. Graham Taylor also joined them. The support rendered by these members of the white civic Establishment now confirmed to the city at large that blacks were the victims rather than the perpetrators of the riot. After raising $12,000 through this defense fund and more than $7,000 among blacks in a separate effort, a successful series of defenses were mounted and the cause of justice was served.[18]

On the horizon, a new decade loomed, and the very uncertainty of life seemed to have a profound and disturbing influence on the altered routines and mindsets of Chicagoans. Anxieties arose from a variety of circumstances: the unsettling pursuit of world peace; labor and racial unrest; anticipated economic recession; and a besieged value system. Prohibition challenged the imagination of those who wished to imbibe in violation of the law, leading to highly organized criminal efforts and the creation of an underworld government under Al Capone's control. Enmeshed in criminal violence and official corruption, Chicago grew to symbolize how ingeniously Americans could thumb their nose at the Constitution. In its fads and fashions, in its unfettered energy and madcap politics, Chicago typified the "Jazz Age" or "Roaring Twenties."

One lingering feature of injustice from the previous decade—race supremacy—continued as a deleterious influence over thought and behavior but with a new emphasis and a new "public problem." The bloody riot of 1919 had transformed the black population from a slightly noticed minority among minorities into the city's number-one problem. In the same manner that the Irish were labeled *the* urban problem during the nineteenth century, and the immigrants from Eastern Europe were so labeled at the turn of the century, the blacks earned this dubious label by the third decade of the twentieth century. Academic and popular analyses contributed to the situation by treating Chicago's black citizenry as an impediment to advancing urban civilization.[19]

Within the South Side black community, a new sentiment also prevailed. There, the "Jazz Age" shared the stage with the "New Negro." As described by African American intellectual Alain Locke, a Harvard graduate and Rhodes scholar, this incipient mindset had its locus in "the younger generation [which] is vibrant with a new psychology; the new spirit is awake[ning] in the masses [too as both transform] what has been a perennial problem into the progressive phases of contemporary life." Locke added: "For generations in the mind of America, the Negro has been more of a formula than a human being—a something to be argued about, condemned, or defended. . . . With this renewed self-respect and self-dependence, the life of the Negro community is bound to enter a new dynamic phase, the buoyancy from within compensating for whatever pressure there may be of conditions from without . . . [even] the migrant masses, shifting from countryside to city, hurdle[d] several generations of experience at a leap."[20] A decade after the metamorphosis began, the NAACP national office made the same assessment and shared it with branch president Dr. Carl Roberts, telling of the growth of black independent thought and a strong mistrust of whites. E. Franklin Frazier saw the riot of 1919 as a watershed in thought in black Chicago, accompanied by the rise of a new professional and business leadership which had "New Negro" sentiments.[21]

And who was this "New Negro," this racial creature with indomitable resolve and titanic abilities? The *Defender* offered the following explanation in 1920: "Much is said of the 'New Negro,' we haven't seen such a critter, just the same old tinted individual, roused into self-consciousness, awakened to his own possibilities, with stiffened backbone, and new ambitions, new desires, new hopes for the future."[22] This assessment coincided with a black Northwestern University graduate's observations in 1927. Frederick H. H. Robb, a law student, wrote: "He is a new type of Homo sapiens psychologically. He believes in preparation, in himself, in fighting but not merely by petitions, orating, and delegations, but in using the courts to insist on his civil rights [as well as] the effective, intelligent use of the ballot to oust those who would disgrace the race. . . . He has no narrow religious creed, supports human principles instead of race prejudice, ignores the unfounded flattery heaped upon the Negro, does not boast, but achieves [and] has a scientific mind. . . . He does not seek philanthropy but an opportunity."[23]

When the "New Negro" expressed his or her interest in race advancement, it was manifested through an individual assertiveness as well as black institutional development. Black Chicago relished the possibility of a Black Metropolis. Nonetheless, the conversion of concept into actuality was muddled because of its complex nature. Drake and Cayton clearly distinguished the multifaceted character of this concept: "To some the dream was inspiring. To many it was a mistake, a substitute for the real American Dream of complete integration into American life. To some . . . the dream seemed a fraud and a delusion. . . . To others, the development of a greater Black Metropolis was a tactical maneuver within the framework of a broad strategy for complete equality."[24]

Importantly, to significant numbers of blacks, the dream of a Black Metropolis seemed useful as a means to an end. The end in question encompassed assimilation into the American mainstream and racial equality. From pulpits, through the press, and over business counters, the message permeated the Black Metropolis. This application of the dream was especially beneficial to the Chicago NAACP and the equal rights movement as it helped the NAACP in realizing its organizational, programmatic, and ideological goals.

In contrast, the dream was also viewed as an end in itself. Implementing a black version of *imperium in imperio* appeared feasible given the circumstances of the twenties. Blacks could remain free of white interference and still live their lives to the fullest extent possible despite the ubiquity of racial constraints. This interpretation incorrectly misapplied the principles of the late Booker T. Washington as well as those of Marcus Garvey's American phase of his Universal Negro Improvement Association plan for the redemption of Africa. While the Black Metropolis concept was not actually nationalistic, the concept shared some of the same strains of separate development under black control and therefore was anathema to many racial egalitarians who believed in interracial cooperation.

Just as significantly, the dream represented a way out from racial dependence and racist humiliation. Although it was impossible for any group to live independent of others in urban America, the world of American racism distorted the American Dream so much that it essentially took on surreal qualities. The emergence of this fantasy, which was contradictory to white racial supremacy, seemed reasonable to some blacks. Acceptance, though, of this view did not bode well for the equal rights movement.

The dream, therefore, in the latter two phases was a nightmare to Dr. Bentley and the rising "New Negro," A. C. MacNeal, who were both staunch egalitarians. The dream was more palatable to Dr. George Cleveland Hall and another "New Negro," Archie L. Weaver, who saw it as a tactic of significant use. In the intertwining of these positions, the branch proceeded on to its historical "rendezvous with destiny."

In January 1920, William C. Graves was impressed favorably enough with the branch to share the following information with Julius Rosenwald: "There seems to be an awakening. I think we are justified in making a contribution or perhaps an offer and then attend meetings again and see whether there is an improvement in the service."[25] By the end of the year, Robert W. Bagnall, the director of branches, reported to James Weldon Johnson, the NAACP's first black National Secretary, that a "new interest has been aroused," confirming Graves's assessment.[26] However, this new interest had to be sustained to generate public attention and support, and this feature of the branch's development still represented a weak point. Moreover, greater efficiency in the branch's administrative operations was essential for stabilization.

The oligarchic character of the Chicago NAACP never appeared so pronounced as it did during this decade. Judge Brown, who celebrated his seventy-third birthday in 1920, proved unable to perform the duties of president of an organization in need of dynamic leadership. Along with Dr. Bentley, who celebrated his sixty-first birthday while in declining health,[27] Brown presided over a paper organization. By June 1921 he vacated his office, leaving Bentley to carry on alone while seeking a replacement from a list of prominent whites. An additional factor now reinforced the oligarchic and inefficient nature of branch operations— Bentley's increasingly irascible personality. His obstinacy impeded the smooth running of the branch and became a source of consternation to national officers in New York.[28] The "doctor" grew so difficult to work with that by the spring of 1922, the national office decided that the fate of the Chicago branch lay between choosing "Dr. Bentley or the branch."[29]

Despite these problems within the hierarchy, and no doubt due to growing support for the cause of racial egalitarianism occasioned by the branch's heightened profile during the successful riot defense cases of 1920, membership in the Chicago NAACP movement stood at 1,896 by 1921.[30] Yet, with the branch on the verge of success, Bentley decided to abandon mass meetings, viewing them as unprofitable from the standpoints of fund-raising and the number of memberships solicited. This unreasonable stance served to hamper growth, since a vigorous approach toward "advancing the interests of colored citizens" was essential. A lowered public interest resulted as the branch failed to meet its constitutionally mandated objective. Younger persons seeking to join, such as the rising semi-professional Morris Lewis, felt stifled even when they were allowed inside the hierarchy.

Bentley personally administered the closed selection process of presidential succession. His technique centered on surveying the small pool of willing and acceptable candidates with two requirements in mind: civic prominence and a white skin. His choice in March 1922 was Harold L. Ickes, a downtown attorney increasingly well known in legal and Progressive Republican party circles. Ickes accepted the presidency, not so much looking for a new challenge, but rather out of a sense of civic duty to what appeared on the surface to be a creditable cause with a viable organization serving it. Obviously not a staunch racial egalitarian of the stripe encountered in the preceding decade, he nonetheless fit Bentley's criteria for acceptable leadership during the twenties. And, according to reports, Ickes "consented to serve with the understanding that the use of his name with the prestige it would carry would be practically all that he would be called on to contribute in personal service."[31] Ickes discovered later that Bentley had misled him in regard to the actual status of the organization, and soon shared his chagrin with Jane Addams, writing: "I don't believe I would have convinced myself that it was my duty to accept this office if I had realized what lay ahead."[32]

Fortunately for the branch, the heightened interest of Morris Lewis, a "New Negro" branch stalwart, transcended Bentley's alternating recalcitrance and benevolent machinations as well as Ickes's reluctance to engage in an undertaking that required so much of him. Lewis joined the Executive Committee in 1921 after having gained a high profile in black egalitarian circles for his work as NAACP "colonel" of fund-raising activities that year. He continued this service in 1922 and worked ceaselessly for the branch even when his civic commitment interfered with his political ambitions. Successive losses in the 1920 and 1922 races for state representative in the Third [State] District (which overlapped the city's Second Ward on the South Side) convinced him to abandon politics. Lewis subsequently turned to the branch for full-time employment in 1922.

Lewis's professional ambitions within the organization contradicted the pattern of volunteerism adhered to by the old elite—the civic volunteer who acted out of a sense of noblesse oblige and ostensibly with no other motivation. But in the racially proscribed milieu of "Jazz Age" America and particularly in Chicago, occupational limitations often forced young black professionals into politics, business, and social service. In Chicago in 1920, only three percent of the black population engaged in professional service despite a slowly growing professional class which was able and willing to enter the city's economic mainstream.[33] In a maneuver that must have infuriated Bentley, Lewis then aggressively promoted himself as employable to the staff of the national office.[34]

Branch secretary A. C. MacNeal had left the branch sometime around the fall of 1920 to pursue a career in journalism at the all-black *Chicago Whip*, run by Joseph D. Bibb, a fellow Yale graduate. Olivia Banks Bush replaced him, and served as temporary executive secretary until the middle of 1922. The presence of Bush and Lewis among the ranks of the hierarchy, even though they lacked the power to direct or modify operations, guaranteed the branch at least minimum contact needed with the egalitarian element of the Black Metropolis. Lewis marveled to the New York office that "the NAACP [had] a wonderful sentimental following in Chicago" and that "the interested people of Chicago of our group [were] waiting, ready, and willing to take a hand in this work."[35] Once Bagnall arrived in Chicago, he saw firsthand the accuracy of Lewis's assessments, observing: "I never saw a city where the people were so ready to respond to the NAACP. I haven't run into a single 'anti' yet."[36]

This interest in the NAACP persisted despite the growing popularity of disparate alternatives within the Black Metropolis. Diversions ranged from working to realize the dream of the Black Metropolis, to building the nationalist Universal Negro Improvement Association, which claimed the loyalty of thousands of Chicagoans, to just enjoying the distractions of urban life during the "Jazz Age." Meanwhile, nearly 900 miles to the east, the national office decided that the branch had to be completely reorganized not only to assure its survival but to exploit its potential for growth. Recruitment was to be initiated even among whites, despite the demise of progressivism and an intense desire to experiment in worldly fads and other pursuits. Democracy was to replace oligarchy, and biracialism with white domination was to be replaced with a mixed black and white leadership, attractive to black professionals, business people, and the rank-and-file black citizenry.

The restoration of vitality would lead to protest activism supported by a large, sustaining membership. Further, this approach met the demands being brought to bear on black-oriented civic bodies by the "New Negro" sentiment pervading the nation. The architects of this reorganization were "New Negro" types in New York—James Weldon Johnson, William Pickens, Robert W. Bagnall, and Walter White—aided by Mary White Ovington, who was chairman of the national Board of Directors. The driving force within the Chicago NAACP appeared to be Morris Lewis, who contributed to Bentley's decline in power as well as to the branch's revitalization.

By November 1922, the Chicago NAACP had completed its reorganization and was ready to enter an active, productive phase in its history. A new Executive Committee was assembled, which comprised able and prominent blacks and whites. In contrast to the situation in 1913, numerical balance existed. Unfortunately, the same problems of age and class resurfaced. Too many of the old names filled the masthead: Willoughby Walling, Edward Osgood Brown, Robert McMurdy, Jane Addams, and Mary McDowell. Harold L. Ickes decided, as well, to remain in the presidency with a reassurance that he would not have to perform any substantive services. Meanwhile, Robert S. Abbott, Dr. Spencer Dickerson, Dr. A. Wilberforce Williams, Irene McCoy Gaines, and C. N. Langston, all major black figures identified with the "New Negro" mentality, joined the branch's leadership. Julius Avendorph, a personal valet to wealthy whites and a recognized social leader among the striving working-class and club-oriented blacks, was added to the committee, no doubt to attract that segment of the population he represented into the branch's membership.[37]

Besides the problems of race and mindset, the selection of meeting times illustrated the width of the class chasm. Many whites, who chose to live in splendid suburbs twenty or more miles outside the city, preferred meetings during daytime hours in the Loop and were reluctant to travel to nighttime meetings on the South Side, which conversely appealed to blacks, whose schedules revolved around daytime work. Quickly dismissed was one impractical suggestion of having two sets of meetings arranged to meet each group's schedule.[38]

In terms of personality, Ickes proved to be the wrong man for the times, irrespective of his skin color. A decade later, as President Franklin D. Roosevelt's choice to lead the Public Works Administration (PWA), Ickes would be described by historian William E. Leuchtenburg as "vain, quarrelsome, suspicious of mankind, a man who saw little but a void of wickedness beyond the arc of his own righteousness" as well as "an unfortunate choice to head an operation which required fast, even reckless, spending if it was to succeed."[39] Considering the needs of the Chicago NAACP, which required immediate, even proactive, planning and decision-making (given the assumption that the passing of a decade had not altered Ickes's basic personality traits), the problem with having him at the helm was obvious. Ickes's dependence on the ailing and aging Bentley (who reached his sixty-third birthday in 1923) merely exacerbated his cautious approach in promoting a movement which lacked widespread public recognition, acceptance, and support.

Another complication arose in 1923 when Ickes became heavily involved in more of his myriad political activities. Direction of the branch's affairs moved centripetally into the hands of the chairman of the Executive Committee, Bentley. At this time, either as a tactical maneuver or as a matter of fortuitous circumstance, Morris Lewis raised the issue of Ickes's perceived lack of sensitivity and commitment. Lewis pointed out that "he is rather ultraconservative," and opined that "he has not got the Negro viewpoint. This is true of most white men." He then concluded: "It is impossible for them to put themselves in our place."[40] It was as though Ida B. Wells-Burnett were active and pleading as she had in New York in 1910.

Between 1923 and 1925, with liberal Harold L. Ickes ostensibly at the helm, the branch continued its perpetual stumble toward organizational relevance and ideological acceptance. These were not momentous years in any sense, nor were they unique. What happened in Chicago seemed to conform to a pattern nationally in which nearly 40 percent of all branches existed in a state of dormancy or near dormancy.[41]

The branch's third reorganization resulted in a modicum of improvements with a revitalized Executive Committee (which was more fully integrated with blacks from the rising "New Negro" group) and even a paid regional secretary to promote greater administrative efficiency. But morale as well as fund-raising, membership, and programmatic activities still languished. Through it all, Ickes remained a reluctant leader, never exerting himself with the NAACP to the extent that he did with his other interests—politics, municipal reform, and conservation. His inclination to identify with and involve himself with liberal personalities and movements persisted; and his activities now followed the same course as that of his earlier involvements with Theodore Roosevelt and the Bull Moose Party in 1912, and with Professor Charles E. Merriam's and Julius Rosenwald's anti-Thompson mayoral campaign of 1915. His attention turned to reform as Democrat William E. Dever challenged a weak Republican substitute for Thompson in the Chicago mayoral election of 1923.[42] Whether this identification with a Democratic candidate angered the voters of the Black Metropolis who saw their salvation as resting with the Republican Party can only be conjectured. It just so happened that the black electorate switched loyalty during this election to prevent Dever's Republican opponent from winning and challenging Thompson in four years.

Elsewhere within the administrative hierarchy, the two branch secretaries between 1923 and 1930, Morris Lewis and Archie L. Weaver, obviously relished the unique social status that the office brought them. Access to the top leadership of the national office made the office of branch secretary one which flattered the ego and eventually elevated Lewis and Weaver into the position of kingmakers. In 1925, Lewis presided at the demise of the Ickes-Bentley clique and ushered in a new leadership.[43] Weaver repeated this maneuver during the presidential succession of December 1932 when Turner resigned his office and was replaced by A. C. MacNeal the following month.[44]

In accordance with the branch's constitution, the secretary's primary duty was to keep the minutes of meetings called by the Executive Committee, which conducted and managed the affairs of the organization. As recorder of all proceedings, the secretary was in a position to interpret and thereby control the flow of information concerning transpired events in much the manner of historians. The secretaries developed a closer relationship with New York than did the rest of the branch's leadership, including the presidents. Like those in other branches, Chicago's secretaries wrote a great deal of correspondence that was personal, unofficial, and often gossipy, and that provided essential information about the branch's dynamics. This unofficial pipeline seemed to delight the national office.[45]

An elevation of status further explained why Chicago secretaries could work so well with the New Yorkers. Both Lewis and Weaver were men of intelligence and talent who lacked professional status in a city where blacks in the fields of medicine and law, as well as certain ones in business and religion, were graduates of prestigious northern universities such as Yale, Northwestern, and Chicago. Far more importantly, a scattering of professional and business people large enough to influence black life in the Black Metropolis was developing.[46] Lewis had a smattering of college training, and Weaver had attended but had not completed college in his native Indiana. Contact with national officers served to raise their social position among their colleagues in civic service, bringing them immense prestige.

Occupationally, neither of the secretaries had a career so enthralling that he could not derive greater satisfaction from the services he performed as part of his branch duties. Lewis performed administrative and clerical duties for the downtown law firm of Ferdinand and Peck, which never seemed to compensate him enough to provide adequately for his familial responsibilities.[47] He desperately needed the full-time employment that his appointment as the branch's first paid regional secretary gave him during 1923. When that position was eliminated a year later owing to the branch's impoverished condition, Lewis moved to the *Chicago Defender* on a full-time basis as circulation editor. He remained at that post until April 1929 when Congressman Oscar De Priest selected him to become his congressional secretary. Weaver, who heretofore had served as financial and acting secretary, assumed full secretarial duties at this point. The nature of Weaver's volunteer service showed he had as strong a commitment as his predecessor. Because he was a postal clerk, he also had a social position in black Chicago that was just as limiting as Lewis's.

Ideologically, both men were devoted to the equal rights movement. Importantly, these Chicago "New Negro" types found their greatest support emanating from the New York office and not from Chicago. After one and one-half decades of association with the egalitarian movement and with basic support among a small segment of blacks, Chicago had still failed to produce results commensurate with the neo-abolitionist dream of 1909. In Chicago's Black Metropolis during this dazzling decade of prosperity and indulgence, there were also many erstwhile egalitarians whose ideology weakened in favor of an experience based on group solidarity as an end in itself. With a sense of fraternity Lewis and Weaver looked to James Weldon Johnson, Walter White, Robert W. Bagnall, and William Pickens, their "New Negro" counterparts in the East, to generate the enthusiasm and leadership that someday was going to establish the

NAACP as the preeminent race advancement organization in the nation as well as in the city.

The symbiotic relationship between the secretaries in Chicago and the officers in New York represented the recognition of centrality that made the NAACP work. It was the essence of this arrangement that produced the joint decision in 1922 that led the branch into its third reorganization the following year. Somehow Ickes reached the same conclusion, that further change was necessary, so he supported the eventual election of a black man as president, which was meant to be a positive sign to the black community that an organization committed to equal rights did not always have to rely on white leadership. It also signaled a negative message about ideological consistency. Instead of choosing along racially egalitarian lines with qualifications and loyalty to ideology being paramount, the branch's hierarchy remained inconsistent by now reserving the presidency exclusively for blacks.

By late fall 1923, Lewis's irritation with Ickes's ineptness as a leader grew to an intolerable level. Accordingly, he proffered the idea of increasing black involvement through the formation of an extra-organizational body in the form of an all-black Citizens Auxiliary Committee.[48] This group's roster contained the names of the most ardent "New Negroes" in the city who supported all-black endeavors. Lewis's idea was not one that was completely grounded in reality when it came to the major issue of who should govern the branch. The locus of power within the branch rested, both constitutionally and in actuality, with the Executive Committee, so any group of this type would be powerless and the change producing it superficial. Insofar as the interest of the black public was concerned, it quickly rejected change that was only symbolic because there were already substantive transformations occurring in black life in political, business, and social spheres.

By the summer of 1924, Ickes suggested again to the national office that he be replaced by a black man who might be able to attract a membership and raise adequate funds for both the national and local efforts. James Weldon Johnson responded positively and made the suggestion that the black presidency be supported by a black Executive Committee.[49] The resulting structural transformation resulted in the virtual elimination of white participation and, in the case of the venerable Dr. Bentley, an ephemeral affiliation only. His poor health and advanced age, combined with the shift in hegemony, relegated him to the sidelines of the movement. No doubt the emergence of an all-black organization rankled him in his last years, as he passed from the ranks of the egalitarians, dying in October 1929.[50]

Nowhere was the evolutionary nature of the branch's status more pronounced than in the implementation of its program. Its leadership during the Ickes-Bentley years brought in more of the inconsistent activism that had plagued the branch since its formation. While incidents involving civil rights violations, such as bombings of black homes and theater discrimination, recurred with regularity, in the early part of the decade these were ignored by the branch's leadership. When there was action, it continued to emanate from the greater black community, outside of the branch's operations. The major protest against home bombings was carried on by a black citizen's committee called the Protective Circle. Its ranks included Black Metropolis luminaries Jesse Binga, Oscar De Priest, Adelbert Roberts, Dr. Carl G. Roberts, and Morris Lewis. Lewis assumed the responsibility for coordinating the "work of the churches, clubs and various civic organizations which [were] fighting to purge the city of the dynamite terror."[51]

The extent of the branch's participation in the controversy over segregated housing had been President Brown's membership on the Chicago Commission on Race Relations. Judge Brown joined Julius Rosenwald, Victor Lawson, Dr. George Cleveland Hall, Edward H. Morris, Adelbert Roberts, and six other black and white men on this body, which was called into formation by Illinois governor Lowden to investigate the causes of the bloody riot of 1919. Their responsibility mandated that they offer recommendations to stem its possible repetition. Despite the intelligence and influence of the assembly that Judge Brown joined, the commission failed in all of its attempts to remove the root causes of housing discrimination and violence. It was successful in remaining bias-free in the presentation of its findings and recommendations, but it was a body that lacked vigor in fighting on behalf of true equality in housing choices, and changes promoting genuine racial equality were neither recommended nor forthcoming.[52]

The general housing pattern throughout the city in the 1920s reflected a determined white resistance at various levels of government, commerce, and neighborhood life to prevent blacks from enjoying residential mobility. The territorial confines of the Black Metropolis therefore remained fixed. As bombings decreased by mid-decade, the restrictive covenant appeared as a means of restricting black mobility. The core of the Black Metropolis, which was filled with some of the oldest housing in the city, took on the appearance of a slum.

Discrimination in public accommodations persistently plagued black Chicagoans. An egregious case of racial discrimination in 1923 involved seating arrangements at the Adams Theater in the Loop. This incident afforded the branch an opportunity to challenge racial discrimination in the city's vaunted central business district and could have resulted in a heightened civic visibility for the branch. Nonetheless, the leadership tandem of Ickes and Bentley declined to act, displaying their self-consuming, conservative attitude toward activism that was reminiscent of the branch's initial stance on the riot of 1919.

Branch secretary Morris Lewis took the case to court as a private citizen to resolve the situation, much to his own discouragement. Meanwhile, Ickes and Bentley disagreed openly with Lewis on several issues. First, the two patriarchs strongly pressured Lewis against taking any action under any circumstances; second, they objected to Lewis's being identified as an official spokesman for the branch; and third, they disagreed with the method of protest employed, suing for monetary damages instead of on principle. Sadly, the duo's criticism was aired publicly in the pages of the *Chicago Defender,* which embarrassed both Lewis and the branch.[53] The national office saw this situation as detrimental to the movement's growth in Chicago and another reason why reorganization was needed.[54]

During the "Roaring Twenties" the city's economy showcased the decade's prosperity through downtown construction and, to a lesser extent, neighborhood expansion at major intersections and in apartment complex construction. At the same time, suburban growth proceeded vigorously. As utilities magnate Samuel Insull, a friend to black banker Jesse Binga, got richer and the city and nation basked in prosperity, so did the Black Metropolis. As Drake and Cayton observed, "The Black Belt became the Black Metropolis in the twenty years between the closing of the First World War and the beginning of the Second.[55]

What were the signs of prosperity that made the economic component of the Dream of the Black Metropolis so alluring and impressive? The black South Side, extending about one-half mile on either side of State Street from Twenty-Second to Fifty-First, boasted two banks with substantial holdings by any other Chicago neighborhood's standards, either old English stock or ethnic. There were three insurance companies by mid-decade, numerous newspapers with large circulations and comfortable profit margins, theaters and jazz spots with citywide reputations, and the usual small businesses found in black communities nationally—restaurants, barber and beauty shops, concession stores, and grocers. An active business organization, the Associated Business Clubs (ABC), promoted entrepreneurship and improved business management. Its leadership boasted of the membership of the Black Metropolis' big three—Robert S. Abbott, Jesse Binga, and Anthony Overton.

The banks with national reputations and ranking among blacks were the Binga State and the Douglass National, which, according to the authoritative *The Negro as Capitalist,* "were the largest banks ever organized by Negroes."[56] These two financial institutions held on deposit over one-third of all the banking resources that blacks possessed nationally, and were completely owned and operated by their respective founders, Jesse Binga and Anthony Overton. Binga came to Chicago in 1895 to start his climb to success, moving from street vendor to real estate owner to private banker by 1908. By 1920, this son of *petit bourgeois* Detroiters had elevated his bank into a state-chartered institution and, probably through Samuel Insull's influence, into membership in the Chicago Clearing House Association. Binga proved true to his word (of which he uttered few) when he announced: "We cannot succeed if we ignore even the smallest fraction of the nation."[57] Accordingly, he invested heavily in his own community, especially in real estate mortgages, which enabled many blacks to become first-time homeowners.

Former municipal court judge and lawyer Anthony Overton moved his thirteen-year-old Kansas City cosmetics business to the South Side in 1911. He expanded the Overton Hygienic Manufacturing Company into a black hair products and cosmetics giant by the twenties. Then he broadened his financial dealings in order to effect greater independence in his financial operations, founding the Douglass National Bank in 1922. Next, he organized the Victory Life Insurance Company and, finally, an advertising organ, the *Half-Century Magazine*, which expanded into the *Chicago Bee* newspaper.

The Supreme Liberty Life Insurance Company, with which Earl B. Dickerson was affiliated, had already started as Liberty Life in 1919 and established itself as the first black legal reserve insurer north of the Mason-Dixon Line. Two insurance firms, Overton's Victory and the Metropolitan Assurance Company, were founded by mid-decade as testimony to the favorable economic climate and lent credibility to the concept of building a self-contained city within a city.

A professional class emerged within a multi-layered society that differed significantly from previous decades. An elite, middle-class, and industrial proletariat had evolved, distinct along socioeconomic lines. Two sets of circumstances contributed. One was the constant migration of southern blacks who wanted to avail themselves of the opportunities and prosperity of the North. Attorneys Sydney Brown and Christopher C. Wimbish came from Mississippi and Georgia respectively in the twenties as part of this incessant wave. Brown earned his law degree at Northwestern University. Attorneys Earl B. Dickerson of Mississippi and William L. Dawson of Georgia had preceded Brown and Wimbish in the city by over a decade. The other source represented the flowering of younger Chicagoans who had completed their professional training in universities within the Chicago area. Physicians Theodore K. Lawless, Arthur G. Falls, and Ulysses G. Dailey graduated from Northwestern University's School of Medicine. In addition, visiting academicians Charles S. Johnson and E. Franklin Frazier, doctoral students at the South Side's University of Chicago, contributed directly to the vitality of the Black Metropolis's image and existence in two ways: through their activities with the Research Department of the Chicago Urban League and their contacts with black Chicagoans; and through their writings on life in black Chicago. Johnson authored the tome *The Negro in Chicago* (1922) virtually singlehandedly, and Frazier wrote incisive material on life in black Chicago and published his doctoral study, *The Negro Family in Chicago* (1930). While the latter's works were somewhat unflattering in tone, their national publication carried a respectability and legitimacy to a news-hungry black America. And, to black Chicagoans, the articles which were published in *The Messenger* and *Opportunity* could always be interpreted as more favorable than they were actually intended to be.[58]

The culture of the Black Metropolis was as extensive as its other components. In arts and letters as well as music—in the paintings of "Scott, Farrow, Dawson, Barthe, and Motley who brought the latest Harmon Award to Chicago . . . to the recital of George Garner," the Black Metropolis, according to Charles S. Johnson, demonstrated that it could produce and appreciate high culture. The hot jazz played along State Street by Louis Armstrong, Robert Rugland, and other musical virtuosos testified to the vitality of the Black Metropolis's attachment to popular culture, which achieved worldwide fame. In the world of the modern visual arts, the filmmaking of Oscar Michaeux delighted black filmgoers at black-owned theaters such as the Vendome on State Street.

Perhaps the most dominant feature of cultural expression appeared beyond the world of aesthetics. Racial consciousness mounted and fed on a renewed sense of personal and group worth. The Black Metropolis acquired another sobriquet in the inspiring and impressive term "Bronzeville," which symbolized the strength and beauty of persons of African descent. The *Chicago Defender* even argued for the use of a new racial title, "The Race." It advocated using "Race Man," and "Race Woman" as substitutes for the confining label of the past several generations—"Negro."[59] The Black Metropolis assumed an existence unique in black Chicago history. In doing so, it inadvertently prepared the way for the Chicago NAACP to transform itself into a major voice for civic advocacy in the city once the branch proved its indispensability to improving the lives of black Chicagoans.

Black involvement within the political sphere during the turbulent twenties unfolded against the backdrop of a political economy which afforded blacks previously unimagined opportunities. The most obvious signs were an expanding pool of office-holders who served the city and especially the burgeoning Black Metropolis. Blacks participated as welcomed members of the city's powerful Thompson Republican faction under separate Thompson regimes that extended through two-thirds of the decade.

The decade had begun in spectacular fashion as Mayor Thompson, "Big Bill the Builder," presided at the opening of the new Michigan Avenue double-leaf bascule bridge in June 1920. This monument to bridge-building marked Chicago as an innovator in the use of double spans. Throughout the decade, Thompson continued to build within the public domain and encourage construction within the private in accordance with Daniel Burnham's vision. And under his successor, Democrat William E. Dever, the city continued to witness the building of monument after monument—some of the most impressive projects being those associated with the city's original lifeline, the Chicago River. Double-decked Wacker Drive followed the contour of the Chicago River along its main artery and south branch; the river itself was straightened south of Twelfth Street; and Samuel Insull's monument to high culture, the Civic Opera Building, rose along its south branch on Wacker Drive.

As part of the NAACP's national network, the Chicago NAACP participated in a lobbying campaign aimed at garnering congressional support for the nation's first anti-lynching bill, the Dyer Bill of 1922. U.S. Representative Martin B. Madden, a white man who was the Black Metropolis's political voice in Congress, was easily enlisted into the cause.[60]

The participation of African Americans in political matters, under the leaderships of Ed Wright until 1926 and his successors Oscar De Priest and Dan Jackson for the remainder of the decade, was marked by its assertiveness. The latter was sorely needed to counteract a web of invidious constraints. In the Chicago Fire Department qualified blacks were limited to duty in one South Side fire house located in the heart of the Black Belt, and this situation was tolerated for another two generations.[61] In housing, city government acquiesced in the face of a popularly supported public policy of racial exclusion that benefited the real estate interests and satisfied white neighborhoods which sought racial exclusivity. The appearance of the restrictive covenant by the late twenties met with no official opposition but rather evolved into official recognition by the late thirties.[62] In the educational sector, overcrowding and attempts at segregation were commonplace in the Black Belt and adjacent areas. Representation on the Chicago Board of Education was systematically denied to blacks until 1939.[63] Overall, in the distribution of political rewards, all constituencies of the Republican machine fared better than blacks, even those of recent arrival such as the Italians and the Poles. According to political scientist Diane H. Pinderhughes, whether blacks confronted a machine or reform government, winning their fair share of the political spoils proved consistently elusive. This was the case even during Thompson's supposedly golden reign.[64]

In spite of the fact that political rewards were denied blacks by the Thompson machine, a contemporary analysis of what they achieved nationally showed that Chicago blacks were in the forefront of black American political advancement. Led by the assertive "New Negro" types, personified by Edward "The Iron Master" Wright, who was Second Ward committeeman and an Illinois Commerce Commissioner, blacks participated as members of an influential, indigenous-led political faction and not as figureheads or puppets. "[Black] Chicago boast[s] a greater degree of Negro political participation and influence than any city, county or state in the nation," asserted Harvard-trained Ralph J. Bunche in 1929. "The toga of Negro political leadership adorns the Illinois Negro. His influence is felt at every election. His voice is often the conclusive determinant in hot races for political office. His reward for support of the successful candidate is the usual consideration condoned by contemporary American political practice."[65]

The black political leadership and organization of Chicago generally reflected at least three tendencies that were at times contradictory. First, they promoted the cause of the Republican machine, which was headed by a corrupt but egalitarian Thompson. The interests of the machine were served by the subordination of the black citizen's interests to those of an organization that benefited whites in the areas of political employment and privileges. However, because of the high level of racial proscription, black demands were never so threatening that whites asked black politicians to support racially exclusive legislation in the City Council. Nor were blacks asked to deny their quest for respect and recognition. Quite the opposite occurred. Blacks joined with ethnics to challenge Ku Klux Klan members in city government. Working together in the city council, they took the first of many governmental steps in Illinois to neutralize the Klan's influence and activities.[66]

Second, black politicians accumulated favors from a machine that allowed them to hold dominant positions in black Chicago and, in turn, grant jobs and favors. A political position, whether elected or appointive, became a sign of racial progress for black America during this period of struggle. To their credit, black politicians in Chicago boasted of having the nation's one and only congressman, one of the nation's two state senators (along with Michigan's), four state representatives, one state commissioner, two city aldermen, two Republican Party ward committeemen, and the nation's first popularly elected municipal judge. Appointed positions included assistant corporation counsels and assistant states attorneys as well as positions with lesser status that were highly remunerative on the competitive municipal pay scale. And, limited (but welcomed for the time), representation occurred on the various boards, commissions, and panels that helped govern the city and state.

If racial politics represented the antithesis of reform politics, there were still circumstances in racist America where it made sense even to the University of Chicago's Charles E. Merriam. The professor and Progressive-Era alderman wrote: "To be willing to exchange the substance of living for the illusions of race representation is not a new phenomenon in the history of race relations. It is in fact one of the indices of a rising sense of dignity and responsibility. To be recognized and represented by a crook is better than not to be recognized or represented at all. . . . This is not in fact the only alternative, but if it seems to be, the result is the same."[67]

Third, as middle-class black Chicagoans, many well-educated and well-trained at competitive northern law schools and on the fields of France as commissioned officers, these black politicians desired those same civil rights that black physicians, dentists, lawyers, and teachers sought. With no political threat to their hegemony over the Black Belt posed by the Chicago NAACP or any other civil rights or civic body, with no obstacles to block them from expressing their displeasure with the racial status quo, and with a personal stake in what the NAACP could do for them, the politicians were supportive of the egalitarian movement generally and of the Chicago NAACP specifically. This condition prevailed out of obvious self-interest. An episode occurred in January 1926 that bears witness to this fact: when Second Ward alderman Louis B. Anderson challenged discriminatory treatment at the Loop's prestigious Palmer House hotel. When he attempted to ride a lobby elevator to his destination on an upper floor, a white bellhop steered him toward a service elevator at the rear of the building. Anderson sensed immediately the reason for this action and resisted with the exclamation: "We are going to use that [lobby] elevator and we're going to use it darn quick or there'll be a houseful of trouble."[68]

Despite the positive contributions that holding political office could bring to the civic arena, the politician as hero to the Black Belt was at the same time persona non grata to the branch's hierarchy. Judge Brown and Dr. Bentley saw only the intrusive nature of venal Chicago politics. In 1922 Bentley wrote to the national office that he "did not want the office of president mixed with local politics for reasons that are obvious."[69]

Only politicians and political activities at the national level received the endorsement and generated the involvement of the branch. Branch members in 1915, for example, were encouraged to write to First Congressional District Congressman Martin B. Madden to express their opposition to black West Indian immigration restrictions that were included in the Negro Exclusion Act, a national immigration bill before the U.S. Congress.[70] In 1920 Arthur Aldis wrote in behalf of the NAACP to persuade congressmen to support anti-lynching legislation.[71] Then, in 1922, the national office encouraged all branches to punish congressmen who had opposed the Dyer Anti-lynching Bill, which the Association had backed.[72]

In its most debilitating form, politics siphoned the enthusiasm and time of blacks away from the egalitarian crusade. Not only were needed funds drained from the branch's coffers, but more importantly, when the branch needed the volunteer fund-raisers the most, they were rarely available. In this connection, Morris Lewis wrote to NAACP national field secretary Robert W. Bagnall in 1922: "There is one point we must bear in mind, and that is the November elections will soon be on and our campaign must be shaped with that in view."[73]

Beyond the branch's association with local black politicians who were all Republicans, the national policy of the NAACP embraced nonpartisanism. In politically charged Chicago, complications invariably arose. In reality, there was an obvious tendency extant in the national office and branches that also favored Republican candidates and policies well into the 1930s. The Democratic Party was anathema to most blacks because of its intransigence on such matters as civil rights, enfranchisement, and anti-lynching along with its self-proclaimed stance in the South that it was the "white man's party." As long as this racism remained constant, there was slight chance that blacks would change their party allegiance.

At the end of the Progressive Decade, the branch was both ideologically and programmatically stronger than anticipated by mid-decade. The flame of racial egalitarianism that had burned so brightly in 1912 and yet flickered by 1917 seemed to rekindle itself by the time of the riot defense of 1919–1920. And a new locus of support existed in the black community where the founders originally hoped it would be nurtured. The branch was now poised to make a difference in the city's race relations. Both internal and external changes during the next decade prepared it well as it advanced a step closer toward institutional status and indispensability in the lives of black Chicagoans.

The changing of the guard between 1920 and 1924 resembled two unresponsive ships passing in the night as a racial succession in leadership occurred. Two conditions were evident. The groups recognized the mutual exclusivity that had developed since 1910. And the burgeoning cadre of "New Negroes" both within and outside the branch challenged the commitment of the branch to become relevant to the changing conditions within the Black Metropolis. The first of two watersheds in the branch's history had been reached.

5

The Black Patriarchy, 1925–1932

I have your letter asking for my analysis of the Chicago branch. The Association in Chicago has so long been regarded as an organization dominated by whites and a few colored individuals that it will take some time to educate public opinion to a realization that it is an organization of [all] the people.

> —Robert W. Bagnall to Dr. Carl G. Roberts, 1925

[Chicago is] in perhaps the worst plight of any of our cities, with school teachers, policemen, firemen, and city workers of all classes unpaid for months . . . . [compounding the problem,] the working class is [even] harder hit, if that be possible, than the professional and clerical class.

> —Robert W. Bagnall to Archie L. Weaver, 1932

THE YEAR 1925 brought the branch to a critical phase in its development—the emergence of a new patriarchy under exclusive black leadership. This hegemonic change was as much generational and ideological as it was racial, with differences in age and the experiences of black Chicagoans who matured during the "New Negro" era assuming great saliency. The new, and first, black president of the predominantly African American Chicago NAACP in 1925 was Dr. Carl G. Roberts, a prominent surgeon. Despite his professional status, Roberts experienced racial prejudice and discrimination like all other black Americans. A grandson of the founder of the famous free, antebellum Roberts Settlement in northwest Indiana, he aspired to live in an America unfettered by racism.

Roberts associated with the cause of equal rights on his own volition and was brought to the attention of the Chicago NAACP by chance. As soon as Morris Lewis met him, Lewis recognized that the branch had indeed found not only a kindred soul, but one worth grooming for future leadership. Describing Roberts as "a thorough N.A.A.C.P. man," Lewis informed field secretary Robert W. Bagnall of this prize who exhibited "such talent and enthusiasm [for the equal rights cause, which] is sorely needed."[1]

In being a "thorough N.A.A.C.P. man," Roberts expressed views that sharply contrasted with the dream of a Black Metropolis, which he regarded as racial separation cloaked in the robe of integration. "Biracialism . . . the proposition [that] the Negro should develop his own economic and cultural civilization, separate and apart from the dominant group surrounding him, implies a strong compliment," expounded Roberts. His detractors ask "him to do something that no other group in history has successfully accomplished [and that is to survive and thrive in isolation from his fellow men]."[2]

That Roberts's view could be counter to what was acceptable in Chicago was explained to him by Robert W. Bagnall in a solicited analysis in 1925, when Bagnall laid emphasis on the "revolutionary change in the psychology of the Negro." The changing mind and mood of the Black Metropolis also caught the attention of Charles S. Johnson and E. Franklin Frazier. The former sarcastically evaluated this mood and found existing along with it a "frontier mind [in the Black Metropolis which] is too suspiciously sentimental about the virtues of mother wit [common sense] and too brutally contemptuous of [a modern, racially pluralistic] culture." Prophetically, his evaluation predated the observations of Bagnall by two years. At the end of the decade, Johnson's colleague Frazier wrote: "The Negro community in Chicago has been very conscious of its place in Negro life. Lately because of this quickened consciousness the leaders among Chicago Negroes have bestirred themselves to make the American public cognizant of their contributions to, and place in, Negro life in America. . . ."[3] What these two scholars recognized in its incipient form, but failed fully to appreciate, was the salutary maturation of a Diasporan people who were progressing systematically beyond the psychological dependence on whites for leadership imposed upon them by their parents, grandparents, and white society.

The black working and emerging middle classes wanted something more closely aligned to what Jesse Binga, the black banker, and Anthony Overton, the black banker-publisher-insurance magnate-manufacturer, wanted—tangible success in a locus under their control, in a black city within a city—the Black Metropolis. Whether the latter existed in their minds as a means or end to race advancement, or just as a fantasy, it carried relevance to their lives. As late as 1925, race equality was still too theoretical and, therefore, too much of an intangible for acceptance by many black citizens of the Windy City.

Within eight months of assuming office, Roberts resigned. His motivation is unknown. It might have been either that he realized what Ickes had realized about the branch's inherent weaknesses or, with his small town background, that he simply was unable to work with the various black personalities with which he came into contact, many grappling incessantly for power and status. His physiognomy (he was light-complexioned enough to be mistaken for a Caucasian) might also have caused him problems in the racially conscious milieu of the Black Metropolis. Ironically, Roberts's announced reason for the resignation cited his need to prepare for the presidency of the National Medical Association, the racial counterpart to the exclusively all-white American Medical Association. Since he did not take up this position until August 1926, his departure in September appeared especially premature.[4] Dr. Herbert Turner, another surgeon and a devoted racial egalitarian, succeeded him.

During Turner's tenure as president (1925 through 1932), the branch received the administrative leadership needed to place it on a sound footing. Turner brought with him a sense of commitment that was ably manifested in his personal fund-raising activities, leadership, and, most importantly, in the length of his volunteer service. Despite the local popularity and national office exposure to the work of the branch secretaries, the locus of power within the organization now lay firmly in the office of the president. Turner directed the branch to an organizational level where committees functioned with both regularity and efficacy. While thoroughly committed to the NAACP ideologically, in administrative matters he questioned the principle of centrality that left the branch in a perpetually subordinate position to the national office in New York.

Turner knew that for the branch to prove its mettle as the protector of the civil rights of blacks, it had to foster change in the racial status quo through successful and highly visible protest activism. So, the Legal Redress Committee energized itself to work as the branch's vehicle for implementation of this mission. The committee successfully attracted practicing lawyers who volunteered their time and expertise, actively solicited cases, and prosecuted these cases to their conclusions. Edward H. Morris, who finally joined the branch's leadership, became chairman of the committee in 1926. Still considered the dean of black Chicago lawyers, Morris's stature attracted some of the most able lawyers in the city into the committee's ranks. Most, but not all, were black. Kentucky-born Morris had served in the Illinois General Assembly representing the old Black Belt for two nonconsecutive terms extending both before and after 1900. His training in law in Chicago took place outside the academy, but this circumstance hardly prevented him from being highly regarded in terms of his knowledge of the law. His past appointment to the prestigious twelve-man Chicago Commission on Race Relations further attested to his elevated stature in the Black Metropolis.

Attorney Henry Hammond chaired the Legal Redress Committee from 1927 to 1930 and included the problem of school segregation among the several activities in which he and the committee were involved.[5] It was during this period that the legendary Earl B. Dickerson joined the Executive Committee, lending his immense talent to its work. Dickerson had fled the South with its economic and personal deprivations during his youth to mature in the more salubrious environs of Chicago. There, he made good an experiential commitment to correct the injustices of racism using the law. After earning his B.A. at the University of Illinois and J.D. at the University of Chicago, he was positioned to attack racism as a member of the Chicago NAACP.

The base of support for equal rights activities broadened noticeably during this decade. The women of the various black communities of Chicago—in the West, North, South, and Far South Sides—worked tirelessly in behalf of the branch during the Turner years. The first permanent women's organization assembled in 1926 when the Flying Squadron was established. Described in the *Chicago Defender* as having the "interests of the race at heart" and as being "an unusual group of smart young women," the group owed its birth to politician Oscar De Priest and his wife. The *Chicago Defender*, although not in official correspondence, also referred to these workers as the "women's division of the NAACP."[6]

In addition to raising funds, these women attracted other energetic young people into the branch and established a voice in branch operations. Because of gender inequality, women did not have full access to decision-making.[7] One indication of their potential and rising influence came after Mrs. Nannie Reed, president of the Federated Clubs of Chicago, joined the Executive Committee. Archie L. Weaver described her to the national office as directing "several hundred and thousand women," adding: "We need her. . . . It is good policy to agree with her even if we do not act."[8]

Perhaps the most important bloc aiding the NAACP movement, other than women, was postal employees. Their annual financial support reached such a level of importance that Daisy E. Lampkin, the national office's assistant field worker, made the observation: "Postal employees, as a class, give greater support to the National Association than any other class. . . ."[9] Throughout the years the allegiance of the employees of the U.S. Post Office remained firm. This relationship was sealed by the similarity of goals of the NAACP and those of the National Alliance of Postal Employees and the Phalanx Forum. Archie L. Weaver's elevation to assistant secretary, which resulted from the democratization of the branch's last reorganization, indicated recognition of this group's contribution.

The distrust the founding branch leaders had of politics and politicians was reversed under the leadership of the first black president who allowed them not only to join the branch's general membership but also to enter the hierarchy. Oscar De Priest served as a member of the Executive Committee and Judge Albert George and Senator Adelbert Roberts joined the Advisory Committee. De Priest's background illustrated why he and other politicians were persona non grata until this period. An Alabamian by birth and a Kansan by upbringing after his family fled racial terrorists, De Priest had experienced racism firsthand, which was an asset toward understanding the severity of the challenge. What was unacceptable about him was his close identification with political opportunism. On one occasion in 1914, Ida B. Wells-Barnett accused him of preventing the election of the city's first black alderman a year earlier because of overriding personal ambition.[10] Charges of political corruption damaged his reputation even more in 1917 as he was forced from his aldermanic post as the city's pioneer black council member.

The passage of time and a change in branch leadership resurrected De Priest, who now appeared as a natural choice for inclusion in the hierarchy. De Priest's presence made the branch more respectable among blacks heretofore considered beyond its influence. The same year De Priest established the Flying Squadron, he was chosen to chair the Citizens Committee that garnered support for the eighteenth annual conference of the NAACP.[11] National Secretary Walter White and De Priest corresponded with some regularity during the latter's tenure in Congress (which began in 1929) on matters of importance to the Association. In vintage De Priest rhetoric, the congressman boasted that without the NAACP he would have never reached the halls of the U.S. Congress.[12]

The involvement of the churches increased as did that of the plethora of fraternal orders which dominated the social life of the Black Metropolis. Support for the branch grew even at a time when the democratization process that had been envisioned in 1925 was subsumed to the promotion of elitism (by the stratum to which Turner and his associates belonged). The all-important branch function of fund-raising increased considerably during the Turner years, helped to no small degree by Mrs. Herbert Turner's annual cabarets, initiated in 1927. These social gatherings grew in popularity, appealing to the younger members of the black elite. While the cabarets played an invaluable role in raising money for the Chicago NAACP, the *Chicago Defender* incorrectly called them "the only opportunity the organization had to secure its [financial] quota due the national body."[13] Overall, the branch met its national assessment in most of the seven years of the Turner presidency, allowing Turner to tout this fact and the independence that black financial support gave the branch. This contrasted with the Chicago Urban League's heavy reliance on white support.[14]

Reorganization in 1925 brought the stability needed for the branch to pursue its struggle against residential and educational segregation with a vigor and effectiveness unseen previously. The branch's concern for freedom of choice in housing extended now to monitoring the use of the restrictive covenant, the infamous legally binding property owners' agreement that made certain neighborhood housing inaccessible to blacks. The growing popularity of covenants prompted the national office to propose building a $3,000 fund to fight them.[15] Restrictive covenants appeared first in Chicago in the West Englewood area, a community located southwest of the expanding Black Metropolis.

The national *cause célèbre* in housing occurred in Detroit in 1925 and involved the family of Dr. Ossian Sweet and their friends who defended the Sweet home against a white mob of over 500 persons. In a gun battle in a previously all-white neighborhood, a mob participant was killed, leading to murder charges against Dr. and Mrs. Sweet and nine others inside the house. The national office of the NAACP took up the family's cause and a national tour for fund-raising and propaganda was arranged prior to the trial. Black Chicago did its part by supporting the Sweets in a series of mass rallies.[16] Coincidentally, Chicago's housing terrorists bombed the Greater Bethesda Baptist Church, which had been recently purchased in a previously all-white neighborhood and was the site of one of the rallies. The influence of the Chicago NAACP extended beyond the city to the trial, where civil rights specialist Clarence Darrow presented his usual brilliant and poignant defense. True to form, Darrow won acquittal for the Sweets. James Weldon Johnson summed up the deep significance of the trial when he wrote that it was Ossian Sweet "upon whose fate hung the right of the black man to defend himself in his home."[17]

While the Sweet case was being heard by a jury in Detroit in June 1926, the branch hosted the NAACP's seventeenth annual meeting. Much like the fourth annual conference in 1912, this event afforded Chicagoans an opportunity to demonstrate just how well the NAACP movement was progressing in the city. W. E. B. Du Bois made the following observation: [The choice of Chicago was] "peculiarly appropriate . . . inasmuch as one of the most serious race riots ever known in America arose [here] . . . as a direct result of attempts at the restriction of the homes of Negroes to segregated areas."[18] As to the proceedings at the conference, they featured intense discussions on topics ranging from housing segregation to southern disfranchisement.

Conference headquarters in 1926 was the Pilgrim Baptist Church located in the heart of the Black Metropolis where the remainder of the meetings were held. An increase of interest among blacks in racial equality counterbalanced a decrease among whites. In contrast to the conference held in Chicago fourteen years previously, whites were scarcely seen. The few familiar faces included Julius Rosenwald, Clarence Darrow, and Theodore Roosevelt, Jr., along with Mary White Ovington and other national officers. Many whites had forsaken the serious cause of race equality for an interest in the aesthetic aspects of Negro life—music, dance, and writing. The more substantive aspects, especially if they projected a bleak picture of America's unkept promises, seemed all too mundane. Chicago's jazz spots along State Street were not unlike Harlem's night clubs which became the magnets attracting erstwhile racial liberals.

Enthusiasm prevailed in the aftermath of the conference, prompting Bagnall to write to Weaver, "I hope the effect of the conference on the Chicago branch will be most telling, and that as a result there will be a large increase in memberships and interest."[19] Beyond the enthusiasm, the recurring problems of big city life remained. One internal NAACP memorandum assessed the situation in Chicago as follows: "There are so many diversified interests in Chicago that the N.A.A.C.P. really suffers greatly from the indifference on the part of the people."[20] Along with racial discrimination, "diversified interests" presented the branch with a major set of challenges which inhibited success.

Discrimination in the city's theaters remained persistent, but unlike its previous reaction in the Adams Theater case, the branch now vigorously fought this civic shame. In an incident at the Tivoli Theater, white ushers assaulted a young black man and forced him and his female companion, a Columbia University student and member of the socially prominent Proctor family of Atlanta, to leave their first-class seats for the isolation of the balcony. The branch took the issue to court with the complete support of the national office, which transported the young lady back to Chicago to testify.[21] An easy court victory followed.

Meanwhile, the Chicago Public Schools system was still the scene of instances of segregation; it appeared that major infractions occurred yearly.[22] And, as the city's black citizenry increased its social interaction with whites, the branch found itself dealing with a spate of cases involving violations of the state's public accommodations law that severely taxed its resources. Since court victories usually came easily, black attorneys from outside the volunteer ranks of the Legal Redress Committee often took on cases. And occasionally the branch championed the cause of labor, although this area was recognized as the preserve of the Chicago Urban League.

Among the "diversified interests" of the Black Metropolis, the branch developed important interorganizational contacts with groups whose interests were compatible with as well as opposed to its own. The branch established a long record of compatible relations with the staffs of the

Chicago Defender and the Chicago Urban League. However, with organizations promoting the ideologies of the Right and the Left, black nationalism and Communism, respectively, contact was marked by competition and conflict.

By the time Robert S. Abbott affiliated himself with the branch as a member of the Advisory Committee in 1926, the *Defender* had logged service of twenty years as a partner in the egalitarian crusade. Abbott had always considered himself a leader, if not the black leader, of the militant crusade for equal rights.[23] During the period 1925–1932, the increased activity of the branch relieved the newspaper of its solitary effort in behalf of fighting discrimination. A unity of purpose was cemented by the 1930s in which the *Defender* was a major booster of the branch, aided by the *Chicago Whip* and *Chicago Bee*. Activities ranging from the purely social to the all-important membership drives received constant coverage and helped catapult the branch into a preeminent position in the arena of protest advocacy during the 1930s.

The Chicago Urban League developed especially close relations with the Chicago NAACP beginning in 1917. By the late 1920s, the sharing that took place between the NAACP's Executive Committee and the League's Board of Directors resembled a civic version of an interlocking directorate. However, both bodies knew where the other's responsibilities lay, and, under the able leadership of the branch's executive secretary, who ran the organization's day-to-day operations, an overlapping of activities was a rarity. If the branch had followed its 1914 guidelines encroachment loomed as a possibility because several of the goals called for interaction with the schools, positions on public demeanor, and assistance with employment problems.[24]

Importantly, a major shift in leadership in 1925 in the League's leadership brought A. L. Foster to the city, replacing T. Arnold Hill as executive secretary. Foster was an activist, unlike the very diplomatic Hill. More importantly, Foster's views on race relations reflected those of the Johnson group in the New York NAACP headquarters; consequently, he related well to Morris Lewis and the branch leadership as it entered its most dynamic phase programmatically. Lastly, what was at stake beyond the organizational pride of these groups was access to the funds of the Black Belt. Quite often, however, fund-raising activities would overlap without creating animosity even as they solicited funds and memberships from the same body of citizens during the same span of time.

The nature of the relationship between the Universal Negro Improvement Association (UNIA), led by Jamaican Marcus Garvey, and the branch was competitive and sometimes blurred. UNIA membership reached several thousand Chicagoans with its appeal of a better life beyond racial prescription and subordination.[25] Its program of complete African liberation both in Africa and wherever sizeable concentrations of blacks were found in the New World appealed to a great many persons of African descent. Several Garvey divisions were frequently seen parading through the streets of the South Side at a time when black pride was on the rise, boosted by the success of the Black Metropolis idea as well as by the UNIA philosophy. What blurred the relationship was the tendency of many residents of the Black Metropolis to hold UNIA and NAACP memberships simultaneously. By 1925, the restrictions drawn up at the UNIA annual conference of 1924 forbade this practice.[26]

Morris Lewis was one branch leader who saw the dual memberships as bordering on the ridiculous, and the nationalist posture as bordering on the insane. He once wrote to New York acclaiming the Association's accomplishments and boasting of the "marked advancement made by our group largely through the efforts of the . . . Association." He went on to say: "Of course, as to Garvey and his position of the hopelessness of the Negro's future in this country, that is all bosh, for if he can't make it here in America, then . . . the case is hopeless."[27] The UNIA suffered a major setback in 1925 when Garvey was imprisoned on federal charges of mail fraud involving his Black Star Steamship Line and deported to Jamaica in 1927. His removal from active leadership resulted in internal breaches within his organization and the challenge confronting the Chicago NAACP diminished. The Chicago Branch of the NAACP had proven it could hold its own against nationalist incursions.

As the 1930s approached, bringing increasing economic distress in the Black Metropolis, the severity of impending Depression diverted attention away from any programmatic solutions that lacked economic relevance. The branch was affected adversely because of its commitment to racial egalitarianism; the nationalist approach, with its preoccupation with a racial solution to all problems, faced a similar fate. In this milieu of economic depression the Communist Party hoped to make its greatest inroads among blacks.

Even before the advent of total economic dislocation in 1925, the party sponsored the formation of an all-black labor group, the American Negro Labor Movement. Led by an avowed black Marxist, Lovett Fort-Whiteman, the party hoped to develop a sense of labor consciousness among the blacks of Chicago to counterbalance the growing racial consciousness of the period.[28] The growth of labor consciousness among blacks in the 1920s was contoured by circumstances which found blacks in disproportionate numbers in menial positions outside of the industrial setting, antagonistic to labor because of racial friction, or joining the growing ranks of the unemployed in the Black Metropolis that began to swell as early as 1926–1927.[29]

Broad-shouldered, perpetually boastful Chicago—hence the appellation "Windy City"—was humbled completely by the Great Depression, which entered its first full year in 1930. In its outward appearance, Chicago looked shabby, with the northern end of the Loop accommodating a Hooverville shantytown. More importantly, the very core of the internal structure of the city, its economy, threatened collapse and stopped functioning effectively during the overlapping Hoover presidency and Cermak mayoralty, 1931–1933. Municipal Chicago faced bankruptcy by 1932 even while a portion of its business community looked forward to A Century of Progress, popularly called the Chicago World's Fair of 1933 (and 1934). Meanwhile, the city's leaderships callously overlooked their responsibility to bolster the city's fragile economy. While the services of policemen and fireman were terminated to reduce the budget, thousands of teachers worked but went unpaid for months. The reasons for this calamity were clear enough. A successful yet devastating taxpayers' strike crippled revenue collections between 1929 and 1932; municipal expenditures continued to climb despite a dearth of funding; and the industrial, commercial, and service sectors released 700,000 workers, representing 25 percent of the city's workforce.[30] Racially, 40 percent of whites went unemployed while 45 percent of blacks experienced joblessness.[31]

The relief rolls filled and grew tenfold between 1930 and 1932. In real numbers, 130,000 families were affected. The city's governmental leadership demonstrated its obliviousness to reality by wavering between inaction and too little action. In response to entreaties for help in October 1930, Mayor Thompson announced in the city council chambers that while "Chicago is suffering from a business depression and unemployment. . . . it [was his] ambition to help correct existing conditions. Relief should take the form of employment which [would] enable a man to maintain his self-respect and his confidence in his ability to provide for himself and his own. . . ." Thompson added that he was "putting 99% of his time to create jobs for the unemployed and 1% for soap houses and charity."[32] In the nation's capital three months later, Congressman Oscar De Priest addressed his colleagues. "I am not asking for public funds to make mendicants of the American people," he boasted to applause. "And I represent more poor people than any other man in America represents. [And emphatically,] I am against the establishment of the dole system in America."[33]

Although these utterances accurately reflected the conservative economic views of President Hoover, the national Republican leadership, and many rank-and-file party faithful, black and white Chicagoans of whatever political persuasion suffered. A nation that once admired Chicago for its productive capacity and inexhaustible energy now felt compassion for the city. Incoming and outgoing correspondence between the branch and the New York office attested to the severity of economic conditions.[34] The Binga State Bank closed its doors in June 1930, never to reopen. A year later Archie L. Weaver lamented to Robert W. Bagnall: "[Twenty] banks have closed their doors in Chicago on Monday and Tuesday. This morning the

Lincoln State Bank closed—these banks . . . all in the colored District. It is terrible. The Douglass Bank is the only bank open in our district."[35] By June 1932, the Douglass National Bank closed its doors permanently. The economic "leg" of the Dream of a Black Metropolis was collapsing.

Next, the political leg crumbled, signaled by Democratic victories in the 1931 mayor's race and the 1932 presidential contest. The Black Metropolis underwent metamorphosis to become Bronzeville—still racially conscious but changing to include an economic consciousness along with a new appreciation of the larger world. Black South Siders realized now, as never before, that racial insularity no longer provided the salvation to their race's future. The branch remained under the leadership of black patriarch Dr. Herbert Turner whose tenure as president extended lengthily from 1925 to 1933. While he held office, Turner was both the titular head of the organization and the dominant force in formulating and implementing branch policy.[36] The same determined worker in the 1930s that he had been in 1925 when he initially assumed office, Turner brought with him certain assets that were essential to the branch's existence. His status as a physician lent respectability to his office and the organization; his profession allowed him the financial independence necessary to carry out his duties as the head of an organization that offered no remunerative rewards as well as to the means to help the organization from his own funds. His and his wife's effective fund-raising activities guaranteed revenue for Association and branch operations, and his contribution of office space, facilities, and a mailing address gave the branch permanency.

Turner's departure from the office after 1932 ended patrician rule. His farewell apparently resulted from internal friction within the branch, related to personality conflicts, along with substantive disagreements over ideology and programmatic direction. His known incompatibility with branch secretary Archie L. Weaver was one factor that led Turner to leave office along with one of his two medical compatriots serving in the Executive Committee, Dr. Charles V. Dudley. The latter served as treasurer for a two-year period beginning in 1931. Another colleague, Dr. Charles M. Thompson, remained active and continued as vice-president under the branch's new leadership.

At the time Turner left office, Archie L. Weaver was both the branch's longest-remaining active member and officer.[37] He was still popular, recognized as "a man of his word"[38] and the link between the branch and the heavily supportive postal organizations. In 1930, Weaver functioned as financial secretary and then, with the prolonged absences of Morris Lewis, who was serving as Congressman De Priest's secretary in Washington, began in April to perform the duties of acting executive secretary.[39] By November, he replaced Lewis as the result of a unanimous vote of the executive committee. Whenever he attempted to retire (and this occurred frequently), his resignation was rejected. As if in testimony to his value to the branch, Weaver was the individual who personally took charge (in the tradition of the intrepid Dr. Bentley) in the move to find a suitable replacement for outgoing President Turner in September 1932.[40]

The Executive Committee peaked with a membership of twenty-six at the beginning of the decade with diversity within its ranks, although its makeup was predominantly black and male. Politicians such as De Priest, Lewis, State Senator Adelbert H. Roberts, and State Representatives William E. King and George W. Blackwell joined lawyers Earl B. Dickerson, West Sider Graham T. Perry, and Theophilus M. Mann. A. C. MacNeal, who was now the manager of the *Chicago Whip,* belonged to the Committee along with ministers and social workers. The Executive Committee met in the most densely populated area of Bronzeville; however, it reached programmatic decisions that aimed primarily at alleviating the plight of the professional and middle strata of blacks.

The disparity between what the branch's program offered and the needs of the mass of Bronzeville's citizenry stemmed from the closed hierarchical character of the Executive Committee. When the people of Bronzeville looked at the Chicago NAACP, they saw an organization that conducted its business as an exclusive club without apparent regard for the divergent interests of the Black Belt's inhabitants, especially in the middle of a Depression. A study of black professionals in the 1930s conducted at the University of Chicago aptly described the Legal Redress Committee as "professionals [who] have assumed the role of protector and guardian for those in the lower and middle strata. They fight for the civil and social rights of Negroes and design most of their activity around the idea of protection to 'unfortunate persons' of their racial derivation. This operation however, is, psychologically, from a distance."[41] Not surprisingly, many ordinary people were simply unaware that the branch or its parent body in New York existed. Transplanted Chicagoan Richard Wright depicted this situation in his classic *Native Son.* As Bigger Thomas, the "typical" brutalized anti-hero of the urban ghetto, conversed with Mr. May, his white attorney and Communist Party supporter, Bigger was unable to personally identify with a black civil rights leadership working voluntarily in his behalf.

The branch obviously needed to clarify its image in the public's mind. One action in that direction was to employ a paid executive secretary to handle branch affairs and expand branch activities.[42] Unfortunately, the recommendation failed to be implemented. Another idea involved the creation of an advisory committee, similar to the one that the Chicago Urban League organized in 1931 and aimed at streamlining the ranks of the leadership. Persons who could not or would not attend meetings but were capable of helping the branch by lending their names and occasionally their advice received notification of a new assignment to this committee. Reassigned were Oscar De Priest and other politicians, the three most prominent black newspaper editors, and Mary McDowell of the University of Chicago Settlement House, a long-time white friend of the Association and a link to the liberal white community. Jane Addams and Clarence Darrow were placed on the National Board of Directors. Addams's lack of activity in the 1930s was due to her poor health, overwork, and devotion to her peace commitments. The branch honored Darrow in June 1930 for his legal contributions to race advancement as well as for his sincerity in dealing with blacks as equals. At that commemoratory dinner, Darrow warned his black friends: "The Negroes must make up their minds to go on alone. The help they've had [from whites] is gone [forever]."[43]

The branch's pride in its members who were politicians surfaced when *The Crisis* incorrectly listed a Michigan lawmaker as black America's first elected state senator of the century. The branch's Adelbert Roberts held that distinction, and Archie L. Weaver wrote with satisfaction to New York to clear up the matter. He claimed the title for Roberts and then proudly described the senator as a "good friend and loyal supporter of the Association."[44] Beyond Oscar De Priest's involvement, there were numerous other politicians who became active in the Association's behalf. On one day alone, April 27, 1930, State Representative William E. King spoke at the Ebeneezer Baptist Church at a morning rally opposing the nomination of Judge John Parker to the U.S. Supreme Court, then introduced Walter White at an afternoon meeting at the Olivet Baptist Church. King spoke before a mass rally in early November to open the annual financial and membership drive, and closed the drive, along with State Senator Adelbert Roberts, in late November. A little-known politician like Herbert Dotson was an Association member and, while assistant attorney general of Illinois, offered his car daily to help in the 1932 annual membership drive. Popular attorney and Republican Party activist Christopher C. Wimbish served the branch as Morris Lewis's secretarial assistant between 1926 and 1928.

If there was one operational unit which successfully pursued the organization's ideological and programmatic goals of bringing about a racially egalitarian society, it was the Legal Redress Committee. In June 1931, the ubiquitous Earl B. Dickerson succeeded attorney Henry Hammond as chairman. The committee's membership of fifteen included some of the city's finest lawyers, among whose ranks of four white attorneys was Elbridge Bancroft Pierce, a member of an old-line Yankee Chicago family, a distinguished attorney and president of the Chicago Urban League. Archie L. Weaver reported in 1932 the committee's members had "served with their time, money and ability without compensation, render[ing] yeoman service to the branch."[45]

During this period of financial exigency, the branch encountered many obstacles in maintaining its operational status, but none was overwhelming. Being spared the necessity of paying a salaried staff and for office space were benefits. But money was always desperately needed for essential goods such as office supplies along with services such as printing, telegrams, and telephone usage. The effort to secure these funds was also a reliable indicator of the community's support and an annual reminder of the branch's need to promote a program that met the needs of its membership and the times.

The annual membership drive, conducted always in November, was one of three principal sources of branch revenue. Its other income came from two sources that were uniquely related to its social and racial composition. The summer cabaret, usually held in June, represented a major fund-raiser and appealed to the middle and upper strata of Chicago's black society. The other source was the personal, nonphilanthropic donations of rank-and-file blacks within Bronzeville.

The quest for adequate financial support presented Association officers with what National Secretary Walter White called the "eternal problem."[46] Throughout the period of the early Depression, the branch had difficulty in meeting both its national assessments and local expenses. During 1930 and 1931, two years of exceedingly high levels of economic deprivation, each year's drive was started on a note of false optimism, probably born of a need to convince both branch workers and supporters in the community of the possibility of success.[47] By 1932, the reality of the Depression with its crushing financial force had set in. That year the drive began on contrapuntal notes of realism and pessimism. Such comments as: "The Depression has hit us all"; "These are tough times"; and "Chicago is one of the hardest hit cities as far as unemployment is concerned" were commonly found in correspondence sent between the Chicago and national office.[48]

The annual fall drive for members ostensibly was carried out to expand the organization's base of support and to raise revenue for local and national operations. In reality, only the latter function was fulfilled and even then with only a modicum of success although the branch's expenses were not exceedingly high. The typical member was an individual who might buy a dollar membership to help the Association in its work locally and nationally. A close affinity for the NAACP movement (as well as an acknowledgment of its necessity as an institution essential for group advancement) rarely existed. Beyond the membership card that he or she carried, there was no meaningful relationship with the organization. In comparison with other groups, the branch's position was not unusual. The Chicago Urban League too was supported by a membership whose responsibility never extended beyond the purchase of a membership card. Although the Communists espoused inclusiveness, dissent and grassroots policy-making were not allowed, so the involvement of its membership can hardly be considered fully participatory.

The branch's membership in 1930 was described by the *Chicago Defender* as "being scant."[49] In answer to this problem, the annual drive was set to increase the membership to 5,000, this for a branch that was described as "not function[ing] to any noticeable extent. You never hear of any of its activities, although there is plenty to be done."[50] The total number of memberships remained low and barely reached 1,500 by the end of the year. At this point in the city's history, there were, however, over 233,000 black residents in the city. Events held to increase membership had ranged during the year from the presentation of free drama at the Wabash Avenue YMCA to mass meetings on the controversial nomination of Judge John Parker to the U.S. Supreme Court. In 1931, the branch once again set as its goal a membership of 5,000 but fell short with only 2,600. Then disaster struck as membership fell below the 300 mark in 1932. As immense resources in the community were being expended in the autumn in behalf of the reelection of Congressman Oscar De Priest and the black Republican state ticket, the Roosevelt landslide swept the country. Little energy remained to launch a campaign to benefit what was largely a protest organization, and the call for volunteers only garnered 500 in 1930, 200 in 1931, and less than 150 in 1932.[51]

The organizations and businesses that did contribute heavily to the branch's coffers and membership remained the several postal employee associations, businesses like the Supreme Liberty Life Insurance Company and the Poro College, and social organizations that included the Phalanx, Appomattox, and the Ambassador clubs. This base of support conformed to Dr. Turner's belief in an independent funding base which "came 90 percent from members of our Race."[52] Indeed, the branch appeared as nearly devoid of a white presence at the membership level as it was in its leadership.

The success of the cabaret rested entirely on the untiring efforts of Dr. Turner's wife, Hazel, and her inner circle of friends. The Turners' social prominence aided Mrs. Turner, who was much younger than her husband, in appealing to those residents of the Black Belt who were professionals, well-off, and active in the "smart set." This group's support brought in $500 in both 1930 and 1931. But by 1932, even the well-off had begun to feel the pinch of the crisis and the cabaret received only two-thirds of its usual support.

The third source of revenue included personal and group donations received throughout the year. The Depression had no effect whatsoever on whether or not the mass of black Chicagoans were going to donate. Their interests lay not just in the attainment of civil rights but in the totality of their existence, which in the 1930s meant they were concerned primarily with employment, housing, relief, and freedom from police harassment. When the branch attempted to get support through donations from the more prominent, older black Chicagoans, such as Robert S. Abbott, Anthony Overton, Jesse Binga, and Edward H. Morris, it failed again. Abbott professed his usual concern with "the masses and not the [well-off middle and upper] classes" and eschewed any close, sustaining connection with the Chicago NAACP, which he considered elitist and whose leadership he disliked on a personal basis.[53] Overton and Morris also appeared to be less than enthusiastic about their racial obligation to make financial contributions to the Association because of their possible personal distaste for the branch's leadership.[54]

As the influence of the Depression became more pervasive, the branch became involved in programmatic activities of an economic character. Yet, despite the enormity of the Depression, not all problems or interests in Bronzeville could be considered economic, or even derivative from an economic root. The branch responded by developing a multifaceted approach that encompassed activities ranging from civil rights violations in public accommodations to police brutality, housing restrictions, and lobbying. Its broadened scope reflected the temper of the times which dictated that a program of legal redress be expanded to include support for economic remedies, no matter how new or novel.

The famous "Don't Spend Your Money Where You Can't Work" campaign of 1930 placed the branch solidly in the middle of direct action protest, a mode of activism completely new and yet fitting for the times. A. C. MacNeal and Joseph D. Bibb, both members of the Chicago NAACP's Executive Committee, led the campaign aimed at getting proportionate hiring for blacks in jobs in their own neighborhoods. Dr. Turner acted as unofficial paymaster for the picketing, boycotting, and soapbox and newspaper propaganda that pitted the *Whip* and segments of the black community against the behemoth F. W. Woolworth Company chain.[55]

The campaign began in earnest in June 1930 and successfully concluded after thirteen weeks of protest. At least two dozen young black females won jobs as counter clerks at the four Woolworth's stores located in the Black Metropolis. Most significant for the branch was its role which prepared it for the full force of the Great Depression's descent on the city. While local in scope, activities such as the *Whip's* direct action campaign did not escape the notice of Bagnall in New York. He directed Mrs. Daisy E. Lampkin, who was traveling throughout the Great Lakes area, to investigate what possibilities these types of activities offered the NAACP if it decided to expand its program.[56]

The *Whip's* campaigning, which developed as a result of black indignation at exclusionary racial hiring, ironically was at variance with the ideological aims of the NAACP. Had the branch been directing the efforts, it would have been expected to advocate the principle of equal opportunity in hiring on the job site. Instead, the *Whip* was fighting for this as well as guaranteed, proportionate hiring as a matter of racial entitlement from white owners and storekeepers who operated their commercial and service establishments in the Black Belt. Pragmatic critics of the campaign saw another inconsistency as well: Protest activities within the Black Metropolis could produce a reverse campaign which would affect African Americans working outside their neighborhoods. As the popularity of the idea moved beyond Chicago, W. E. B. Du Bois predicted that the possibility of a boomerang effect or backlash was too real to overlook.

Just as the *Whip's* campaign was winding down as the result of an anticipated victory over the Woolworth Company, the "street car riots" began. The direct result of unemployment, these episodes generated an even higher level of activism in the streets than the *Whip's* campaign. In September 1930, employment in the city's transportation system seemed possible. Black men had worked for the various transportation lines in the city as outdoor laborers in the early twentieth century but had not held those positions since the end of World War I. In the interval between the war and the Depression, the city government hired approximately 1,200 black men for street work every summer.[57] With the Depression, blacks saw those jobs as a means of reducing unemployment. They were urged on by the *Chicago Defender,* the *Chicago Whip,* and the Chicago Urban League, which molded popular opinion to expect some sort of political solution to help ease the economic crisis.[58]

The first phase of the work in Bronzeville began on surface line extension on September 8, with the Fifty-First Street line being extended one-half mile beyond South Park heading eastward to Cottage Grove Avenue. To the disappointment of blacks, all the workers on the site were white and unionized. Meanwhile, in the confines of Washington Park, almost a square-mile expanse of verdant recreation area, black men were meeting daily to discuss and complain about the high unemployment. Their leaders and the exhorters were residents of Bronzeville and recognized as legitimate racial spokesmen. One agitator for employment rights for blacks was willing to use force if necessary to secure those rights. He had been a labor organizer in the Panama Canal zone and was labeled by the *Tribune* as being under the influence of the Communists.[59] Another leader believed that the system could be reformed and would be if blacks exerted enough pressure in their own behalf.[60]

On September 16, hundreds of black men, angry over the lack of success in securing jobs by the Urban League, the *Whip,* and the *Defender,* marched from the park to the Fifty-First and South Park worksite. There, encouraged by agitation and previous strategy sessions, they took the tools from the hands of the Italian-speaking laborers. The white workers wisely withdrew to the safety of the Fifty-First Street sidewalks. With this retreat of only twenty or thirty feet, the potential for a full-scale riot, surpassing the mayhem of 1919, decreased.

While some of these black activists saw the issue of unemployment in terms of personal and racial survival, others perceived the confrontation as a stage in the class conflict between the forces of capital and labor. For the non-Communists, the enemy at Fifty-First Street was primarily a group of foreign-born white men who held the jobs they sought, and not the Chicago Surface Lines. Communists saw the transportation companies as the culprit. Both identifiable leaderships molded the direction into confrontation nonetheless.

The street car disturbances, which had brought near riots, aimed at securing jobs for unemployed black workers. Notwithstanding the initial appearance of success, sociologist Oliver Cromwell Cox estimated that not more than one hundred black laborers out of the thousands who wanted work were hired in 1930. At a Fifty-First Street site, there were twenty-five men who were hired outright. At another site on Fifty-Second Street, ten men were hired immediately with a promise to add fifty additional workers. By 1932, it was reported, however, that "there were only about 50 colored men working three days a week part-time for the lines."[61]

The significance of this particular direct action campaign extended beyond the number of jobs secured, which was small, to the use of direct action both within and outside the confines of Bronzeville. Although the branch made no overt gesture in behalf of this new street activism, sympathy existed.[62] While the Chicago NAACP maintained its equilibrium, the Great Depression crushed the branch's sister organization, the Chicago Urban League. By 1932, the League had suspended its operations to such a point that it was moribund.

Across the ideological spectrum, economic distress provided the Communists with an opportunity to recruit disenchanted workers of both races who sought immediate redress from the economic crisis. In implementing its program, the Communist Party looked for issues, hopefully sensational and provocative ones, upon which to build its organizational base in the Black Metropolis and the city as a whole.[63]

As could be expected, Anton Cermak's administration was also treated in an adversarial manner by the party. The mayor stood trial in absentia in November 1931 at a mock tribunal for his complicity in promoting what the Communists regarded as police terror. Twelve months later, Herbert Newton, a black Communist running against De Priest for Congress, presented a petition to Cermak in the name of the 50,000 persons who had marched on City Hall demanding limits on relief payment cuts; free gas, water, and fuel; and an end to housing evictions and foreclosures.[64] Not unexpectedly, these demands failed to spur the government into action.

Marches inspired by Communist propaganda and organizing efforts brought most black and white workers together in a unified cause for the first time in their lives and further served to strengthen the Communists' claim to being staunch supporters of the principle of racial equality.[65] Overall, the Communist Party encountered as much difficulty in recruiting blacks into its ranks as did the Chicago NAACP. This befuddled the Communists because, according to the theory of class struggle, the Black Metropolis should have provided a fertile ground for Marxist propaganda.[66] Even when the masses listened, they selectively associated themselves with the humanist component of Marxism-Leninism that pertained to racial equality, not the prophecy of inevitable class struggle. Blacks, whether integrationists or nationalists, were *racially conscious* and believed that the elimination of racial barriers meant an end to their problems. And, whether protest- or political-oriented, racial solidarity was a key component in both their actions and thoughts. The Communists, on the other hand, viewed American racism as being a secondary problem for blacks, that is, as a by-product of the capitalistic exploitation of the working class. Such terms and concepts as the proletariat, the revolution, the dictatorship of the proletariat, and the international were new and exotic to the black masses, "and if they were to become associated with aims and ideals of the Negro world . . . . [they had to be] symbols [that] furnished an important escape or release for the suffering, humiliation, and restraints which were the common lot of most Negroes."[67]

Communist Party membership among all Chicagoans during the early part of the decade at no time could have exceeded 500 to 600 persons;[68] and, in fact, this level declined at a time when the economic crisis was worsening. In 1930, following a recruitment drive, the number of blacks reached 113.[69]

Since both the Chicago NAACP and the Communist Party sought to lead the black community in the fight against discrimination, "in the final analysis one organization could succeed only at the expense of the other."[70] The Chicago NAACP made its position clear to the Communists after they disrupted a protest meeting held in behalf of building support for the nine Scottsboro boys in June 1931. The branch planned to prosecute the disrupters in court while the national office was advising Archie L. Weaver: "We shall have to prepare for those fellows."[71]

While the unemployed were being evicted from their homes in large numbers between 1930 and 1932, the branch under Turner's patrician leadership felt it was powerless to act. Since the branch perceived the problem of evictions as primarily social and economic in nature and not a legal and civil rights problem, whenever it expressed sympathy for the plight of the working class it did so privately and intangibly. Meanwhile, the tensions generated as a result of the evictions were so explosive that they culminated in a major riot on August 3, 1931, which involved scores of demonstrators and over a thousand spectators who were incited by the members of one of the Unemployed Councils to challenge the sheriff's bailiffs. During the melee, three protestors were killed; several protestors and policemen were injured, and many persons were arrested.

While the city's leaders feared a replay of the calamitous riot of 1919, the branch's leadership under Turner saw it as an event beyond the scope of its mandated responsibilities and repeated the branch's inaction of 1919.

Dr. Turner adamantly refused to act in a matter that was not clearly discernible as violating the civil rights of blacks. Accordingly, he wired New York that the riot was "not racial but radical" in nature.[72] Again, prodding from the New York office forced the branch into changing its position to at least lend partial assistance to the defense of the riot defendants. Earl B. Dickerson, representing the Chicago NAACP's Legal Redress Committee, helped provide that assistance by interacting with the ACLU affiliate in the city, the Chicago Committee on Civil Liberties. In a fitting climax, the defense teams were successful and the false imprisonment of innocent defendants was prevented.[73]

In the heart of the Depression, the core of the branch's activities remained that of its noneconomic pursuit of social justice. As the new decade began in January 1930, the Chicago branch reported that it was actively pursuing its program in behalf of cases involving "bus discrimination, public schools, public bathing beaches, help [for] servants from the South, public places of accommodation, etc."[74] Twelve months later, it again laid claim to the "great accomplishments of the branch" in those same areas.[75] When the Legal Redress Committee prosecuted major cases involving discrimination at places of public accommodation such as theaters and restaurants, they were disposed of easily and successfully.

Relations between the police department and Chicago's black citizenry continued to be strained. The advent of the Cermak political regime in February 1931 merely exacerbated, in the popular mind, the image of the policeman as a "Cossack." Cermak—the Democratic replacement to Bill Thompson as mayor—had a blind spot when it came to seeing the people of Bronzeville as a collection of decent citizens with diverse lifestyles, overwhelmingly moral and legitimate. Cermak's famous crackdown on the policy racket in 1931 seemed to be both a continuous blanket raid on an entire community and, to many blacks at least, retaliation against a political bloc which had been steadfast in its support of the Republican Party for years.

The NAACP's Legal Redress Committee responded vigorously in this matter, in contrast to its stance on evictions. While admitting that gambling and policy raids were justified, the committee noted that "police officers ha[d] taken upon themselves to break into homes, beat up citizens and search people on the streets without probable cause or legal process."[76] Perhaps one of the most important factors to note is that the type of citizen being abused was the homeowner, the businessman, and other members of the emerging middle class.[77]

One criminal case, in particular, left an indelible imprint in Earl B. Dickerson's memory. He remembered it vividly one-half century later because it involved the unusual convictions of two black men and a black woman for the alleged rape of a young suburban white woman in a Bronzeville apartment. It included a sordid cast of characters and bizarre circumstances in what became known as the "De Vol Affair." The white woman was party to a plan to abort her unwanted pregnancy by having aggressive sexual intercourse with De Vol, a white man who was her sister's paramour. One of the two black men was paid to join the orgy. The black woman and the other black man provided the apartment for this sordid rendezvous and became active supporters of the depravity. Following the encounter, the young woman's family contacted the police and the four participants were arrested. De Vol posted bond and fled the city before his trial, leaving his three black accomplices to face the white criminal justice system. The conviction, which had the ingredients of a northern-style lynching, incensed the branch's leadership. Dickerson personally led the defense, which sought to nullify the decision through judicial appeal. The Illinois Supreme Court deliberated the case, overturned the convictions, but refused to comment on the details of the case because of their moral offensiveness.[78]

Beyond the Depression's influence in producing wholesale evictions, Bronzeville experienced overcrowding of its dilapidated housing stock. Any territorial expansion resulted in interracial conflict. East of Bronzeville stretched the Hyde Park and Kenwood areas with an invisible dividing line between the black and white communities at Cottage Grove Avenue (exactly one mile east of State Street). Throughout the twentieth century, the residents of Hyde Park and Kenwood opposed the movement of blacks into their community and, as early as 1908, the wealthiest residents established the Hyde Park Improvement Protective Club to keep the area as free of blacks as possible. Shockingly, whites encouraged blacks already in residence to sell their homes or surrender their apartment leases.[79] By 1918, the Hyde Park Property Owners Association aimed at keeping the area racially exclusive and the community evidently was covered by covenants before the Depression decade. By 1930, the Chicago NAACP became aware of another threat to blacks—that of a boycott against black workers. The Hyde Park Property Owners Association pressured white apartment house and hotel owners in Hyde Park to refuse to hire or retain blacks who lived outside of Bronzeville's confines.[80]

This exclusionary pattern extended into the area adjacent to Hyde Park and south of Bronzeville, the Washington Park subdivision of Woodlawn. As early as 1928 the Woodlawn Businessmen's Association and the University of Chicago enacted an agreement to halt the movement of black Chicago into the area.[81] The signs of their success were obvious as the black population in 1920 was virtually nonexistent. By 1930, it was a minuscule .07 percent, but still it was a source of concern to whites.

The severity of this situation prompted the director of branches in New York to issue a stern warning: "This and other attempts make all the more clear the utter hopelessness of the Negro's fate unless he will organize in sufficient numbers to combat these attempts to debar him from earning a living and living decently."[82] By the time a copy of the Hyde Park covenant reached New York in 1931, 39.6 percent of all the covenants were in force; throughout the remainder of the decade, another 37.4 percent would be added to that list.[83] Upon examination, the legal problem appeared to be too complicated and costly for immediate action. The national office directed the branch to curtail its activities for the time being and to concentrate on gathering information pertinent to initiating an effective legal campaign in the future.[84]

In the more salutary portion of an oft-menacing scenario, politics combined with protest for racial advancement in 1930 as organized opposition to the nomination of Judge John Parker of North Carolina to the U.S. Supreme Court built into a groundswell. As the *Defender* would summarize the Parker fight at its conclusion, it was "the most imposing political demonstration ever staged by the Negro in the United States and [was] the impressive forefront of a sharp attack, not only upon the administration's lily-white policy, but upon nullification of the 14th and 15th amendments to the Constitution."[85]

A statement by Parker in 1920, questioning the capabilities of blacks to intellectually and morally exercise the franchise, brought Congressman Oscar De Priest and the national NAACP in the forefront of the challenge, alongside organized labor. Jointly, the two developed a well-coordinated, but not unified, campaign. While this type of issue neither appealed to nor had relevance for the Thompson machine, blacks saw Parker's nomination and possible confirmation as a threat to their right to participate politically in the governance of Chicago, the state, and the nation. Oscar De Priest took an especially active role in the campaign, resisting pressures emanating from the White House while lobbying among members of the Senate.

In the fragile relationship between politics and civil rights advancement, change was no longer taking place incrementally but with alacrity as the Depression created new relationships. Politics as an external organizational challenge loomed as potentially ominous as the Communist threat. Although the NAACP's and therefore the branch's policy regarded politics as *verboten*, it was still possible to embrace nonpartisanism. But in Chicago, as in other locales, this did not manifest itself in noninvolvement. As the Association reiterated its nonpartisanism, the organization was now perceived as pro-Democratic. To clear the air, Walter White enunciated the Association's position: "We don't support candidates, we oppose those that are anti-Negro . . . we are watchdogs."[86] The *Chicago Defender* took up the organization's defense: "The National Association for the Advancement of Colored People is not a political organization, but like the

Defender it has sometimes found it necessary to fight the enemies of our Race, even in the parties in which large numbers of our voters are enrolled. When it fights the Democrat . . . some are likely to think that the Association favors Republicanism; and similarly, when it fights Republicans who are judged to have betrayed the Race the charge can be heard that the Association favors Democrats. The Communists, when they felt the opposition of the Association, as in the Scottsboro cases, charged that the Association was capitalistic, which means both Republican and Democratic . . . [proving that] a nonpartisan position is really more difficult to maintain, and explain, than is the partisan position."[87]

In the same vein, any accusation of partisan affiliation made against national officials affected both the branch and the national organization, usually adversely. The issue surfaced in 1932 during the annual membership drive when national officers William Pickens and Daisy E. Lampkin were branded as disloyal Republicans by some branch volunteers.[88] Any case of perceived disloyalty affected the outcome of the fund-raising effort. Yet, to the normally astute and perceptive William Pickens, black discomfort with the change in the city's political status quo appeared to border on the foolish if not the childish. Pickens's correspondence with the national office showed a complete misreading of the Chicago situation. In one letter to Robert W. Bagnall that was illustrative of the outsider's view, Pickens stated: "It is strange how seriously colored people [in Chicago] take white people's politics. The white people do not take their own politics so seriously: even Mr. Hoover and Mr. Roosevelt can get together after their very heated campaign is over. Colored people have a lot to learn, but I believe they will learn it. Meanwhile, we will have to pay the price of helping to give the lesson."[89]

What Pickens witnessed was the deleterious effect that politics had on branch operations before World War II. In Chicago, almost every year seemed to bring some political contest, and with each one, the number of volunteers, fund-raising activities, and memberships decreased. In 1931, a mayoral campaign was conducted that changed the character of Chicago politics up to the present. Of ultimate significance, Republican control of City Hall ended with Thompson's defeat. In successive even-numbered years, biennial contests for control over the First Congressional District seat occurred. And, in addition to the 1932 presidential campaign, the fall of 1930 had witnessed a draining U.S. senatorial campaign.

Political influence acted as a negative force in other ways, overwhelming the branch in 1932 and almost bringing disaster. The national office was already aware that 1932 would be a difficult year in which to proceed with the Association's tasks when the city was hosting the conventions of the two major political parties along with that of the Communist Party. Robert W. Bagnall wrote to Daisy E. Lampkin: "I don't suppose you would get to Chicago until after the election, for prior to that I doubt that effective work could be done there."[90] In October, Archie L. Weaver confirmed this to William Pickens: "All of the active people of Chicago more or less are busy in politics. Politically, colored people are more highly organized in Chicago than anywhere else in the United States. It is now and has been for some time, a very difficult thing to have a complete or even good attendance at a Committee meeting due to the interference of politics. Many were absent from our Executive Committee meeting . . . they decided that all were so busy with politics that I should meet you . . . "[91]

As the nation chose between Hoover and Republican traditionalism and Roosevelt and his willingness to experiment, all matters irrelevant to individual, group, and national survival seemed to lose their importance. Weaver summed up the situation in the 1932 Annual Report: "The public's vital interest made it impossible to secure the ordinary attention and assistance from those who otherwise are genuinely interested."

The formidable and pervasive influence of the Great Depression affected the Chicago branch of the NAACP in a manner that inextricably linked it to external forces, both economic and organizational. Nonetheless, its primary struggle remained that of the development of a viable organizational structure from which to launch a relevant civil rights program. As the Depression continued, it affected the branch's ideological and programmatic features by degrees, causing its structure to alter correspondingly. In demonstrating that racial equality could exist on a practical level within its ranks, the Communist Party inadvertently bolstered the branch's ideological efforts. And, the rise of the Democratic Party to all-pervasive influence, on the other hand, placed it in a position to offer the branch's leadership and membership incentives that could distract them from their commitment to the Chicago NAACP's mission to fight primarily for equal rights.

6

A. C. MacNeal and the "Whole Loaf or None at All," 1933–1937

I, personally, am ready to abandon everything that is Jim Crow because it has certainly been proven that "we can by being separate demonstrate our greatness and break down the barriers" is a washout. It has reinforced the barriers. I am committed to the "whole loaf or none at all" policy. The half loaf is getting too small via the Jim Crow and separatist route. . . .

—MacNeal to White, 1934

It must be remembered that in Chicago there are a large number of competing interests and an event has to be something that everyone WANTS or is in the nature of a "natural." Civil rights are not yet popular like policy or Joe Louis and cannot be considered as a natural drawing card.

—MacNeal to White, 1937

A. C. MacNeal's ascendancy to the branch presidency in January 1933 propelled the Chicago NAACP into a fully modern, activist stage of programmatic activities. As one of about 400 branches in the nation, the Chicago NAACP developed an organizational maturity between 1933 and 1937 that was linked directly to the personality and vision of MacNeal. Serving as the branch's third black president, he was its first leader from the ranks of the professional middle class. Moreover, MacNeal represented the generational link between several key elements in branch history—between the "Young Turks" legal corps in the contemporary branch of the New Deal period and their predecessors among the "New Negroes" in the Black Metropolis in the 1920s as well as to the neo-abolitionist, biracial founders during the Progressive Era. With the exception of the trio of Earl B. Dickerson, Dr. A. Wilberforce Williams, and Archie L. Weaver, no one could claim to be a more active and direct product of neo-abolitionist thought and zeal than A. C. MacNeal. Along with Dickerson and Williams, he was considered in December 1932 as one of the possible successors of the outgoing president, Dr. Herbert Turner.

Dr. Williams, who was a life member of the Association, seriously considered taking the office;[1] however, he was looking forward to celebrating his sixty-ninth birthday in 1933 and was ending a long, distinguished career in medicine. The strains and demands of the branch presidency presumably did not look very appealing. Dickerson was busy in electoral politics as a Democrat and expected appointment to the post of Assistant Attorney General of Illinois, a position he did receive in February 1933. The branch's established tradition of occupational elitism automatically excluded Weaver from consideration for the presidency. MacNeal, the final choice, embodied the anxiety brewing within the branch; the anticipation of Roosevelt's initiation of the New Deal added to a festering factionalism.[2] Moreover, MacNeal possessed the physical, occupational, ideological, and administrative requisites to lead the organization at this time. The period of white and black patriarchical leadership had ended; the reign of the middle-class professional had begun.

MacNeal left a lasting imprint on branch history, the result of both his personality and achievements. His personality was unusual and so, also, was his physiognomy. He was described by one contemporary who had worked with him at the *Chicago Whip* as resembling "an old Colored Ichabod Crane."[3] His light complexion was attributable to his having descended from mixed racial ancestry in Louisiana. The frustration of not achieving his lifetime goals of personal and professional distinction because of his color and African ancestry acted as stimuli to a person like MacNeal, driving him to engage in actions to change the racial status quo in Chicago and the nation.[4] The promise of racial equality promoted by the National Association for the Advancement of Colored People throughout the country provided MacNeal with the vehicle through which he could both personally and collectively achieve the recognition denied him and his group for so long. This fusion of organization and man produced an unwavering loyalty to the Association and an ideological zeal for racial equality that was unshakable.

MacNeal thrived as an advocate of the "whole loaf or none at all" faction within the Association, which zealously fought racism among whites and voluntary separatism among blacks. Yet, in a city like Chicago, there was so much diversity among blacks in thought and behavior that the ideology of racial equality held by the NAACP still met opposition more than two decades after its rebirth as "neo-abolitionism." The desire among blacks for racial equality was ambivalent, as shown in the various strains of thinking within the ranks of the supporters of the fading Black Metropolis concept. Other blacks in the city disdained contact with whites as much as they could and took a passive stance on the problem of racial caste.

MacNeal's irascibility in pursuit of racial equality assumed a legendary status in local civic, political, and press circles. Combining this trait with his other attributes of tenacity, intensity, thoroughness, and courage, the new president proved to be a thorn in the side of racists and other opponents, real and imagined, of black racial advancement. His personality was such that one contemporary described him as a man "born with a sour stomach which has never been cured."[5] In 1936, Roy Wilkins wrote this paean to an equally caustic letter writer: "I had begun to feel that you had lost your penchant for sharp and forthcoming expression. It is a distinct relief to know that my mail last morning is likely to contain a little Tabasco Sauce along with the doses of skimmed milk I receive."[6]

MacNeal led the branch from January 1933 through October 1937 as its president (and served from January 1938 through January 1939 as its secretary). During this five-year period, he sacrificed professional interests and suffered financially for the cause of equality. MacNeal doggedly pursued Sears, Roebuck and Company and the Rosenwald Foundation in 1933, whom he charged with racial discrimination at the former's Loop store, in much the same manner that he had pursued the Woolworth chain in 1930 while at the *Whip*. He harassed the children of Julius Rosenwald (an ideological nemesis to whom he was personally unknown), hoping to influence Sears's executive leadership to end discrimination. At the opposite pole, in 1933 he targeted the leadership of a local National Guard armory that permitted discrimination at polo games. MacNeal pursued them through the upper echelons of the Illinois National Guard to U.S. Army headquarters in Washington.[7]

MacNeal's plans called for the branch to increase its prosecution of the "fight against [discrimination, making] the Chicago Branch of the Association a necessity for Chicago."[8] The substance of MacNeal's plans was found in "Notes and Proposals of the Executive Committee," which he prepared in February 1933. "Notes and Proposals" represented a highly incisive documentation of the branch's concern for strategic planning. Moreover, these concepts appeared as the first evidence of a written plan since the branch contemplated its formation in 1911. The five major administrative concerns had to do with clear policy formulation, sound financial oversight and increased resources, democratization of the membership and leadership, solid organizational structure, and aggressive programming.

Organizational policy was designed in such a manner as to leave "no doubt in the minds of officers, membership and the public as to what the Branch can and will do and what it cannot and will not do."[9] The changes in public sentiment that occurred during the Depression years required a comprehensive, fixed policy on the part of a stable organization. To this end, MacNeal envisioned and implemented a "planned and definite program." The treasurer was bonded to stabilize finances, whereas authority to disburse funds was controlled through the secretary, acting on behalf of the Executive Committee. Analysis followed, which explored different ways of raising funds, ranging from year-long membership solicitation to cabarets.

MacNeal next focused on the problems of achieving a quorum, increasing attendance at meetings, improving punctuality, and maintaining a permanent office. Significantly, democratization was broached head-on. He wrote: "People who [were] not of the so-called elite but who [were] valuable people with followings and the willingness to work" should fill the Executive Committee's membership. He stated further that this "should be considered in the light of removing the stigma of 'high-brow' from the organization. [The branch should even] consider the matter of having a known Communist on the Executive Committee."[10] Meetings of the membership at large were scheduled quarterly instead of annually, with well-known speakers featured as drawing cards. Branch-affiliated neighborhood leaders within the various black neighborhoods of the city were expected to carry the Association's message throughout the metropolitan area. Finally, a formal women's auxiliary was envisioned, while the Advisory Council of well-known but inactive, noncontributing members faced abolition.[11]

Targeting the stagnancy found among the volunteer leadership of the branch in the Executive Committee, MacNeal transformed the committee by dropping many of the old members and by enlarging its size overall, at first from seventeen to thirty, then ultimately to fifty members. Although Dr. Turner had pledged to remain active with the organization, his departure from the presidency led to the end of his activities once the new administration began instituting its plans.[12] Turner later claimed that "Big Bill" Tate, the well-known Bronzeville pugilist and picketer in the "Don't Spend Your Money Where You Can't Work" campaign, confided in him that MacNeal wanted him out of the branch. When Turner departed his office in January, the resolute physician unfortunately left carrying a grudge.[13]

MacNeal worked stoically to keep Turner's forecast of impending organizational doom from becoming reality. He labored diligently to assemble a volunteer group that would lead the branch to the zenith of its operations structurally and programmatically, seeking volunteers who would remain with the branch for a lengthy period as well as demonstrate themselves to be assiduous workers. The impressive number of young attorneys taking joint membership on the Executive and Legal Redress Committees attested to the prevalence of this trait. Prominent, civic-minded black professional women were sought out and inducted into the leadership. Attorney Edith Sampson joined in the early 1930s and Madame Azalia Mahone of cosmetics fame joined the committee by the middle of the decade. Volunteers served on other committees, including education, membership, finance, publicity, and press.

The effectiveness of volunteerism also served as a wedge against an unresponsive community or overbearing central office. When local citizens complained about the branch or, more frequently, ignored its pleas for financial assistance, branch spokesmen were quick to inform them that their civil rights were being protected by fellow citizens who served without compensation. In 1936, branch secretary Carl A. Hansberry took the national office to task for complaining about its workload when the volunteers of the branch had "but ONE paid clerk and likewise a large volume of correspondence."[14] Writing to Walter White in 1937, MacNeal bared his soul: "I sincerely hope that this letter will not lead you to feel that we are lacking in sympathy, or un-cooperating," he confided; "but it is to point out that local people who give their time and service without compensation have a perfect right to indulge their attitudes and preferences in respect to the work of the Association."[15]

The major drawback to volunteerism seemed clear. Because time and service were given freely, workers were immune to supervisory pressures found in a remunerative situation. The branch broached this problem in 1936 when it formulated its "Proposal for Establishment of a Regional Office": "Volunteer service must of necessity be intermittent because of the intervention of personal interest."[16]

Although the gender imbalance on the Executive Committee received the attention it demanded and was being corrected, a racial imbalance remained. Almost all the whites who belonged to the leadership were found among the ranks of the lawyers of the Legal Redress Committee. In part, that fact confirmed the accuracy of Clarence Darrow's assessment that whites had abandoned the egalitarian movement. Whites were indeed more likely to join economic-focused groups working to counter the problems of the decade. In addition, there had been an upsurge of support for social justice (which included racial equality) among the city's Roman Catholics; their choices, organizationally, were those groups affiliated with their church.[17]

In a movement dedicated to the advancement of blacks through racial tolerance, respect, and cooperation, MacNeal exhibited an ambivalence toward white participation. His past suspicion of whites had not abated one iota. Yet his "Notes and Proposals" called for greater contact with white liberal groups in the city to broaden the support for racial equality. In the aftermath of the annual conference of 1933, he supported white and black race egalitarians who lambasted interracial "do-nothing" tea groups.[18] He severely criticized former NAACP Board Chairman Mary White Ovington in 1936 for "living in the dim past of 1913," and considered her views on race advancement to be anachronistic and useless.[19] He chided Jane Addams for remaining aloof from the branch for over two decades, but seemingly welcomed the support of Addams's longtime friend and NAACP supporter Sophonisba Breckenridge.[20] MacNeal continued to be suspicious of Julius Rosenwald and his foundation; the philanthropist remained his favorite target among well-to-do Jews as he continually questioned their collective motives for involvement in the NAACP. His analysis of the Rosenwald Fund showed that it promoted black preparation for advancement rather than advancement itself.[21] In contrast, his sensitivity to the mistreatment of German Jewry led him to pledge his support to alleviating their plight, seeing in their victimization a case parallelling black America's.[22]

Reorganization during the MacNeal years also led to the displacement of black Executive Committee members dating from the Turner presidency, much to the exasperation of national field secretary William Pickens, who considered many of those removed his personal friends. Pickens became prolific in his criticism of the branch throughout the decade; on one occasion, he confided to Walter White: "The new officers are active, but confidentially, they made a mistake by ousting so many of the former workers and 'abolishing' groups like the 'Flying Squadron' and the 'Advisory Board.' The abolishment gained nothing and certainly lost something."[23] Pickens did not explain further what was lost because he could not. His antagonism toward MacNeal overshadowed his ability to reason in this matter. In the meantime, the branch operated at a higher level of efficiency than ever before under MacNeal's leadership.

The field secretary's animosity toward the new leadership stayed consistent; consequently, during the next year, there was a running feud between him and Chicagoans MacNeal and Irvin C. Mollison (now the former's alter ego in the Illinois State Conference of the NAACP as well as leading spokesman for racial equality on the Executive Committee). Pickens assessed the status of the branch in June 1934: "I doubt that the Chicago Branch is better because it has young officers instead of Dr. Turner and others. Certainly the young officers did not show any superiority over the old officers when we met there last summer."[24] Ironically, Pickens had accused these same friends among the old officers, and especially Dr. Turner, of "sitting down" on the job in December 1932, leaving their successors very little, organizationally, upon which to build.[25]

During MacNeal's tenure, the branch secretaries still maintained a high visibility with the public, the national office, and the branch's hierarchy and membership. Archie L. Weaver served until January 1934 when

Carl A. Hansberry assumed those duties for four years. Hansberry shared neither Weaver's close relationship with the national office nor a lengthy affiliation with the Association (he entered the racial egalitarian movement in 1932 upon election to the Executive Committee). For Hansberry, dealing with local issues loomed as matters of greater importance than cultivating the friendship of easterners. It was not surprising that Hansberry was very readily identified with the Chicago court case involving housing discrimination that followed his purchase of a home in the Washington Park division of the Woodlawn community.

MacNeal set as his priority the enlargement of the branch's membership from which a democratic base of support would develop.[26] The branch even increased its informational meetings in an attempt to broaden its popular appeal. But the overwhelming number of blacks in Chicago at the advent of the New Deal were primarily concerned with matters of the palate and the digestive tract, not of the intellect. These gatherings, as opposed to mass protest meetings involving issues with emotional appeal such as the Scottsboro defense, appeared to have met with only limited success. As a barometer of popular support, membership throughout the New Deal period hovered slightly above the 1,000 mark on an annual basis.[27] This small membership illustrated the influence of competing ideologies and organizations as much as it did the limited, but growing, appeal of the branch.

The low level of memberships in the branch represented the failure in the branch's development more glaringly than its inability to develop a program. Despite advances in organizational stability and program activism, the pattern continued during MacNeal's reign. This unfortunate circumstance was cited in a branch press release: "[While the branch was fighting for the] ordinary rights of colored people it is found that over 90% of the cases handled for colored people in Chicago were for people who were not members of the Association and this is in a city of 250,000 persons, [where] 10,000 members or $10,000 is a small amount for protection of the fundamental civil rights [we seek]."[28]

For the first time in its history, the branch approached the ranks of organized labor for assistance and a reciprocal promise to also support its interests. Slowly, the branch became more clearly identified with the union movement in both its pre-CIO and CIO stages. Though the peak years of industrial trades support for the branch were not to be reached until the 1950s, support from other unions developed earlier. Retail clerks gave their support to the branch in 1933; and by 1936, workers in the pressing and dyeing industry entered the branch's membership.[29] Postal workers continued as the most valuable support group, so even as Weaver was leaving the branch's leadership, their financial contributions increased.

The commitment of black churches grew even stronger, and one clergyman, a Reverend Nicholson, was inducted into the Executive Committee in 1933. A myriad of black churches proclaimed June 25, 1933, "NAACP Sunday," with the hope that all churches "would cooperate in this effort to make Chicago fully N.A.A.C.P. conscious and therefore fully race conscious as the first step toward an intelligent plan to bring colored people in Chicago together along all lines."[30]

"Notes and Proposals" called for a frontal assault on discrimination in unions, governmental bodies, transportation, and housing. Omitted from the document, but not from the activist program initiated almost immediately, was the branch's most important target—discrimination in public places of accommodation and in commercial establishments. Protest advocacy of the New Deal period centered around the fight to eliminate what Drake and Cayton called the "color line" in Chicago. Blacks emigrating to the city anticipated encountering less prejudice than in the South, but they found that Chicago "had always been somewhat uncertain about what place Negroes should have in the city's life. The result [was] a color-line which mark[ed] Negroes off as a segregated group deemed undesirable for free association with white people in many types of relationships. The color-line also serve[d] to subordinate Negroes by denying them the right to compete, as individuals, on equal terms with white people for economic and political power."[31]

Programmatically, the branch had come of age in fighting what political scientist Charles V. Hamilton has called the "dual agenda of the civil rights movement"[32]—the noneconomic and economic targets of injustice that had to be overcome before a racially egalitarian society could evolve. The branch's new program activism resulted in the processing of 8,000 cases of racial discrimination between 1933 and 1939. Of the scores of cases taken to court, none was lost. Using only one paid clerk among its unpaid volunteer corps of attorneys and other professionals, the branch's staff provided service to a virtually endless throng of blacks with complaints about the color line. Daisy E. Lampkin was one officer who could attest to the energy Chicagoans were expending in promoting the advancement of civil rights in the city. On one occasion, she reflected on this occurrence: "As I sat in the office conducting the campaign, I was amazed at the number of people who came in with their problems and cases. It is the first branch that I have seen function to this extent, and shows the possibility of what a well-salaried NAACP officer could do."[33] The branch's success so impressed Walter White that he requested fifty copies of its 1936 service brochure to distribute to other branches as a "how to" or demonstration manual.[34]

The Legal Redress Committee prosecuted the discrimination cases brought to the office, maintaining its function as the primary vehicle for civil rights advocacy. The committee always had at least twelve members and was predominantly black.[35] To their credit, the volunteer lawyers took scores of cases to court during the New Deal period and earned the sobriquet given by Ralph J. Bunche of "Young Turks." The lawyers found their bulwark against racial discrimination in the Illinois Civil Rights Act of 1885, which had been periodically amended by racially progressive black and white legislators throughout the twentieth century.

One common type of case pursued by the lawyers involved the refusal of service or exorbitant pricing at restaurants on the periphery of the black neighborhoods of the South Side. Discriminatory restaurateurs were Greek, Jewish, Chinese, Irish, and Nordic (or Anglo-Saxon), united by a common bond of protecting their financial investment from a group they considered to be deserving of their animus. The blacks most affected were middle-class, usually professional, people in social work, education, or similar fields. That this group of cultured and assimilated Americans were denied their rights made the affront all the more egregious to other successful persons within their ranks.

Using a tactic employing maximum coercive power, the branch sued plaintiffs for punitive damages to teach them the strongest lesson possible. One lawyer explained the approach as follows: "We hope to make it so expensive to discriminate that the offenders will stop as soon as the word gets around."[36] Suing for monetary damages instead of for principle contrasted sharply with the tactics in the Adams Theater case of 1923 and exposed the lawyers to the unfounded charges that they sought out cases for personal profit. No evidence has ever been presented to substantiate this charge and, in fact, Earl B. Dickerson argued that the opposite circumstance prevailed.[37]

In civil rights cases that did not require a lawyer's attention, a telephone call or a letter penned by A. C. MacNeal, proudly identifying himself as president of the NAACP branch in Chicago, worked effectively. Cooperation with the local black press helped the branch institute an effective, hard-hitting propaganda network. Letter writing proved useful against the racial ridicule of blacks over the airwaves as well as in publications, movies, and plays. Branch action resulted in apologies for or refraining from the use of "nigger," "darky," "Sambo," and other such words over local radio stations.

Racial discrimination in the major Loop department stores, such as Marshall Field's, Wieboldt's, and Sears, Roebuck and Company proved regrettably commonplace. The branch actively pursued redress through contrition and a promise to end the practice. Complaints about deliberately slow service or clerical surliness toward black women and their families in Sears's shoe and women's clothing departments reached the branch, which immediately contacted the family of the late Julius Rosenwald. MacNeal's complaints to one of the sons, Lessee, so incensed him that another son, William, wrote to Walter White to curtail what the

Rosenwald family considered unwarranted harassment. The Rosenwalds felt that letters of pique written to them about a department chain over which they no longer had control were an unnecessary intrusion into their lives. With his considerable leverage, William Rosenwald convinced White to persuade his overzealous Chicago leader to curtail his activities temporarily. MacNeal reluctantly agreed, but only with White's assurance that the matter would not be held in abeyance indefinitely. With this assurance, the campaign against discrimination at Sears ground to a temporary halt.[38]

When the Chicago World's Fair opened in June 1933, the branch belonged to a federation of several dozen, mostly professionally led, black organizations from the South and West Sides which comprised the Colored Citizens World's Fair Council. The Council handled most of the contact with the fair's management including cases alleging racial discrimination. Within its arsenal, the council included conciliatory as well as protest weapons.[39] The growing presence of white Southerners in the city, both as permanent residents and summer visitors, increased the tendency of certain concessionaires to cater to the Southerners' regional customs.[40] One major incident involved Chicago Urban League board member and activist, Catholic, egalitarian Dr. Arthur G. Falls who, while in the company of his wife and an out-of-town guest at the Pabst Blue Ribbon restaurant on the fairgrounds, was denied service. The party dined only after Falls threatened the manager with immediate police action under the Illinois Civil Rights Act. Faced with this embarrassment, the manager ordered the party served. The next day Falls wrote the director of the fair, the Hon. Rufus G. Dawes, to complain about the affront. Within twenty-four hours, Dawes's staff contacted Falls, and the restaurant manager guaranteed that this type of incident would never recur. Falls, for his part, made it clear that if it did, he would seek revocation of the restaurant's license.

The slow prosecution rate of reported civil rights violations at the fair angered the branch to such an extent that it led a delegation from the Council to the offices of the Cook County States Attorney to protest. The official on duty acted cavalierly and only appeared to be willing to respond with civility to Earl B. Dickerson, who was recognized as a fellow Democrat and Illinois Assistant Attorney General.[41] However, because of a promise of fairness agreed to prior to the fair's opening as well as the alert action of the Council and its members, similar incidents were kept to a minimum for the duration of the fair.

The scope of the branch's civic mission was still expanding; consequently, it began to include more of the interests of all classes of black Chicagoans. Further, as the branch's efforts moved from dealing with restaurant cases outside the Loop and with housing discrimination cases in white neighborhoods to instances of police brutality and civil rights violations, the branch was safeguarding the rights of the rank-and-file citizens of black Chicago as well as the middle class and the elite.

The branch's 1936 brochure entitled "Your Civil Rights in Chicago" stated: "No other fight is more important at this time as the right to live where one is able."[42] With this slogan as its battle cry, the branch initiated a campaign designed to open up housing for blacks that lasted five years in its legal stage and even longer in its legislative phase. The campaign to dismantle the restrictive covenant as an effective instrument of racial proscription began in earnest in 1937 after the branch's secretary, Carl A. Hansberry, and his family (which included future playwright Lorraine) were harassed by white vandals into fleeing their recently purchased home in the Washington Park subdivision of Woodlawn. The local white improvement group sued the Hansberrys and the white seller for violating a standing restrictive covenant that forbade the sale of property to Negroes. The branch's Legal Redress Committee combined the Hansberry case with two others and the newly expanded case found its way into the local and state courts. Consistent with decisions rendered previously in cases involving culpability with regard to broken covenants, the white seller and the Hansberrys were found guilty.[43] The branch continued building a local defense fund to support the struggle, raising money annually until the case, *Hansberry v. Lee,* reached the U.S. Supreme Court in 1940. There, a favorable decision resulted in a bar specifically against the restrictive covenant in the Woodlawn community.

Beyond the struggle for equal housing, which was initiated locally, other noneconomic concerns, generated from New York, did not produce as much support from the branch's leadership. A case in point was the national office's attempts to get the branch involved in its on-again, off-again interest in the Scottsboro case.[44]

The most surprising of the new program components that developed during the New Deal period involved the struggle for jobs. Traditionally, the Association's founders avoided this sphere because of a past commitment to economic liberalism, passed on to the branches as a negative feature of local policy. However, new conditions produced a new perspective. The 1933 Amenia conference held at Joel E. Spingarn's Troutbeck estate in New York state emphasized the need for the Association to adjust its program to reflect the economic issues of the day. Although the cerebral MacNeal and other similarly endowed black Chicagoans were not invited for reasons that are unknown, and therefore were not present to express their views, their convictions were in many respects similar to those of Ralph J. Bunche and Abram Harris of Howard University, who did participate. At Amenia, these future leaders called for greater participation on the part of the Association in tackling economic issues head-on, and this injunction included its entire network of branches.

While theoretically the branch's program was designed to fight discrimination in both the private and public sectors of the economy as well to promote unionism among black workers, in actuality it did not advance the cause of organized labor. This inaction contrasted greatly with the role that the Detroit NAACP assumed as its ranks split into pro- and anti-labor factions.[45] Unlike the Chicago Urban League, which moved assertively again during the New Deal to place workers into the newly revitalized private sector, the branch fought only racially discriminatory practices that blocked employment for job-seeking black workers. One case in August 1933 brought the branch into conflict with the A & P and National Tea food chains, which had advertised for 2,900 men to fill vacant jobs. Reflective of the times, all announcements contained the offensive wording that applicants "must be white."[46] MacNeal immediately sent a letter of protest to the food chains and counseled with the members of the Executive Committee to discuss the feasibility of organizing a boycott. In spite of the high level of economic deprivation that existed throughout Bronzeville, one alternative suggestion prevailed on black consumers to shop at independent grocers.

The capacity of the branch to grow in the area of economic involvement again led it to take an assertive stance on the employment issue. In 1936, it called on corporate America to create 25,000 new jobs.[47] The need to protect the rights of the masses of organized labor was also explored with the branch's membership at one of the quarterly forums sponsored by the Education Committee. Guest Paul Douglas of the University of Chicago (and a future member of the U.S. Senate) spoke persuasively enough to garner branch support from the forum for needed amendments to the Wagner Labor Act. The branch responded by contacting Bronzeville Congressman Arthur W. Mitchell, Oscar De Priest's successor, to investigate the matter and introduce appropriate legislation.[48]

Yet the branch's attempts to attract members from the ranks of organized labor reflected its dilettantism in this sphere. It did not have an action program that led it to do any more than verbally espouse the rights of labor to organize and gain compensation for its production through first the AFL and later the CIO. In addition, the branch neither recruited nor signed up workers for the unions. If the branch deserved credit for having made a contribution in the economic sector it was in its active fight against discrimination in the New Deal agencies where Roosevelt created thousands of jobs. Using the power of his pen, MacNeal regularly fired off letters to the heads of the innumerable alphabet agencies—the WPA, CCC, FEPC, NRA, and others—to challenge them to end racism in their ranks.[49] The branch's flair for the dramatic was further manifested in a resolution it introduced and had passed at the 24th annual conference Chicago hosted in 1933. The resolution called on the president of the United States to either redistribute jobs on an equitable basis or face the possibility that "blacks

[would] appeal to the League of Nations" for redress of their grievances."[50]

As organizational stability under Turner and then MacNeal grew, so
did the national office's attempts to maintain centrality. While always a
potential source of intra-organizational conflict, contention over centrality
affected relations between the national office and the branch in Chicago to
a point at which the nadir was reached in November and December of
1939, when revocation of Chicago's charter was threatened. This confrontation occurred as the culmination of a series of contentious encounters
beginning in 1933 over, first, the limits of internal governance and national
reorganization; second, ideology; and, third, fund-raising and apportion-
ment. The MacNeal regime interacted with Walter White's administrative
team—Roy Wilkins, William Pickens, Daisy Lampkin, and the secretary
himself—who staunchly believed in the validity of James Weldon
Johnson's policy of treating the branches like minor league baseball teams.
Within the unitary structure of the Association, branches were to be guided
in their activities, supported to the fullest, but ultimately led from New
York.[51]

Significantly, at no time did branch officers contemplate revolutionary
changes within the operations of the Association. Their insistence was
solely on a branch's right, whenever prudent, to approve or disapprove of
activities and proposals taking place under national auspices. This position failed to get a positive response from New York, so this sore point
festered throughout the decade.

Another major source of contention was the famous "Chicago Revolt"
which originated in 1933 as soon as A. C. MacNeal assumed power.
MacNeal, Mollison, Murray, and others espoused a level of ideological
purity that they euphemistically labeled the "whole loaf or none at all"
approach. It was an uncompromising, zealous approach that produced
factionalism. They vehemently opposed segregation and even tackled
both the concept and existence of the Black Metropolis. In the minds of
these advocates of racial equality, there were true believers and there were
traitors, and most of Chicago, the Association, and the nation fell into the
latter category. However, MacNeal's ideological purity did not reflect the
branch's collective thinking. Archie L. Weaver, Earl B. Dickerson, and
others questioned this approach, seeing little value to combining impru-
dence with ideological commitment.

MacNeal once wrote, "the only reason that I, personally, am ready to
abandon everything that is Jim Crow is because it has certainly been
proven that 'we can by being separate demonstrate our greatness and
break down the barriers' is a washout. It has reinforced the barriers. I am
committed to the 'whole loaf or none at all' policy. The half loaf is getting

too small via the Jim Crow and separatist route. . . ."[52] MacNeal regarded the "Negro National Anthem [also known as "Lift Every Voice and Sing" and written by James Weldon and J. Rosamond Johnson] as a 'Cradle Song' and hangover of the confused and muddled thinking and approach of the NAACP in its beginning."[53]

As one who had been present at the beginning, the venerable W. E. B. Du Bois created a tumult in 1933 and 1934 in a spate of speeches, comments, and editorials in *The Crisis* articulating his misgivings about the economic course that the Association was taking in the middle of a debilitating, worldwide Depression. He questioned the organization's longstanding reluctance to tackle economic problems as well as its insistence that all forms of racial separation, forced or voluntary, be opposed.[54] As Du Bois assessed the situation in 1933, the economic exigencies of the Depression dictated a change in Association policy. The plight of blacks in the aggregate was so severe that he foresaw mass starvation as a real threat. Du Bois, though, was not advocating "a program of complete racial segregation [or] even nationalism among Negroes." On the contrary, he was stressing the real point that "economic discrimination [was] fundamental and advised concentration of planning" as a solution to the black plight during the Depression,[55] something commonly accepted in the Black Metropolis phase of Bronzeville's existence. In the fall of 1933, Du Bois supported a New Deal measure calling for the establishment of a separate federal agency to oversee the social and economic progress of black Americans—something akin to the Bureau of Indian Affairs. MacNeal considered it a new "Emperor Jones scheme."[56] To MacNeal's and Mollison's ears, Du Bois's pronouncements sounded like apostasy.

The emanation of this argument from Chicago in 1934 led Du Bois to dub the assault upon him from within the Association the "Chicago Revolt."[57] William Pickens discovered that some branch leaders considered Du Bois's acceptance of voluntary separation and certain vestiges of segregation as merely a tactical maneuver during an economic crisis. "These leaders do not interpret it as Mollison interpreted it," Pickens wrote. "As one said, we take it that Du Bois means that we should *get our team together* and smash the opposition with an organized team. At the same time, they believe in the Association's need to stand for equal rights for Negro Americans."[58] In Chicago, Archie L. Weaver questioned the fairness of the verbal onslaught on Du Bois because of all of his past contributions to the development of the Association,[59] and objected to the intensity of the attacks. Dickerson clearly saw the difference between what was impractical ideologically and what could be reasonably achieved. He had, after all, served as officer in the all-black Eighth Illinois Regiment (redesignated the 370th Infantry Regiment) during World War I; and he was soon to lead the all-black Cook County Bar Association as its president in 1939. And in their very commercial pursuits, Black Metropolis businessmen and future branch presidents Charles Murray and Ira Williams were calling into question the validity of the purist approach. As to the Du Bois affair, it ended in June 1934 as Du Bois resigned from the organization under external pressure and amid some self-generated fanfare.

The branch's relationship with the two dominant political parties and the politicized Chicago city government always represented a potentially dangerous threat to the Chicago NAACP's direction as well as to its future. Even during an economic Depression, politics remained the vehicle through which black Chicagoans ultimately believed their most important racial advances were to be made. Throughout Bronzeville, political considerations such as party loyalty and racial solidarity at the polls overshadowed economic realities.[60] By 1933, the Democratic Party assumed a greater control over city politics than any local political organization had ever previously envisioned with the advent of the New Deal. Bolstered by the largesse of Franklin D. Roosevelt's New Deal, party loyalty shifted to make Chicago a Democratic stronghold. The Second, Third, and Fourth Wards now constituted both the major exceptions and the heart of the political representation of the Black Metropolis. Even with this pervasiveness and dominance, it is incorrect to assume that political influence determined the course of civil rights activism during the New Deal period.

As the branch applied pressure on its own initiative nationally, statewide, and locally, it never threatened the political status quo. MacNeal guided the branch in such a manner as to keep it free of partisan politics and from a direct confrontation with the Democratic political machine, headed jointly by Mayor Edward Kelly and Cook County Democratic Party Chairman Patrick Nash. MacNeal's need to preserve the appearance of neutrality if not nonpartisanism was easy to understand. First, a partisan stance, which before 1931 had meant a Republican affiliation, could have considerably eroded popular and financial support of the branch, which was always struggling because of its elitist image and its ideological "purity." Second, the branch's leadership was already divided politically, albeit peacefully, between the Democratic and Republican parties. Irvin C. Mollison, for example, who was president of the Third Ward Regular Republican Organization, shared an office with Earl B. Dickerson, one of several leading black Democratic spokesmen on the South Side. Dickerson was active enough in behalf of the Democratic Party to receive the position of Assistant Attorney General for Illinois in 1933. Through careful cultivation of the ideological issue of racial unity and the avoidance of flagrant partisanism, the branch prevented politics from becoming an impediment to its program.[61]

However, during the same period, others within the Association realized the volatile nature of partisan politics and warned of harmful consequences in the wake of such a stand in Chicago's Black Metropolis. Roy Wilkins warned Walter White to avoid any confrontations with Illinois Democratic Congressman Arthur A. Mitchell, even if White was asked to oppose him by the Chicago branch.[62] Avoiding Mitchell proved difficult. In its role as a pressure group for civil rights, the Association and Chicago NAACP found themselves diametrically opposed to the presence, actions, personality, and policies of Bronzeville's Congressman Arthur W. Mitchell. The latter won De Priest's seat by riding on Roosevelt's lengthy coattails in the 1934 congressional elections and by winning predominantly white support from the northern end of the district.[63] After his election, however, Mitchell publicly proclaimed himself to be a proponent of Booker T. Washington's moderate racial ideology. He evinced an embarrassing obsequiousness in his contacts with almost all whites except for those Republicans in his district who opposed the New Deal. To them, he exhibited an uncharacteristic aggressiveness and often acted with deliberate hostility. Consistent with his ideology of obsequious conciliation, considered "fawning" in Bronzeville, he engaged in behavior and sponsored legislation viewed as detrimental to race advancement. Because of the strategic implications, the Chicago NAACP and Association feared that a public altercation with Mitchell over ideology and program might be construed by the black public to mean that the organization opposed the ameliorative programs of Roosevelt's New Deal. As it turned out, Mitchell was neither recognized as a national spokesman for America's black citizens nor even as a racial leader by black Democrats in Chicago. His limited domain was the South Side's Second Ward, which wavered between Republican and Democratic control.

Controversy over the best way to pursue race equality legislatively engulfed two of Mitchell's proposed bills in 1935. The first of these was an industrial bill that would have set up the equivalent of a Bureau of Indian Affairs for blacks and the second was an anti-lynching bill that the NAACP national office regarded as too weak to be effective in the fight against legalized, community-sanctioned mob action. Mitchell's first piece of legislation was House Bill 5733, which called for the establishment of an industrial commission to oversee black economic progress during the New Deal period and afterward. With alacrity, the national office criticized both Mitchell and his bill. Mollison and the Illinois State Conference also attacked it, considering it "unnecessary and unwarranted."[64] In June, Mitchell contacted MacNeal, seeking his understanding of if not cooperation and support for the bill, and called the Association's opposition "foolish."[65] MacNeal's response to his new-found ideological antagonist was predictable. He helped write a resolution condemning Mitchell's bill as a piece "of class legislation . . . for 12,000,000 American citizens . . . [and declared further that] under such terms a bill of rights and privileges which are inherently the rights of ALL American citizens could be compromised and abridged." In his peroration, he protested that "the passing of this bill [would] set the Americans who happen to be Negro back seventy-five years [and] establish a Black Code."[66]

By August, Mitchell wrote a supporter (of which there were many throughout the nation despite his equally numerous detractors) condemning the Association's leadership: "The N.A.A.C.P. is fighting this bill for all that it is worth, not because it is a bad bill but because it is not their bill . . . [and it] has fallen into bad hands and can no longer be regarded as an institution interested in Race uplift."[67] Mitchell was correct in assuming that the Association could never support a bill of this type given its ideological mission of integrating blacks into the American mainstream, not further isolating them from American life. The Association had solid backing in opposing the bill, but Mitchell had impressive numbers in support throughout the nation.[68]

Advocates of racial equality found the Mitchell Bill offensive beyond its flirtation with voluntary separation. Its provisions condemning subversive activity and propaganda produced apprehension among civil rights supporters because of both the need of the NAACP to continue its propaganda against racism and the rising tide of European fascism, which was ushering in rigid totalitarian controls. For years southern racists and other opponents of the NAACP had accused it of being subversive and of spewing propaganda while purportedly seeking racial justice. Once the Association assessed the chances of Mitchell's bill being considered during this session of Congress as slim, it toned down its criticism. The bill, along with several similar ones, eventually languished in committee.

The relations that had developed between the congressman and both the national and the Chicago NAACP offices over the industrial bill made future cooperation unlikely. For his part, Mitchell had a personal reason for not wanting to cooperate with the branch which he shared eventually with MacNeal. While a virtual newcomer to the city before 1933, the congressman had been denied a seat on the Executive Committee, and that still rankled.[69] Mitchell was a person who neither forgot nor forgave, so no relaxation in the level of mutual antipathy could be expected. Being so challenged by his actions, the branch characteristically intensified its attacks on Mitchell. By May 1936, the branch requested the national office to send it all the information that it had on Mitchell and this was done, no doubt, to help the De Priest reelection campaign in violation of the branch's operating policy of nonpartisanship.[70] Mollison subsequently attacked Mitchell in Walter White's behalf before an audience in Lincoln, Illinois, and MacNeal urged White to counterattack Mitchell "using bricks, not powderpuffs."[71]

The Mitchell Anti-Lynching Bill which the congressman introduced in 1935 fueled more conflict. He received extensive congressional support among liberals and moderates who were confused over who spoke for the interests of blacks. Was it Mitchell, now maneuvering to become *the* political voice for black America by virtue of his congressional seat, or the NAACP with its nearly three decades of service? Many of Mitchell's colleagues went along with him, including members of the Illinois delegation. They observed the rules of congressional courtesy which dictated that congressmen support another lawmaker's bills when they received inquiries or pressures from the latter's constituents. This placed the branch and the national office in a precarious position when it came to getting support for the measure they supported fully, the Wagner-Costigan Anti-Lynching Bill. Mitchell wrote to one congressional colleague that "personally I do not approve of their [the Wagner-Costigan] bill. I certainly do not approve of their tactics. I question their sincerity in this matter. It seems to me that the most they are interested in is making a gesture or creating a ruckus."[72] Throughout 1936 and 1937, the NAACP stalwarts in New York, Chicago, and elsewhere challenged Mitchell in both the Congress and throughout the nation over the relative merits of the bills.

Mitchell openly denounced Walter White as being "mentally unbalanced" and as "bordering on insanity."[73] The congressman also had criticism for MacNeal, which was mild, however, in comparison with White's.[74] For his part, Walter White developed total disdain for Mitchell, writing in 1936 that "the Afro-American congressman from Illinois has done a disgusting job as a man Friday for the most reactionary elements of Southerners in the House of Representatives."[75]

As the Mitchell bill became more of a major impediment to the passage of the Wagner-Costigan Bill, the national office directed the Chicago branch to apply pressure on the Kelly-Nash machine to have Mitchell desist in his efforts.[76] Simultaneously, the branch was called on to contact Illinois congressmen to see if they could convince Mitchell to abandon his obstinacy.[77] The branch also worked within the Illinois State Conference to persuade the various statewide branches to apply local pressure on legislators in their congressional districts to support the Wagner-Costigan Bill. In the end, this bill met the same fate as the Dyer Bill of the 1920s; the U.S. Congress never enacted any anti-lynching legislation.

By 1935 and 1936, new organizations appeared in Bronzeville, representing both more support for and yet a greater menace to the branch's pursuit of hegemony over the city's civil rights movement. In 1935, the Chicago Council of Negro Organizations was organized under the auspices of the Chicago Urban League. Significantly, MacNeal held a post within its leadership. The Council functioned as a clearing house for information and resources, and as a lobby for black issues in areas that ranged from civil rights to employment. The next year, the National Negro Congress (NNC) convened its first annual meeting in Chicago. From the time of its initial appearance, the Congress showed it had the potential of becoming an all-inclusive civil and economic rights organization. Ironically, its leader, John Davis, had been feted six months earlier by the Chicago NAACP at the Wabash YMCA in the heart of Bronzeville.

Now, in the dead of winter, in January 1936, Davis and his National Negro Congress were being viewed as threats to the hegemony of the Association and its branches. The national office grew suspicious of its intentions and sent Roy Wilkins to the opening session to monitor the proceedings.[78] In contrast to relations the previous year, the branch grew suspicious of John Davis's motives and deferred on any association with the Congress.[79] MacNeal's assessment of the Congress was ominous. He wrote: "[The] Congress is what the Negro wants but the National Negro Congress [alone] cannot deliver. Only with the energy of the Communists could it hope to succeed."[80] Later that year, as the Congress established a national network of local councils and attracted widespread support under the leadership of its president, A. Philip Randolph, the national office confirmed the branch's opinion and now considered the Congress as a major rival.[81]

By the end of the organizing conference in Chicago, the Congress had also developed a local, autonomous council to actively fight for the rights of blacks. The worst fears of the branch came true as the Chicago Chapter of the National Negro Congress began to crowd the already full civil rights field. Competition between the Chicago NNC and the Chicago NAACP began in earnest and extended into the next decade, until such time as the branch proved triumphant. Another group, again sponsored by the Chicago Urban League, appeared in 1937. The Negro Labor Relations League channelled the energies of the militant young semi-professionals and high school–trained men and women of the South Side into protests aimed at securing employment in such occupations as projectionists at local theaters, milk truck drivers along routes in Bronzeville, and telephone operators.

The MacNeal years began with a flurry aimed at organizational and programmatic revitalization and ended at the same pace. By the time MacNeal left the presidency he had transformed the Chicago NAACP by bringing it closer than ever before to becoming "a necessity" in the life of Chicago. Institutional status for the branch beckoned, requiring only that the organizational patterns reflect a true democracy.

7

Crises of Charter and War, 1938–1945

Any city of over 260,000 Negroes that has as much difficulty as Chicago is having trying to sell the NAACP has something fundamentally wrong.

— E. Frederic Morrow to Walter White, 1939

The war demands all-out cooperation and unity, if we are to win it. Among the ideals that are at war, [is] the ideal which will give all persons the opportunity to make a decent living on the basis of their ability to work, [and this] is the ideal that must be victorious.

— Oscar C. Brown to Anita McCormick Blaine, 1943

DESPITE A. C. MACNEAL'S resignation in October 1937, the branch moved closer to a second watershed in its history as it crossed the divide between black hegemony and organizational democracy. The branch operated without a president for a three-month period until Charles Murray, a cosmetics manufacturer of growing wealth, assumed office in January 1938. One of his first acts in office was to state his public commitment to continue MacNeal's policy of the "whole hog [loaf] or nothing."[1] Since he was the first president to come from the ranks of the Black Metropolis business class (which depended so heavily on exploiting the segregated nature of the black South Side market), this announcement served to highlight the contradictions inherent in black Chicago's thinking. During the one year Murray spent away from his business pursuits, the antithetical gap between professed ideology and demonstrated action apparently left him unaffected.

Intense activism undertaken in behalf of equal rights continued under Murray's leadership, with the branch taking action in 1,264 cases involving civil rights violations.[2] Instances of police brutality or false arrest persisted, involving the branch in eighty-nine cases of alleged abuses.[3] One report also included three extradition proceedings in which the branch prevented two endangered black men from being returned south.

As Chicago's black population grew to exceed one quarter of a million, the problem of housing discrimination reached crisis proportions with "the Negro population . . . herded into an area that should contain only one-fourth its number."[4] Locked in Bronzeville's confines, blacks faced exorbitant rents and an ever-increasing shortage of habitable housing. Racism extended to proposed public housing (the South Park Garden Apartments, now known as the Ida B. Wells Homes) which were delayed by problems involving land acquisition, construction, and politics. Preparation for the proposed 1938 opening became a nightmare that ended only when the first tenants moved into their homes in June 1940.

The year 1939 ushered in a new president in the person of Ira Williams. A Bronzeville real estate broker, former branch treasurer, and member of the Executive Committee since 1935, Williams followed Murray's paradoxical action of committing himself to the ideals of the Association, namely, the ideological purity as upheld by MacNeal, and the firm belief that there were financial benefits to be gained in a racially captive market. As Europe entered its second conflagration within a generation, Williams led the branch during its darkest hours of upheaval when the annual fundraising campaign of November and December 1939 ended disastrously.

Like many events of historical importance, the charter crisis of 1939 had a beginning free of controversy and any premonition of doom. In 1938, the branch attempted to build a local defense fund by sponsoring a baseball benefit featuring an all-black professional baseball team, the popular American Giants. This benefit was approved by the national office. The branch anticipated receiving 50 percent of the proceeds, an amount President Ira Williams initially considered exceedingly low.[5]

The benefit promised to be a guaranteed financial success since Executive Committee member Mary Cole's husband owned the Giants. The anticipated large turnout materialized on game day with an estimated 10,000 persons attending. The lucrative gate receipts, however, were not realized. A star chamber proceeding ensued during which Mrs. Cole was summarily accused of theft.[6] Humiliated by the incident and emotionally distraught (while perhaps betraying her precarious socioeconomic status as a member of the nouveau riches), Mrs. Cole immediately sought revenge, not redress, for the perceived insult. Her friends rallied and initiated a whispering campaign against the branch that almost caused its demise.

To vindicate Mary Cole's besmirched reputation, these aggrieved matrons targeted the membership drive in fall 1939. The annual campaign was conducted amid dissension and ended in a debacle. Total receipts for the campaign reached $600 of which only $117 were available to meet local operating costs after expenses. This financial failure, accompanied by rough treatment accorded E. Frederic Morrow, the national office's replacement for Daisy E. Lampkin, attracted national office scrutiny that threatened charter revocation.[7]

Locally, a disheartened President Ira Williams had grown just as frustrated, threatening to disband the branch completely if sizable public support was not forthcoming. Beyond the misguided effort of the whispering campaign, the public still had not fully acknowledged the work the branch was doing for black advancement. Addressing those who had benefited so much but were willing to return so little, Williams declared that "the day is past when just a few people should sacrifice time and energy in order to provide protection for Race in Chicago. . . ."[8] Significantly, Williams's threats proceeded simultaneously with, yet independently of, similar action from the national office.

Charter revocation was the final administrative remedy to correct serious or egregious local difficulties and deficiencies. The discussion therefore produced disparities in the responses among the national leadership. Walter White assigned newcomer Morrow the task of reconstructing the national office–branch relationship and examining the branch's most recent activities.

With this opportunity to assess the branch's status, Morrow recommended revocation. Citing both the branch's current failure to perform effectively in the fall campaign and its well-documented historical difficulties, he reported that the branch's current condition rested on the "culmination of a series of vexing episodes over the years."[9] Young, intelligent, forceful but naive, Morrow had walked into a hornets' nest in Chicago during the 1939 membership drive. Only a seasoned national officer could have been expected to bring order into this chaotic scene, and the most effective field officer, Daisy E. Lampkin, was assigned elsewhere. Moreover, based on the vitriolic tone of massive amounts of correspondence from Chicago to White, Wilkins, and Pickens, Morrow opined that the branch had always opposed cooperation on the issue of centrality. Morrow also surmised from his limited experience in Chicago that what he saw of the branch represented the totality rather than a capsule view of the branch's status and operations.

Morrow's assessment could not have been further from the truth. In its current program, the branch had reached a new level of effectiveness in addressing the diverse needs of Bronzeville. Constituent groups ranged from the well-to-do to the unemployed, and each formulated its own agenda. From its involvement in the "Don't Spend Your Money Where You Can't Work" campaign to its support of black pre-CIO union membership, the Chicago NAACP assertively identified itself with workers' rights. And, from legal assaults on the restrictive covenants to attempts to end downtown department store discrimination, the branch was responding to the needs of middle-class blacks as the latter perceived them.

Yet, Morrow thought something was amiss in Chicago; he wrote perceptively about Chicago's troubles in the midst of a seemingly favorable setting for civil rights advancement. As he approached various occupational and social groups throughout the city—beauticians, for example—he was told that they "felt they weren't on the right social plane to be with us [the NAACP]." Something was wrong, and it did impede Chicago's development. Perhaps Morrow, because of the very successful campaign he had completed in Detroit, was perturbed at not realizing the same high expectations for Chicago.[10]

In contrast, Daisy E. Lampkin had grown to appreciate the intense programmatic initiatives of the branch and the enigmatic personalities who led the movement. By the mid-thirties she had made peace with Weaver, MacNeal, and Mollison, admitting that there was disagreement but she "most certainly would not call it hostile."[11] She finally advised the national office to take a cautious approach, and to forget revocation.

Thurgood Marshall succeeded Charles H. Houston as special counsel in 1939 and rendered his opinion that the branch was not contributing to the movement and was made up of people "who looked for every advantage to thwart the Association's efforts."[12] Marshall's evaluation reflected two of the contributing factors to the friction. As a newcomer in the national office he readily accepted unbridled centrality as a method of governance. Further, he quickly embraced the probability that the Chicago branch was guilty of culpable behavior.

As the intraoffice debate about charter revocation continued to brew, William Pickens's consternation boiled. He recounted the years he had battled MacNeal, Mollison, and others over centrality, politics, and personal issues. The veteran officer supported Morrow's view: "I have no doubt that what you say is true, judging from the almost constant attitude of the Branch for the last ten years or more."[13] To substantiate his recollections, Pickens even contacted Chicagoan Claude A. Barnett, the head of the Associated Press and his colleague over the years, but who, importantly, was not a branch member, to assess the branch's status over the decade and following the winter debacle. Barnett suggested that political involvement and opportunism explained the disaster, but Pickens did not accept that explanation, given the personalities involved.[14] In the midst of chaos, Roy Wilkins saw the Chicago case as an opportunity to bring order by modernizing the Association's structure along lines having been under consideration for years.[15] This meant, no doubt, increasing local democracy and engendering interoffice harmony while retaining the essential features of centralization.

For his part, Walter White reacted viscerally. He regretted both Morrow's agonizing experience and what he had uncovered through research of official files that seemed to confirm his suspicion "that the branch would eventually end up where it was."[16] The branch was, in fact, at the threshold of organizational success, but this was not made clear until the end of the following year's membership campaign. The issues of centrality, most prominently exposed by the debacle of 1939—lack of cooperation with the national office on a personal level and inadequate fund-raising—were being resolved on a local basis. In the end, the branch retained its charter as rationality in New York overcame passion.

Bronzeville businessman Ira C. Williams entered his second year as branch president in 1940, more firmly committed than ever before to correct the conditions that had produced the charter-threatening debacle of 1939. Speculation permeating Bronzeville that his reelection was not a personal accomplishment, though, surely tormented him. It appeared likely that his reslating occurred because of a scarcity of candidates for office rather than to any renewed sense of confidence in his administrative abilities. If indeed there was a void in leadership, the new blood quickly being infused into the branch's hierarchy acted as a corrective. Homemaker Mrs. Cora Patton became the first female since the 1920s to fill the position of branch secretary, and attorney Oscar C. Brown, Sr., accepted membership on the Executive Committee. Both were destined to be future presidents.

Despite Williams's management style, characterized by the term "weak sister," from 1940 on the branch regularly exceeded its apportionments and became the third largest contributor among branches.[17] During the annual fall drive of 1941, Williams led the branch to a fund-raising record of over $6,000.[18] Along with these accomplishments, the branch enjoyed successes with program activities and with its efforts to democratize the branch through a growing membership and inclusive hierarchy. The membership ranks became filled with persons who previously had viewed the branch from a distance but were now willing during membership drives to tout the branch's needed role in the black community. Increases were recorded in 1940 and 1941 with 5,000 members on the rolls in the latter year, a branch record.[19] Despite these gains, in the eyes of some supporters and leaders of the branch, Williams provided only inefficient leadership. The president accordingly received criticism instead of plaudits.

As the United States entered the Second World War after Pearl Harbor, the lessened confidence of the Executive Committee in Williams's abilities manifested itself fully. The branch elected popular newcomer Oscar C. Brown, Sr., to succeed him in 1942. With recognition of his administrative skills growing and because of his personal dynamism, Brown became the logical choice to lead the branch during the war years. Whereas Brown exuded a quiet dynamism in contrast to MacNeal's irascibility and Williams's low-key persona, he was still described by one national officer as "a live wire, and highly respected in Chicago."[20] Forty-six years of age when elected, Brown possessed the maturity and experience necessary to direct an organization that was on the verge of reaching its programmatic potential. Importantly, he was the fourth successive branch president with middle-class, professional roots. The influence of the black bourgeoisie on the branch's future was entrenched.

Experientially, Brown had seen racism at its worst in his native Mississippi, but within a supportive family setting he quickly developed the mettle to confront this evil head-on.[21] Reared in a milieu that stressed assertiveness and achievement as a means of realizing personal fulfillment, he manifested the leadership traits of decisiveness, analysis, and compassion. When the First World War began, Brown volunteered and received his officer's training at the segregated Des Moines, Iowa, army officers training facility. There, he accepted the compromise of second-class treatment in order to fight in behalf of his country along with the promise of first-class citizenship some day later. After serving in France with the 351st Machine Gun Battalion of the 92nd Division, he was mustered out as a first lieutenant. His proud return home in uniform to rural Edwards, Mississippi, exposed him to the danger of joining the ranks of a dozen or more returning black veterans in the South who were killed by white racists. In the postwar South, wearing a soldier's khaki garb, with its undeniable claim to the rights of full citizenship, invited white reaction, ranging from verbal assaults to bodily harm to lynching.

One episode cemented his commitment to mass involvement in the struggle for equal rights. Brown recalled over one-half century later how three black strangers befriended him at a train depot in Vicksburg, "expressed pride in [his] being a commissioned officer . . . [and showed concern] about [his] safety throughout the balance of the night." He reflected that "these men were a part of that vast underprivileged population sometimes referred to as the 'masses' . . . From this group the successful ones of us ascend, and the height of our ascendancy is dependent upon them as our foundation-base. Therefore, as heavy a load as it may seem to be, we must pull them up and along as we try to climb."[22]

With this particular facet of his developing ideology intact, Brown went on to finish his college training at Howard University. He became one of five Brown brothers educated in the challenging academic climate of Howard, Chicago, and Northwestern. Upon graduation, Brown held degrees in economics and law. As if in training for future service beyond his professional interests, he was elected to the presidencies of his fraternity and of the Howard chapter of the NAACP. During his post-collegiate years, he accompanied his brother, Sydney, to Chicago, where they entered into private law practice in 1925 after passing the Illinois bar. He soon joined his brother in the law firm of Temple, Brown, Harewood, and Wimbish, which was comprised of some of the rising stars of Bronzeville's professional class. Later, during the Depression, he became a partner in Brown, Brown, and Cyrus (destined to be one of Bronzeville's most influential and prestigious law firms).

Still uncertain of his ideological direction, Oscar C. Brown did not immediately join the city's egalitarian movement. He experienced a conversion after his precipitant and disappointing association during the 1930s with the quasi-nationalist Forty-ninth State Movement. A combination of concern and frustration about the plight of the black working class during the Great Depression had convinced Brown and other professionals of the necessity of making plans for an independent nation.[23] The charter of the movement called for "the ultimate establishment of a new state . . . wherein, at least, a portion of the Negroes in the United States can have an opportunity to work out their own economic, political, and social destiny unhampered and unrestrained by ruthless artificial barriers, wherein they can have a chance to raise the lot of their poor masses from exploitation, insecurity and wretchedness." By the end of the decade, Brown and the other leaders underwent a waning in enthusiasm for their movement as it failed to move beyond the conceptual stage. At his wife Helen's urging, Brown now became involved with the Chicago NAACP.[24]

Brown came into office with a commitment to building a branch that was inclusive and that functioned as a people's organization rather than one which harbored exclusivity. He even promised to be more effective than A. C. MacNeal in attracting the attention and support of the black rank and file. His methods were totally plebeian as he used massive picnics and church visits, along with contacts from his personal network, to direct the branch toward democracy and institutional status. He remolded the branch's leadership to include more women, middle-class professionals, and clergy. He was adamant that his three predecessors in office—MacNeal, Murray, and Williams—remain active in the branch as members of the Executive Committee.

As important as the presidency had been and had remained since the founding of the organization, branch operations required efficient, day-to-day management by a full-time executive secretary. During a time when most of the big-city branches—Philadelphia, Detroit, Baltimore, Cleveland—experienced difficulty in filling these positions in the 1940s, the Chicago NAACP hired two dedicated and able executive secretaries. The first was Harry J. Walker, a native Pennsylvanian, who brought a new perspective to Chicago. Educated at Fisk, Oberlin, and the University of Chicago, and with credentials in research and race relations that seemed to qualify him better for an Urban League post than for a position as executive secretary, Walker served during 1943–1944. His successor was Eugene O. Shands, who had worked as a postal employee but who had sacrificed his job after devoting himself completely to the branch's work full-time. For his civil rights service and sacrifice, he earned public recognition and received the title of "Race Man."[25]

The presence of a full-time executive secretary relegated the status of the offices of secretary, financial secretary, and assistant secretary to ceremonial status. At this juncture, women began to fill these positions. In contradistinction, these appointments occurred when the financial contributions and campaign efforts of women reached a new level of importance. The largest numbers of women were found in the Women's Auxiliary, from which the branch's most successful fund-raising activities emanated. While the Association's network suffered without viable or extant auxiliaries,[26] Chicago's grew with increased stature because of its success in filling its and the national office's treasuries.

Overall, the role of women became more highly visible, with their numbers on the Executive Committee rising to a high of seven in 1943, decreasing to four in 1944, and climbing back to six in 1948. Women had gained representation but only limited input into policy making due partially to their former affiliations, which were mainly social and civic in nature and rooted in club work rather than in business and the professions. With the exception of attorney Jewel Rogers,[27] the daughter of a branch leader, none was in law, politics, or medicine. Among these women, at the half-century mark, gender advocacy had not taken root; racial ideology still enjoyed its primacy.

The growing acceptance of the Chicago NAACP developed just as much from the energies, support, and quiet leadership of these women as it did from the efforts exerted from the presidency, the Legal Redress Committee, and the postal employees. The Advanced Guard from the early 1930s was succeeded by the Women's Auxiliary from 1935 into the 1940s. Now, middle-class women with widespread social and civic support dominated the leadership of the women's groups. Popular community club woman Cora Patton filled the presidency of the Women's Auxiliary in 1940 and schoolteacher Ethel Hilliard assumed the office in 1941. At the same time, Patton and Hilliard acquired seats on the Executive Committee. Mrs. Helen Brown's presence and effective volunteerism also played a major role as she gave her husband's tenure an added dimension not seen since the Turner years. As impressive as it was when the Rev. Clarence Cobb of the First Church of Deliverance was induced to take out a $500 life membership,[28] when the Rev. Mary Evans of the Cosmopolitan Church joined in 1941, she recruited 700 of her 826 members for a mass enrollment.[29]

With Brown's leadership emphasizing inclusivity, the branch annually produced membership enrollments of over 12,000 supporters. The membership peaked when the branch recorded 18,500 wartime memberships, including servicemen, in 1945.[30] As imposing as these figures were for Chicago, Detroit recorded an Association high of 33,000 memberships. One national officer used the challenge from Detroit as an incentive to spur Chicago forward. "Detroit will top its goal," he wrote to Brown "I do hope Chicago will aim at the same number."[31]

An increase in financial support quite naturally went along with the rise in memberships. The branch's financial status continued to improve until exceeding a national office goal of $1,000 became a matter of course. The 1942 effort netted over $8,000; the 1943 effort, over $13,000. The branch raised over $26,000 in 1945 and produced enough collateral revenue to finance its own local initiative against the restrictive covenant.

Realizing that the branch's program was the most effective instrument through which to attract community support, Brown promoted an activism that touched on the most important concerns of the membership. In contrast to the previous wartime period, programmatic activities were intensified. With the advent of war in Europe in 1939 and an upswing in defense orders from the Allies by spring of 1941, the national office directed Chicago and the other large city branches to selectively picket companies with defense contracts in order to promote fair employment practices. This attempt to democratize the defense industry proceeded with the cooperation of the Chicago Urban League and the Chicago Council of Negro Organizations and anticipated the success of the March on Washington Movement later in the year. Grim-faced pickets with placards that embodied the frustration of black America marched outside the Bauer and Black plant in Chicago. One placard read, "Hitler Must Run This Plant—They Don't Employ Negroes." By the end of the year the branch legitimately claimed credit for its contribution in opening defense work for blacks.

The widening of the war in 1941 brought yet another protest organization to the forefront, this time to challenge the federal government on its commitment to provide economic opportunity for all American citizens. In January 1941, A. Philip Randolph, president of the Brotherhood of Sleeping Car Workers, organized blacks into a broad-based, popularly supported, all-Negro group, the March on Washington Movement

(MOWM). The MOWM committed itself to eliminating all discrimination in American industry, appropriate, given the irony of the times, in that there was a shortage of white workers and an abundance of able and willing black ones. With the assistance of the national office, and with the Chicago NAACP's aid, Randolph planned a protest march on the nation's capital for July 1, 1941. Randolph especially sought change beyond a governmental pledge, so he called for the creation of the Fair Employment Practices Commission (FEPC) to monitor the defense industry's compliance with the anticipated new federal policy.

From New York, NAACP Secretary Walter White celebrated success along with Randolph in June 1941 when President Roosevelt acquiesced to the MOWM's demands. The branch's support of the MOWM approximated symbiosis as it helped organize black Chicago. Of the five members of the FEPC, one of only two black members selected was Earl B. Dickerson of the Chicago NAACP. Further demonstrating his boundless energy in pursuit of racial justice, the ubiquitous Dickerson was also serving as alderman of the Second Ward as well as president of the Chicago Urban League and the Cook County Bar Association. As black civil rights forces nationally reached a consensus that the FEPC had to be protected as well as enhanced in its powers, FEP Commissioner Dickerson convened hearings on the subject in the Chicago City Council chambers as part of a long-term NAACP strategy.

The branch supported Dickerson's effort at the national level during the war and at the state level afterwards. Meanwhile, Chicago NAACP Executive Committee member Elmer W. Henderson contributed his skills and time as the head of the Chicago Citizens FEPC Committee, as did former branch secretary Morris Lewis, who succeeded him in May 1945.[32] Concomitantly, Congressman William L. Dawson, who represented the city's Loop and black South Side, cooperated by introducing H.R. 3986 in support of FEP in January 1944.[33]

As the branch engaged in grass-roots, mass pressure, it was propelled into a new dimension of organizational and democratic inclusion within its own ranks. Chicago NAACP branch members could be found passing out leaflets at defense plants to garner support for a permanent FEPC in 1945. One problem peculiar to Chicago involved the question of how to distribute the leaflets in such a manner as to avoid offending white plant managers by passing out pro-FEPC materials inside the buildings, or white workers by ignoring them in the presence of their black co-workers outside the plant gates. This was a matter that perplexed branch secretary Eugene O. Shands, but was of little interest to the national office.[34] The volatile nature of wartime race relations in Chicago made this an issue that had to be handled diplomatically to avoid future untoward consequences.

With the war's end in 1945, black and white liberal proponents of equality in employment feared a retreat from the spirit that had pervaded since 1941. In Chicago, the branch's position was succinctly expressed in a flyer that received general distribution. It read in part, "If it is unfair to discriminate in wartime, is it not equally unfair to discriminate in peacetime?"[35] Consequently, the branch spent a great deal of time in 1945 and in subsequent years working in support of an FEPC for the state of Illinois. The effort was extensive and was spearheaded by the black Chicago state legislators. House Bill 353 was introduced in March 1945 and included language that called on an FEPC "to make equal opportunity to seek employment a civil right."[36]

Another part of the branch's economic agenda took it beyond the struggle for passage and support of a FEPC. The branch championed the cause of black employees of the Chicago Post Office, one of the nation's largest, in which racial slights bordered on the egregious. While black workers were employed in large numbers at the clerical level, qualified employees with managerial aspirations were systematically denied advancement because of their race. The result was that only twelve supervisors, or 2 percent, out of 600 on duty at the post office were black. Then, adding insult to injury, less qualified whites were being promoted.[37] At the urging of the National Association of Postal Employees (NAPE), the Chicago branch led a delegation to the office of Postmaster Ernest A. Knuetgen in early March to discuss the matter. The delegation included representatives from the Chicago Urban League, the CIO, the Mayor's Office of Human Relations, and other groups. "We consider this grossly unfair and in view of the gallant fight that Negroes are making to help the war effort we seriously urge you to use your influence to correct this awful situation," was the gist of the message that the branch's executive secretary sent to the entire Illinois congressional delegation.[38] Also, the NAPE leadership advised Congressman William L. Dawson "to go through with [his] plan to call the Chicago congressional delegation together and lead them. . . ."[39] Meanwhile, Dawson had co-sponsored a FEPC bill.

The wartime economic opportunities in which blacks had shared allowed them to gain a foothold in the mainstream American economy. Gains in the city appeared nothing short of spectacular. The protection of a permanent FEPC seemed absolutely essential with more than 40 percent of the black workforce engaged in economic activities outside domestic and service employment. Black workers found employment in the food processing industry (including meat packing), the iron and steel industry, and wholesale and retail establishments.[40] The sting of racial discrimination during the demobilization of 1945, however, pricked the dream of many blacks that the jobs they held in 1941–1945 would be theirs forever.

Inequality in housing opportunities continued to plague the black community as another major economic evil. Blacks were still being stacked one on top of another as the lure of defense work brought 70,000 to 100,000 additional black workers from the South to the city between 1942 and

1945.[41] This demographic explosion increased the density of population in the South Side's Black Belt to 375,000 persons living within 4.2 square miles by 1945. *The Crisis* in 1940 described the circumstances that forced these blacks into an area that should have contained only three-fourths of their numbers in a feature essay.[42] Aptly titled "The Iron Ring of Housing," it reported that there were 85,000 excess persons living in the limited space in which blacks were restricted legally by race. Conditions could only be expected to worsen given the open racial hostility against housing expansion for blacks.

Blacks, securely locked in Bronzeville, faced exorbitant rentals and an ever-increasing shortage of habitable housing. Racism in rent gouging extended to racism in public housing. The newly opened Ida B. Wells Homes catered to blacks exclusively while all the other units in the city excluded blacks from occupancy. Throughout the city, blacks occupied 10 square miles but were denied access to 40 additional square miles due to enforcement of the restrictive covenants.[43] Eliminating the restrictive covenant was the key to opening up housing throughout the city.

The fight against the restrictive covenant, which had begun in earnest in 1937, reached the nation's highest tribunal on October 25, 1940, when Earl B. Dickerson argued the case of *Hansberry v. Lee* before the U.S. Supreme Court. Dickerson's strategy involved challenging the validity of the particular covenant used in the Washington Park subdivision of the Woodlawn community. He cited the fact that it had insufficient signatories among the affected white home owners. The Supreme Court ruled that because the required 75 percent white signatories had failed to sign the document, the covenant under review was invalid.[44] As significant as the decision was, it had failed to attack either the legal principle upon which protection of the covenant rested or the practice of denying the right to due process to Negroes under the Fifth and Fourteenth Amendments.

Nonetheless, the decision rendered in November became a local *cause célèbre*. While the *Chicago Defender* predicted that a favorable result would be far-reaching and that 500 homes would be opened up as a result of the victory,[45] it was left to the case's champion, Dickerson, to place the victory in perspective. At the time Dickerson cautioned blacks that "victory of the Hansberry case assure[d them] only of the right to live in the Washington Park area ... [but that they] must continue to fight to live anywhere [they] please[d]."[46]

Dickerson and the lawyers working with him—Francis Stradford, Loring B. Moore, Irving C. Mollison, and Truman K. Gibson—had also wanted all covenants invalidated as well as the principle of *res judicata* (this case serving as legal precedent for all cases of this class) inferred. However, their desires proved to be fruitless. What the decision achieved was simply to lay the groundwork for future assaults against the covenant, of which the brunt of the work was to be shouldered by the national office. The ultimate victory was won in the 1948 U.S. Supreme Court case of *Shelley v. Kraemer.*

Winning a battle against one neighborhood covenant merely signified that others in the Englewood, Hyde Park, Oakwood, Kenwood, and East Garfield Park communities still would have to be eliminated. Much of the joy associated with the *Hansberry* case dissipated quickly as the Chicago Title and Trust Company, the city's major land deed repository located in the Loop, refused to stop issuing titles with restrictive covenants included. And, at the University of Chicago, the institution with the biggest interest in housing in the Woodlawn community, resistance to black housing expansion remained unabated. Throughout the city, the realty groups were just as steadfast as ever in denying blacks their right to live wherever they wanted and could afford. The branch, meanwhile, stood just as undaunted in its efforts and carried its struggle against the restrictive covenant to the Illinois General Assembly. In 1941, Bronzeville Senator William Warfield aided this effort by introducing a bill to stop the restrictive covenant in the far south Roseland community, located approximately four miles south of the Woodlawn area.[47]

The legal fight against the restrictive covenant also proved expensive. Under Brown's leadership, over $25,000 was raised to pay permanent legal counsel attorney Loring B. Moore for his services. [48] With the pervasiveness of the covenants, the costs seemed almost reasonable to many. To eventually eradicate the covenants, the branch spent $35,000 in court and legal fees between winter of 1944 and the early postwar period.[49] Even during the war, the branch raised and spent thousands of dollars in pursuit of fairness in housing. Oscar Brown passionately summed up the situation to Walter White in February 1945: "There is unusual activity on the part of whites to put in effect more and better restrictive covenants. *Our backs are to the wall!* [emphasis in the original]. Our organization finds itself with the tremendous problem of breaking restrictive covenants or so prosecuting or defending suits to get the right for Negroes to live out of their present ghettos that we must immediately go to the public for a war fund for this purpose."[50]

Protecting the right of black children to enjoy a decent education became another wartime concern of parents and the branch. Overcrowding in classrooms as well as idle, unsupervised school children were commonplace problems at certain predominantly black South Side schools. The Chicago Board of Education refused, however, to allow transfers from any schools with a heavy concentration of black youngsters to ones that were predominantly white because of white resistance to any mingling of the races. In 1943, the branch publicized the information that "segregated schools are a fact" in Chicago. Its solution reflected the nation's overseas preoccupation with bigotry and racial hatred by calling for an effort to "de-Hitlerize the Chicago school system."[51]

Peace in Europe and the Pacific in 1945 was followed by turmoil at home as the white students at the racially mixed Englewood High School used direct action to demonstrate their displeasure with an increasing number of black classmates. This student strike was more representative, however, of their and their parents' hostility toward blacks in housing, employment, education, and other spheres of interracial contact. For decades the Englewood community had accommodated a limited number of blacks in the school, but the change in their numbers precipitated a backlash. An investigation by the American Council on Race Relations recommended increased interracial contact and understanding as well as freedom of choice in housing. The branch watched this incident from the sidelines as well as a student strike that took place at Calumet High School south of Englewood. Two years later, a racial confrontation at Wells High School on the North Side did bring branch involvement.

Despite the branch's fixation with the restrictive covenant campaign, its Education Committee remained active with a corps of dedicated teachers in its ranks. Veteran teachers, such as Madeline Morgan Morris and one of the branch's few active Caucasian members, Faith Rich, served on the committee. Rich was a New Englander who joined the branch in 1942 and blended her early Vermont exposure to racial egalitarianism with learned scientific humanism to become the branch's leading educational stalwart for the next several decades. Rich had earned a doctorate in classical literature at Bryn Mawr and used her skills of fact-finding, analysis, and narrative to the branch's advantage in both this decade and the next.

As support grew for the branch, the organizational dream of presidents, from A. C. MacNeal to Oscar C. Brown, of making the branch "a necessity" materialized. With a predominantly black middle- and working-class orientation throughout its hierarchy and membership, the racial sensitivities of Bronzeville's citizens now fused with the soul of the branch. The branch leadership's attitude simply insured that no complaints of civil rights violation would be overlooked. The admonition of branch secretary Morris Lewis a generation previously about developing such an awareness flowered into realization because to blacks any racial slight, regardless of the severity, was considered devastating to their psychological well-being. When persons with problems involving race to any degree came to the branch's office, they were served directly or received a referral to an agency that could assist them.

The scope of the complaints of racist intimidation ranged from the substantive to the ridiculous, from physical assault to imagined stares. When sharecropper Samuel Miller fled his native Mississippi to escape debt peonage, little did he realize that in the middle of a global conflict, Mississippi police officials would pursue him to Chicago. Sheriff V. R.

Barnham of Sunflower County, his deputy, and two constables came to Chicago to complete extradition proceedings. Miller discovered that he had been charged with larceny for stealing two radios, a common offense which provided Southern officials the justification to file for extradition. The Legal Redress Committee investigated the charge and assigned the unflappable Henry William Huff to stop the proceedings. After securing three separate writs of habeas corpus, Huff successfully won permanent freedom for Miller.[52]

Restaurant and theater discrimination continued, as did derogatory usages such as "nigger" and "darkey" in public and private advertising. The branch investigated all of the charges. By 1945, the Chicago NAACP cooperated with a new group devoted to direct action in civil rights matters—CORE (the Congress of Racial Equality, founded in Chicago in 1942). The branch pursued legal charges against the operators of the White City Roller Rink after CORE initially publicized the discriminatory practices.[53]

Court action, legal suits, picketing, lobbying, and publicity continued to be indispensable tools in the branch's arsenal as its tactics changed dramatically during the war. During 1945, CORE attempted to persuade the national office and the Chicago NAACP to consider adding nonviolent, direct action to its choice of tools, solidly convinced that if the NAACP did so, the masses would become involved as never before. As CORE assessed current Association tactics, acts of discrimination which were frequently resolved through court and legal action as well as through education and fellowship were never tested for their effectiveness. CORE suggested that sit-ins or other demonstrations would prove decisive if civil rights were attainable. It would be another twenty years, however, before the branch would employ these tactics.

Besides familiar programmatic activities, one event in particular bore the imprint of Oscar C. Brown's democratization campaign as well as a strengthening of national office–branch relations. In 1944 the Chicago NAACP hosted the thirty-fifth annual conference of the Association over a five-day period beginning July 12. Following a pattern set by the last two conferences that Chicago had hosted, in 1926 and 1933, the meetings were held exclusively within the black community. At the Metropolitan Community Church, proceedings carried an assertive, enveloping African American essence. Not surprisingly, the conference took "a theme of militant determination to carry its campaign for a 'Negro Bill of Rights' to the grass roots of America." Roy Wilkins could not have found a more propitious setting than this to caution against what he considered the dangers of racial consciousness run amok.

Befitting the occasion, Chicago's mayor, Edward Kelly, opened the conclave with a warm welcome to the delegates. A. L. Foster of the Chicago Urban League and home care manufacturer (and future millionaire)

S. B. Fuller of the Chicago Negro Chamber of Commerce followed with their greetings. When national Secretary Walter White spoke he deplored the racial contradictions abounding nationally, finding it ironic that "the white world clings to the folly of white supremacy despite the war for democratic equality." At the working sessions, the 600 delegates from 46 states produced resolutions that demanded an end to segregation in the armed services, expanded wartime and postwar employment opportunities, a permanent fair employment practices law and an agency to promote it, along with equality of opportunity in housing and education.

The highlight of the conference was a first—a mass, outdoor assemblage on Saturday, July 15 in the city's expansive, verdant Washington Park. It was chosen as a site of last resort by Brown because of the overcrowding of other city facilities tied up by the Republican and Democratic party conventions. Use of the park represented a gamble because of Walter White's fear of a small crowd and Brown's of possible inclement weather.[54] The weather held, and anywhere from 15,000 to 30,000 persons participated in the conference's closing ceremonies. Dr. Charles R. Drew of Howard University, the genius behind the nation's wartime blood plasma program, received the Association's Spingarn Award.

Despite Oscar C. Brown's insistence on and success with an activist program, as the war neared its end and with enthusiasm for activism mounting, he began to appear too cautious to some of the younger, more militant labor and working-class members of the branch. They regarded his approach in calling the nation to task on the issue of equality as too moderate. Their agenda and Brown's placed the two sides on a collision course.

To other members, the branch appeared to be a one- or two-man operation which had to be replaced, preferably with themselves or members of their faction. One person with a pressing grievance was attorney Henry William Huff, a self-made lawyer and friend of political iconoclast Arthur W. Mitchell. Huff went public in the pages of the black *Chicago World* newspaper, accusing attorney William Temple, the chairman of the Legal Redress Committee and former law partner of Brown, of being out to discredit him professionally.[55] Charges that "evil-hearted" lawyers within the committee were ignoring the needs of the ordinary citizen, while catering to the whims of the privileged few, characterized Huff's views of the state of the branch under Brown's leadership. Huff's ultimate response was to challenge Brown for the branch's presidency in December 1943 in a race that the former lost by a four-to-one margin. In reslating the membership for the 1944 Executive Committee, Huff lost again.[56]

Brown's aggravations did not end with internecine squabbling. Centrality ceased to be as severe a problem as it was in the 1930s, but it did occasionally contribute to tension between Chicago and New York. The

Chicago position was essentially a straightforward effort to improve both the Association and the process of centrality. Before this stance was fully understood by the New Yorkers, President Brown commented thusly on the feelings of Chicagoans: "[The] successful women and men, who occupy responsible places in our community . . . [and who] make important decisions for themselves in their business and personal and business affairs . . . [are people] our community expects [are] able to do so for the Chicago Branch, NAACP. The need to get 'permission' from someone a thousand miles away in order that we may accept from our own community money we raise is hindering."[57]

Bronzeville's *modus vivendi* between the civic and political spheres rested on two preconditions that remained constant until the postwar period. First, as long as the level of political rewards and recognition was low in the Black Belt, there was little likelihood of a discernible breach in the arrangement between black civic advocacy and black politics in and peripheral to Bronzeville. The scarcity of large scale, tangible incentives such as governmental positions merely bolstered the level of racial consciousness among blacks as this political deficit illustrated the depths of racism. Second, the absence of personal and ideological friction between the leaderships of the various civic and political organizations coupled with a shared sense of racial destiny to hold the two groups in balance. Growing altruism in behalf of better race relations never emerged as a threat to the self-centered features of machine politics. Both in terms of probability and possibility, conflict was virtually unimaginable until the 1940s brought greater occupational opportunities and an expectant sense that a color-free America might be nearer.

On the national level, the Democrats had little to offer blacks in 1940, since the appeal of Roosevelt's first eight years in office focused on the economy.[58] By 1944, the personal magnetism of Franklin and Eleanor Roosevelt overshadowed a Democratic Party platform that was much weaker in the area of race advancement than the Republicans'.[59] The Republicans made clear their commitment to black citizenship by supporting a permanent FEP as well as a federal anti-lynching bill[60] while the Democratic convention produced a mild plank on race advancement to mollify the disparate elements within its ranks.[61] The reality of the war years was manifested in segregation in the armed services and by racial violence at home. Yet the confidence of blacks rested on the possibility of what could be achieved by a Roosevelt-led America, based on their New Deal experiences, as well as on their growing anticipation of their ability to promote change in American society.

Locally, the branch's fragile nonpartisanship had been threatened earlier in 1942. With so many Republicans within the ranks of the membership, the branch's leadership walked a political tightrope. Words of praise attributed to Walter White and Thurgood Marshall were used by Democratic Illinois Congressman Robert McKeough's campaign staff to enhance his standing among black voters in the Illinois U.S. Senate race. McKeough's campaign featured a full-page *Defender* layout [62] which angered Republican branch members so much that they sent a telegram to the national office: "Scores of your intimate friends and supporters . . . are throwing away their NAACP buttons in utter disgustful protest against the NAACP endorsement of McKeough for senator against C. Wayland Brooks who has championed the cause of our people on every occasion . . . . The endorsement will cause you . . . to lose the most valuable support of hundreds of loyal members of the organization in Chicago and the state of Illinois."[63]

Shortly thereafter, Daisy E. Lampkin repeated Pickens's 1936 mistake of misconstruing Chicago political behavior. She told Walter White to ignore the protest and added: "Do not let it disturb you. I would personally give the telegram [credence] if it were not so terribly exaggerated,"[64] leaving Oscar C. Brown with a major problem to resolve. Brown advised White that it was necessary to publicly disavow NAACP support for candidates along partisan lines.[65] The election results in November illustrated the formidability of Republican strength in Bronzeville as Brooks beat McKeough in both the Second and Third Wards.

A bright spot now shone from the Congress. U.S. Rep. William L. Dawson, who replaced Arthur W. Mitchell in 1943 after he forced the latter's retirement, offered a refreshing contrast to his predecessor's gradualism and rancor. Dawson remained in office until his death in 1970 and began his tenure by speaking in behalf of all of the nation's 13 million black citizens as De Priest had done in 1929. (Harlem's Adam Clayton Powell did not arrive in Congress until 1945.) Although Dawson's political career was built partially on the ruins of race egalitarian Earl B. Dickerson's, he began his national career in a positive manner. His victory statement in November 1942 was militant as he exhorted his fellow blacks to "stand together united as one in striving to attain final integration into American life" or suffer the continued indignities of the racial status quo.[66] Nevertheless, Dawson was emerging from his "race first, party second" mold and moving toward a position that was just the reverse.[67]

The branch began its revitalization following the financial and charter debacle of 1939 without severe opposition from the Left. By the early 1940s, the threat of the Communists subsided as the party changed its tactics from opposition to cooperation with mainstream civil rights groups. The Communists now supported new "front" groups organized to help fight against fascism in Europe. With the temporary end to this threat, the branch had outlived both the NNC and its Chicago chapter.

As the Depression decade neared its end, the city's black South Side had been changed forever, and with it, the Chicago NAACP. The insularity of black life with the possibility of success in a biracial world proved to be an idea whose time had come. Once Bronzeville accepted the challenge of change, the branch conducted its activities in a milieu that was more conducive than ever before to its message, extolling the virtues of racial equality. Despite the threat of the war to the nation's security and the loss of many loved ones during the course of the fighting in the Pacific and European theaters, African Americans could happily point at its conclusion to a war economy that had produced economic opportunities in the form of new jobs and with them, a new sense of power associated with increased earnings, purchasing capabilities, and, importantly, assertive action. Moreover, blacks gained recognition as a major voting bloc. In addition, a new creed, endorsing racial equality, was creeping across the land. The branch's image, membership, and status improved considerably while led by a one-term president, a supposed "weak sister," and a "live wire." A more inclusive America as well as a democratic branch made these good and expectant times.

Democracy at Work, 1946–1953

*Many of the complaints we receive appear minor
in light of the bigger problems, but to the
individual involved his problem is always
important. For this reason, we have a policy in
the office that no problem is too small for us to
listen to. Sometimes it is not a case for [the]
NAACP. In such cases we make the proper
referral, always giving an assurance of our
interest in their troubles.*

—*Henry W. McGee, 1947*

*No one else [the Communists] will under any
circumstances be permitted to interfere in the
management of the Association's affairs.*

—*Walter White, 1948*

*The timely intervention of the NAACP [in
Cicero] has won a new prestige for our local
branch by bringing its prompt action sharply
to the attention of an aroused public.*

—*Walter White, 1951*

DURING THE POSTWAR PERIOD, the Chicago NAACP shared the nation's trauma
as it prepared to meet new challenges from within and without. The presidency of Oscar C. Brown extended until June 1946 when he resigned
abruptly in a manner similar to Roberts in September 1925 and to MacNeal
in October 1937.[1] Brown felt the pressures of running a professional-level
volunteer organization lacking both adequate levels of support from

Bronzeville's citizenry and effective administrative support from his Executive Committee and the national office. As for the latter, the national office served as much as a hindrance to local initiative as anything else.[2]

Oscar Brown resigned as president when ideas became more plentiful than workers to implement them. As he explained to Walter White, "the board . . . had tremendous legislative capacity, but very little time 'to do the leg work' that the Chicago Program required."[3] In comparison, the differences in organizational structure and programmatic expectations between the branch and the local affiliate of the Urban League illuminated a great deal of what ailed the branch. The Chicago Urban League employed a professional staff which could initiate action without having to consult its board. In addition, its program of job placement and urban adjustment was also moderate enough until 1947 to be achieved without disturbing the racial status quo within the city.

Despite an increase in membership and financial support during Brown's four and one-half years in office, certain underlying problems endemic to administering to the needs of a racially proscribed group persisted. Within the splintered Executive Committee, there were members who expected too little of American society and, therefore, moved cautiously; individuals who acted out of self-interest, in variance with what was expected of volunteers committed to the equal rights movement; and activists who expected too much, too soon (or so it appeared to the "conservative" middle-class leadership). The younger, activist-oriented, more militant members of the branch experienced a heightened sense of racial mission, so they constantly put pressure on Brown, who was hardly a conservative. Significantly, in their estimation, he was not the consummate democratic activist he thought himself to be. Over all, the various factions applied enervating pressures on Brown, which prevented the branch from acquiring the administrative vitality it needed.[4]

Throughout it all, Brown's maturity, personal aplomb, and pragmatism served him well until he tired of what he perceived to be collective, inordinate expectations accompanied by petty bickering. Moreover, Brown was troubled by the entrenched indifference harbored by large segments of black Chicago's population which still did not support the equal rights movement fervently enough. Along with the rampant discrimination throughout the city, the president encountered mounting new problems to solve. One important one was the demand for money to fight restrictive covenants which drained the branch's fund-raising capabilities.[5]

Brown's successor was his able and energetic vice-president, Henry W. McGee, who by his own accounts strongly admired Brown.[6] McGee's appreciation for Brown's methods and commitment to democratic rule meant that there would be a semblance of continuity in governance. The tone and image of branch operations would shift, nonetheless, even more toward a mass orientation.

McGee was a postal clerk who had risen to become a national postal employees' leader and organizer. A working-class migrant from Texas, having arrived in Chicago at age seventeen in 1927, he faced hurdles at age thirty-six that were formidable, to say the least. These included, most challengingly, an inheritance from Brown of major financial and administrative headaches. Two other factors seemed important at the moment. He was the youngest man ever to assume the presidency, and he was relatively unknown within NAACP circles.

Yet, McGee's seasoning as the president of the National Alliance of Postal Employees (NAPE) had prepared him to cope with many of the new problems awaiting him. This administrative training also formed the basis of his *modus operandi*. NAPE chapters were whipped into line by McGee, who seriously believed in the organization's motto, "*Ad Mortis Fidelis.*" As a militant, egalitarian employees' organization within the U.S. postal service, NAPE vigorously pursued economic justice for blacks throughout the postal ranks. Its goal during the 1940s was advancement for men who were systematically excluded from moving into managerial ranks.[7]

Moreover, in the year preceding his ascendancy to the branch's presidency, McGee had remained in constant communication with the Association's New York office on matters concerning NAPE's efforts to establish a permanent Illinois FEPC.[8] His Chicago branch of NAPE "was nationally acclaimed for its militant effort to eliminate racial discrimination,"[9] so his elevation to the helm of an organization with a similar agenda boded well.

McGee's ascension to the presidency proved essential to the evolution of the Chicago NAACP for three reasons. First, it marked an end to a tradition of occupational snobbery, the most notable incident of which saw long-time branch stalwart Archie L. Weaver excluded from consideration as a presidential candidate in 1933. When McGee was elected, Archie L. Weaver was reported to have exclaimed, "I never dreamt that I would see the day when a postal employee would become president of the branch!"[10] Second, McGee's installation permanently established the Chicago NAACP as a democratically constituted movement. In the wake of his holding office, ministers, women, unionists, "shadies," economic radicals, both Communist and Socialist, and others could aspire to, and, within a decade, did hold this office. Opposition to McGee, based on his postal affiliation, did surface, but it was insignificant and did not, in any way, deter either him or his supporters from performing their duties. Third, McGee became the branch's first president from the ranks of labor. It was his background in labor protest that shaped his militant support of FEP and open housing, two areas of concern to black Chicago's working class.

By the end of 1947, the vigor that McGee brought to office served him well as he successfully eliminated the previous year's budget deficit.[11]

Then, with the branch's new democratic thrust, he opened the doors of membership to organized labor on an extensive basis, writing proudly to Thurgood Marshall that "we have a very strong labor committee now."[12] He also continued Brown's practice of welcoming whites, both Jews and gentiles, into the membership ranks.[13] However, very few of the city's whites took up the branch's offer because of their dispersion among other white-led liberal groups, such as CORE, the Council against Religious and Racial Discrimination (CAD), and the plethora of Protestant, Catholic, and Jewish social justice organizations. Consequently, the Chicago NAACP remained basically a black egalitarian organization while some of the other liberal groups and the Chicago Urban League sustained mixed racial memberships.

Paralleling McGee's rise to the presidency of the Chicago NAACP was Cleveland's Sidney A. Williams's selection as executive secretary of the Chicago Urban League in January of 1947. He shaped a militant agenda for housing and employment reform, replacing an approach that was so cautious in the employment sector that the League refused to take a stand before the 1950s in favor of FEP because of its pro-business ties. Williams's positions were far in advance of those of his organization but very much in accord with the aspirations of the citizens of Bronzeville.[14] It was not uncommon for Williams to personally speak out in favor of FEP and open housing despite opposition from his own board of directors.[15] He wrote Oscar C. Brown in March 1947 to solicit support for his idea of fighting housing bias by persuading blacks to remain in the heart of American cities instead of moving to peripheral neighborhoods.[16]

Meanwhile, the Chicago NAACP's pressing need for an executive secretary (a position left almost perennially vacant) forced McGee to combine the responsibilities of that position along with those of the presidency. At the conclusion of his term in December 1947, McGee left the presidency to return to full-time employment in the U.S. Post Office. He remained active on the Executive Committee well into the 1950s, leaving as an important part of his legacy a presidential report on the branch's structure, finances, and program that stands as a model of organizational planning and analysis.[17] The end of the Brown-McGee years now exposed the branch to two of its most perilous challenges—the renewed incursion of the Communist Party from without and the debilitating, internecine power plays stimulated by a rising socioeconomic status among African Americans from within. These were disruptions that the branch scarcely withstood. Interruptions in programming and membership fluctuations resulted.

In a city now populated by nearly 400,000 African Americans in need of dynamic leadership in order to advance their civil rights, attorney Genoa Washington, former chairman of the Legal Redress Committee, succeeded McGee. Unfortunately, he served only one term in office, fulfilling his duties intermittently between January and December 1948. To the detriment of both his reputation and the branch's operations, Washington had taken on major responsibilities in the presidential campaign of Republican governor Thomas E. Dewey of New York. His overriding political responsibilities led him to forsake his branch duties well in advance of the expiration of his term.

Even before Washington's demanding campaign commitments in the summer and fall months, indecisiveness and a lack of resourcefulness marked his attempts at leadership.[18] This crisis in leadership unfortunately occurred at a time of internecine struggle for control over the Chicago NAACP. Early charges from one branch member referred to a devious clique within the organization which apparently sought to perpetuate its own interests at the expense of the equal rights movement.[19] Whether this group was Communist, Democratic, militantly pro-labor, or even the partisan Republican following of Washington, it was one of several which sought to fill the leadership vacuum caused by the president's inattentiveness to his duties.

Significantly, for the first time in its history, the Chicago NAACP lacked leadership altogether. Neither the Executive Committee nor the general membership held meetings regularly. In retrospect, branch founder Dr. Edwin C. Bentley's exclusionary policy (which three decades previously sought "like-mindedness") had been superseded by some of the worse features of an open, broad-based, diversified organization. With Washington's absence for months at a time because of his political campaigning and without an executive secretary to attend to necessary administrative duties, the branch lacked the leadership to supervise the part-time office staff, meet branch expenses, and keep the membership and public informed of its activities. The national office experienced *déjà vu* in dealing with Chicago as the enervation of national presidential politics replicated the membership debacle of 1939 with its subsequent organizational disarray. For the second time in less than a decade, it considered closing the branch.[20] The defeat of Washington's candidate, Governor Dewey, provided the final irony because it allowed the beneficial Truman civil rights revolution to continue unabated. This dynamic president's federal assault on racism ushered in a national acceptance of equal rights which, in turn, further legitimized the branch's struggle over the previous three and one-half decades.

As the disastrous year 1948 drew to its end, fifteen members of the Executive Committee felt compelled to act decisively to save the organization. They authorized the fourth vice-president, Mrs. Mary Ann Parker, to call a meeting facilitating the formation of a 1949 nominating committee. Levi Morris, first vice-president and a Washington supporter, tried initially to stop the meeting. Next, he attempted to circumvent the power of the nominating committee by arranging for nominations from the floor. Possibly Washington and Morris feared some type of takeover from untoward elements, probably from the Left, and thought that an open meeting posed fewer dangers for their rule and the branch's future.[21] Or, they simply might have wanted to retain power. The group, represented by Parker, was aware of suspicions about their intentions, so they acted cautiously as they proceeded publicly,[22] going to the extreme of publicizing actions of an internal organizational nature in local newspapers.[23]

The threat of expanding Soviet-based Communism fed a postwar hysteria that also influenced the branch's internal operations. Parker's group reacted with a test for patriotism that required a candidate's statement of loyalty both to the United States of America and to the NAACP. The national office responded swiftly and condemnatorily, labeling the branch's action as illegal in light of the spirit of both the United States and NAACP constitutions.[24]

For its part, the Communist Party continued its activities, attempting to wrestle control of the branch, using its traditional "boring in" tactics. *Counterattack*, a fervidly anti-Communist, national publication, edited by former FBI agents, warned the NAACP that it was a prime target of the Communists and that party members had been advised "to behave discreetly . . . to refrain from pushing the party line conspicuously . . . and thus quiet the suspicions of Walter White."[25] White, for his part, was alert and active in warning the branches of the danger: "What has taken 39 years to build can be destroyed in a far shorter time if any political party should succeed in capturing control of any NAACP branch. No one else will under any circumstances be permitted to interfere in the management of the Association's affairs."[26]

In Chicago, the branch established a good track record in meeting the Communist challenge for the second time in two decades. In one notable instance shortly after the war, the Chicago NAACP outmaneuvered the Communists by organizing veterans under its own auspices. The branch openly challenged United Negro and Allied Veterans of America (UNAVA), which was organized in April 1946, and hastened its demise.[27]

Beyond the threat of Communist infiltration, the branch tried to salvage what was left of the organization following Genoa Washington's abandonment of his office. On December 30, 1948, the rump leadership of the Executive Committee called a special meeting and declared the office of president vacant. Clarence Dawson, a close associate of Oscar C. Brown, Sr., both within the branch and in the erstwhile Forty-ninth State Movement, was chosen chairman of the Executive Committee to run the branch until a president could be elected in January.[28]

Not unexpectedly, the irregularity of the succession process that saw one president removed but not immediately replaced also had serious effects on the branch's internal operations. Affected adversely were fundraising, membership recruitment, staff payrolls, and organizational image. The debacle of 1948 with the presidency signaled a new organizational reality: an able executive secretary, who acted as a day-to-day manager, potentially could run the branch on a regular basis with efficiency in virtual disregard of internal and external diversions. Additionally, the liberal political climate, which had done so much to promote racial egalitarianism, now fostered a backlash of conservatism with regard to the type of change that the branch espoused. This made attracting viable leaders difficult. The added liability of Communist meddling in the branch's affairs made the branch look especially militant to the city's respectable, and very conservative, white civic leadership.

Sometime during early 1949, the Chicago NAACP elected its first president from the ranks of the clergy. Methodist minister S. Marion Riley, Jr., was apparently a compromise candidate elected as a caretaker awaiting the installation of a permanent leader of higher professional status. Yet the Rev. Riley saw himself as having the requisite skills to lead the branch forward to its organizational salvation. He was recognized by those who supported him as a man possessing high integrity, committed to the cause of racial equality, independent of the more mundane ambitions prevalent in Bronzeville, and competent administratively. Perhaps most important in a society in flux, Riley proved to be a good leader during his first and only term in office. But his not being an "insider" who was acceptable to the "movers and shakers" of Bronzeville rendered his days in office short.

Luckily for the branch, Riley's assumption of the presidency in 1949 brought a needed restoration of normality to its operations. The Executive Committee that served under Riley included some of the same stalwarts that had steered the branch through the tumult of 1948–1949. Henry W. McGee remained an active member, as did the last full-time executive secretary, Eugene O. Shands, who was now first vice-president. Beatrice Hughes Steele served as second vice-president while Mary Ann Parker and Cora M. Patton served as members of the Executive Committee. The situation appeared calm up to the time of the annual election of officers.

The preparations for the election of the winter of 1949–1950, during which Riley was to be reslated, proved to be especially fraught with frustrations. They were aptly described in correspondence with the national office as being "a mess."[29] There was first the recurring fear that the Communists might take over the branch.[30] Then, Riley became suspicious that certain members of the Nominating Committee might exploit the hysteria over Communism to remove him from an office that carried more and more prestige in the black community.

The branch's constitution mandated that a duly selected Nominating Committee take the responsibility of returning a slate of officers to the fully assembled branch for consideration either at its annual meeting in December, or, if delayed, at its January meeting. Furthermore, the Nominating Committee was now empowered to screen candidates and publicly release the names to the newspapers in an effort to eliminate Communists. It became obvious that the place at which to influence any election was from this body since most branch members who participated in voting considered the committee's slate as having the stamp of officialdom. Once apprised in late November of the names of the nine persons elected by the membership to sit on the Nominating Committee, Riley quickly rejected them. Among this group were past president Henry W. McGee; labor leaders representing building tradesmen, electrical workers, typographers, and transportation service workers; a minister; and a schoolteacher.

Seeking normality and a return to the halcyon days when Oscar C. Brown, Sr. was president and before, the Executive Committee searched for its own Eisenhower two years before the nation chose to enter a period of calm under the general's leadership. The criteria set forth called for a leader with a firm commitment to egalitarianism, a familiarity with the Association's and branch's operations, acceptability to the branch's leadership as a fellow insider, a personality that was amicable and low-key, and an absence of personal ambitions which might threaten the branch's integrity or overshadow its agenda. Digging deep into the pool of stalwarts who had served in the past and would be willing to serve despite the increased internecine squabbling that accompanied democratization, the committee chose attorney Nelson Willis.

Willis had worked actively on the Legal Redress Committee under Earl B. Dickerson's leadership during the 1930s and had assisted in the notorious De Vol case. He was still closely associated with Dickerson, who at this time was at the peak of his influence within Bronzeville's civic circles. Dickerson's credentials and civic service included being a victorious U.S. Supreme Court litigant, former alderman, prospective congressman, former FEPC commissioner, past head of the Cook County Bar Association, and second-term president of the Chicago Urban League (after having been called to the fore again in a time of organizational crisis).[31] Dickerson was in his tenth year of service on the NAACP's national board of directors and accordingly cast a giant shadow across Bronzeville's civic life.

The coterie of "like-minded men" to which Dickerson, besides Willis, belonged, included Robert Ming, Jr., from the University of Chicago Law School's faculty, Loring B. Moore, Harvard Law–trained George N. Leighton, and members of the influential Cook County Bar Association. In the tradition of first-generation branch leader Dr. Charles E. Bentley, Dickerson influenced the branch's direction by assisting in its choice of leaders. His choices usually were men of the modern Niagara Movement stripe, committed to their group's uplift along the rigorous standards associated with a first-class existence. As neo-patricians they were also representative of and considered themselves the best and the brightest in the nation's, not just black America's, pool of leaders.

The new president, Nelson Willis, was elected and inaugurated as scheduled in January 1950, and the branch entered the fifth decade of its existence resolved to overcome its most recent period of disruption. In his own right, Willis was successful in the legal and mortgage fields by making contacts with the rising black legal elite of the nation. In 1950, he recommended Judge William H. Hastie, who was nominated by President Truman in October 1949 to be the nation's first black federal judge, to the U.S. Senate's Judiciary Committee.[32] Once Willis was in office, NAACP Director of Branches Gloster B. Current in New York informed him that he was expected "to place the Branch on an even keel and start it toward its former place as one of the largest Branches of the Association."[33] Almost immediately, local conditions impeded Willis's ability to comply. Outgoing president Riley challenged the results of the December 1949 election, charging that Willis's control over the Nominating Committee tarnished the election and brought the latter into office under questionable circumstances.[34]

Dissatisfied with an election process that denied him the presidency, Riley contacted the national office to seek its intervention. Association officers in New York responded immediately and appointed a special investigating committee to decide the legitimacy of Riley's concerns. The national office's logical choices to conduct this investigation were the two distinguished Chicago attorneys who also sat on the national board of directors, Earl B. Dickerson and Robert Ming, Jr. Riley, on the other hand, perceived this move to be a conspiracy. Buttressing his suspicions were Roy Wilkins's refusal to answer his letters and Gloster Current's ignoring his pleas for information and cooperation.[35] The process that produced Willis's election was ruled fair and binding, and Riley faded from the roster of the branch's leadership.

Willis concluded his first term in office without any further challenges and successfully won a second term. His tenure as branch leader, though, was short-lived, as untoward business circumstances forced him to reduce the amount of time he spent on his administrative duties. By late summer, it was obvious that his tenure in office was being affected adversely; so, given an opportunity to serve in the presidency for a third consecutive term, he declined. In his place he sponsored a young, assertive attorney who was a relative newcomer to the city, George N. Leighton.

Leighton came to Chicago at the end of World War II at the suggestion of his mentor, Earl B. Dickerson. He was a second-generation American whose non-citizen, farm worker parents were natives of the Cape Verde Islands (located in the Atlantic Ocean off the west coast of Africa). He was born George Leitao in 1912 in New Bedford, Massachusetts, and reared in New Bedford and on Cape Cod. Successful as a 1946 Harvard Law School graduate, he had never completed elementary school, having been drawn into a world of migrant fruit work with his parents and later to sea on an oil tanker. It was self-motivation, along with an appetite for reading and a thirst for knowledge, that led him to Howard University in 1936 and finally to Harvard in 1940.[36] Upon graduation from Harvard, he was ranked by his dean as "one of the most conscientious and brilliant students of the institution."[37]

By the time Leighton's name was mentioned a decade later as a possible leader of the Chicago NAACP movement, he had established himself in legal and civil rights circles by handling the difficult defense of the victims of race rioting in Cicero in 1951. Yet, the election of Leighton as Willis's successor was not accomplished without obstacles. A spirited campaign and election took place between Leighton and a young, aspiring black businesswoman, Naomi Hughes Roland. Roland had headed the Membership Committee in 1949 but did not hold a seat on the Executive Committee, and consequently lacked a base of support with substantial power to influence branch elections. She encountered increasing difficulties in her quest and became convinced that the hierarchy was an exclusive body, cliquish and unresponsive to the needs of the black community in general. In writing to New York in search of a sympathetic ear, she accused Willis of conspiring against her and concluded that "there is a relatively slim chance for a fair election."[38]

As to the election contest itself, it represented another milestone in branch history, garnering significance for its contribution in helping to open the branch to an even wider spectrum of socioeconomic groups now visible and emerging within the transforming black community. Roland represented the rising group of black business people that appeared in the aftermath of World War II. Capital, accumulated but not spent, stood ready for use in a variety of entrepreneurial endeavors. It produced a new class of aspiring community leaders that replicated the cycle after World War I when the "New Negroes" appeared. Mass production and mass consumption, the energetic twins of American material progress, propelled the nation into its headlong flight to prosperity. This decade brought a consensus of opinion that contentment and placidity characterized the lives of working- and middle-class white Americans who enjoyed suburbia, increased purchasing power, and satisfaction with an unalterable promise of linear progress. To black Americans, however, expanding opportunities within the economic sector collided with their unmet expectations of advancing their civil rights.

Among black Americans, a rising socioeconomic status even in an imperfect America meant new ideas, attitudes, goals, and a changing and discernible class structure. E. Franklin Frazier described the decade as one in which "the prosperity which the U.S. enjoyed as a result of World War II and the war economy during the Cold War has trickled down to the Negroes, especially since the barriers to the employment of Negroes have been lowered." He continued with some specificity that "Negroes were beginning to secure employment on an unprecedented scale in the marketing branches of white businesses. White firms have found it extremely profitable to employ Negroes in advertising positions for Negro consumers."[39]

In postwar Chicago in the late fall of 1948, erstwhile Chicago Urban League researcher Frayser T. Lane pictured a bright new economic milieu for blacks, filled with the possibilities of their living the American Dream and extending even beyond Bronzeville into its northern, southern, and western appendages. Wartime migration, bringing thousands of able-bodied, energetic workers into the city—perhaps 100,000 for the decade—fed the ample job opportunities and understandably produced an appetite for more living space. Instead of envisioning an expanding "ghetto," Lane spoke of an ever-enlarging residential area composed of old and new housing stock and populated with homeowners who appreciated property values. The Washington Park subdivision of Woodlawn became both increasingly African American and physically improved. The same occurred along the city's beautiful, tree-lined boulevard system. Employment gains during the war were not only being maintained but enlarged upon afterward with "rapid infiltration into new fields of commerce and industry (including transportation operations and personnel jobs)."[40]

By the 1970s, sociologist William Julius Wilson presented a more analytical description of the 1950s, pinpointing statistically the extent to which occupational mobility had grown. He began by noting an increased participation in labor unions, which accounted for a rise in semi-skilled and skilled positions from 17.2 percent in 1940 to 29.1 percent in 1950. Wilson then proceeded to identify other factors that contributed to the growth of a solid, industrially based black working class along with a service sector middle class. The number of black males over fourteen years of age in working- and middle-class jobs also grew from 22.3 percent in 1940 to 37.6 percent by 1950. Pivotally he pointed out that "the most dramatic changes in black mobility, however, occurred during the decades of the 1950s and the 1960s. Whereas 16.4 percent of black males were employed in middle class occupations in 1950, 24 percent held such jobs in 1960 and 35.3 percent in 1970."[41] The picture of occupational status was positive, with the number of black males holding "lower class jobs" showing a decline from 62.1 percent in 1950 to 50.7 percent in 1960 to 36.4 percent by 1970.

In Chicago, salaries and wages from professional, skilled, and semi-skilled work appeared to explain both the burst of enthusiasm on the part of blacks for the chance to enjoy more of mainstream American life and the dissatisfaction with discrimination and prejudice. As plentiful as opportunities appeared in a relative sense given past limitations, in absolute terms racial injustice in the workplace still loomed ominously. The Industrial Department of the Chicago Urban League, reporting early in the decade, gave the following self-congratulatory account of conditions: "The general employment situation in 1950, happenings in the Chicago area, as well as the national and world atmosphere, were all of a nature to be conducive to the success of a 'gentle' approach such as the Urban League's. The employment level was again attaining an all time peak and qualified Negroes were being welcomed into many previously all-white firms because few competent white workers were available. In 1950, the small staff of the Chicago Urban League succeeded in placing Negro employees with 108 firms which had never hired Negroes before, and in 1951 the number was nearer to 188."[42] In 1951, the League announced further that a certain Loop store was "in the process of integrating Negro workers as an administrative assistant, [a] comptometer operator [as well as] furniture handlers."[43] Yet, this rosy picture was misleading since entry level managerial positions were difficult, if not almost impossible, to obtain and even clerical jobs in downtown banks were denied qualified black applicants.[44]

Leighton's first term in office was marked with relative calm and stability within the organization. Outside, the Chicago NAACP's programmatic activities continued against a backdrop of Jim Crow practices throughout Chicago. Tension within soon matched the frenzy outside once the branch was financially able to select and compensate a full-time executive secretary. The person selected, Benjamin Bell, Jr., initially appeared to be the proper choice. From the standpoint of his commitment to egalitarianism, Bell was eminently qualified. He surveyed the landscape of the nation and the status of race relations and declared, "Racism is democracy's bitterest enemy."[45] But temperamentally, Bell was unsuited for the administrative duties he assumed. As the first executive secretary following the departure of Eugene O. Shands, Bell was expected to bring order to the branch headquarters (now located on Bronzeville's main east-west axis, East Sixty-Third Street) and to display loyalty to the administration that brought him into its ranks. Instead, he brought disorder through self-generated dissension.

The intensity of Bell's volatile nature was revealed when he once physically attacked Leighton at a meeting. Another sign of impending trouble surfaced within three months of his being hired in July 1952. Bell sent a telegram to the national office complaining of the supposed machinations of an alleged Willis-Leighton faction.[46] His disloyalty also revealed itself quickly as he aligned himself with labor leader Willoughby Abner, who had been envisioning an assumption of power from the time he joined the branch in the middle of the previous decade. Abner had planned a coup to coincide with the year-end elections scheduled for December 1952 or the following January.

Bell's meddling and his repeated failures to perform his administrative duties finally led to the termination of his services. Undaunted and infuriated, Bell left the branch as ordered but resurfaced in time for the branch's pre-election campaigning. As fate would have it, the volatile Bell missed his showdown with the branch's leadership. Weeks before the election he accidentally shot himself in the groin while cleaning his revolver.[47]

Within the branch itself a tense but nonviolent anticipation of the election grew. On the evening of January 9, 1953, the forces of President George N. Leighton had their head-on confrontation with the militant labor faction of Willoughby Abner. In a major shift of influence, Abner's allies dominated the all-important Nominating Committee and reported a slate of officers that excluded Leighton and promoted long-time branch supporter Cora Patton as president. Leighton countered with his own slate presented from the floor. Perhaps the most decisive factor at the meeting was the presence of Earl B. Dickerson in the chair. He delayed the proceedings long enough to allow Leighton time to have his slate printed and distributed among the assemblage. White Executive Committee member Faith Rich protested to Walter White later, accusing Dickerson of either chicanery or incompetence.[48]

The *Chicago Defender* described the contest as one which lasted for more than four grueling hours: "Seldom during the meeting were voices subdued or parliamentary procedures followed . . . both groups yelled charges of fraud, labeled the other as 'Red-dominated,' and grew brusque with each passing second."[49] When the balloting ended, Leighton had won by a scant thirty votes. The triumph, however, disturbed the incumbent because of the pyrrhic nature of his victory. His entire slate, including attorney Jewel Stradford Rogers, the branch secretary, had been defeated. Not only was Leighton isolated among the new officers of the Executive Committee, but his power had been significantly diminished by Abner's having been elected chairman of this group. This new office of chairman undermined the president's authority throughout 1953 and led Leighton to refer to the arrangement as the "two heads."[50]

After six months of leading the branch with this division of authority, Leighton admitted to Gloster Current that "the 'labor boys' are giving me a hard time."[51] Their field general was Willoughby Abner and this blockage accomplished exactly what Abner's faction desired. The "labor boys" belonged to the militant United Packing House Workers Union–CIO. Despite their militant label, which applied more to their passion in the cause of civil rights and selected tactics than to any other features, their motives paled when compared to those of the Communist faction within the branch. The latter's intentions, tactics, and strategy aimed at either destroying or subverting the branch. The members of the labor faction, however, were the purveyors of a level of dissension that tore at the fabric of the branch and added to its decline in both spirit and organizational image.[52] Rumors abounded. One circulated that the Abner faction wanted to sabotage the fall membership drive to keep the membership rolls low for future use as a campaign issue.[53]

The appearance of Oscar C. Brown, Jr., late in 1953, when the campaign for the election of new officers for 1954 began, introduced a new complication for an organization badly in need of balm instead of agitation. Brown, Jr., joined the Executive Committee in 1950 carrying the banner of the Communist Party. He envisioned converting the branch into a tool of the Party and making it responsive to the immediate socioeconomic needs of Bronzeville's masses. However, he and his cohorts were thwarted and their activities subsequently abandoned. In defeat, the Party realized that a united liberal and labor front could easily neutralize any Communist attempt to control the branch. Since the Communists irritated certain liberal Catholic and Jewish groups, such as the Catholic Interracial Council and the Anti-Defamation League, who regularly cooperated with the branch in its protests against racism, the list of their enemies grew.[54] It was left to the members of the Socialist Workers Party, who were more moderate in their approach to change, to carry forth the doctrine of class struggle, and they fared little better.

The impending election resembled a battle royal as dissension from within the ranks of the non-labor, non-Communist stalwarts also materialized. Henry W. McGee and A. Miles Cartman managed to enrage the always irascible Henry William Huff by, according to Huff, casting aspersions on the integrity of the branch's attorneys.[55]

The presidency as the locus of power and status was now rivaled by the Executive Committee as the locus of democracy. The most prominent names of the Black Belt were no longer in banking and financial enterprises but were found in politics, law, medicine, labor, and religion as well as in public education. The blossoming of a new class structure in Bronzeville was never more apparent. This socioeconomic differentiation among groups of blacks primarily reflected wartime gains, buttressed by the opportunities of the 1920s "New Negro" era. The new members of the committee also mirrored these changes. The number of women increased. Whites appeared on the roster of the Executive Committee as active members for the first time in two decades, although not in significant numbers. Protestants, Catholics, and Jews joined the Executive Committee between 1942 and 1948, although never in appreciable numbers to match their numbers during the Progressive Era. In 1947, Rabbi Jacob Weinstein and labor leader Meyer J. Myer joined the branch's hierarchy to become the first Jewish members since Julius Rosenwald and Rabbi Arnold Hirsch belonged a generation previously. In 1945, Joseph Genne joined the board and brought along his extensive talents in fund-raising. Correspondence and inquiries to the branch from whites, who were, to say the least, enthusiastic about joining the egalitarian crusade, proved to be accurate indicators of the changing and salutary temper of the times regarding race.[56]

By 1949, the limited support of organized labor in days past grew into massive labor representation. For the first time, the Packinghouse Workers Union, Steelworkers, Retail Clerks, United Transportation Service Workers, Building Service Tradesmen, and others became part of the NAACP team. The influential Chicago Industrial Union Committee–CIO urged all local CIO unions to join this crusade. In one statement a representative of the trade union movement declared that "the CIO joins with [the] NAACP in . . . battles to secure justice and equality for the poor and oppressed, to obtain equal opportunity for the 15 million colored people in the United States and for an end to the vicious discrimination against Negroes."[57] Part of the credit for the work done among unionists had to go to the national office which sent assistant field director Herbert Hill, a white man with entrée to the unions, to drum up the support needed.

The move toward organizational democracy revealed certain limitations and flaws as well. A racial and gender imbalance still marked the branch's hierarchy, with black males dominating both its proceedings and committees. Women reached their highest percentage of representation in 1950, when they held fifteen of thirty-seven seats. After that numerical peak, the numbers slipped but were always respectable. Beyond the presidency and the chair of the Executive Committee, the next most important office in the branch was that of executive secretary, always envisioned as the major administrative position in branch operations. In many other branches in large cities, the executive secretary virtually ran the branch.[58] In Chicago, ultimate power and prestige still lay with the presidency but with a growing potential for the accouterments once reserved for the presidency accruing to other offices.

Since the executive secretary handled the branch's day-to-day operations and reported to the part-time Executive Committee on the state of the branch, the position carried immense status and influence. With black occupational opportunities limited by racial proscription to public education, social work, and federal governmental service (if they eschewed two of the major products of segregation—machine politics and Bronzeville businesses), applicants eagerly sought the office which paid an annual salary of $4,000 in 1952 and $7,500 in 1959. The major impediment to filling the position was the branch's finances, since salary and benefits were linked to local conditions affecting fund-raising.

During 1951 and 1952 the branch tried to fill the vacancy and undertook an exhaustive search for a person with the requisite educational, administrative, and interpersonal skills. Several applicants were screened and rejected. One of them was Executive Committee member A. Miles Cartman, who, while popular among many members of the Executive Committee, ultimately disqualified himself because of earlier statements made at a convention in the 1940s that showed that he favored voluntary separation for black business advancement in the South. Public relations consultant Joseph F. Albright, who arrived in the city in 1952, had twenty-seven years of service in behalf of the NAACP and was ready to compete for the office. What he saw when he arrived in Chicago did not discourage him, and he felt that he could rectify it "with proper executive action."[59] But he did not get the position, for reasons not clearly explained in NAACP records. Instead, Benjamin Bell, Jr., of the West Side's East Garfield Park community, who had also accumulated an impressive résumé, was hired. However, his previously mentioned termination left the secretary's position open for several years.

The branch's committee structure continued to grow to keep pace with the needs of the burgeoning black population. Traditionally, the most active committee remained Legal Redress. It bore the brunt of the branch's program against the restrictive covenant, peonage, and extradition, along with assuming responsibility for instituting action against incidences of discrimination in restaurants, public accommodations, transportation, and the workplace. A Labor Committee was organized which represented two aspects of the changing nature of branch interests. One included a combined economic and civic focus. The other encompassed recognition of the upgraded status blacks enjoyed in the economy as a result of high-paying wartime and post-wartime work. Willoughby Abner of the UAW and James Kemp of the Building Service Employees International Union brought a commitment and leadership to the branch that would surface fully in the 1950s. A. Miles Cartman headed the newest committee formed in 1947 to bring administrative efficiency, that of Office Management and Personnel. It was from this body that the administrative shortcomings of Genoa Washington were first officially reported to the branch at large as the day-to-day operations of the branch ground to a halt.

At mid-century, the branch's membership comprised people of all classes, religions, and races. Churches were especially prominent in their solicitation of memberships. Large and small segments, on the South Side and West Side, of the black religious community gave their financial support, as well as their stamp of approval, to the NAACP and its mission. The black business community was more receptive than it had ever been. Many companies depended on an all-black market to solicit large numbers of members annually and sought to give back something to their clientele as well as to protect their own rights. John H. Johnson's publishing company was one; Earl B. Dickerson's Supreme Life Insurance was another. Insurance broker Walter L. Lowe took out life memberships for each member of his family of four as well as pledging his company's support. Realtor Dempsey J. Travis, a future branch president, supported the movement because he felt "Negro businesses, especially in the Real Estate field, are indebted to the NAACP for its victory in the 'Restrictive Covenant' case in '48 which has made it possible for Negro real estate men to sell property in these new areas where Negroes could not formerly buy." Impressed moreover by the branch's aggressive stance in the Cicero housing episode, the Travis Realty Company signed on to the Chicago NAACP effort with a life membership of $500.[60] And, of course, the ranks of organized labor were well represented, being measured by the hundreds early in the decade and by the thousands at its midpoint.

The goal of Brown and McGee of increasing the membership through a broad-based, vigorously pursued, militant program was met. Organizational size became a visible factor in the organization's popular appeal and success. McGee observed that "in volunteer organizations one of the big attractions is size . . . [and] people like to be connected with something big. Often the caliber of leadership is determined largely by the size of the organization."[61]

The mid-year resignation of Brown in 1946 temporarily disrupted the branch's momentum which was reflected in a drop in memberships to 14,743 at the end of the year. The campaign of 1947 produced approximately 15,000 memberships. The sporadic and precarious leadership of Washington in 1948 halted this growth pattern and the membership barely topped 10,000 that year. One branch leader observed that the membership campaign of 1948 was a relative failure because "the pulse of the community is that the local branch of the Association is doing nothing."[62]

The postwar period produced its disappointments as decreasing finances caused by both internal organizational problems and a national economic slump were coupled with skyrocketing expenditures necessary for the organization to meet its needs. The four major sources of fundraising were the annual, profitable Freedom Fund Dinner, held in the spring in the Loop; the spring tea; Tag Day; and the annual membership drive in the fall. The Freedom Dinner appeared to be the brainchild of Chicago branch leader Robert Ming, Jr.[63] Originating in 1953, in Chicago and in Detroit, it spread nationally as a major source of funding for the Association's coffers, producing large sums of money. The tea continued as the Women's Auxiliary's major benefit (along with Tag Day), the 1953 affair contributing one-quarter of what the branch took in for that entire year. Any financial drain occasionally forced the leadership to go into its own pockets to finance the branch's operations whenever funds were low. On one occasion, Archie L. Weaver, who returned to active service as treasurer for one year only in 1953, advanced $1,000 from his own limited resources to keep the branch operations continuous.[64]

Women continued to play an integral role in the financial status of the branch. Hundreds were recruited each year for work as taggers on street corners as well as for sponsors of tables at the annual tea held annually each spring beginning in 1941. The major group was the Women's Auxiliary which was analogously identified as the branch's unofficial Finance Committee by Archie L. Weaver. Weaver was always shrewd enough to realize that recognition of the contributions of women had to be publicized to keep their morale high, especially since they were denied important offices. This action was appropriate at a time when only they as a group dutifully supported the branch in its many hours of financial need. Weaver's effusiveness was demonstrated in the monthly treasurer's report he filed in October 1953: "Aside from our membership receipts, we depend on our Women's Auxiliary to keep the Branch in some sort of [healthy] financial condition. All praise and glory to these—our own fine WOMEN." His report also lent insight into the indispensable role of women in the African American community—whether in politics, civics, religion, social life, or the family—as he added: "They furnish the power behind the works."[65]

A. L. Foster, as Executive Secretary of the Chicago Urban League from 1925 to 1946, had worked closely with community-minded women and had grown to depend on their skills and diligence at fund-raising. It is no wonder that Foster performed successfully as the branch's campaign director for 1953. Weaver wrote: "We expect this because it is A. L. Foster. . . . The men are standing with him but his greatest assets are the women. Yes, again our N.A.A.C.P. would die without them."[66]

The precarious level of support from the black community continued to perplex Henry McGee but he formulated one explanation for the problem, relating it to competing interests. "Are they dissatisfied with the program of the NAACP? No! On the whole, they express satisfaction with the program. The problem . . . is a problem of primary and secondary interests. Each organization [church, block club, or social group] is interested first in its own program and generally spends most of its time achieving that purpose,"[67] he stated. Loyalty to the Chicago NAACP's efforts, not self-serving but community-serving, often came in second.

Faith Rich had a different view, however. Hers was a concern that the branch did not afford the membership the opportunity to participate in making civil rights a reality. With this assessment, Rich called for a citizen-level involvement that approximated CORE's. The Chicago chapter of CORE remained active and cooperated with the branch on numerous occasions, despite some major differences between the two. In 1947, its president invited both Chicago NAACP youth and adults to join CORE in its workshops on nonviolent, direct action. The next year, Chicago CORE led picketing against Goldblatt's department store in the Loop in protest against employment discrimination. The campaign nevertheless ended amid charges that the protest bore the taint of anti-Semitism.[68]

National office–branch relations remained at the same level after the war as they had been before, with the germs of cooperation as well as conflict always present. At the 1946 conference held in Cincinnati, one-half of the branches, with Chicago actively involved, voted to make changes in the constitution that would have enhanced the branches' ability to raise more funds for their local defense campaigns.[69] Additionally, the Chicago branch challenged the oligarchic nature of the Association, calling the structure "self-perpetuating."[70] When McGee took over the presidency, there were occasions when he and Roy Wilkins disagreed over minor points that they were nonetheless able to resolve to each other's satisfaction. McGee even traveled to New York to meet Wilkins to discuss some of these matters. The refreshing visit to New York, undertaken by many of the branch presidents, always ended in a greater appreciation by branch leaders of the value of a unified and smooth-running Association.[71] Further, the recurring problem of inexpeditious handling of membership cards produced the perennial tension that always elicited the branches' inquiries into when the new subscribers would become bona fide Association members.

Despite the seemingly inordinate amount of time spent on administrative matters, the Chicago NAACP pursued civil rights advocacy at a furious pace. The branch pressured for expanded employment opportunities, open housing in both the private and public sectors, and parity in public education. As the prime mover for racial change in Chicago, the Chicago branch of the NAACP eschewed the Chicago Urban League's "gentle approach," the Communist Party's revolutionary agenda, and CORE's direct action but legally defenseless program. Perhaps the real key to the branch's success in transforming itself in order to reach institutional status was its concern for the "little man's" problems. Henry W. McGee showed this concern in 1947 as he demonstrated awareness of the absolute necessity to treat every one of Bronzeville's citizens and his or her racial complaints with the respect due him or her.[72]

When the postwar governmental policy of the Office of Price Administration (OPA) compounded the discomfort and misery of blacks struggling against the psychological effects of segregated living, the branch responded in a timely and appropriate manner. The OPA raised the ceiling on rental units nationally in 1947 and opened the doors to exploitation by landlords regardless of hue. Black workers were forced to accept the skyrocketing rates or face eviction. At the same time, a joint congressional subcommittee scheduled hearings in Chicago in October 1947, and branch president Henry W. McGee spoke for the branch and black Chicago in telling the subcommittee that the highest rents in the city were found in Bronzeville. He explained that the racial containment of over 300,000 of the city's 400,000 black citizens in Bronzeville's restrictive confines produced a seller's market where any price was abnormally higher because of the inordinate demand for goods and services emanating from such a concentrated population. McGee demonstrated that unemployment had risen and that black families spent $68 a week in inflated prices while it took $32 per week to live on the normal price scale affecting whites. He concluded that a price rollback to the June 1946 level was the only way to insure a decent standard of living for working families.[73]

While McGee was doubling as president and executive secretary, he converted the branch into an efficient pressure group working cooperatively with the Chicago Urban League, organized labor, and other liberal groups seeking equal opportunity in employment.[74] Optimism was high, and recognition came as an NAACP FEPC Day was celebrated in April 1947.[75]

In contrast, with ineffective leadership during the Washington presidency, most Chicago NAACP protest advocacy came to a halt in a situation described as "program disintegration."[76] Fortunately, the momentum generated by the struggle for an Illinois FEPC was such that lobbying continued without the NAACP's involvement. Black politicians cooperated in behalf of FEP so in consecutive sessions of the General Assembly between 1948 and 1962, employment opportunities bills were introduced. Plans were made, nonetheless, for a mass rally in order to raise funds to lobby for FEP as the successors to Washington assumed power two days before the new year of 1949.[77]

In the housing arena, the end of the war failed to bring a change in residential freedom, and so tensions resumed. White tactics ranged from nefarious legal means to flagrant acts of violence. Reminiscent of the post–World War I period, returning black veterans became the first victims of Chicago's post–World War II violent housing crises. In December of 1946, the Chicago Housing Authority (CHA) attempted to integrate veterans in a housing development near the western suburb of Cicero, called Airport Homes. As a part of a deliberate plan, a designated number of units were left open for black veterans while the screening of applicants took place. White squatters moved in during the lull. Once the new black residents arrived, rioting ensued, and blacks were threatened and beaten. City government proved to be as derelict and powerless as always, so the situation continued to deteriorate. Henry W. McGee and members of the Chicago Council against Religious and Racial Discrimination (CAD) met with Mayor Edward Kelly and received his pledge to intervene through the Corporation Counsel's office. Speedy prosecution of rioters was promised and, most importantly, the branch's six-point program for relieving racial tensions was accepted. "For two weeks the Negro families courageously lived in the projects under guard. Then they succumbed to the pressure and moved away," one report chronicled.[78] In what was to become a familiar pattern involving white mob action during the postwar period, no blacks ever returned to the development.

In what was described by contemporaries as "racial terrorism," arson fires, stone throwing, and personal assaults replaced rioting on the West and South Sides. Black citizens resisted as best they could without the full protection of law enforcement officials.[79] The police showed their greatest effectiveness in keeping blacks out of white neighborhoods through official passivity in the face of lawbreaking. For its part, the branch investigated fifty-nine terrorist attacks against individual Negroes in so-called white areas in the twenty-four months preceding 1946.[80]

As a new year dawned, tensions built and violence erupted. Early during the spring of 1947, an anticipated ruling from the Illinois Supreme Court increased anxiety among black homeowners and renters in contested racial areas. Over 3,000 blacks worried about the court's validation of a restrictive covenant case that threatened their being evicted from predominantly white areas on the South Side.[81] Another peculiar aspect of the covenant campaign surfaced. In Chicago, there was continuous grumbling among some blacks that the covenant fight benefited the middle class more than it did the working class and the impoverished.

The branch tackled the restrictive covenant on a case-by-case basis until, by January 1947, Special Counsel Loring Moore was handling twenty-three cases. While the national office voiced support for the Chicago effort in general, what Chicago experienced lacked strategic value beyond the city. What New Yorkers wanted was the prosecution of certain selective cases with a potential for substantive, national impact.[82] They saw this happening in some cases being handled by the Los Angeles branch. When the Association was ready to proceed all the way to the U.S. Supreme Court, it was one of the California cases, chosen among a total of six, that led to the landmark *Shelley v. Kraemer* decision of 1948.

While the campaign that led to the *Shelley* decision was being mounted, the national office did see enough tactical merit in the Chicago effort to use the city as a meeting place for an all-branch conference concerned with devising the best strategies for all participants. But by the time the Supreme Court reached its decision, the Chicago NAACP was unable organizationally to capitalize on the opportunity to press the case of residential freedom. Most importantly, with an end to the covenant struggle, blacks and other minorities—Jews, Native Americans, and Asians—were able to enjoy their rights of citizenship to live in a place of their choice and means.

The summer of 1947 brought new violence to the Fernwood Park public housing development on the city's far southwest end. Mobs, with numbers in the thousands, defied the police and engaged in three successive nights of violence. City Hall responded with 1,000 policemen but mob rule still triumphed. The branch pursued complaints from thirty-five black automobile assault victims through the Legal Redress Committee, but without satisfactory results. NAACP General Counsel Thurgood Marshall, in town for the annual membership drive, likened the acquittals of rioters to the freeing of lynchers in a recent South Carolina incident.[83] McGee saw the incident at Fernwood in a broad sense as a "threat to [the Negro's] very well being." He pleaded that "it could happen to any Negro.

I call up every red-blooded citizen, not just to get mad, but get SMART and join [us]."[84]

The precariousness of the black quest for housing was dramatically illustrated again in 1949 in the Park Manor area, located immediately south of Bronzeville. In July, massive demonstrations erupted with crowds numbering in the thousands producing continuous disturbances. Concerned citizens felt that the only response to this racial violence was to legislate against it. Newly elected Alderman Archibald J. Carey, Jr., from Bronzeville's Third Ward offered an ordinance in the city council which would make it illegal for any person owning or managing property acquired from a land clearance action to discriminate. This ordinance covered both private and public developments, such as the proposed Lake Meadows complex in the north end of Bronzeville, near the Loop, and at all CHA sites. Carey's argument was persuasive to liberals but fell on mostly deaf ears. He proposed that "where the people's money and people's power are used to create something, that all the people, regardless of race or creed, shall be entitled to share in the benefits without discrimination."[85]

The branch was in its disorganized stage when the ordinance needed the Chicago NAACP's support the most. However, supporters of the ordinance included Jewish, Catholic, Protestant, labor, civic, and social groups, and this effort toward residential equality represented the liberal coalition at its best. Those resisting change unrelentingly pressed their case, however, and the ordinance failed. The climate generated by the conflict did produce a decision by the developers of the Lake Meadows Apartments on the South Side to voluntarily add a non-discrimination clause in their rental agreement.[86]

The movement for equal access to housing evolved against a backdrop of the city's historical pattern of centrifugal residential movement. White residential mobility, or "white flight," originated in the exigencies of nineteenth-century Chicago territorial expansion when initial changes in the economy made the periphery of the city more attractive than the core.[87] The best illustration of the process is found in the demographics of the area. By 1950, the city's overall population reached 3,621,000, which represented a 6.6 percent increase since 1940 but a decrease within the metropolitan area in which 5,600,000 persons lived. Meanwhile, the black population increased appreciably to 492,265. By 1960, the city's total dipped to 3,550,404; the metropolitan level rose to 6,794,461, and the black population reached 812,637, up 65 percent from 1950.[88]

As housing and employment opportunities in the suburban areas beckoned upwardly mobile whites, housing conflict arose from among those whites who did not wish to move or share their racially exclusive neighborhoods with non-whites. All black residential movement was described by the euphemism "Negro invasion." One has to wonder which "alien force" concerned white Americans the most, the Soviets and Chinese and the possibility of their invasion under the banner of Communism, or black Americans who sought equal rights. The next decade gave a particularly disturbing answer to this question.

The branch began the decade of the 1950s examining the suspicious character of slum clearance. In the Second Ward, blacks were convinced that once their homes were demolished to make way for the privately financed Lake Meadows development they would be priced out of the area. As far away as New York, Walter White commented that "many believed that what the white man wants always turns out to be harmful to the Negro—that after the slum was cleared, the whites would turn the centrally located Lake Front district for their own use, as certain whites had publicly advocated, leaving the Negroes nowhere to go."[89] Taking the offensive, branch president Willis demanded that any housing project undertaken on the South Side had to demonstrate its obvious community benefits before support was forthcoming.

Blacks who fled overcrowded South and West Side neighborhoods weekly, however, found themselves in previously all-white neighborhoods that were filled with tension and actual violence. In the summer of 1951 housing riots broke out in suburban Cicero, located on the city's western periphery, becoming a national *cause célèbre*. Over a two-day period, beginning July 11, hundreds of white youths and adults from both the suburbs and Chicago battled local and state law enforcement forces for control of the streets of Cicero. What precipitated the rioting was racial prejudice against blacks which ran unabated without official condemnation. In June 1951, the four-member Clark family—Harvey, Johnette, Michelle (age 8), and Harvey III (age 6)—tried to live out part of the American Dream by moving from overcrowded housing on East 46th Street in Bronzeville to healthier and roomier quarters in Cicero. They prepared to trade a single-room apartment without windows for a commodious apartment actually fit for human habitation. As members of the decade's growing black college-trained middle class, the Clarks eagerly grasped at the American Dream. Their enthusiasm unfortunately overshadowed their unawareness about Cicero and its 70,000 residents, all of whom were Caucasian and would use any means at their disposal to keep it racially exclusive.

Ex-serviceman Harvey Clark felt that because he was a veteran, Cicero's residents could not "afford to deny him his civil rights after he had made such a sacrifice and helped win the war and . . . establish the safety of those who live[d] in Cicero."[90] Resistance came as quickly as the Clarks moved their furniture, accumulated over nine years of marriage, into their apartment on June 23. Cicero's police chief, Ervin Konovsky, personally barred their entry and threatened Mr. Clark, warning him to "get out of Cicero and don't come back . . . or you'll get a bullet through you."[91] At this point Harvey Clark sought the assistance of the Chicago NAACP. Attorney George N. Leighton, who chaired the Legal Redress Committee, skillfully obtained a federal injunction against the Village of Cicero mandating that it afford all the protection the Clarks needed to enjoy their rights as citizens. Then he filed a suit for $200,000 in damages against Cicero and its officials for having conspired to practice racial discrimination.

By mid-July, the Clarks tried to move into their apartment for a second time but were met by a series of bullying crowds on Tuesday, July 10, which degenerated into a mob the next day. The white families in the apartment complex moved away to safety after having been warned beforehand of impending trouble. Planned rioting against the police began ironically against men who themselves possessed ambivalent feelings as to their professional commitment and racial sympathies. When challenged by the mob, the police offered only token resistance which, in turn, spurred on the racial agitators. The mob's vengeance was partially satiated only when the entire steel and brick apartment building which had housed twenty families lay burned and gutted. Personal damages for all the residents were high, and the Clarks lost $3,000 in valuables.

The mob's yearning for excitement and violence flared again the next night, forcing Illinois authorities to dispatch five companies of the National Guard with a total strength of 500 men to the scene. They met a mob that totaled in the thousands. Using fixed bayonets and tear gas, the guardsmen dispersed the rioters by night's end following four hours of violence. Before the violence was curbed and the streets cleared, 117 persons had been arrested. The next morning, the military order of the day called for the erection of an encircling barbed wire barrier to cordon off the area around the apartment building. In this tense milieu, enemies of the NAACP intimated that somehow blacks and perhaps even the NAACP itself had precipitated the crisis. For his part, attorney Leighton shrugged this off as diversionary, convinced that the violence was part of a well-planned effort by whites to deny the Clarks their civil rights.

However, it was left to Cook County states attorney John Boyle to exacerbate the situation beyond ratiocination. In the same mean spirit of the riot of 1919, the first indictment handed down by a grand jury following the rioting overlooked the actions of the white rioters and charged that George N. Leighton "unlawfully, maliciously and wilfully conspired to injure the property of a large number of people . . . [by] wilfully and maliciously [causing] a depression in their market selling price."[92] This outrage spurred national Executive Secretary Walter White to ask the man known as "Mr. Civil Rights," NAACP National Counsel Thurgood

Marshall, to fly to the city to lend his expertise and the Association's full prestige to the Chicago NAACP and its beleaguered Legal Redress chairman. Once in Chicago, Marshall personally assisted branch attorneys in preparing Leighton's defense. An outraged Walter White described the situation as one in which "the plain import of the Cook County grand jury's action is that any person who in any fashion advises, encourages and assists any Negro citizen in moving into a so-called white neighborhood is guilty of inciting to riot; and that any white mobbist who takes the law into his own hands to prevent an American citizen from moving lawfully into his own home is guiltless of a crime."[93]

At this point, the city's white liberal coterie raised a hue and cry resulting in condemnation of the grand jury's action. Federal action followed from the Truman White House. Shocked by the local miscarriage of justice, U.S. Attorney General J. Howard McGrath ordered a federal grand jury to investigate both the riot and the conduct of the Cook County grand jury. This episode also exposed the nation to the breadth of the Association's civil rights agenda, enhancing its image as an issues-driven body. The significance of this historic episode was found in Walter White's assessment that "in a way, Chicago [was] the key place so far as the NAACP [was] concerned as a result of the focusing of world attention on that area by the Cicero riot."[94]

Decisive action strengthened both the Chicago NAACP's resolve and its hold on the mantle of protest leadership in the city. The branch provided the legal protection the Clark family needed and extended its assistance to the extent that it raised funds to sustain the Clarks on a daily basis. One internal memorandum proclaimed: "The timely intervention of the NAACP has won a new prestige for our local branch by bringing its prompt action sharply to the attention of an aroused public."[95]

Unfortunately, the tragedy of Cicero was as much a triumph for injustice as for justice in 1951. The Clarks were forever banned from living where they wished, and racial exclusion has persisted there to the present. According to White, the gutted apartment complex stood as a mute reminder of the triumph of rule by the mob. Under the combined leadership of attorney-presidents Nelson Willis and George N. Leighton between 1950 and 1954, the branch settled in for a continued struggle in the courts with cases related to Cicero and with other emerging civil rights challenges.

The racial hostility and violence of Cicero represented only a small portion of the specter of housing discrimination. During one span in 1953, one-third of all the city's policemen were on details throughout the city attempting to prevent or quell major racial confrontations. And by summer 1953, a new international *cause célèbre* in housing discrimination exceeding Cicero's notoriety unfolded in the southernmost extremity of the city at the federally subsidized Trumbull Park Homes.

Trumbull Park was an all-white public housing project filled with townhouses. Its completion in 1938 took place over the objections of the whites in the area who did not want blacks in what they considered their racially exclusive community. Through a tacit understanding the townhouses were to remain virtually free of non-whites, while providing housing to over 400 white (and a few Mexican) families until the arrival of the first black families in 1953. Two racial incidents in 1952 were harbingers of the depth of racial antagonism at Trumbull Park. In March, an Argentinean family with dark complexions was forced out of the housing complex because the whites "thought they were Negroes." Six months later, blacks attending a Chicago Housing Authority (CHA) flower festival were the targets of a racial assault. Then, on July 30, 1953, the four-member Howard family moved in—Donald Howard, 25; his wife, Bettye Ann, 22; Cynthia, 4; and Donald, Jr., 2. CHA officials who rented the apartment townhouse no doubt presumed that the Howards were white. Mrs. Howard had a light complexion, and she was the only family member present during the application interview.

Within six days, the chanting crowds, morbidly curious at first, degenerated into aggressive mobs which assembled daily. Their plan bordered on devious simplicity, and called for the use of any means available short of direct physical attacks on the Howards to drive them from their townhouse. Noisy, powerful and frightening fireworks called "aerial bombs" were exploded overhead nightly; fire alarms were repeatedly pulled, both to add to the mob's strength and to divert the policemen from their defensive positions; and arson fires were set both inside and outside the perimeters of the housing development. Once the police were deployed to counter the violence, one local report said the area "resembled a besieged fortress."[96] On the periphery of the development, passing black motorists faced the constant threat of assault. S. B. Fuller, the millionaire member of the Chicago Negro Chamber of Commerce, was one such victim. This particular attack bore bitter fruit later in the year.

The police guard grew from scores of men to hundreds to a peak of 1,200 around October 13. The normal allotment after October ranged from 100 to 250 officers, manning their posts over a twenty-four-hour shift. To insure the safety of the black residents, whose numbers had grown to five families by the end of the year, every black person was escorted to and from his or her home by several policemen, either on foot or in police wagons. Injuries to police personnel mounted, reaching twenty by the end of the first six months of white resistance. Neither Cicero nor any other area showed "local hostility as intense or long-lived as Trumbull Park," reported the Chicago Commission on Human Relations (CHR).[97]

The Trumbull Park crisis produced a confrontation between three major forces in sustained disturbances that extended to the end of the decade. First, certain key agencies of the city of Chicago involved in governance and law enforcement were caught in the middle of the conflict instead of properly directing their attention to eliminating both the root causes of the trouble and the immediate problems of lawlessness and racial misunderstanding. These agencies included the mayor's office, the CHA, the corporation counsel's office, the CHR, and the Chicago Police Department.

Second, the Chicago NAACP cooperated with black and white liberal groups as allies on behalf of implementing integration. As early as the fall of 1953, the Howards asked the Chicago NAACP to assist them in their predicament. Branch president Leighton and his law partner, Robert Ming, Jr., responded and provided whatever legal assistance was needed. In addition, the branch drained its treasury to cover mounting court and bond costs. For its part, the Chicago Negro Chamber of Commerce issued an indignant report on the situation: "The Howards and other Negroes in the project personally have done nothing to anyone. The rioters are not aiming their assaults and attacks at these individuals [alone]. . . . The attack is against the Negro people; and the Negro people must not be the last ones to realize this fact. This injustice has been inflicted upon the whole society, upon every citizen who cherishes democracy in America. The Negro families at Trumbull Park exemplify the determination of the Negro people in America to continue, with the greatest haste, their advance toward full citizenship rights in America. To the overwhelming majority of Negroes, sick of discrimination and the suffering it brings, it is abundantly clear that there is nothing to gain from further compromises or retreats at Trumbull Park or anywhere else in the land. We shall not be moved!"[98]

From 1953 through 1958, as the harassment of the up to thirty black families in residence remained constant, so too did the Chicago NAACP's unrelenting pressure to eliminate housing discrimination, utilizing every legitimate form of protest imaginable. Assistance was provided on a timely basis, ranging from financial support for daily sustenance to personal interaction and legal support. A suit for $100,000 was filed against the CHA to force the integration of the remaining all-white Bridgeport and Lathrop Homes projects.

Third, numerous, well-organized white groups coalesced in order to bring about greater efficiency in their protest. They ranged from the narrow-minded South Deering Improvement Association, to the race-supremacist White Circle League, to the *Daily Calumet*, from which pages a daily venom of racial prejudice flowed. The head of the South Deering Improvement Association, Louis Dinnocenzo, made this truculent appeal to resisting whites: "We can win this fight by keeping up the pressure [of mass demonstrations]. They [the blacks] can't face people like you. . . . Make it necessary to keep the police out there [at the housing project]. Other districts over the city are screaming mad about the loss of police protection." He later added: "Moving in another (Negro) family only increases our resistance. . . . We're in their hair and we're going to stay there."[99] While Dinnocenzo publicly decried the use of violence, the crowds degenerated into lawless mobs, which were perhaps more useful to his cause. Overall, all parties involved were determined, and so they settled in for a long campaign that would, in effect, last throughout the decade.

In the private housing sector, one case in particular illuminated the perpetual blind spot in the branch's handling of those civil or criminal rights cases in which interracial conflict was absent. Just as the branch had been reluctant to act in the wake of the riot of 1919 because it feared for its reputation by getting involved in possible criminal cases, and in the eviction riot of 1931 because an economic rather than a racial motive was involved, so, in 1947, the branch acted with great circumspection in the heart-wrenching Hickman case. James Hickman was a black steelworker who suffered at the hands of an unscrupulous black landlord in a West Side slum area. The Hickman family of nine was crammed into an attic cubicle that measured 14 by 14 feet, without water, light, or gas lines. Ominously, the family did not have access to a fire escape. It had been acceptable to the Hickman family only because it was the best housing available. As Hickman described the conditions, "we lived like rats in a hole."[100] When the landlord tried to persuade them to move so that he could make even more money from more devious spatial modifications to the property, the Hickmans declined. And it was at this point that the landlord threatened drastic action.

The drastic action translated into an arson fire that killed four of the seven Hickman children, while Mr. Hickman and an older son were at work. Six months later, Hickman learned of the landlord's complicity, contemplated revenge, and fatally shot him. An interracial defense committee formed immediately that included Hollywood actress Tallulah Bankhead and award-winning Chicago novelist Willard Motley. When the Chicago NAACP was asked to join formally as an organization, McGee refused "since both Hickman and the man killed [were] colored."[101] Since this decision reflected the Association's policy on incidents involving injustices among African Americans, the branch's leadership could only join the legal defense effort as individuals. Accordingly, President Henry W. McGee and several others quickly did so.[102] Hickman eventually was released from jail and was sentenced to two years' probation. A persistent irony of black life in America had surfaced again. The organizational strength of the NAACP was unavailable in a case that mirrored the horrors of racial restriction and individual greed just because of a similarity in skin color between victim and victimizer.

If the branch still had its limits during its most expansive organizational phase, what was the fate of its two closest ideological allies? During the Cicero disturbances of 1951, the branch's sister organization, the Chicago Urban League, experienced a completely different pattern of development. The League grew weaker as the NAACP was being propelled to its apex. The League's Executive Secretary, Sidney Williams, described his activities as being "limited to keeping the National League informed, working through the N.A.A.C.P. and The Committee Against Racial Discrimination, and commending the Governor for calling out the militia." When the Trumbull Park riots followed, the League was again "on the sidelines. Its activities were restricted to consultation with the organizations working to curb the violence."[103] This work with the NAACP involved "the establishment of an Urban League–NAACP liaison committee to facilitate releases and cooperation between the two agencies."[104] Williams spent his last five years of tenure with the League in continuous opposition to the wishes of his board of directors.

Compared to the activities of the Chicago NAACP, CORE's paled. What is especially ironic in the case of CORE, is that CORE had always considered the Chicago NAACP, generally, to be the more inefficient body; but by 1950, it was the Chicago chapter of CORE that was virtually moribund.[105] Its organizational atrophy was attributable to the failed protest directed against Goldblatt's Department Stores in 1948 as well as in general to the political and racial climate which fostered an anti-Communist hysteria and black mistrust of white intentions. Some members of the Chicago NAACP, such as attorney Jewel Stradford Rogers and Faith Rich, held dual memberships, while trying to benefit from the best of both groups. Other activists, such as the iconoclastic Roosevelt University student Joffre Stewart, kept the spirit of protest alive with his constant run-ins with shopkeepers and the police over his right as a citizen to equal treatment in Loop barbershops and restaurants.

Education exemplified perhaps the third most important item in the activist agenda during this period. Faith Rich served on the Textbook Subcommittee which at this juncture in the branch's and Chicago's history fought primarily for fairness in racial depiction in school textbooks. The subcommittee contacted publishers and argued, always persuasively and sometimes successfully, for an unbiased portrayal of blacks based on historical fact. By focusing on changing the image of blacks, first during slavery and then during the modern period, they hoped to bring about an elimination of prejudice as well as an acceptance of modern anthropological theory of racial equality. Rich felt the latter would be helpful in showing blacks as "human equals struggling for their just dues from the colonial beginning to the present time."[106] By 1946, the subcommittee could claim credit for either having assisted or prepared a "Supplemental Unit for the Course of Study in Social Sciences" for the Chicago Public Schools.

As to the possibility that educational inequities might end some day, excitement filled the air in 1953 as the nation awaited the decision of the U.S. Supreme Court on a series of school segregation cases brought before the nation's highest tribunal by the Association during the early 1950s. It was presumed in civil rights circles that the decision, once rendered some-time in late 1953 or early 1954, would be favorable to the cause of equality. It was also forecast that in its influence it would be a major breakthrough signaling a new day in race relations for black Americans.

An unforeseen and dramatic transformation within the American po-litical economy, which began during the war years and continued through the prosperous 1950s, indelibly altered the nature of the civic-political relationship within Bronzeville. The death of Franklin D. Roosevelt in April 1945 brought Harry S Truman, an avowed pragmatist and budding race egalitarian, to the presidency. In an almost miraculous fashion, and in the face of deep-rooted black skepticism, Truman steered the nation on a course toward racial equality for the first time in its history.[107] This change in the course of American politics was dictated to a great extent by both the actual and the potential voting strength of black Americans. In addition, popular sentiment at the war's end precluded any return to the racial status quo *ante*. By December 1946, the die was cast for major black ad-vancement after Truman appointed a presidential commission to investi-gate and recommend the necessary changes to protect the civil rights of black Americans. The commission reported its findings in 1947 under the title, *To Secure These Rights*, a position report of far-reaching scope and recommendations. As a blueprint for racial equality, it exceeded the aspi-rations of the legislation of the early Reconstruction Era. Further, Truman desegregated the U.S. armed services by issuing Executive Order 9981. Almost simultaneously, the U.S. Supreme Court rendered its decision in *Shelley v. Kraemer* in 1948, making discrimination in housing unenforce-able under the Constitution.

At the Democratic convention in 1948, white supremacists walked out in disagreement over the party's adoption of the strongest civil rights plank in its history. At a time when the Progressive and Republican parties saw fit to challenge Truman's motivation on the issue of civil rights, the black electorate overwhelmingly chose Truman over Dewey and mightily contributed to the election upset of the century. Chicago blacks, spurred by the efforts of Dawson's growing organization, continued to shift to the Democratic ranks in larger numbers than ever before. Now considered the nation's civil rights president among blacks and white liberals, the Mis-sourian received 71.8 percent of the votes cast by Chicago blacks, who led the city's and state's voting percentage in ballots cast for the Democratic presidential ticket.[108]

Chicago's liberal Democratic mayor, Edward Kelly, who acted in the tradition of Republican Bill Thompson, contributed further to the growing black support for the National Democratic Party, as well as its local unit. The fundamental base of black political support expanded primarily because of the tangible increase in benefits at the local level which were manifested in more jobs for the working class and upscale political offices for the aspiring middle class. Under Kelly, African American Robert Taylor was appointed as chairman of the Chicago Housing Authority, and Dr. Midian O. Bousfield was made a member of the Chicago Board of Education. Other such appointments, support for a local FEPC ordinance, and a close identification with the call for white Chicagoans to follow both the law of the land and the promise of equal opportunity established Kelly as a friend to blacks and a conduit for opportunities. For his devotion to fair play, Kelly was targeted for defeat by white racists within the party in the primary election of 1947.[109]

The influence of these newly proffered political opportunities on the volunteer-driven Chicago NAACP meant that more talented lawyers could pursue professional advancement to judgeships after serving in the offices of the Cook County States Attorney and Chicago City Corporation Counsel. Moreover, this breakthrough in occupational mobility adversely affected the pattern of volunteerism, which had made the branch's Legal Redress Committee always a well-staffed legal bureau in the NAACP's crusade against discrimination. Another change diminished, at least conceptually, the need for high-intensity volunteerism except for fund-raising purposes. That was the public office-holding of dedicated egalitarians (or at least newly committed dilettantes) to the cause of racial equality. As blacks placed a larger number of effective public administrators in office, the need for pressure groups to work for systematic change from the outside ostensibly lessened.

Demographics, moreover, surely favored blacks in politics as the swollen populations of the Second and Third Wards guaranteed continuous black representation. Newcomers emerged and new faces in politics manifested the political transformation. Democratic municipal judges Wendell E. Green and Fred (Duke) Slater were elected in 1944 and 1948, respectively. Black control over these wards continued as William Harvey replaced the Second Ward's Earl B. Dickerson in 1943, and won reelection in 1947. In the Third Ward, long-time egalitarian and political opportunist Oscar De Priest defeated Democratic political reformer Benjamin Grant in 1943. Within four years, Archibald J. Carey, Jr., ousted De Priest.

Being elected into office in Bronzeville still required that all candidates pass the litmus test of race. Political scientist Hanes Walton's paradigm of black political culture as a sphere unto itself explained why no politician in or from Bronzeville could ever have been elected to office in the 1940s without some identification as a "Race Man." Black politicians differed, however, as to the level of their activities in behalf of civil rights because of both their involvement in Democratic machine politics and various levels of commitment. The aldermen serving the Second and Third Wards had to endorse civil rights advancement publicly. The half-dozen state legislators in the Illinois General Assembly continued their tradition of advancing race equality and forcing the issue of job opportunities through the passage of a state level Equal Jobs Opportunity law. In successive biennial sessions from 1944 to 1952, black efforts in the lower house of the General Assembly were fruitful. In the upper house, the traditional bulwark of conservatism in American politics, the employment bills perpetually languished.

Relations between the branch and Congressman Dawson remained amicable so long as (1) the branch continued its non-threatening profile in Chicago politics, while simultaneously raising its profile as a racially oriented advocate for black advancement; (2) the political situation remained fluid within both parties; and (3) Dawson lacked a firm political base beyond his Second Ward Democratic organization. On the one hand, the branch appeared unintrusive and non-threatening in its relationship with the world of politics. In 1947, in a manner somewhat reminiscent of the service De Priest's secretary Morris Lewis provided the branch, Dawson's secretary, Bill Wall, acted as co-chairman of the membership drive. Wall was considered by contemporaries as being totally apolitical when engaging in civic affairs. Joining Wall was the recently elected Republican alderman of the Third Ward, Archibald J. Carey, Jr.

Ironically, the latter's father had been excluded from consideration for the branch presidency and initially its hierarchy because of his partisan political affiliation in the 1920s with "Big Bill" Thompson. Carey, Jr., experienced a somewhat similar fate as he was dropped from the Executive Committee. His removal, however, resulted from his inactivity caused by his partisan involvement in behalf of Republican presidential candidate Thomas Dewey. Carey's departure from the ranks of the Executive Committee proved fortuitous because it no doubt helped the branch steer clear of Congressman Dawson's scrutiny.

The branch's partisanship was all too apparent throughout this period, despite its facade of neutrality. Then, too, its level of involvement intensified. This bred an image of intrusiveness, by way of its being affiliated with persons seeking political office, or associated with certain political causes or campaigns. An escalation of open political warfare between rising political master William L. Dawson and civic leader–reform politician Earl B. Dickerson had characterized the middle of the decade. Alarmed at the level of this conflict, the *Defender* warned the politicians and its readers: "There is no time for inner struggles of men whose cause is one and the same. It is clear that only our enemies can profit by such a struggle as it is now taking place. Both men are too big for such a thing."[110]

One ingredient that linked Dickerson and Carey partially sparked the conflict—the desire to represent Bronzeville's First District in Congress, made easier with impressive civil rights credentials. Dickerson's ambitions were brought to President Roosevelt's attention as early as 1941–

1942[111] and Carey's to his cousin in 1947 as he shared his dream—"the real reason I am running [for alderman] is because I want to go to Congress."[112] The dual desires of these racial egalitarians, elevation both for their race in the attainment of citizenship rights and for themselves in terms of higher office, obviously worried Dawson and were not to be treated lightly.

Also infuriating to Dawson had to be the sight of the core of the branch's leadership, which included President Genoa Washington and his two most immediate subordinates, becoming so involved in the presidential election of 1948 on behalf of the Republican Party that they neglected their branch duties altogether. Their being associated with a losing cause, albeit one that caused Democrats concern until the last ballots were counted, could have done very little to console Dawson.

The eight years of postwar organization-building that the Chicago NAACP experienced beginning in 1946 clearly established democracy within the branch. The best results were inclusiveness both within the hierarchy and in the general membership, more effective fund-raising, and better service to the cause of civil rights. The worst results were increases in internecine squabbling, lapses in fund-raising, and interruptions in protest advocacy. Overall, what the branch weathered during this period would be intensified in the years to follow. Importantly, the Chicago NAACP stood ready to engage in triumphant struggle.

At the Apex of Militant Activism,
1954–1957

We believe that such situations as have occurred
in Trumbull Park would not have done so had the
traditions of Abolitionist Chicago and the
contributions of Negroes to Chicago been kept
alive during succeeding generations.

> —Cora M. Patton to Mayor Martin H.
> Kennelly, 1955

There are many ways to fight for civil rights, I
have mine and they have theirs.

> —U.S. Congressman William L. Dawson

ALTHOUGH THE PAST relationship between the branch as an agency of civic protest and the black Republican and Democratic machines indicated the possibility of harmony, the character of the period evidenced the probability of open hostility. What evolved into a confrontation had its genesis in 1954 as two influential and incompatible personalities, controlling two disparate movements, clashed. Chicago NAACP leader Willoughby Abner challenged veteran South Side political leader William L. Dawson over the future direction of black racial advancement in Chicago.

Abner's entry into the ranks of the Chicago NAACP's leadership resulted from the 1954 election of branch officers held in December 1953. The contest pitted George Leighton against Cora Patton in a rematch of the previous years, with Abner once again controlling the Nominating Committee. Patton ran with the trappings of legitimacy, while Leighton carried the stigma of an interloper. The results were dictated by the energetic efforts of the trade union forces, and Patton won handily. Abner accompanied Patton into office as first vice-president as well as chairman of the Executive Committee. Militant trade unionist rule achieved its birth. Within the branch, factionalism would persist, but never at the level of previous years. Moderate and militant members of the branch's leadership who disagreed with the branch's direction would more often than not leave the organization rather than engage in Machiavellian schemes for control. When the latter scenario next occurred, it would be the result of Bronzeville politics invading the civic sphere.

The trade union phase centered around an activism that carried the branch to new heights of protest advocacy. For all practical purposes, Willoughby Abner ran the branch for the next four years, first as chairman of the Executive Committee, and then through the presidency, which he won outright in successive elections in 1956 and 1957. Abner had suffered without influence through the leaderships of mid-forties militant Henry W. McGee (who won victories over the Establishment but always too slight for Abner's liking), and then under legal moderates, from Washington through Leighton (who believed ultimate advancement was possible through the legal system). Now the strategy and orientation of the branch changed to challenge any force that perceptibly impeded the advancement of black citizens into the American mainstream, whether through open hostility, enervating benevolence, or suffocating indifference.

Abner's approach endorsed direct confrontation with the forces of racism, with no holds barred. Extremely ambitious, courageous, and uncompromising, he drew strength from among his supporters based on these personal qualities and his articulate, gentlemanly, persuasive manner. He did not exhort; rather he cajoled and won over a crowd through the logic of his message, his winning smile, and his generally compelling demeanor. "While popular with his loyalists," an observer reflected, "he never wore the cloak of arrogance." His plan was basically to remain "outspoken and unintimidated in the struggle for racial justice."[1]

Willoughby Abner's emergence as the city's foremost agent of protest advocacy coincided with a major socioeconomic transformation of Chicago's black society. This process figured prominently in political scientist James Q. Wilson's study, *Negro Politics: The Search for Leadership.* Wilson described a growing number of well-educated, upwardly mobile blacks who were frustrated with a civic and political leadership that failed to lead them in attaining a place in the American mainstream commensurate with their talents and expectations. Because of the leadership's lethargy, connivance with the white power structure, and cowardice, they were alienating middle-class blacks. The aspirations of the black strivers were, in fact, closely associated with the Chicago NAACP's modernized program, which originated with A. C. MacNeal in 1933. A generation later in the 1950s, the ideological heirs of these upwardly mobile strivers were described by a fellow Chicagoan as being part of another wave of "New Negroes."

In the civic arena, forces advocating winning the "whole loaf" of citizenship rights sought to methodically push aside those persons willing to compromise on the pace and scope of racial advancement. The same was observed in the political sphere. "A new Negro voter has arisen as a result of educational, economic and social progress," reported one analyst for *The Nation.* "There are school teachers, doctors, lawyers, artisans, civil servants and others who can now afford the 'luxury' of voting on a candidate's stand, or lack of one, on an ideological issue."[2] Yet tension was inevitable, according to political scientists Edward Banfield and James Q. Wilson, because "in the north the goals of lower-class and middle-class Negroes [were] often in conflict and the political process tend[ed] to exacerbate the process."[3] Dawson molded his political agenda to cater to the needs of the lower class and sought to meet its "welfare" or basic needs. The middle class, having had its basic needs met, sought "status needs" that the machine could not deliver without greatly disturbing the economic and racial status quo. Though the branch at the mid-century mark experienced the same tensions emanating from a heightened racial restlessness that political organizations experienced, as an activist group it could address them aggressively, frontally, and openly.

When Abner assessed the political domain which supported the racial status quo, he had no alternative but to challenge politicians from both parties, from the president to the governor to Bronzeville's Congressman Dawson. He opposed the political machine because it stifled the "natural expression of the needs and aspirations of Negroes."[4] His tactics were often the polar opposites of the legal approach of the former several decades as the branch now stressed boycotts and picketing when circumstances dictated, along with negotiations, letter writing, and intensive publicity. Not since A. C. MacNeal two decades earlier had the branch been directed by such an iconoclastic leader.

As important as Abner's ascension to power was, Cora Patton's election as titular head of the Chicago NAACP (1954–1956) broke a precedent extending back to 1913 when the first male became the branch's chief executive. Her election represented the culmination of two disparate trends of great significance. First, the democratization process acted to extend the important role of women, which was more recognizable than ever before, especially because of their indispensable role in fund-raising. Second, labor involvement had increased to such an extent that labor insurgency, leading to control of the branch, was imminent. And militant labor forces were willing to topple moderates even if it meant having a woman from outside the ranks of organized labor as the organization's head. As a result of the interaction of these influences, Patton never functioned as the supreme branch leader even though she was elected to two consecutive terms in office. It is important to note, however, that no evidence indicates that she objected to this arrangement. As chair of the Executive Committee, Abner controlled the organization, so, more often than not, official statements concerning the branch, its operations and activities were given by him. Decision-making, in all probability, followed this pattern also.

Cora Patton deserved to be president regardless of the circumstances leading to her election. There was growing sentiment within women's ranks that the time had come for one of their group to be recognized. The Nebraska-born leader proved herself to be an able fund-raiser and mover of people. The highly successful Tag Day was initiated during her presidency. She had come into the ranks of the NAACP in the 1940s from the vast network of national women's clubs while she was president of the Gaudeamus Women's Club, and was personally acquainted with national clubwoman and NAACP field administrator Daisy E. Lampkin. Her affiliation was probably as much social as it was ideological. The personable Patton had the ability to work with all people and obtain concessions when they were needed.[5] With extensive club connections, she helped increase the branch's visibility as an organization that was essential to the advancement of black people.

During Patton's tenure in office, Archie L. Weaver continued in his self-prescribed role as the grand old man of the local movement. He wrote regularly to the national office about conditions in Chicago, observing in the spring of 1954 that the branch "is a closed corporation—very much .... Much of the public is disgusted. Have we got a president? Who runs the organization? I do not go near the office. I must protect my own name and reputation."[6] As the months passed and the influence of Abner increased, so did the perception of his domination over the branch. By the summer of that year, Weaver wrote to Current that "this is truly a one man organization—[only Beatrice Hughes Steele] asserts herself as to [her] office."[7] The latter served as corresponding secretary until 1945 when she was inducted into the Executive Committee as branch secretary. Her fund-raising reached legendary levels, and she continued her service until her death in 1991.

Weaver's involvement in branch affairs ended with Abner's attempts to control a special Elections Supervisory Committee in 1956. The three-member committee was formed to regulate the procedures for the election of the branch leadership for 1956. Abner openly interfered in the election process, not only because the exceptionally cerebral Abner wanted to improve his chances for victory, but also because of his perceptions about the competence of the members of the committee. Weaver's displeasure grew with this affront to protocol, and he warned Abner that untoward circumstances could overtake the branch because of it.[8]

Abner's activities notwithstanding, a surprisingly quiet, uneventful election followed. He had calculated correctly that victory could be guaranteed by strategically arranging the ballot positions if this plan were combined with a heavy labor turnout. When Cora Patton subsequently questioned the results of the election, she demanded nothing beyond a recount of the ballots.

The gender barrier was breached again by early 1957, when attorney Willie Whiting became the first woman to serve permanently as executive secretary. Her preparation for office came after joining the branch's leadership three years previously as a member of the Legal Redress Committee. In something that was also rare for the branch in a city of migrants, she was the first Chicago native to climb this high within the hierarchy. Whiting was born on the South Side, was partially reared and educated on the West Side, served the nation in Europe during the war, and was educated at Roosevelt University and John Marshall Law School. Capable, assertive, determined, attractive, but somewhat naive as to survival in an organization in flux, she immediately made crucial missteps. As executive secretary, she attempted to bring a semblance of order into a body which had grown accustomed to inefficiency as its operating norm. Her intent to correct the organization's system of accounting for memberships caused widespread consternation. Under the system in operation, the branch was doomed to a low membership as both potential and past supporters held back their volunteer and financial support. In 1957, both the Supreme Life Insurance Company and a key worker on the West Side expressed reluctance to support the branch because of its poor bookkeeping practices.[9]

The lifestyle of many of the members remained middle class, even among the representatives of organized labor, who were more often articulate spokesmen for the working class rather than members of it. And the democratization process remained constant despite the perpetual criticisms of domination by one clique or another. The first white officer since 1925 took his seat in 1956 as Walter Nielubowski, a labor representative, became fourth vice-president. Also in 1956, Robert Birchman again applied for a job within the NAACP's administrative ranks as Illinois Field Secretary. West Sider Faith Rich chaired the Education Committee for several years, during which time the branch challenged discrimination in teacher's testing and *de facto* segregation,[10] and Edward Holmgren in Hyde Park served as chairman of the Hyde Park Unit's housing chairman as did Deborah Meier. Hyde Parker Alberta Ackerman served both the unit and state conference as an officer.

The membership of the branch peaked during this period of militant activism under Abner in 1956 and 1957. The branch lumbered along with a membership slightly below the 5,000 mark until Abner captured the public's imagination with his assaults on an indifferent, as well as sometimes antagonistic, white Establishment and what he considered its pitiful black sycophants. Black discontent with the ubiquitous racial status quo was fueled by major events, such as the disturbances at the Trumbull Park Homes on the Far South Side between 1953 and 1957, the 1955 murder of fourteen-year-old Chicagoan Emmett Till while he was on vacation in Mississippi, and the epochal year-long Montgomery, Alabama, bus boycott. The only organization that concerned itself with all of these problems without regard to the consequences was the Chicago NAACP. Through its fearless advocacy, it achieved both institutional status and primacy among protest organizations during the decade. One sign of organizational relevance and success was a return to the halcyon days of impressive fundraising. The branch raised over $115,000 in two years under Abner's leadership before he was eventually defeated in the branch election of December 1957.

Moreover, the Chicago NAACP felt comfortable enough with centralized authority to petition the national office for assistance, guidance, and even intervention when election irregularities were feared or had actually transpired. Because of factional disputes, this contact occurred on an annual basis. The national staff officers wisely steered clear of any involvement in a local affair that was resolvable at that level or that might involve the national office in a situation in which it would be forced to take sides. The use of the good offices of Dickerson and Ming in the dispute of 1950 was one such example. Branches were also encouraged to solve their own financial problems, so when the national office became aware of the fact that the Chicago branch had raised enough money to support an executive secretary without difficulty, appropriate suggestions were made to achieve that end.

In December 1956, Abner won his reelection bid with almost unanimous support after driving out contenders from the ranks of the leadership. The major result of Abner's two terms in office (1956–1958) was a level of branch involvement in programmatic pursuits that resembled the activism of the New Deal years. Activism producing change was just what the bulk of concerned black citizens wanted in the way of an improvement in the quality of life. This list of proposed changes to the branch's agenda included an end to overcrowding and double shifts in the public schools; state passage of an FEPC; job opportunities on the periphery of Bronzeville as well as in the Loop; and adequate police protection in racially contested neighborhoods where bombings had supplanted verbal abuse and the restrictive covenant as methods of racial intimidation.

While the black politicians, under Congressman Dawson's influence, counselled accommodation with the status quo, interracial tensions were exacerbated by increased racial contacts, and at some point proactive measures would have to be considered if not instituted. The interests of upwardly mobile blacks in Chicago, especially on the South Side, which encompassed Dawson's congressional district, called for dramatically changing the fabric of race relations. This segment of the citizenry demanded access to housing, improved educational opportunities, personal safety, the removal of the "job ceiling" in public and private employment on an immediate basis, and, perhaps just as important, a modern, twentieth-century political representation which could bring about the attainment of the American Dream. What the old-stock Americans had achieved generations ago, and persons of immigrant strains were benefitting from during the postwar period, black Americans still sought. And, if black and white politicians were not willing to accept the challenge of the age, the Chicago NAACP showed, through its extensive activist program, that it was willing.

The fates of the branch's two most prominent allies, the Chicago Urban League and CORE, were adversely affected by the very same conditions that propelled the branch forward. League secretary Sidney Williams was viewed with such antagonism by the white power structure that he was forced out of his position after 1954. He committed the unthinkable by condemning the Catholic Church, the unions, and the corporate community for failing to support racial justice. The conservative leadership of the League faced the troubling situation of having to remove a man who had built a considerable following among working-class blacks. Williams's superiors solved their problem by closing the League during a reorganization phase extending through 1955. With Williams gone the board selected a Seattle Urban League official, William "Bill" Berry, to fill the executive secretary's slot.

In demeanor, Berry was much like T. Arnold Hill, the League's first secretary in the twenties, in that he was "articulate, skillful, and diplomatic [with prominent whites]."[11] Determined to work on the cause of problems rather than the effects, Berry turned out to be more activist-oriented in the long run than his employers had imagined. At this juncture, though, he took a moderate stance but used a conservative tone in controversial issues, a compromise which his civic and political opponents could tolerate. In the meantime, CORE allegedly "suffered from an intense factional fight over an anarcho-syndicalist clique" and this further weakened its organizational structure.[12] One former activist member, however, remembered differently. Joffre Stewart recalled that the chapter was overwhelmed by moderates who steered the group clear of confrontation and thereby neutralized its effectiveness.[13]

Attaining institutional status brought the branch into direct confrontation with local and national white authority as it pursued a policy of attacking housing discrimination in suburban Cicero in 1951, in the Trumbull Park Homes from 1953 through 1959, and everywhere else housing discrimination raised its ugly head in the city. The branch's program expanded to transcend the concerns of one class, for the most part, so open housing, fair employment opportunities, and quality education were at the core of equal rights thought and action. When Korean War veterans returned home, for example, with less than honorable or dishonorable discharges caused by racism in the armed services, the branch showed that it had matured enough to embrace even their cause. All of these areas of concern were interpreted and categorized conceptionally as "status needs" versus "welfare needs." In reality, they were often indistinguishable in the eyes of black Chicagoans who saw them in the aggregate simply as rights that were being denied.[14]

At the beginning of the new year, 1954, when the branch changed leadership, it changed the tactics it had been using in the anti-discrimination housing campaign at Trumbull Park. In the hands of labor activists Willoughby Abner and Charles Hayes, successful tactics from the labor arena were grafted onto the branch's legalistic tactics and strategy. Acceptable new methods included confrontation and direct negotiating, letter writing, telephone campaigns, and, if necessary, "pressure in the form of boycotting and picketing."[15] This labor faction also adopted a "1954 Action Program" which organized the city, precinct by precinct, section by section, into NAACP units for integration. In the Trumbull Park campaign, the branch was so closely involved in the lives of the residents that a subcommittee on education scheduled and held its meetings at Bettye Ann Howard's home. During this same period, Abner personally led a group of residents to a baseball field to demonstrate that public grounds anywhere in the city were the preserve of all of its citizens.[16]

By mid-January 1954 the CHA attempted to evict the Howards based on the allegation that they had falsified their income statement to gain admittance to the housing project. Attorneys Leighton and Ming repudiated this charge immediately. They held that this action was prompted by race prejudice and, if left to stand, "would deprive [the Howards] of their rights under the 14th amendment."[17] Simultaneous with this court action, branch president Cora Patton and Executive Committee chairman Abner contacted the offices of the Illinois Attorney General, Cook County States Attorney, and the City's Corporation Counsel to investigate the conspiratorial involvement of the South Deering Improvement Association and the White Circle League in the continuing disturbances.

By February, President Patton, Abner, and several other branch leaders met with Chicago's politically complacent and racially insensitive mayor, Martin H. Kennelly. He was asked to make a personal plea for compliance with the law and an end to white racially based resistance to black housing aspirations, not only in Trumbull Park but throughout the city. Kennelly in his eighth year in office was the same recalcitrant man he had been during the housing disturbances of the late forties. A man of supposedly pure character, he still had a blind spot when it came to equal opportunities for black citizens. Not surprisingly, the delegation was unsuccessful in its entreaties.

In order to force a resolution of this impasse, Patton acted in advance of this meeting to broaden the branch's appeal for assistance. She sent letters to President Eisenhower and U.S. Attorney General Herbert Brownell asking for federal intervention in light of the fact that Trumbull Park had been federally built and subsidized. From New York, Walter White added the national office's influence by also writing to the president and attorney general several days later. White also asked the FBI to investigate the nature of the protracted struggle; subsequently, the Civil Rights Unit of the Justice Department promised to look for any federal violations. The crisis of Trumbull Park eventually reached the desk of the president.[18]

The pace of activism quickened during the following month. A mass rally, called by the branch in collaboration with the Ministers Alliance of Community Churches, took place on March 7 to protest inadequate police protection and dilatory political action. An assemblage of 1,500 swelled the sanctuary of the Metropolitan Community Church, hoping to end assaults and other forms of intimidation against black residents. Willoughby Abner presided over the meeting and stirred the crowd with an oratory that appealed both to the intellect and the senses. As expected, Abner's rhetoric made racial integration seem logical, legitimate, desirable, and imperative. A face rarely observable in public gatherings was also present—that of Congressman William L. Dawson. When Dawson took the lectern, he urged the crowd with his usual directness to vote politicians (such as Mayor Kennelly whom he did not name specifically and did not like personally) out of office if they did not uphold the law.[19] Successful in its own right, this mass assemblage encouraged other groups to show their displeasure with what appeared to be deliberate governmental inaction.

After the meeting, the branch sent new protests to Kennelly, the states attorney, and the police commissioner. All entreaties proved unsuccessful as the Democratic political machine deliberately remained noncommittal as well as oblivious to the deepening, long-range implications of the crisis. Several days later, Third Ward Republican Alderman Archibald Carey, Jr., took the floor of the city council chambers to ask the mayor to clarify his position on the Trumbull Park situation. Carey inquired first about the pace and scope of prosecutions that found only 167 arrests over seven months when 50,000 to 60,000 demonstrators had been involved, and second about the expenditures of $2 million for law enforcement (which was more than the project itself had cost).[20] By April, Carey had introduced a resolution, calling for city council support for open occupancy throughout the city irrespective of race, color, nationality, religion, or creed. It passed with surprisingly little difficulty but it lacked the power of enforceable law along with a strong base of support among white Chicagoans.

Less than two weeks after the Metropolitan Church rally, the Chicago Negro Chamber of Commerce, now headed by former branch president Oscar C. Brown, Sr., conducted its own mass demonstration. This time, a mass mobilization of blacks and sympathetic whites marched around City Hall. The announced base of support was broad with over 200 groups involved or invited to participate, including the Chicago NAACP. The mere thought of this demonstration was so unnerving to Mayor Kennelly that he attempted to persuade the leaders of the effort to cancel it. To convince them of his new-found interest in the matter, he issued a statement condemning the lawlessness at Trumbull Park. It was so mild in tone, however, that it was rejected by everyone involved. Cora Patton felt that the statement "lacked specificity and firmness." She also added these sentiments: "While violence has apparently ceased at Trumbull Park Homes, the violence against Negro families moving into new areas is spreading to other sections of the city, to Rosemoor and now the West Side. The tension was sure to spread as a result of months of laxity on the part of city officials and without strong prosecution and penalties. . . ."[21] The mass mobilization itself went forward and an estimated 500 to 1,500 persons participated in what was described as a significant action by the organizers: "Never before in Chicago had so many citizens picketed City Hall on such an issue."[22] Part of the agenda that day called for the simultaneous dispatching of delegations to Washington, D.C., Springfield, and various departments of city and county government to plead for tougher law enforcement at the housing project and for freedom in the general housing market. This agenda wastefully duplicated already extant NAACP efforts.

The upcoming 1954 spring countywide elections provided the branch with another opportunity to apply pressure on the political Establishment. In a series of forums and through questionnaires, the branch sought to ascertain the extent of possible support for open housing as well as to determine what politicians should be targeted for defeat in the election. One candidate for county clerk was veteran Democratic committeeman and future mayor Richard J. Daley. His response was appropriate if not stronger than any of Kennelly's pronouncements.[23]

By May 6, at a second NAACP mass rally, the branch issued an ultimatum to the mayor and other officials which, if not answered promptly, promised continuous citywide demonstrations. This form of protest paralleled the seemingly successful tactics of whites used at Trumbull Park to neutralize black efforts. The meeting had one unexpected and obviously unwelcome intrusion in the form of a telegram from the White Circle League, which read: "Your org[anization] and all its interlocking race mixing groups are through over running white neighborhoods in Chicago. . . . *You are disturbing the peace* (emphasis added)."[24]

Just one week later, the peripatetic branch leaders were back at Police Chief Timothy O'Connor's office. This time they left with more assurances about the safety of the Trumbull Park residences and information about the extent of police efforts that were normally not made public. One amenity had been added: residents were now to be driven to and from the development in police cars rather than windowless police wagons. The next day, the group met with Cook County states attorney John Gutnecht and his first assistant but left this meeting less assured than when they met with O'Connor.

Broadening the base of support for the branch's housing campaign, Cora Patton took the cause of Trumbull Park and open housing in general to the NAACP's national conclave in Dallas, Texas. Describing the situation in Chicago, Patton pleaded: "It is inconceivable that we will be able to destroy segregation in the most hostile backward sections of the Jim Crow South until we can defeat it in a northern metropolis like Chicago."[25] A resolution condemning the discrimination against the besieged black families of Trumbull Park finally reached the floor of the national conclave. The Chicago delegation then met in special session with Walter White and Thurgood Marshall, pressing them for more vigorous action at the national level. Within weeks, White wired U.S. Attorney General Brownell that "if the Trumbull Park affair gets out of hand it will develop into another Cicero."[26]

Once back in Chicago, Patton bolstered the branch's campaign by assigning to three lawyers from the Legal Redress Committee the task of vigorously pursuing civil suits for damages against both civilians and policemen who abused black residents. One attorney handled civil suits against individual citizens; another pursued legal action against places of public accommodation in the neighborhood that practiced discrimination; and the third focused on policemen who failed to do their duty out of sympathy for the mob. The complaints from black residents varied, ranging from that of one lady who was attacked by a white woman wielding an umbrella outside a Catholic Church after mass, to that of a man who was denied service at a neighborhood liquor store. It was at this point that branch leaders also became the official spokesmen for the residents. The branch immediately issued a press release explaining to the city at large that the black residents of Trumbull Park would under no circumstances be intimidated or moved from what they now considered to be their homes.[27]

In the third year of the crisis, in 1955, much of the tension dissipated but there was still the matter of final resolution. To this end, the branch intensified its efforts in the political sphere by pressing for a just and final arrangement to the lingering crisis, which was now envisioned as part of a larger scenario of racial discrimination throughout public housing as well as in the private sector. The upcoming mayoral primary offered an excellent opportunity for pressure group activities, so the branch sponsored a rally on February 6, 1955, to question candidates on the pressing civil rights issues of the day. Participating were two of the Democratic Party's most popular ethnic candidates, Richard J. Daley and Benjamin S. Adamowski, along with Robert E. Merriam, the WASP Republican candidate. All announced their support for an open city with regard to residency as well as backing for fair employment practices.

Daley was the eventual winner, and in July he made good on some of his campaign promises by appointing a twenty-four-member Emergency Committee on Community Welfare to investigate the Trumbull Park situation and other contentious interracial situations. The committee was representative of the influential men of the city and included three blacks—John Sengstacke of the *Chicago Defender,* Claude A. Barnett of the Associated Negro Press, and Robert Taylor of the CHA. While this committee was being organized, the branch questioned four of the five black aldermen as to their stand on support for an all-city citizens watchdog committee for civil rights. President Cora Patton articulated the branch's position and determination at this point: "It cannot be considered solved until you and your families can walk down the streets in peace; can pray in your church together with your family; can participate in PTA and other community activities as other parents and citizens [do]; and can be at home without a background of exploding bombs."[28]

Additional pressure from Chicago was also directed toward the national office. Chicagoans were overwhelmed and admitted it. Assistance came in the form of constant, informative written responses, and, most importantly, of regular visits of Madison S. Jones, the newly appointed specialist on housing. By late July, Thurgood Marshall had arrived in the city, consulted with branch leaders, and returned to New York to meet with Walter White while the national executive secretary was planning a fall meeting with influential Chicagoans.

Many blacks who were conscious of conditions in the South referred to Trumbull Park as a "Little Mississippi."[29] As a response, Abner led anywhere from 200 to 4,000 demonstrators (depending on the source) around City Hall in peaceful picketing and forced the mayor to flee inconspicuously through an uncovered street exit.[30] Unknown to most demonstrators and bystanders, 120 additional policemen were in place in the event trouble should ensue. The NAACP demonstrators, denouncing racism, clearly embarrassed Daley, and the episode chagrined the ultramoderate Dawson,who usually eschewed overt confrontations with whites.

By the end of the year, the branch declared victory. Abner met with Commissioner O'Connor again and the latter declared the Trumbull Park area secure. Blacks now walked the streets of the development without police protection and rode to and from home in vehicles other than police cars. Willoughby Abner was satisfied with the progress and considered "this action [as] the first step forward in the process of securing full exercise of their civil rights by the Negro tenants in Trumbull Park."[31] Tensions lessened and whenever Trumbull Park was mentioned in branch meetings and correspondence, it appeared as part of the broader question of how to integrate all of the city's public housing.

Whereas the crisis at Trumbull Park grabbed headlines, along with draining the branch's energy and finances, the problem of public housing, which was in itself egregious, still represented only a small part of the problem of open residency. Only 1 to 2 percent of the city's total housing stock was under the control of the CHA. Nonetheless, the effort to tackle discrimination was important and intensive. The CHA had over 12,000 apartments under its control and projected a total of 20,000 by 1960. Of the three factors determining eligibility for these units, race supposedly played no part. Clearance priority, veteran's preference, and registration number were officially and legally the sole determinants. In practice, however, one report confirmed that "until the recent past, race ha[d] been used by the CHA as a major selector among applicants." As a result there were all-black, all-white, and a few mixed projects. On the West Side, all-black Robert Brooks Homes on Roosevelt Road was located directly across the street from virtually all-white Jane Addams Homes. At the Lathrop, Bridgeport, and Lawndale Homes, as well as at Trumbull Park Homes until 1953, only whites qualified for housing.

A report on the situation at the CHA, possibly prepared for the branch, summarized the situation as follows: "The policy and practice of a quota on Negro families or of maximizing white families in occupancy involved the by-passing of many Negro families with slum clearance and/or veterans' priority with low registration numbers in favor of non-priority white families who had recently registered. It involved keeping many apartments in existing projects vacant for extended periods until white occupants could be secured. It involved delaying total occupancy of new projects, located in Negro communities, until a significant proportion of white families had moved in. It involved the application of lower standards of desirability for white families than for Negro families."[32]

The argument for endorsing a policy of integration as opposed to one that was color-blind was very complex and filled with contradictions. Should integration, with artificial restraints, exist and give the city a demonstrable example that racial coexistence was possible? Or should a color-blind policy be followed that would inevitably result in a virtually all-black CHA and resegregation due to the impoverished condition of large numbers of blacks? A sixty-percent black occupancy rate in the mid–1950s was estimated to grow to eighty or ninety percent with this policy.

What the future brought illustrated that the eventual acceptance of the latter position produced a more abject resegregation than was ever imaginable.

The deep-rooted feelings of racial hostility in the city, coupled with the trouble in Trumbull Park, served notice to bigots that other such forms of antisocial thought and behavior were permissible. As a result, a vicious race riot erupted in the vicinity of Trumbull Park Homes in the recreational area of nearby Calumet Park in July 1957. To the city's embarrassment, the racial explosion in Chicago was publicized in the national news wires and newspapers as an example of how the city failed to curb racial violence. *U.S. News & World Report* was quick to attribute the violence to the pressure cooker of housing.[33] Apprehensions of major, widescale confrontation were such that additional policemen were sent to nearby Trumbull Park just in case trouble flared.

The branch responded to Calumet Park as it did to all incidents during this period of program activism. A mass meeting was held in Washington Park, but on this occasion, Abner was unable to attend. Instead, under a banner reading "Remember Trumbull Park," the Rev. Morris Tyne read Abner's prepared statement to the crowd. The words of Abner struck a sober note to those in attendance. He called on the city to spend as much time in a campaign of bettering race relations, a "Make Chicago Democratic" campaign, as it did on "Make Chicago Beautiful." Additionally, he called for immediate public hearings on the disturbances, put officials on notice that the branch would be closely monitoring their activities on this matter, demanded beefed-up police protection, and promised a return to the picnic site before winter began.[34]

The Chicago NAACP's concern for equality of educational opportunities ranked secondary only to housing as a major program issue. On May 17, 1954, the dream of three generations reached a level of fulfillment. In *Brown v. The Topeka, Kansas Board of Education,* the high court ruled that the legal foundation of national Jim Crow for fifty-eight years, the "separate but equal" doctrine, was unconstitutional in public education, and, by logical extension, in all other forms of public accommodation.[35]

Following the 1954 U.S. Supreme Court's outlawing of legalized school segregation in the southern and border states, the expectations of Chicagoans for fairness in the city's schools soared. Black Chicagoans scanned the segregated American educational landscape and were appalled to see some of the same vestiges of injustice occurring locally. The high expectations did not translate automatically into program and policy, so the branch's stance on the issue evolved throughout the remainder of the decade and into the next. At the time of the *Brown* decision, branch reports on education took on an optimistic tone, bordering almost on naiveté. One branch report read: "It is our understanding that the Board of Education

hopes to end double shifts next year but that present plans are not sufficient for possible future population changes. We know that Superintendent Willis is making a thorough analysis of the statistics to avoid the
double shift in the future."[36]

Under scrutiny, the contemporary scenario offered little grounds for
optimism. Over 10,000 black children attended school in basically all-
black neighborhoods on a double shift while vacant classrooms were
available in adjacent all-white neighborhoods. With 11,000 new students
entering the system annually, the problem demanded, but did not receive,
an instant remedy. The branch still focused its interest on the "mental
segregation" that racially biased textbooks inflicted on the well-being of
the city's school children. It reasoned that if knowledge of brown-skinned
Jean Baptist Pointe Du Sable's contribution to the city as its first permanent
non-white settler were made available, racial pride among black students
and a greater awareness of black accomplishment among white children
would result in better race relations.

With the 1954 *Brown* decision, the pace for racial equality quickened
everywhere in the nation. In Chicago, what the branch needed was an
updated policy and a relevant program. The branch acknowledged that
there were predominantly black schools in the city that prepared students
adequately and met the highest academic standards. However, this was
not the case system-wide; *Freedom's Call*, the branch's monthly organ,
argued "that in spite of the many fine schools attended by Negro children
. . . for the average Negro pupil the facilities were not the same as those
available for the average white student. . . . The most serious inequality is
the crowded classroom and the double shift school."[37]

The branch launched its major effort in education against this particular, local problem of racial inequality, which was quite different from the
southern problem except in consequence. Also, unlike in the South, the
nature of this inequality had neither been properly examined nor categorized and labeled. This became the task of the Education Committee, still
steadfastly headed by Faith Rich. By spring, the Education Committee
called for an investigation and survey of segregation and discrimination in
the Chicago schools in the scientific manner that Du Bois had found so
useful at the turn of the century. Cooperation and guidance from the
national office proved indispensable. The northern branches were told of
the successful modes used in New York City to battle educational inequality. New Yorkers even coined a new and fitting label for this practice—*de
facto* segregation. Chicago, encouraged and energized, was fast nearing
the development of an educational policy.

In addition to lobbying local bodies for educational change, the branch
brought pressure to bear at the state and national levels on government
which had not moved toward the implementation of fair educational

policies. The branch made a plea for citizen support of a $50 million bond issue to help all schools while it petitioned the Illinois congressional delegation to vote in favor of the Powell Amendment, a legislative rider which banned the use of federal funds in school districts where there was noncompliance with the 1954 Supreme Court decision. Ominously, Congressman William L. Dawson of the First District rejected this approach as perhaps helpful to blacks but detrimental overall to the interests of all Americans.

The painstaking work of gathering information on the schools proved difficult and frustrating for Faith Rich's small band of West Side unit investigators. When the Board of Education claimed that it lacked needed data on school enrollments and attendance by race, Rich responded by collecting the data through two creatively constructed networks. One was the PTA councils throughout the city into which she could tap because of previous contact. The other was the corps of white school engineers who gladly provided information to concerned fellow whites on the number of black students "invading" their schools. Very meticulously, the committee accumulated information on the racial character of the school system. In the meantime, the branch both probed and planned, anticipating the day when it could act decisively. Contact was made with the Board of Education to determine how it spent the taxpayers' money while overcrowding ran rampant. And by August and October 1956, the branch's second annual planning session and conference on education, respectively, were convened.

Resolution still proved elusive. Exactly one year later, in August 1957, Willoughby Abner reported his conclusions: "We have seen that in Chicago and New York the tangible factors of experienced teachers and small schools and classes are not equal between the races; and the march of the Negro educational ghetto continues unbroken by any plan for integration."[38] Branch leaders neglected to ask one major question—to what extent black parents, some of whom were branch members and leaders, wanted quality education in their own neighborhoods even if integration were not achieved. Myrtle Brooks, member of the Women's Auxiliary and wife of board member (and future president) Albert Brooks, recalled that her major concern was overcrowding and the harmful effect it was having on their two children at the Willard School. The Brookses desired a quality education for their children in whatever school they attended.[39]

As fall began, Rich and her workers completed their work on the school system and released their study, "De Facto Segregation in the Chicago Public Schools." The study analyzed school size and determined that a great disparity existed: the average all-white school enrollment was 669 pupils; the average mixed school had 947 students; and the average size of an all-black school was an outrageous 1,275 pupils. Of 22,462 students suffering from double shifts, 81 percent were black. At this juncture Rich commented: "It is a nice point whether the school time lost to the Negro child is not almost as great in Chicago as it is in Mississippi." Countering the argument that housing segregation produced segregated neighborhood schools, the report demonstrated that high school districts with heterogeneous populations did not always have similarly composed student bodies.[40] The finger of guilt pointed squarely to the school board, which catered to white racial fears and presumptions of racial superiority to produce a dual school system in the city. With evidence in hand, the branch now moved to build a program around it while the nation read of the situation in *U.S. News & World Report*.[41]

By the end of the year the Executive Committee met and adopted the report in its entirety. From this point on, the branch's policy recommendations to the Chicago Board of Education were, first, to redistrict school boundaries to utilize available classrooms wherever they existed in disregard of race, and second, to transport students to the nearest school wherever they were located. The North Side unit of the NAACP added its weight to solving the school crisis by recommending to the board of education at its annual budget hearings that no new schools be built, but rather that old vacant ones be utilized fully. The Executive Committee examined and included this stand, which opposed new construction to perpetuate segregation, into its policy also. Finally, with a policy to guide it, the branch spent the rest of the decade trying to get the Chicago Board of Education to implement the changes it recommended.

In the middle of the prosperous 1950s, job discrimination hung over the city like a pall. The branch's 1954 Action Program called for "a vigorous campaign [to] be developed to break down employment discrimination in Chicago firms and business establishments such as stores, banks, and medical institutions. Special attention [is to] be directed against those locations in the Loop and those locations on the periphery of the so called 'Black Belt.'"[42] As could be expected, with the branch under labor control, it intensified its support of EJO. In 1955, Willoughby Abner spoke in Springfield as a representative of both the NAACP and organized labor. One branch campaign even began with a promise to obtain 100,000 signatures on petitions for equal opportunity. Yet job discrimination remained so pervasive that in 1955, 16 percent of all firms still refused to employ blacks at a time when black workers were streaming into the city at the rate of 1,000 per month. Worried about a charge of the Chicago NAACP's overaggressiveness, the national office challenged the branch's methods, no doubt overlooking its cooperative activities with allied groups in the state capital.[43] Notwithstanding the inquiry, the branch cooperated with liberal groups as diverse as the League of Women Voters, the American Jewish Council, the Chicago Council of Negro Organizations, the Catholic

Interracial Council, the Japanese-American Citizens League, the ACLU, and organized labor in pursuit of economic civil rights.

Opposition was formidable. The vast network of manufacturers that dominated the economy of the state represented the major obstacle to equal opportunity in the workplace. Allied with the Illinois Republican Party, this formidable set of adversaries consistently blocked passage of fair employment codes until 1961. Their motivation was a combination of racism and a conservative dislike of governmental interference, which they turned into a strategy of effective obstructionism. Since Republican governor William Stratton acted in accordance with this party's dictates in helping to stymie passage of legislation, the branch threatened him with political retaliation on more than one occasion. This gesture proved futile given the growing support of blacks for the Democratic Party. But if the branch could not punish the governor, it could at least criticize him as it did during his visit to the Soviet Union after promising support for EJO among Republican state senators. A sarcastic branch press release read: "We hope he can explain to the Russians why his state failed to pass a law guaranteeing the right of nearly a million citizens to obtain work."[44]

Additionally, the comprehensive branch program included expanding the base of adequate, accessible health care in Chicago. Pervasive discrimination was the rule throughout the city. Some hospitals excluded blacks altogether, while others segregated the few that were admitted. "Few hospitals had Negro physicians on their staffs . . . [acting] fairly was Michael Reese, a Jewish-run hospital of 908 beds on the edge of the Negro slum," cited Banfield in *Political Influence*. "There, Negroes comprised 15–25 per cent of all patients, and a number of colored physicians were staff members."[45] Candidates for public office in 1955 faced the branch's inquiry as to their positions on a proposed amendment to the Chicago Municipal Code to ban discrimination in hospital service. Outside the city, the branch worked with state legislators to produce a law banning discrimination in area hospitals.

Nestled under the umbrella of the Chicago NAACP's Council of Organizations (later transformed into the NAACP Civil Rights Legislative Council) in 1955 was the Committee to End Discrimination in Medical Institutions. Well-known integrationists and liberals such as Earl B. Dickerson, the Rev. Homer Jack, Percy Julian, and Drs. Quentin Young, Ruth Lerner, and A. M. Mercer worked to implement the committee's six-point program, which included a ban on racial discrimination in all area hospitals. The Council's chair, Gerald D. Bullock, belonged to Willoughby Abner's inner circle.

A proposal by the Cook County Board to build a South Side branch hospital to replace the central public facility, the West Side's Cook County Hospital, brought up a recurring dilemma. Probably the last concern of the commissioners on the board was race, their focus being economy and overcrowding. But to blacks, a dichotomous set of concerns existed. Civil rights advocates adhered to the principle of securing "a whole loaf"— unfettered access to medical facilities throughout the Chicagoland area for both patients and physicians irrespective of race—or "no loaf"—meaning that they uncompromisingly opposed a desperately needed branch hospital for the South Side if it meant racial segregation.

The need for any type of hospital facility in the midst of the health crisis gripping Bronzeville dictated either organizational silence in opposition or open support for a pressing need of the black masses. The Chicago Urban League opposed the hospital branch openly on the grounds that it fostered racial segregation while the *Chicago Defender* covertly supported it because of community need. The branch's position paralleled that of the Dawson machine but emanated from a different starting point. Promoting the "status" interests of the branch's leadership and part of its membership dictated that integrated health care and professional opportunities for black physicians take precedence, at least theoretically, over the necessity of building a facility in the heart of Bronzeville. The branch, despite its commitment to enforcing a ban on hospital discrimination, remained silent on the branch hospital. The absence of any documentation on this issue in *The NAACP Papers* coupled with an abundance of information on the anti-discrimination campaign in medical facilities, locally and statewide, tends to indicate a deliberate silence. Meeting the desires of the bulk of the branch's membership (which coincided with the desperate needs of Bronzeville's masses) required vocal support for the medical facility. Barring that, silence seemed appropriate. Dawson was also deliberately silent, either out of deference to the wishes of Cook County Board of Commissioners president Daniel Ryan,[46] a powerhouse among county Democrats, or because patronage was involved, and the status quo was preferable to job losses.

Discrimination in public accommodations continued to be a recurring problem for African Americans, with restaurants regularly refusing service to blacks who sought it either alone or as part of racially mixed groups. Branch cooperation with other groups grew as the Japanese American Citizens League accompanied the branch to court in 1957 to protest a denial to public accommodations based on race. Likewise, instances and complaints of police brutality never ceased. The Chicago Police Department's reputation for acting like antebellum-era patrollers continued as officers enforced discipline and instilled fear of white authority among the descendants of slaves. Around the time the Calumet Park riot took place, the branch was flooded with complaints about harassment of black motorists and pedestrians by the special crime task force, dubbed the "Flying Squad."[47] Racist policemen even claimed Archie L. Weaver's grandson as a victim. Yet, Attorney Robert Ming's response moved beyond indignation and protest to preparing more African Americans for leadership roles on the police force. With this plan, the branch undertook the training of police officers for the sergeants' exams in 1957.

Events taking place outside Chicago also fell within the branch's purview. Perhaps no event provoked so much passion and so many calls for activism during the period as the killing of fourteen-year-old Chicagoan Emmett Till in 1955 near Money, Mississippi. Till was visiting relatives for the summer and ran afoul of Mississippi's racist taboos as he was kidnapped and lynched for an allegedly flirtatious remark made to a white woman. Till's body was fished from the Tallahatchie River after over a week—bloated and decayed. Once Till's remains were returned to Chicago, near riots ensued in and around the South Side funeral home where he lay at rest. On the streets of Chicago, indignation regrettably gave way to hostility and acts of violence aimed at whites.

The murder became another international *cause célèbre*, both embarrassing the nation and positioning the branch to lead the city in protesting to the federal government. The lawyer who handled the Till family's affairs in Chicago was Henry W. Huff, veteran fighter against southern racism and now the chairman of the branch's Legal Redress Committee. Huff still remained the expert in extradition cases and served several Southerners who had fled southern oppression. As to the Till case, protest meetings followed during which the branch demanded that federal troops occupy Mississippi while the U.S. government assumed control over the affairs of state government.[48] Meanwhile, Willoughby Abner had already suffered through Dawson's silence in 1955 in the aftermath of the Till murder and on matters concerning education and housing discrimination, but this action proved to be the breaking point, and the Abner faction openly denounced Dawson's seeming cowardice in failing to act in behalf of their race's interests.[49]

Late in the same year that Emmett Till was killed, the African Americans of Montgomery, Alabama, began a successful boycott of that city's bus lines. Chicagoans tried to do their part by following the lead of Willoughby Abner, Charles Hayes, and the Rev. A. Lincoln James, who went directly to the Chicago headquarters of the National City Lines to register their protest by sending money to the Montgomery Movement or by pressuring National City Lines through an extensive letter writing campaign to all of its subsidiaries. More dramatic, though, was the rally held at the Chicago coliseum on April 11, 1956, which featured Montgomery's Rev. Ralph David Abernathy and the Association's Roy Wilkins. The meeting attracted a large crowd and raised $2,500 in support of the boycott.

The network of branches continued to prove that their combined strength worked as an effective force in confronting racism. This interregional network provided Thurgood Marshall with the opportunity to exhort Chicagoans at the annual Freedom Fund Dinner "to fight just as hard for civil rights here as they're fighting in the South."[50] With relatives in the South and Chicagoans regularly visiting them, Jim Crow transportation arrangements were targeted for elimination by the branch. Blacks were routinely forced to switch train cars when they reached Memphis heading south and this affront was challenged throughout the decade. Early in the decade, attorney George N. Leighton scored a legal "first" in this battle by appearing as a party in a suit against the Illinois Central Railroad. Then, later in the decade, the branch enthusiastically supported the Association's "Bundles for the South," an effort that provided needed foodstuffs and clothing for black Southerners in need due to their resistance to racism.

As Abner prepared to campaign for a third successive term in office in 1957, his supporters lauded his achievements: "In the two years that Mr. Abner has served as president, the Chicago Branch has engaged in more programs, become involved in more activities and initiated more projects than in any comparable period.... We who have worked with [him] ... can attest to his courageous and forceful leadership in all aspects of the civil rights struggle."[51] Most importantly, the dream of A. C. MacNeal in 1933 of the Chicago NAACP's becoming "a necessity" in the lives of black Chicagoans had been realized.

In terms of both harmony and disharmony the tenuous relationship between the black civic and political spheres unfolded predictably. Early in the decade, the altered character of civic protest (operating within an environment shaped by a political liberalism counteracting conservatism, and a burgeoning economy) resulted in escalating tensions between the races and within the civic-political association. Harmonious relations between the black civic and political worlds were the rule until the Dawson-Abner confrontation of 1957. Several examples are notable. The joint chairmanship of the 1952 annual membership drive was shared by the aldermen from the Second and Third Wards, Democrat William Harvey and Republican Archibald J. Carey, Jr., respectively. The reclusive Congressman Dawson appeared at the 1954 mass rally in behalf of justice at Trumbull Park; speaking before a mass assemblage, he urged the group to vote out of office any politician who did not serve black interests. His target was plainly Mayor Kennelly, who he blocked from getting party reslating for a third term in 1955. The mayor, for his part, gave evidence of indifference toward the responsibility of chasing down the housing terrorists who bullied blacks citywide, while showing zeal for ridding the South Side of its legendary illegal gambling operations, especially policy operations. Policy, as a financial resource, provided Bronzeville's political machine with an independent funding base, free of interference from the Irish-dominated Democratic Party of Chicago and Cook County.

Based on decisive black support in 1955, Richard J. Daley triumphed in his first campaign as mayor. A congenial, mutually supportive relationship between blacks and the mayor initially appeared possible. Optimism grew, based on Daley's reputation for racial fairness stemming from his actions in the General Assembly in the 1940s as well as from the fact that Daley owed black voters repayment for their support in his recent election.[52] Perhaps the high point in branch enthusiasm for the mayor followed issuance of a proclamation declaring May 29, 1958, "NAACP Tag Day." Volunteers on street corners sold NAACP tags to passersby on a citywide rather than sectional (South Side) basis. Daley's recognition of the effort represented an acknowledgment of the legitimacy of both the Chicago NAACP and its pursuit of racial justice. Aware of its news value, the national office of the NAACP directed its chief of publicity to maximize the issuance of the mayor's proclamation.[53]

At this early juncture of the decade, the branch invited the leading Republican and Democratic candidates to a 1952 fund-raiser which attorney Robert Ming considered an especially appropriate signal of cooperation. Then, carefully avoiding any reference to the debacle that involvement in the 1948 national elections had produced, George Leighton wrote to Walter White that "Chicago was [destined to be] the pivotal point of this [1952] election year. [The Executive Committee wanted to be active and] influence the thinking of liberal minded citizens . . . [in support of] progressive provisions in the planks of the two major parties."[54] Continuing to walk a tightrope of nonpartisanship in 1954, the branch queried potential judicial candidates as to their stands on racial justice before the bench. The branch hosted a community forum during the next year at which all of the leading candidates for mayor, including Daley, were questioned about their support of equal rights. Prospective council members from the South Side received questionnaires about their positions on six important civil rights issues, including housing, education, and access to medical care.

The deleterious influence of partisan politics continued to deprive the branch, however, of its volunteers at campaign time and subjected the organization's name to misuse. In 1952, a combination of internal friction and national politics adversely affected the branch's fall membership drive.[55] Gertrude Gorman, who succeeded Daisy E. Lampkin as regional secretary, wrote: "Due again to the election many of our best workers will not be able to do anything for the NAACP until after November 6."[56] As the branch reached institutional status and rose to prominence along with the national body, the organization's famous initials were subject to misuse. In 1957, one candidate for the State Senate who lacked either branch or national affiliation distributed flyers that read "The National Assn for the Advancement of Colored People Asks Your Support for the Election of Michael Hunt." The flyer was signed by a fictitious "J. R. Evans, Director, N.A.A.C.P."[57] The branch quickly disavowed any link to this printed material.

After having achieved institutional status because of its aggressive programmatic and organizational activities, the branch conformed to

Hanes Walton Jr.'s model of NAACP branches as dynamic forces within the political sphere.[58] As a pressure group, the Chicago NAACP expanded its efforts to change the character of race relations locally and in support of southern blacks. The branch evolved beyond pressure-group activities into a quasi-political organization, a shadow political body with the potential to do for black citizens that which its elected officials, such as Dawson, could not or would not do. The tactics of protest advocacy became more stringent, more demanding on the total society, and more confrontational. The call for mass demonstrations, mass meetings, and massive letter-writing campaigns, coupled with the branch's propaganda and informational barrage, raised the public awareness, by 1954, of the contradictions between what the polity was supposed to do and what it actually accomplished in behalf of citizens. One such meeting was described in this manner: "The mass meeting which is being supported by numerous civic and community organizations will launch a campaign for the passage by the 69th Illinois General Assembly of a 6 point legislative program to combat segregation and discrimination in Illinois."[59] Abner attacked both Dawson and the Daley machine with which he collaborated. He was vehemently opposed to machine politics, on principle and in practice, since it stifled any real expression of black aspirations.

Well-organized protest advocacy required extensive citizen involvement, so the method of organization resembled a pyramidal structure, relying on cohesion at its basic level, the political precinct. Along with churches, unions, civic and social clubs, and neighborhood groups—the citywide units (North Side, Hyde Park, and West Side) planned to galvanize a new level of activist protest. Using surveys, questionnaires, and telephone inquiries, the branch members discovered they were intimidating machine politicians accustomed to dealing with a passive public.

The targets of protest were governmental agencies and officials at all levels—local, state, and national. Although lobbying at the national level was left mainly in the hands of New Yorkers and the Washington NAACP bureau, the branch supported the national calls enthusiastically and on occasions, in the tradition of Chicago, initiated high profile protest independently as it had done with Trumbull Park and the Till murder case. The branch also supported the national office's voter registration campaign but added a twist of its own. In contrast to the Dawson machine, which relied on a small, controlled vote, the branch appealed " for a record turnout of Negro and liberal white voters in the 1956 primary election." Abner also used the poignancy of a Southern appeal to spur voters. He wrote: "Negro citizens . . . many of whom fled north from the terror and violence that is so bravely being resisted in the South today, should be the last to take for granted the right to vote. . . . Cast your ballot to help win freedom for your brothers in the South." He continued: "An outpouring of voters will serve as a warning to all politicians, that Negro and white liberal citizens of the north want action, not words."[60] Later that year, the branch mailed out tens of thousands of its monthly organ, *Freedom's Call*, which included useful information to be used as guidelines for evaluating the two parties. Dawson recognized a threat when he saw it and explained his position: "I don't think that a civil rights organization should be used as a political platform. I feel that a volunteer association that is agitating for *certain* [emphasis added] civil rights goals is, in effect, tampering with politics."[61]

In many aspects, the Dawson-Abner confrontation of the mid–1950s was a replay of the Du Bois–Washington dichotomy of 1903–1915, with differences of personality, public image, tactics, strategy, and political orientation assuming the same importance as they had assumed in earlier times. The answer to the question as to why there was a gulf between the two men and their movements lay in different constituent perceptions reflecting their disparate economic needs, statuses, and strivings. Analyzing black politicians who appealed to a predominantly working-class electorate, Banfield and Wilson wrote in *City Politics* that "matters involving Negro rights in the abstract do not interest them, however. These concern militants, but they are not the base upon which the machine builds."[62] In *Negro Politics*, Wilson diagnosed Dawson's approach similarly and explained that Dawson led the fight to obtain the basic need of jobs, housing, favors, and privileges essential to improve the socioeconomic well-being of the masses, while Abner directed an organization which pursued the status goal of integration, along with some basic needs, which appealed to a more highly mobile group of individuals.

Dawson, as a machine leader, was "mindful of the fact that he [was] a Negro, elected largely by Negroes, and must keep tending the fires of [mass] Negro interest, [so he never completely abandoned racial politics]."[63] Dawson's power and influence lay in his control over his political appointees, his large electoral bloc, and the personal loyalty from admirers among the masses and middle class who had received major to minor considerations over the previous two decades. To the average resident of racially proscribed Bronzeville, being the recipient of concessions in the form of a job or a promotion often became more important than improving the overall life chances of the entirety of Bronzeville. Dawson saw this desire for individual as well as group material advancement as part of the conditions as they existed. He was incapable, by temperament and experience, of delivering a vision of what could be. Abner's power lay in his principled, uncompromising approach and in an awareness of the need to harness the dynamic forces of change in order to construct a better future. He saw a threshold which afforded progress and which could not be ignored if one of those prized moments of history, when the ultimate in opportunity appeared, was to be exploited. Contemporarily, some of his detractors labeled his thoughts and actions in a different light, seeing them as either masking his clear political designs on Dawson's congressional seat, or as aiming at establishing dominion over Bronzeville.[64]

Meanwhile, citywide, major political and governmental change ensued with Richard J. Daley's ascendancy in 1955. All city and county patronage and favors were being centralized under Daley's control. He followed a personal agenda that allied him with the city's corporate leadership for decades to come. His dictum was encapsulated in his slogan, "good government is good politics." Restructuring the delivery of the machine's largesse as well as endorsing and appointing professionally qualified, "blue ribbon" candidates for high office instead of party loyalists served to undermine committeemen throughout the city. In Bronzeville, Second Ward committeeman Dawson seethed at this arrangement, which seriously compromised his power as the Daley years progressed.

This study, however, is fundamentally concerned with the Daley-Dawson relationship only until 1957, and therefore focuses on Dawson at a time when he was basically free of irresistible pressures from an external locus of power. And during this period Dawson's organization was at its peak of political efficiency. For a generation of political science researchers primarily coming of age after Wilson's contemporary work on Dawson was published in 1960, the congressman was a product of post–World War II racial politics whose claims to power were exaggerated. These conclusions question the extent to which Dawson had any influence or bargaining power at all, given the hegemony of the Democratic machine which carefully cultivated subordination from its racial and ethnic lieutenants.[65]

Without a doubt, by 1959 Dawson had to comply to City Hall directives when Daley won reelection and controlled the patronage and privileges of forty-seven of the city's fifty aldermen. One incident was especially pertinent to illustrate this impending drain on Dawson's influence. At the time Dawson was preparing to confront militant blacks, he was faced with a direct threat to his political power from within the Democratic hierarchy. Political scientist William Grimshaw's account of this pivotal event places it in 1958 when Dawson bloc alderman Claude Holman agreed to support an open occupancy ordinance because it was ostensibly the correct civic response to his constituents' needs. Politically, it was advantageous to Holman since it embarrassed Dawson by exposing the latter's compromising, moderate stance. Holman achieved this independent action over Dawson's objection because the latter was unable to punish him. The centralization underway within the Democratic Party under Daley's leadership allowed Holman to reverse himself the next year but he did so because of Daley's inducements rather than Dawson's threats.[66]

Yet as concerned as Daley was about black South Side politics as part of his citywide plan of centralization, he played no part in the Dawson-Abner conflict. Dawson and Abner were on a collision course based on which direction black Chicago would take for racial advancement. In addition, Charles S. Stone observed that many blacks viewed Abner "as the rightful successor to Dawson in the new era of black awareness."[67] At this time, the country was becoming more aware of Dawson's acceptance of a philosophy of accommodation to power, and *The Nation* assessed his politics as follows: "The emphasis for years—right through the New Deal—has been on concrete economic and social benefits rather than political 'equality' which superficially, at least, seems absurd. Voting for a man or party who adheres to fine sentiments on civil rights is a political luxury; voting for a man whose power is useful for bread and butter advantages is a necessity."[68] Experientially, more so than his younger detractors with their northern regional focus, Dawson had witnessed the results of political powerlessness as a youngster in his native Georgia, and it affected him deeply. An observer remarked: "He remembered when the school for Negro children was open only when they weren't needed in the fields." Accordingly, he sought to be a major player in the sphere of power politics to the greatest extent that a black man could hope for in the 1940s and 1950s. "As Dawson saw the problem . . . then . . . the Negro's only hope was through [involvement in] the white political structure. A half loaf . . . if need be. . . . The alternative? Further and deeper inequality and oppression."[69]

Dawson did have a civil rights philosophy and it was promoted, but usually quietly as men of influence often do. Two examples illustrate this fact. In 1956, the congressman blocked an attempt in the District of Columbia to slow integration from within the Congress. Georgia representative James A. Davis tried to undermine school integration by investigating his claim that it produced "racial mongrelization." Dawson went to the law books and dug up an obscure ruling that found the existence of Davis's committee to be illegal since Congress was not in session. Against House Speaker Rayburn's advice, Dawson personally marched into the hearing and dispersed the group. By 1961, he would speak impassionedly in one of his rare appearances on the floor to denounce the Winstead Amendment, which favored resegregation of the armed services.[70]

Dawson also strongly rejected the label "Uncle Tom." In defense of his position, he elaborated: "Yes, they called Booker T. an Uncle Tom. They said he was a detriment to the race and a traitor. But today the bust of Booker T. Washington is displayed in the Hall of Fame. Congress has just approved an appropriation to help preserve his birthplace for posterity while the names of his detractors have long since been forgotten. . . . Yes, there are many ways to fight for civil rights, I have mine and they have theirs."[71] It was in this ideological context that Dawson felt justified in 1956 in voting against Congressman Adam Clayton Powell's amendment outlawing federal funds used for discriminatory purposes. Political scientist Charles V. Hamilton's biography of Powell showed how the Harlem congressman's use of his blocking amendment could frustrate even white civil rights allies both inside and outside the Congress.[72]

Unlike Booker T. Washington, Dawson neither catered obsequiously to nor sought favor with white political, corporate, and civic leaders. As to the latter two categories of white leadership, Dawson distrusted them both as self-serving power brokers for corporate Chicago and as white men. Wilson interviewed Dawson on the subject; the congressman stated: "I won't break bread with them. They invite me to big dinners and the like. I won't go. Why should I? I know what they want from me. I don't need a meal from them, and I am not flattered by their company."[73] If categorizing of political action and thought is essential, Dawson is best understood, then, as one among many types of moderates on race. He was no conservative, obviously having nothing to conserve as a member of a proscribed group; but he personally and politically saw little value in direct confrontation which to this point had not accomplished racial change. In his own eyes and those of a substantial number of black Chicagoans, Dawson appeared to be moving the black racial agenda appreciably forward. A contemporary remarked: "One of Dawson's supporters, a brilliant attorney who ha[d] served as a[n] assistant states attorney, explained his loyalty: 'I have never seen a political decision that Dawson made that he did not regard as in the public interest of the American Negro.'"[74] As to tactics, the "Old Man" preferred negotiating and bargaining and, as could be expected, opposed public, high-powered, flamboyant activism.

Scholars and journalists have been quick to compare Dawson with Harlem's Adam Clayton Powell, who in his rhetoric more than in his actions made militancy seem equatable with effectiveness and consistency in behalf of civil rights.[75] Powell has also been revealed as a politician who could compromise the cause of civil rights to suit his own needs and interests. Powell demonstrated these proclivities when he unexpectedly backed down from criticizing American racial policy during the Bandung Conference in 1954; firmly backed Republican President Eisenhower in 1956 for reelection; and slowed down civil rights legislation through his own egotism and inattentiveness during his watch as a congressional protector of civil rights.[76]

Ironically, by the fall of 1957, formidable opposition to Abner mounted within the branch. Earl B. Dickerson moved openly to replace him, a turn of events with significance because of Dickerson's status as a civic kingpin.[77] Abner for his part started to exhibit less and less of his usual enthusiasm for campaigning. Gertrude Gorman described him: "[He acts] like Ike; he feels that he will not be able to succeed himself. He will not take speaking engagements and if he does he will cancel them at the last minute."[78] In a wearying pre-election campaign that was waged throughout the white and black media, in meetings halls, and on street corners, Abner was accused of running a dictatorship. He was even charged with deliberately antagonizing state and city officials. His retort to this charge and to one alleging that he was becoming a dictator was clear and defiant: "I make no unilateral decisions. My actions are always approved by the board."[79]

Archie L. Weaver believed that Abner and his supporters were caught off balance by the growing intensity of the opposition. So, when the nominating meeting was held in November, they were ill equipped to defend their turf. Abner's challenger was businessman Theodore A. Jones, who had been a protégé of Earl B. Dickerson at the FEPC during the war and at the mammoth Supreme Life Insurance Company in the 1950s, which at that time anchored the north end of Bronzeville both financially and spatially. Jones became Dickerson's third choice of the decade to lead the branch because Dickerson envisioned him as a president who would pursue a prudent course that was both a rational and an effective means to change the racial status quo.

Jones had grown up in Chicago, experienced racial injustice, and had become determined early to do everything in his power to bring about change compatible with his beliefs and training.[80] Taking advantage of every opportunity that a changing American society offered, Jones was graduated from the University of Illinois with an accounting degree. Significantly, Jones's candidacy pleased Dawson because of his moderate, businesslike approach. Moreover, Jones maintained close ties with the leaders of Bronzeville's business and political interests of which Congressman William L. Dawson was an indisputable protector.

Abner lay ill during the month of December, but may in fact have sensed that a broad-based counteroffensive was afoot to dislodge him. The magnitude of the opposition would have stunned him had he been aware of its formidability. The national office, the neo-patricians led by Dickerson, and traditional labor allied themselves with some of Abner's erstwhile supporters. In this world of shifting alliances, Weaver ran as an Abner delegate, solely to protect the moderate position if Abner were to be reelected. He confided afterwards to Gloster B. Current in New York, however, that he voted for the Jones slate.[81]

Dawson's response to Abner's challenge on the appropriate means and timing for racial advancement came on Friday evening, December 13, 1957, at the NAACP annual election of officers. That fateful evening started out as routine for many of the first few persons who filed into the Du Sable High School auditorium in the heart of Bronzeville. Some early arrivers might or might not have anticipated that this year's annual election of officers for the Chicago branch of the NAACP would be contentious. Obviously, they hoped for exciting oratory and perhaps expected the machinations so common at recent branch elections. Several highly charged and significant questions hung in the air. How strong would incumbent President Willoughby Abner's forces be during this year's election, especially since there were rumors of a major attempt to unseat him? Would civic kingpin Earl B. Dickerson have enough support for his presidential choice, Supreme Life Insurance Company colleague Theodore A. Jones? Would the members of the Left, either Communist or Socialist Workers Party, stage a demonstration in protest of creeping reaction as they saw it? Just how large would the turnout be?

The auditorium filled quickly enough, with everyone who was upwardly mobile and included in the expanding galaxy of Bronzeville's stars in attendance. The assemblage swelled despite the temperature; it was a typically chilly Chicago Friday evening with a temperature in the twenties. Future judges, congressmen, business magnates, civic and political leaders were conspicuous by their presence. It was an hour into procedural business when future U.S. Congressman Augustus "Gus" Savage noticed that the hallway outside the auditorium was filled with political workers from the camp of Congressman Dawson, an unusual occurrence, to say the least. And the response that Savage got from one person to whom he spoke surprised him. Six hundred of Dawson's precinct workers had descended on the NAACP meeting. Their goal was simple—participate in the election as bona fide branch members of thirty days' standing and dislodge Abner, a bane to the congressman because of his militant, unceasing civil rights advocacy.[82]

The Rev. Archibald J. Carey, Jr., spoke eloquently in his denunciation of Abner whom he depicted as representing a threat from the Left to the branch's existence. Vociferous speeches followed in behalf of both candidates. But what was transpiring unknown to most regular NAACP branch members was a carefully orchestrated plot to overthrow Abner, his supporters, and all activist challengers to the racial status quo. Although Earl B. Dickerson had hand-picked Jones, the latter also represented Dawson's choice and even that of the Communists in attendance. What united these disparate groups (except for the Communists, who envied Abner's popular appeal to the masses) was the realization that Abner could lead the NAACP along the same course as that on which Sidney Williams had directed the Chicago Urban League—into organizational demise.[83]

As the voting concluded, the assemblage became acutely aware that an event of historical importance had transpired. With the ballots finally counted after midnight, Jones claimed victory. And from that day on, the Chicago NAACP would never again challenge the racial status quo to the extent that it did under Abner. Another future congressman confirmed this new fact involving Chicago power relationships. Charles Hayes recalled that "the invaders of the NAACP were elected to make certain that no one in the newly elected NAACP hierarchy or their successors would ever rock Daley's political boat. . . ."[84] For at least a generation to come, the long-term victor was a nonresident of Bronzeville—first-term mayor Richard J. Daley.

As it is sometimes popularly recalled in the lore of black Chicago, an alleged "political takeover" of the branch that night by Dawson's formidable organization culminated with the absorption of the branch into his political machine. However, there never was an actual takeover of the organization in the aftermath of the election. Dawson achieved his goal with incumbent branch president Willoughby Abner's ouster, so he did not interfere directly in its operations in the months and years that followed.

Despite its being an event of singular importance, this confrontation represented neither the beginning of the end, nor the organizational demise of the Chicago NAACP. Its significance lay in its relevance as evidence of organizational evolution. Appearing along a historical continuum, it showed both how far the branch had progressed since the dawn of the new century and how well equipped its leadership was by 1957 to further the NAACP mission, no matter what the opposition or consequences.

Congressman Dawson, now undisputed leader over the civic and political domains of Bronzeville, reflected on his action contemporarily to James Q. Wilson, who related that "the new president was not an agent of the machine; he was only an acceptable alternative to a thoroughly unacceptable leader."[85] Several years later Dawson confided to realtor Dempsey Travis, the branch's president in 1960, "I'm not interested in controlling the NAACP or its policy making body. However, I do want to see the 'right man' as president."[86]

Translating Dawson's explanation strategically and tactically, it dictated the scope and means civil rights activism would take in the city for years to come. Protest advocacy would continue, but it would be more moderate and less disruptive in the eyes of the leaders of the city's political economy as well as Bronzeville's. Yet, there was a level of acceptability to many blacks in what Dawson was asking, for they, like he, were moderates at heart. While not a black patriarchy, this group constituted the Bronzeville Establishment—middle class and elite, professionally inclined and moderate to the core. As Dawson's power over the South Side was subordinated more and more into Daley's citywide Democratic machine, Daley gained the means to weaken protest advocacy directly both within and outside the branch. Compromised completely because of this interorganizational struggle, the Chicago NAACP prepared to serve its constituents in the future without control either over its own destiny or that of racially progressive black Chicagoans.

The branch's successful implementation of its program positioned it to sustain its institutional status. To maintain this standing, the branch assumed a confrontational stance and sought situations that contributed to the successful accomplishment of its role. A clash with Dawson's political machine therefore became inevitable. Significantly, Dawson's action neutralized the city's primary civic force at a point in the city's history at which it appeared that, if Chicagoans were to experience racial equality, it would come as a result of the Chicago NAACP's succeeding in its ideological mission along militant lines.

10

Epilogue: The Era of the "Civil Rights Revolution," 1958–1966

The family, clique, and associational structures of Negroes in Chicago have been very little affected by the trend toward "integration."

—*Drake and Cayton, Black Metropolis,* 1962 revision

IN THE DECADE following the ouster of militant Chicago NAACP president Willoughby Abner, the branch's crusade for full citizenship rights underwent a transformation that was most noticeable as far as its emphasis on protest advocacy remained viable. As expected, the incoming administration of Theodore Jones in January 1958 produced a shift both in the form and in the intensity of protest. The fate of the high-principled, uncompromising "whole loaf" equal-rights ideology and its program, however, rested as much with acceptance by the burgeoning rank and file of old Bronzeville as it did with moderate Congressman Dawson's views.

One thing was certain after Dawson's election-night assault: the branch would be hard pressed to replicate its ability and will to challenge the racial status quo, as it had done for the previous two and one-half decades. When Abner participated in new president Jones's installation to signify a continuity of leadership, the latter spoke in conciliatory tones; the transition in 1958 from Abner's activism to Jones's controlled protest appeared calm on the surface. However, once in office, Jones committed himself to reversing what he considered the strident militancy of the Abner years, and he accordingly substituted alternate tactics associated with moderation. In his approach, he paralleled that of William "Bill" Berry, his counterpart at the Chicago Urban League. Both men shared the assessment that the only reasonable way to transform the city's race relations structure was to confront diplomatically the powerful figures found in the corporate boardrooms and the mayor's office. In this, they echoed the view held by the black civic leadership in the Chicago Negro Chamber of Commerce, the insurance companies, the service and undertaking industries, the churches, and the fraternal orders that talking with those in power was better than shouting at them. Especially important was the fact that one-on-one negotiating replaced mass meetings. Predictably, measured calm replaced fervor. Moreover, like the black politicians, they were willing to gently rock but not threaten to sink the boat as Abner and the Urban League's Sidney Williams had done.

Jones's tenure as president began with many familiar faces returning to the ranks of the Executive Committee. Cora Patton returned to office as Jones's first vice-president but succumbed to a terminal illness in August 1958. Attorney Robert Ming, Jr., returned to head the Legal Redress Committee. Harvard-trained attorney William Cousins took over the Legislative Committee, joining labor advocates Charles Hayes and James Kemp who now headed the Finance Committee. Willie Whiting continued to serve as executive secretary after having helped forge the alliance that elected Jones. Jones led the branch, still seeking change in the areas of housing, education, and jobs, so the agenda remained untouched; only the level of intensity had been altered. "As a group whose principal weapon is protest, we are liable to be misinterpreted by both the unknowing and the unscrupulous," Jones then explained. "It is therefore critical that we make our objectives and our basis of action clear in whatever case."[1]

Abner's plan to lead blacks back to Calumet Park during the fall was postponed until 1958, when, under the banner "Return to Calumet Park," blacks were to have dramatized their perseverance in using public facilities wherever and whenever they desired. Changing administrations resulted in shelving the plans. Despite the urging of the Hyde Park Unit and the University of Chicago Youth Chapter, Jones remained steadfast and refused to approve the demonstration.

On the housing front, the restructuring of the branch in 1954 had provided both the necessary impetus and means to fight for an end to discrimination in private housing. The unit system evolved to deal with particularistic neighborhood concerns about private housing. On the West Side, NAACP members organized to stabilize the rapid change in the racial composition of the North Lawndale and East Garfield Park communities. Along the lake on the South Side, the Hyde Park group took on the challenge of slum clearance and open occupancy.

The West Side unit was led during its short existence by the Rev. Arthur Austin and his successor, Carter A. Jones, Jr. Comprising African Americans and liberal whites, the unit concentrated its energies on solving several basic or "welfare" issues with which the average citizen could identify—housing, education, and employment. The problem in promoting open housing involved white hostility and the other side of the coin— "white flight" by liberal elements. If whites resisted blacks as they had on Hamlin Avenue, requiring police protection, integration was stymied. If white neighbors agreed to work cooperatively to build a truly American neighborhood through integration but did as Jones witnessed—early one morning at 1:00 or 2:00 A.M.—which was to move out at that ungodly hour so that their other neighbors would not know of their true intentions, integration would also be thwarted. The general result of the black influx was white outmigration and a resegregated West Side.[2]

Middle-class whites dominated the Hyde Park group; nonetheless, the unit involved itself in an issue that affected the black working class more than any other segment of citizens. The Hyde Park community, which was surrounded on three sides by bulging Bronzeville to the north, west, and south, had been undergoing rapid racial change since 1948–1949. By the mid-1950s, the University of Chicago became alarmed by the quick racial change in the community area it controlled, especially on its western boundary.[3] It responded with a plan for slum clearance and urban renewal. Blacks, who had accounted for 6 percent of the community's population in 1950, were 37 percent by April 1956.[4] With a great many working-class people represented in these figures, the area quickly took on the appearance of an expanding slum.

The members of the unit distrusted the university's motives and saw the plan as resulting in the indiscriminate removal of blacks from the area. Although nearly one-half of the 20,000 persons to be relocated were white, they would be allowed to remain in Hyde Park, but the blacks who left the area were to be forced back into the already overcrowded black neighborhoods from which some had so recently moved. Working closely with the branch's Housing Committee and the national office's housing advisor, Madison S. Jones, the Hyde Park unit adopted the national office's position on slum clearance. That stance did not "oppose slum clearance, it [did] oppose any effort that extend[ed] and perpetuate[d] the barrier of segregation or bec[ame] 'Negro clearance.'"[5] After unit housing chair Alberta Acker spoke before a Chicago City Council committee examining housing, success was apparent. Then Alderman William Harvey, Dawson stalwart, voted against the slum clearance measure when it reached the floor of the city council on March 14, 1957.[6] A correct and principled stand notwithstanding, slum clearance and Negro removal did take place; and, metaphorically, the University of Chicago simply bulldozed the unit, the branch, and the Association.[7]

The Hyde Park unit also worked on the problem of open occupancy with the national office and local politicians, actually formulating the branch's housing policy. To liberal, racially integrated Hyde Parkers, integration was tangible, practical, and democratically necessary, not abstract and unattainable. The issue of open occupancy throughout the city was therefore never allowed to become dormant. Also, with the city of New York already pioneering in this effort, the national office endorsed the Chicago policy. The result was the strengthening of the lines of communication with the national office even when the latter incurred the displeasure of the branch's leadership over circumvention and dilution of branch authority. Then an ordinance, conceived by black machine alderman Claude Holman and liberal Jewish alderman Leon Despres, from Hyde Park, moved unofficially through the Chicago City Council. Whatever the motivation for this political tandem, it was welcomed by open housing advocates.[8]

Despres enunciated an uncharacteristically pragmatic but not very idealistic position that the ordinance should only be presented to the council when public sentiment citywide appeared more supportive. He subsequently urged all concerned citizens groups to work at earnestly building a base of mass support for open occupancy. When an ordinance was introduced and voted on in 1963, it did so with the open endorsement of Mayor Daley. Although it passed, it was so unpopular with white Chicagoans that the white alderman Daley had forced to present it became *persona non grata* among his constituents and decided not to run for reelection.[9]

Meanwhile, Theodore Jones was particularly disturbed by the growing independence and influence of the three neighborhood units. Originally approved by the national office in 1954 as a way to increase NAACP membership by taking the civil rights movement to the people, the units acted with a sense of autonomy that lacked the sanction of either the branch or the national office. Fearing a weakening of branch authority, Jones abolished the unit system altogether, but not without severe criticism from within his board, NAACP supporters at large, and active workers among the general membership.[10] The usually mild-mannered treasurer, Beatrice Hughes Steele, lambasted the action publicly in the pages of the *Chicago Defender,* calling the abolition "a destruction of the grass-roots heart of the branch."[11] Jones argued that he had an administrative imperative to maintain organizational discipline. In desperation, he raised the specter of Communist infiltration without offering any evidence. National board chairman Channing Tobias tried to comfort one disgruntled critic by saying that "in the end, [the action] should bring order out of chaos."[12]

The dissolution of the neighborhood units spurred the supporters of Abner and Larry Bullock into concerted opposition against the Jones administration to recover the branch's democratic base. Abner now vigorously supported Bullock for president at the next election. North Dakota–born Bullock loomed as a formidable challenger with previous leadership experience with the Chicago Teachers Union and the Independent Voters of Illinois, the latter the bane of machine politicians. To counterbalance this growing opposition, Jones called on the support of the Bronzeville Establishment once again.[13] The December 1958 election was an especially bitter one with Jones soundly defeating Bullock. With the post-election air filled with allegations of rampant fraud, the national office aggravated the situation by rejecting the charges.[14]

With a new year in 1959, the first branch historically now proudly claimed the mantle of supremacy over a thousand branches in being the NAACP network's largest, with 20,000 members.[15] Although it received accolades at the national convention (that year held in New York), its achievements were kept in check by the manueverings of the national office, bent on maintaining centrality.[16] Back home, the Chicago NAACP faced its day of reckoning. The branch's monthly membership meetings, transformed during the postwar period into fully democratic assemblies, remained battlefields as Bullock loyalists sought to control the branch. President Theodore Jones countered with rulings from the national office outlining the scope of his authority which, in fact, indicated that branch meetings had never been intended to become forums for policy formulation.

Meanwhile, the white Establishment—the dominant force impeding racial change—remained as formidable as ever. This cluster included manufacturers who systematically denied jobs to black workers and lobbied against FEP; realtors and their associations which exploited racial fears and profited from residential segregation; and local governmental officials who displayed an insensitivity toward fairness in housing and education. Even Theodore A. Jones's calmer approach of 1958–1959, surprisingly matched by School Board Chairman R. Sargent Shriver's promise of change, failed to break through the board's unspoken commitment to preserving a racial status quo built on *de facto* segregation.

It would be left to a different set of advocates of educational equality and open housing in the next decade to effect change, using different tactics, including boycotts and street demonstrations. So the educational climate in the city in the next decade remained antagonistic because of the overcrowding in black schools, the shift of experienced teachers to white schools, the unfairness in teacher examinations, and the exclusion of talented black students from citywide educational opportunities. Furthermore, the housing climate was depressing.

What was especially new for the times with regard to its program focus was the branch's interest in ending its isolation from racial controversies in which criminal charges were pending against an African American. The senseless murder of a white teenager by a black youth on a South Side elevated platform produced cries of indignation and sympathy from throughout the city and from all persons. However, the branch also demanded sensitivity to, and an effort to eliminate, the conditions that produced the criminal and his action. While the white newspapers labeled the alleged murderer an animal, the branch had "concern for [the total] society, the total social matrix, which succor[ed] hypocrisy and g[ave] haven to 'respectable dishonesty.'"[17] An event later that year gave credence to the branch's concerns. A relative of former Congressman Oscar De Priest was killed by a youth while driving his bus through a white neighborhood. After the police refused to arrest the accused, the branch remonstrated, but beyond issuing a public statement, it neither intervened legally nor acted demonstrably. The invisible line of moderation held firm again.

Perhaps believing that the only victories possible were pyrrhic, Jones declined to run for a third term and the Democratic organization and business groups approved real estate broker Dempsey J. Travis as his successor. Bullock challenged the moderate bloc again but suffered his second straight defeat as Dawson political workers voted in large numbers against his faction. Bullock was a double loser because he also lost the respect of Roy Wilkins and the national office as a result of a pressure campaign, directed against the national office's supposed partiality.[18]

The Chicago NAACP continued to adapt to its new role in the equal rights struggle during the 1960s, which has been dubbed the era of the "Civil Rights Revolution." The branch neither disappeared nor became moribund but as branch leaders and members engaged in this struggle, it was often outside the parameters set by the branch's consistently moderate leadership.[19] Faith Rich went on to head CORE in 1960. And Executive Committee member Charles A. Davis, Sr., recalled recently how the branch, along with the Chicago Urban League, collaborated in 1961 to establish the Chicago Council of Community Organizations (CCCO), which provided the Chicago civil rights movement with an independent structure from which to challenge *de facto* segregation in the public schools.[20] With an Executive Committee filled with persons having direct ties both to the Bronzeville Establishment and the white Establishment, the branch lacked the unfettered vitality it needed for the times. Notable in this category were labor leader and branch treasurer James A. Kemp as well as National Baptist Convention president the Rev. Joseph H. Jackson of the Olivet Baptist Church.

Although former branch president Dempsey J. Travis has written retrospectively that "the branch ceased to articulate black expectations except in toothless rhetoric that was designed not to offend,"[21] Travis served the cause of civil rights passionately as the branch's first native-born Chicago president during 1960–1962.[22] Interestingly enough, Travis credited the branch under his leadership with not bowing to untoward political pressure in the attainment of its program goals. Travis organized successful open-housing panels in 1960 on which discussions of the beneficial aspects of fair housing in both the city and suburbs took place. The panels followed an especially embarrassing incident in the northern suburb of Deerfield in which well-to-do blacks were the victims of discriminatory housing practices.

Just as in the 1930s, social change produced a proliferation of new groups and personalities participating in the protest arena. Activists were younger, militant by temperament and choice of tactics, uncompromising on the issue of full citizenship rights on an immediate basis, and, importantly, without ties to the leadership of Bronzeville's institutions. As early as 1962, under the leadership of the new president, the Rev. Wilbur N. Daniel, the branch cosponsored an *ad hoc* militant effort aimed at desegregating the schools. Perhaps most importantly, in that year the Student Non-violent Coordinating Committee (SNCC) became active in the city. Meanwhile, CCCO took the leading role in the successful, well-coordinated effort to break the back of school segregation and overcrowding in the Chicago Public Schools system.

In Chicago, 1963 became *the* pivotal year in the city's modern civil rights struggle. In both the civil rights and political spheres, insurgency appeared. For years, the branch had enthusiastically looked forward to the centennial year of the Emancipation Proclamation as a watershed year marking black progress. The question now uppermost in members' minds was this: "If equal rights and freedom are not attainable now after 100 years of struggle, when will they be attained?" Civil rights activism in the South generated a heightened sense of urgency once the Birmingham demonstrations and the March on Washington concluded triumphantly. Back in Chicago, the branch not only prepared to eliminate Jim Crow conditions but also to host its fifth national convention. Sadly, under the leadership of the Rev. Wilbur N. Daniel, its tendency toward moderation acted as an internal hindrance as the month of July ushered in a summer of embarrassments. First, Mayor Daley and the Rev. Joseph H. Jackson were booed viciously during the NAACP convention during an open air meeting in Soldier Field on the lakefront. Young militants from the Revolutionary Action Movement (RAM) initiated a cacophony of discontent that prevented both men from speaking. By mid-month, Daniel was denounced for statements he made criticizing the progressive civil rights stand of Hyde Park liberal alderman Leon M. Despres. Irate letter writers lambasted Daniel's "sincerity," which, they said, obviously ". . . [lay] with the status quo forces and not with those who . . . [were] seeking full citizenship rights for all persons."[23]

By fall, the branch's fortunes had improved. As a part of CCCO, the branch supported massive student boycotts, street demonstrations, media campaigns, and confrontations with leading public officials to force the resignation of Superintendent Benjamin J. Willis, who had become *the* symbol of racial recalcitrance.[24] The branch promoted the first of two school boycotts involving thousands of children but withdrew its backing of a second boycott called for November 1963. Ostensibly the boycott interfered with a voter registration drive the branch had planned in advance of the announced protest action.[25] Then the branch's representative to CCCO, Charles A. Davis, Sr., withdrew from the coalition because of a disagreement over the choice and timing of activities. Whatever the reason for the branch's action, the mix of personalities and organizations with different agendas and levels of resources to commit to any campaign had to play a major part. Despite charges of inconspicuous posture during this period, the branch suggested its own boycott to demonstrate its disapproval of Mayor Daley's reappointment of an unpopular black board member. The pledge of support from participating organizations hinged on the duration of the boycott. CORE and SNCC suggested five days and the Chicago NAACP suggested two. Ultimately, it was CORE and SNCC which broke away.[26]

The political arena also featured independent action from an unusual source, and at a level unseen previously. A grass-roots organization of dedicated, educated progressive activists initiated the "Protest at the Polls" campaign. This coalition of South and West Side black progressives, including professionals, wanted to "contribute to the civil rights movement in Chicago by adding to its new thrust the decisive element of electoral action, . . . the least developed facet of the Freedom movement." At its core, "Protest at the Polls" embraced a new generation of political leaders committed to public service that would eventually overwhelm the Dawson style of machine politics. Furthermore, politics influenced administrative shifts within the branch, illuminating the temper of the times. President the Rev. Wilbur N. Daniel resigned his branch office after one and one-half years to run against U.S. Rep. Dawson in the First Congressional District as a Republican in the November 1963 election. The Daniel candidacy reflected the sentiment building against the congressman's moderate civil rights stance during the school boycotts. First vice-president Albert Brooks, an officer in the National Alliance of Postal and Federal Employees, succeeded Daniel.

What the branch encountered in its former, exclusive protest domain were new faces such as those of Albert Raby of CCCO, Lawrence Landry of SNCC, Robert Lucas of CORE, Jesse Jackson at SCLC's Operation Breadbasket by 1965, and the irrepressible, peripatetic Dick Gregory. After branch secretary the Rev. Carl Fuqua left his post in 1964, Sydney Finley, the new NAACP regional officer for eight central states, assumed the former's local duties. As acting executive secretary, Finley brought to the branch a penchant for activism which belied its later 1960s image of an effete organization floundering in the middle of civil rights revolution. However, it took Dr. Martin Luther King, Jr.'s presence in the city in June 1965 to solidify a new coalition with even more new faces and ideas.

Invited to Chicago by Al Raby and Syd Finley to speak in behalf of the anti-segregation school crusade, King addressed over 30,000 demonstrators whom he led to City Hall in protest over the city's resistance to equal opportunity. With the movement's demands on city government largely ignored, King returned in 1966 to formally organize the Chicago Freedom Movement, which comprised CCCO, SCLC, the Industrial Union Department of the AFL-CIO, and some smaller organizations. Although, with Democratic Party hegemony, there was no power vacuum in the city, because of it, there was a discernible moral void. Dr. King aimed to fill it with the help, primarily, of the city's black and white clergy and social justice activists. As the Chicago Freedom Movement became more visible, the national aura of SCLC began to overshadow that of the CCCO,[27] much in the same manner that the Chicago NAACP seemed to disappear in the crush of activism at the opening of the decade.

Nineteen sixty-six will long be remembered as the year Dr. King both resided and protested in Chicago. Although a transient, because of his travels to other parts of the nation as well as overseas, and rarely at home in his South Hamlin Avenue apartment on the city's West Side, he did break bread with the masses as well as break protocol in dealing with the city's powerbrokers. Dr. King dared to champion the cause of the city's neediest citizens as well as fight the same attitudes, mores, and beliefs that prevailed in the South.[28] He originally envisioned that he would lead a broad-based campaign aimed primarily at Chicago's *de facto* school problems. Instead, the resignation of Superintendent Willis diverted the movement into a fight against slums and the conditions that bred them. While Mayor Daley denied that a ghetto or slums existed, he showed as early as 1963 that he could adjust to changing politics. He pushed an open occupancy ordinance through the Chicago City Council by a 30–16 vote that, as we have seen, eventually cost the white alderman who sponsored it his seat. Now fully aware of the white ethnic backlash that accompanied concessions to blacks, Daley adopted a more rigid hands-off policy to racial change.

Under King's leadership, an interracial, interorganizational housing coalition emerged that included the Chicago NAACP but in a minor role. This impressive coalition directly challenged segregated housing both in the city and the suburbs. King's efforts bore immediate fruit as he signed a housing agreement with the city and realty groups in August 1966 and thereby won a limited housing victory. However, as he was leaving the city, King suspected correctly that he had been outmaneuvered by Mayor Daley.[29] The summit agreement contained promises that were never meant to be kept. Yet King cannot be faulted for bargaining with integrity. Moreover, the agreement set the stage for future advancement as well as the mood for more militant demands and programs rooted in the reality of existing circumstances.

The most unfortunate consequence of Daley's political chicanery occurred in the wake of King's departure. In having defeated King and virtually forced him from the city, many younger Chicagoans now viewed nonviolent, direct action as having passed from the scene also. For this group of black Chicagoans, with neither family, clique, nor associational structure through which to channel their desires, both their future and that of the greater society boded ill.[30] The ultramilitant ideology of Black Power loomed on the horizon, to be attended by increased street violence and racial distrust. The branch, along with the Chicago Freedom Movement, was shoved back even farther into the protest landscape.

As the expectations of black Chicagoans continued to rise, the place of the branch as a major vehicle for change diminished accordingly. This development paralleled the decline of black political empowerment that, by 1966, found Daley's pet black aldermen becoming the infamous "Silent Six" on matters of importance to black advancement. The confrontation between the proverbial immovable object of the white Establishment, comprising corporate, civic, religious, political, and municipal leaderships, and the irresistible force of black advocacy uncovered the weakness left by the Dawson-Abner clash of 1957. With the exception of the small independent political movement, located primarily on the South Side, and the growing civil rights component in Chicago that acted in accord with the national movement, the Chicago scene was distressing indeed. That the Chicago NAACP and its professional leadership had played its part in moving the black civil rights agenda to the center stage by mid-century where it had to be addressed is undeniable. Its role of prime mover, however, was limited to the period of foundation-building in that span of time before 1960.

NOTES

Preface

1. Christopher R. Reed, "Black Chicago Civic Organization Before 1935," *Journal of Ethnic Studies* 14 (Winter 1987): 65–77.

2. Edith Abbott, *The Tenements of Chicago, 1908–1935* (Chicago: University of Chicago Press, 1936), p. 118, writes: "in the face of continued manifestations of race prejudice, the Negro has chosen to acquiesce silently on civil rights...." From Abbott's minimization of African American protest advocacy, four works mentioned programmatic activities only, compartmentalizing the Chicago NAACP's mandate: Chicago Commission on Race Relations, *The Negro in Chicago* (Chicago: University of Chicago Press, 1922), p. 148; Allen F. Spear, *Black Chicago: The Making of a Negro Ghetto* (Chicago: University of Chicago Press, 1967), pp. 87–89; Charles Flint Kellogg, *NAACP: A History of the National Association for the Advancement of Colored People 1909–1920* (Baltimore: Johns Hopkins University Press, 1967); and Harold F. Gosnell, *Negro Politicians* (Chicago: University of Chicago Press, 1935), pp. 113, 328.

3. Alan B. Anderson and George W. Pickering, *Confronting the Color Line: The Broken Promise of the Civil Rights Movement in Chicago* (Athens: University of Georgia Press, 1986), p. 27.

4. Black works specifically dealing with the NAACP, its activities, and its leadership—derived from *The Papers of the NAACP*—are Kellogg, *NAACP*; Barbara Joyce Ross, *J. E. Spingarn and the Rise of the NAACP, 1911–1939* (Boston: Atheneum, 1972); August Meier and Elliott Rudwick, eds., *Along the Color Line: Explorations in the Black Experience* (Urbana: University of Illinois Press, 1976), and *Black Detroit and the Rise of the UAW* (New York: Oxford University Press, 1979); Darlene Clark Hine, *Black Victory: The Rise and Fall of the White Primary in Texas* (Millwood, NY: TKO, 1979); Robert L. Zangrando, *The NAACP Crusade against Lynching, 1909–1950* (Philadelphia: Temple University Press, 1980); Sheldon Avery, *Up from Washington: William Pickens and the Negro Struggle for Equality, 1900–1954* (Newark: University of Delaware Press, 1989); and Kenneth Goings, *The NAACP Comes of Age: The Defeat of John J. Parker* (Bloomington: Indiana University Press, 1990). General works that have included appreciable information on the NAACP from the *Papers* are Harvard Sitkoff, *A New Deal for Blacks: The Emergence of Civil Rights as a National Issue, Volume I: The Depression Decade* (New York: Oxford

University Press, 1978); Nancy J. Weiss, *Farewell to the Party of Lincoln: Black Politics in the Age of FDR* (Princeton, NJ: Princeton University Press, 1983); and Mark Naison, *Communists in Harlem during the Depression* (Urbana: University of Illinois Press, 1983). A specific study of a solitary branch during the 1930s is H. Viscount Nelson, *The Philadelphia N.A.A.C.P.: Epitome of Middle Class Consciousness* (Los Angeles: Center for Afro-American Studies, UCLA, 1972). Some of the activities of the Cleveland branch are mentioned in Kenneth L. Kusmer, *A Ghetto Takes Shape: Black Cleveland, 1870–1930* (Urbana: University of Illinois Press, 1976).

5. St. Clair Drake, "Churches and Voluntary Associations in the Chicago Negro Community" (Chicago: W.P.A. Study, 1940, mimeographed), p. 105.

6. Spear, *Black Chicago,* chs. 3 and 4, are devoted to exploring the ideological and socioeconomic differences between an old elite and a new business leadership.

7. See Kusmer, *A Ghetto Takes Shape,* p. 103.

8. Robert H. Wiebe, *The Search for Order, 1877–1920* (New York: Hill & Wang, 1967), p. 112.

9. St. Clair Drake and Horace R. Cayton, *Black Metropolis* (New York: Harcourt, Brace, 1945), p. 529.

10. See Nancy J. Weiss, "From Black Separatism to Interracial Cooperation: The Origins of Organized Efforts for Racial Advancement, 1890–1920," in Barton J. Bernstein and Allen J. Matusow, eds., *Twentieth Century America: Recent Interpretations* (San Diego, CA: Harcourt Brace Jovanovich, 1969), pp. 64–66. Weiss maintains that it is more reasonable to treat internecine squabbling as a feature common to emerging groups actively seeking specific goals and grasping for power at a particular point in their historical development than as a characteristic of black organizations.

11. Contemporary references to this unique American phenomenon are numerous. See Charles S. Johnson, "These Colored United States, VII—Illinois: Mecca of the Migrant Mob," *Messenger* 5 (December 1923): 926–928; E. Franklin Frazier, "Chicago: A Cross-Section of Negro Life," *Opportunity* (March 1929): 70–73; Ralph J. Bunche, "The Negro in Chicago Politics," 17 *National Municipal Review* (May 1928): 261–264; and Gosnell, *Negro Politicians.* One of the most probing essays into this subject in recent decades is Martin H. Kilson, "Political Change in the Negro Ghetto, 1900–1940s," in Nathan I. Huggins et al., eds. *Key Issues in the Afro-American Experience* (New York: Harcourt Brace Jovanovich, 1971), pp. 167–192. A major study is Charles R. Branham, "The Transformation of Black Political Leadership in Chicago" (Ph.D. diss., University of Chicago, 1981). Important, current theoretical work on the significance of black political culture is found in ch. 2 of Hanes Walton, Jr., *Invisible Politics: Black Political Behavior* (Albany: State University of New York, 1985). The most recent assessment from the University of Chicago's sociological ranks is that "Chicago blacks never let whites define their lot as one of complete dependence on white paternalism." See Gerald Suttles, *Man-Made City: The Land Use Confidence Game in Chicago* (Chicago: University of Chicago Press, 1991), p. 268.

12. August Meier and Elliott Rudwick, *From Plantation to Ghetto* (New York: Hill & Wang, 3rd ed., 1976), p. 232, and Kenneth L. Kusmer, "The Black Experience in American History," pp. 121–122, in Darlene Clark Hine, ed., *The State of Afro-American History: Past, Present, and Future* (Baton Rouge: Louisiana State University Press, 1986).

1. Prologue: Making the NAACP "a Necessity" in Chicago

1. "Notes and Proposals," 1933, NAACP MSS., Branch Files.

2. Ross, *Spingarn*, p. 104.

3. E. Franklin Frazier, "The American Negro's New Leaders," *Current History* 28 (April 1928): 59. See also Wilson Record, "Negro Intellectuals and Negro Movements in Historical Perspective," *American Quarterly* 8 (Spring 1956): 3–20.

4. Ross, *Spingarn*, pp. 25, 26. See also James M. MacPherson, *The Abolitionist Legacy: From Reconstruction to the NAACP* (Princeton, NJ: Princeton University Press, 1975).

5. Robert Gruenberg, "Dawson of Illinois: What Price Moderation?" *Nation* 183 (September 8, 1956), pp. 197, 198; Edward C. Banfield and James Q. Wilson, *City Politics* (Cambridge, MA: Harvard University Press, 1963), p. 309; and James Q. Wilson, *Negro Politics: The Search for Leadership* (Glencoe, IL: Free Press, 1967). In ch. 8, "Goals of Negro Leaders," without designating them as such, he addresses the manifestations of class differences in instances where "welfare" and "status" needs separate the actions of black leaders.

6. See Howard Zinn, *SNCC, SNICK, Student Nonviolent Coordinating Committee: The New Abolitionists* (Boston: Beacon Press, 1964). Ch. 1 describes the "new abolitionists" of the 1960s who were unique, most significantly, in their youthfulness. However, zeal and sacrifice in the cause of civil rights appeared as an indispensable element throughout the NAACP's history. See also Record, "Negro Intellectuals," p. 18, to appreciate just how far the Chicago NAACP had come by the late 1950s in broadening its program to include the concerns and needs of the working poor along with those of the solid working class, middle class, and elite.

2. Progressive-Era Chicago, 1900–1919

1. Edward R. Kantowicz, "Carter H. Harrison II: The Politics of Balance," in Paul M. Green and Melvin G. Holli, eds., *The Mayors: The Chicago Political Tradition* (Carbondale: Southern Illinois University Press, 1987), p. 28.

2. Spear, *Black Chicago*, p. 12.

3. W. E. B. Du Bois, *The Souls of Black Folk* (Greenwich, CN: Fawcett Publishing, 1961), p. 81.

4. First Annual Report, NAACP, January 1, 1911, Blaine MSS., NAACP File.

5. Ibid. Kantowicz, "Carter H. Harrison II," pp. 23, 29.

6. Charles E. Bentley to Frances Blascoer, June 24, 1910, NAACP MSS.

7. Jane Addams, *Social Control* (New York: NAACP Publications, 1911), p. 1, in Blaine MSS., NAACP File.

8. Steven J. Diner, "Chicago Social Workers and Blacks in the Progressive Era," *Social Science Review* 44 (December 1970), p. 404.

9. Oswald Garrison Villard, "The Objects of the National Association for the Advancement of Colored People," *The Crisis* (May 1912), p. 81, 82.

10. First Annual Report, NAACP, January 1, 1911, Blaine MSS., NAACP File.

11. *Chicago Defender,* March 13, 1915, p. 4. At this point, Judge Brown blamed his pessimism on the war in Europe.

12. *Chicago Tribune,* January 16, 1915, p. 1; *Chicago Defender,* January 16, 1915, p. 4 and April 17, 1915, p. 1.

13. Arvarh H. Strickland, *History of the Chicago Urban League* (Urbana: University of Illinois Press, 1966), p. 6.

14. Thomas Lee Philpott, *The Slum and Ghetto: Immigrants, Blacks, and Reformers in Chicago, 1880–1930* (New York: Oxford University Press, 1978; Wadsworth, 1991), pp. 295–303; Ross, *Spingarn,* p. 27.

15. See Spear, *Black Chicago,* pp. 84f., and Strickland, *History of the Chicago Urban League,* pp. 34ff., for views that support the idea that a split among the black elite existed and was of great importance in black Chicago. For a view that holds that the split was of major importance on a national scale, see the definitive work on the subject by August Meier, *Negro Thought in America, 1880–1915: Racial Ideologies in the Age of Booker T. Washington* (Ann Arbor: University of Michigan Press, 1963), especially ch. 10, "Radicals and Conservatives."

16. "Opinion," *The Crisis,* March 1914, p. 227. The view of Spingarn as the uncompromising champion of egalitarianism and carrier of the torch of "New Abolitionism" is best described in Ross, *Spingarn,* pp. 21–48.

17. *Chicago Defender,* January 10, 1914, p. 4 and *Chicago Broad-Ax,* September 7, 1912, p. 1.

18. Archie L. Weaver to A. L. Foster, September 18, 1953, NAACP MSS., Branch Files.

19. Reverdy C. Ransom, *The Pilgrimage of Harriet Ransom's Son* (Nashville, TN: Sunday School Union, 1947), p. 164.

20. Drake, "Churches and Voluntary Associations in the Chicago Negro Community," p. 125.

21. Interview with Earl B. Dickerson in his corporate office on March 21, 1984, in Chicago. Dickerson knew both Washington and Du Bois, having taught at Tuskegee in 1914 and having interacted with Du Bois as a fellow NAACP supporter. Dickerson led the Legal Redress Committee of the Chicago branch between 1930 and 1933 and the legal team that prepared the ground-breaking *Hansberry v. Lee* case (1940), and served the NAACP on the Board of Directors for over three decades.

22. Louis R. Harlan, *Booker T. Washington: The Wizard of Tuskegee, 1901–1915* (New York: Oxford University Press, 1983), pp. 359–478, 427, 435–437. The com-

plexity of the disagreement was such that matters of personality could over-shadow differences of principle, tactics, and strategy.

23. Spear, *Black Chicago*, p. 60.

24. Juvenile Protective Association, *The Negro in Chicago* (Chicago: Juvenile Protective Association, 1913), n.p.

25. Untitled editorial, *Half-Century Magazine* 11 (August 1916), p. 4. See also "Observations about the Need of Business Enterprises among Colored People," December 1916, p. 9, and "Lest We Forget," March 1917, p. 3, as well as "Business and Segregation," May 1917, p. 16, all in *The Half-Century Magazine*.

26. *Chicago Defender*, March 27, 1915, p. 8.

27. Lawrence A. Levine, *Black Culture and Black Consciousness: Afro-American Folk Thought from Slavery to Freedom* (New York: Oxford University Press, 1977), pp. 429–440. See MacNeal to White, June 1, 1937, NAACP MSS., Branch Files: "It must be remembered that in Chicago there are such a large number of competing interests and an event has to be in the nature of a 'nature.' Civil rights are not yet popular like policy or Joe Louis and cannot be considered as a natural drawing card."

28. Harlan, *Booker T. Washington*, p. 98.

29. Fannie Barrier Williams, "Social Bonds in the 'Black Belt' of Chicago: Negro Organizations and the New Spirit Pervading Them," *Charities* 15 (October 15, 1905): 41.

30. Ibid., p. 44.

31. Alzada Comstock, "Chicago Housing Conditions, IV: The Problem of the Negro," *American Journal of Sociology* 18 (September 1912): 250, 257.

32. James R. Grossman, *Land of Hope: Chicago, Black Southerners, and the Great Migration* (Chicago: University of Chicago Press, 1989), p. 161.

33. *Chicago Broad-Ax*, October 26, 1912, pp. 1, 2. See also Harlan, *Booker T. Washington*, pp. 290–294, regarding his trip to Europe in 1910.

34. *Chicago Broad-Ax*, August 24, 1912, p. 2.

35. Ransom, *Pilgrimage of Harriet Ransom's Son*, pp. 131, 132.

3. From Vigilance Committee to Branch, 1910–1916

1. *The Crisis* (August 1914): 185 and Kellogg, *NAACP*, pp. 297–299.

2. "Du Bois on the National [Negro] Conference, 1909," in Herbert Aptheker, ed., *A Documentary History of the Negro People in the United States*, 2 vols. (New York: Citadel Press, 1968), 2:926. Also see Weiss, "From Black Separatism to Interracial Cooperation," pp. 72–78, for black suspicions of whites in an interracial setting.

3. "Remarks by J. Max Barber," in Aptheker, ed., *Documentary History of the Negro People*, 2:921.

4. "Du Bois on the National [Negro] Conference," ibid., 2:927.

5. Alfreda M. Duster, ed., *Crusade for Justice: The Autobiography of Ida B. Wells*

(Chicago: University of Chicago Press, 1970), pp. 323–326. See also David Levering Lewis, *W. E. B. Du Bois: Biography of a Race* (New York: Henry Holt, 1993), pp. 396–397.

6. Duster, *Crusade*, p. 325. See also *The Crisis* 2 (June 1911): 11 (September 1915): 238–239; (December 1929): 423; "Du Bois on Niagara, 1905," in Aptheker, *Documentary History of the Negro*, 2:904.

7. Center letterhead for 1908, Blaine MSS., Frederick Douglass Center File.

8. Wells-Barnett to Spingarn, April 21, 1911, Spingarn MSS. Wells-Barnett File and Duster, *Crusade for Justice*, pp. 238–288 and 327–328. See also Mary Church Terrell's concern about being locked out of black leadership by Du Bois's growing stature among whites, in Terrell to Villard, September 14, 1913, NAACP MSS., Branch Files.

9. See Walling to Addams, April 1, 1909, Addams MSS., which contain a portion of the Jenkin Lloyd Jones Papers, Meadville Theological School of Lombard, Illinois; Bentley to Blascoer, January 28, 1911, NAACP MSS., Branch Files; Kellogg, *NAACP*, p. 124.

10. Allen F. Davis, *American Heroine: The Life and Legend of Jane Addams* (New York: Oxford University Press, 1973), p. 129.

11. Addams, *Social Control*, p. 2.

12. Addams to Jones, October 20, 1903, Addams MSS.

13. Davis, *American Heroine*, pp. 131–134.

14. Staughton Lynd, "Jane Addams and the Radical Impulse," *Commentary*, July 1967, p. 57.

15. Davis, *American Heroine*, p. 134.

16. Philpott, *Slum and Ghetto*, pp. 299–301.

17. Edward O. Brown, "The Nation's Duty," *The Crisis*, May 1912, pp. 84–87.

18. Interview with Earl B. Dickerson on March 21, 1984, in Chicago.

19. Frederick Douglass Center, Fall Calendar, 1907, n.p., Blaine MSS., Douglass File.

20. Duster, *Crusade for Justice*, pp. 279–288. See also Calendar, 1907, of the Frederick Douglass Center, Blaine MSS., Douglass File and *Chicago Defender*, March 27, 1915, p. 8.

21.Frederick Douglass Center, Fall Calendar, 1907, n.p., Blaine MSS.

22. Bessie Louise Pierce, *A History of Chicago*, vol. 3 (New York: Alfred A. Knopf, 1957), p. 450.

23. *Chicago Defender*, February 21, 1914, p. 8.

24. Memorandum, W. E. B. [Du Bois] to Spingarn, April 2, 1915, Joel E. Spingarn MSS. which contain the James Weldon Johnson Collection, Beinecke Rare Book and Manuscript Library, Yale University Library, New Haven, Conn. See also Bentley to Spingarn, March 29, 1915, Spingarn, Bentley File, and Christopher Robert Reed, "Organized Racial Reform in Chicago during the Progressive Era: The Chicago NAACP, 1910–1920," *Michigan Historical Review* 14 (Spring 1988): 82, n. 16, for the far-reaching implications of these documents on the view that the Chicago branch of the NAACP was either directly or indirectly under the domination of supporters of Booker T. Washington.

25. Bentley to Blascoer, January 28, 1911, NAACP MSS. Branch Files.

26. Robert McMurdy, *The Upas Tree* (Chicago: F. J. Schulte, 1912), pp. 82, 83, 285, 286.

27. MacPherson, *Abolitionist Legacy*, pp. 342, 353.

28. Bentley to Blascoer, January 28, 1911, NAACP MSS. Branch Files.

29. Gilbert A. Harrison, *A Timeless Affair: The Life of Anita McCormick Blaine* (Chicago: University of Chicago Press, 1979), p. 49.

30. See Kellogg, *NAACP*, p. 124; Ross, *Spingarn*, pp. 25, 31; Thomas C. Holt, "The Lonely Warrior: Ida B. Wells-Barnett and the Struggle for Black Leadership," in John Hope Franklin and August Meier, eds., *Black Leaders of the Twentieth Century* (Urbana: University of Illinois Press, 1982), pp. 54, 61.

31. *The Crisis* (May 1912): 89.

32. Rosenwald to Villard, July 2, 1914, Rosenwald MSS., NAACP File.

33. Comments in *Notebooks* to the Rosenwald MSS.

34. "Notes of February 23, 1915 on the activities of the Chicago party at Tuskegee [Institute, Alabama]," in Rosenwald MSS., Box 54, Tuskegee 1915 File.

35. Bentley to Spingarn, March 29, 1915, Spingarn MSS., Bentley File and *Chicago Defender*, March 13, 1915, pp. 1, 4.

36. *Notebooks* to the Rosenwald MSS. Also see Charles Edward Merriam, *Chicago: A More Intimate View of Urban Politics* (New York: Macmillan, 1929), p. 146.

37. Addams to [Blaine], August 7, 1913, and Addams to Evans [for Blaine], June 15, 1914, both in Addams MSS.; also, Rosenwald to Villard, August 18, 1913, and July 2, 1914, both in Rosenwald MSS., NAACP File.

38. W. C. [Graves] to Rosenwald, January 26, 1920, Rosenwald MSS., Chicago Urban League File.

39. W. C. [Graves] to Rosenwald, April 8, 1914, Rosenwald MSS., Chicago Urban League File.

40. Scott to Williams, February 1, 1910, Washington MSS., Spec. Corres.: Williams.

41. Williams to Scott, October 25, 1910, Washington MSS., Spec. Corres.: Williams.

42. Spear, *Black Chicago*, ch. 3. Chicago's black population totaled 30,000 persons in 1900. See Floyd Hunter, *Community Power Structure: A Study of Decision Makers* (Chapel Hill: University of North Carolina Press, 1952), for a major model used to determine what persons within any community made up its leadership. Missing from Spear's catalogue of leaders were most ministers, especially the clergy of the Olivet Baptist Church, the "mother" church of Chicago black Baptist churches; the hierarchies of the fraternal orders; neighborhood spokespersons; clubwomen; and the entire social structure of the West Side.

43. Bentley to Blascoer, June 24, 1910, NAACP MSS., Branch Files.

44. Helen Buckler, *Doctor Dan: Pioneer in American Surgery* (Boston: Little, Brown, 1954), p. 232.

45. See Brown, "The Nation's Duty," pp. 84–87. Also, A. C. Chatfield-Taylor, *Chicago* (Boston: Houghton Mifflin, 1917), pp. 34, 43–44, 96, 111, 128–129. Also, Pierce, *A History of Chicago*, vol. 1, pp. 24f., for information on the strong anti-

slavery sentiment that pervaded early Chicago. The New England influence and its promoters are described on pp. 176, 177, 231, 402, and 403. Also, Drake and Cayton, *Black Metropolis*, pp. 32–51.

46. His son, Northwestern University professor Norman Dwight Harris, authored *The History of Negro Servitude in Illinois and of the Slavery Agitation in That State, 1719–1864* (Chicago: A. C. McClurg, 1904).

47. George Edwin Mowry, *The Era of Theodore Roosevelt and the Birth of Modern America, 1900–1912* (New York: Harper, 1962), p. 61.

48. William L. Sullivan, comp. and ed., *Dunne: Judge, Mayor, Governor* (Chicago: Windermere Press, 1916), p. 143.

49. Ralph F. Pearson, "Charles S. Johnson and the Chicago Commission on Race Relations," *Illinois Historical Journal* 81 (Autumn 1988): 214–215.

50. Chatfield-Taylor, *Chicago*, pp. 41, 50, 51, and 70.

51. *Crusade for Justice*, edited by her daughter, Mrs. Alfreda Duster, with the assistance of Professor John Hope Franklin, is the most eloquent testimony to Ida B. Wells-Barnett's uncompromising commitment to social justice. Beyond it, Holt's penetrating essay, "The Lonely Warrior: Ida B. Wells-Barnett and the Struggle for Black Leadership," pp. 39–83, in Franklin and Meier, eds., *Black Leaders of the Twentieth Century*, is recommended. A doctoral dissertation that relied on the Wells-Barnett Papers for its interpretation, Mildred Isabelle Thompson's "Ida B. Wells-Barnett: An Exploratory Study of an American Black Woman, 1893–1930" (Ph.D. diss., George Washington University, 1979), is very useful also.

52. Wells-Barnett to Spingarn, April 21, 1911, Spingarn MSS., Wells-Barnett File.

53. Duster, *Crusade for Justice*, p. 327.

54. Ibid., pp. 327, 328.

55. Mary White Ovington, *The Walls Came Tumbling Down* (New York: Harcourt, Brace, 1947), p. 106.

56. Duster, *Crusade for Justice*, p. 283. Also see ch. 33.

57. Clifton O. Dummett, "Charles Edwin Bentley: A Genuine Emancipator," *The Crisis* (April 1979): 134.

58. See Alfred F. Moss, *The American Negro Academy: Voice of the Talented Tenth* (Baton Rouge: Louisiana State University Press, 1981), pp. 75, 76, 115, 116.

59. S. Laing Williams to Emmett Scott, October 25, 1910, Washington MSS., Spec. Corres.: Williams. For a fuller sketch of Williams's life, see Spear, *Black Chicago*, pp. 66–69.

60. Harlan, *Booker T. Washington*, p. 357.

61. Wells-Barnett to J. E. Spingarn, April 21, 1911, Joel E. Spingarn MSS., Ida B. Wells-Barnett File, Moorland-Spingarn Library, Howard University, Washington, DC.

62. A. N. Marquis, ed., *The Book of Chicagoans: A Biographical Dictionary of Leading Men* (Chicago: A. N. Marquis, 1917), pp. 9, 266, 520.

63. Bentley to Blascoer, June 24, 1910, and Bentley to Blascoer, January 28, 1911, both in NAACP MSS., Branch Files; also, First Annual Report of the NAACP,

January 1, 1911, and Addams to Blaine, February 30, 1911, both in Blaine MSS., NAACP File. For a view that questioned the organization's tenuous existence, see Williams to Scott, October 25, 1910, Washington MSS., Spec. Corres.: Williams.

64. First Annual Report of the NAACP, January 1911, Blaine MSS., NAACP File.

65. Kellogg, *NAACP*, pp. 42, 61; Ovington, *Walls Came Tumbling Down*, pp. 109–111; Ross, *Spingarn*, pp. 56, 57, 68, 69.

66. Kellogg, *NAACP*, pp. 90, 91. The birthdates of some of the Chicago leaders were: Jones, 1843; Brown, 1847; Bentley, 1859; Addams and McMurdy, 1860; and Wells-Barnett, 1862.

67. Bentley to Blascoer, January 28, 1911, NAACP MSS., Branch Files.

68. Ibid.

69. Kellogg, *NAACP*, pp. 43, 44.

70. W. E. B. Du Bois, "The Niagara Movement," in *The Voice of the Negro*, September 1905, pp. 144–148, cited in Philip S. Foner, ed., *W. E. B. Du Bois Speaks: Speeches and Addresses, 1890–1919* (New York: Pathfinder Press, 1970).

71. Bentley to Bagnall, March 13, 1922, NAACP MSS., Branch Files. For correspondence which shows Bentley's early influence over who should assume the leadership of the branch, see Bentley to Blascoer, January 28, 1911, NAACP MSS., Branch Files.

72. Wiebe, *The Search for Order*, pp. 292, 293. Before the decline in enthusiasm within the progressive ranks, Wiebe pinpointed its "floodtime" in 1912, p. 208; Richard Hofstadter, *The Age of Reform: From Bryan to F.D.R.* (New York: Alfred A. Knopf, 1955), p. 273; Otis L. Graham, Jr., *An Encore for Reform: The Old Progressives and the New Deal* (New York: Oxford University Press, 1967), pp. 151, 158, 159.

73. *Chicago Defender*, March 20, 1915, p. 1, and Ovington to Addams, October 23, 1922, NAACP MSS., Branch Files. Addams declined to participate in the Association's fourteenth annual conference earlier in the year. See Addams to White, March 2, 1922, NAACP MSS., Spec. Corres.: Addams.

74. *The Crisis*, April 1913: 297.

75. Graves to Rosenwald, November 23, 1917, Rosenwald MSS., Chicago Urban League File and Graves to Rosenwald, January 26, 1920, Rosenwald MSS., NAACP File.

76. *The Crisis* (March 1914): 228 quotes the *Chicago Tribune*, n.d.

77. *The Crisis* (March 1916): 255, 257.

78. Ibid. (June 1915): 97.

79. *Chicago Defender*, March 21, 1914, p. 8.

80. Bagnall to Johnson, January 2, 1920, NAACP MSS., Spec. Corres.: Bagnall.

81. *Chicago Defender*, August 29, 1914, p. 5 and September 5, 1914, p. 4. Also, *The Crisis* (August 1914): 25. Raising $400 in 1914 was quite a feat and placed the branch on solid footing in terms of meeting its expenses. This event also heralded the active participation of postal worker Archie L. Weaver, a person whose importance becomes more notable as this narrative proceeds. His relationship with the branch lasted until his death in 1958.

82. Graves to Rosenwald, April 8, 1914, Rosenwald MSS., NAACP File.

83. Duster, *Crusade for Justice*, pp. 335–337, and Wells-Barnett to Spingarn, April 21, 1911, Spingarn MSS., Wells-Barnett File.

84. *Chicago Broad-Ax*, September 24, 1910, p. 1.

85. Drake and Cayton, *Black Metropolis*, pp. 32–36. See also Richard C. Wade, *Slavery in the Cities: The South, 1820–1860* (New York: Oxford University Press, 1964), p. 224.

86. *Chicago Defender*, August 27, 1910, p. 2, and September 24, 1910, p. 1; *Chicago Broad-Ax*, September 24, 1910, pp. 1, 2; *The Crisis* (November 1910): 14; Duster, *Crusade for Justice*, pp. 335–337. To follow the documentary circle of self-affirmation, see Duster, *Crusade for Justice*, p. 337, n. 1, which cites Kellogg, *NAACP*, p. 63, n. 73: for his part, the latter relied on the accuracy of Wells-Barnett to Spingarn, April 21, 1911, Spingarn MSS., Wells-Barnett File. Kellogg's interpretation of the latter correspondence assumes that Wells-Barnett not only initiated all protest but implemented and completed it as well. Significantly, she did claim this honor. Further clarification is reached through Bentley to Frances Blascoer, June 24, 1910, NAACP MSS., Branch Files.

While Wells-Barnett was credited by Charles Flint Kellogg, the major historian on the early NAACP, and John Hope Franklin, the scholar who guided the editing of Wells-Barnett's autobiography, with almost single-handedly managing the affair to its successful conclusion, this was not the case. Her autobiography, along with contemporary evidence other than her correspondence, disclosed that a complex series of interrelated activities beyond a single individual's effort brought about this victory. A black grass-roots movement composed of civic and political interests operated beyond the direction of, but in complete ideological harmony with, the fledgling, biracial Chicago NAACP vigilance committee which, on this occasion, received ample financial support from the national office in New York. See also *Chicago Defender*, October 12, 1912, p. 1.

87. Villard, "Objects of the National Association for the Advancement of Colored People," 81–84.

88. Brown, "The Nation's Duty," 84–87.

89. *The Crisis* (May 1912): 89.

90. The *Tribune* reported that "on the authority of a well known member of the honorary Chicago conference committee[,] the most rabid opponent of race equality could not have failed to observe the easy refinement of the mixed assemblage." The *Chicago Defender* called it "the most significant and important gathering for race welfare since the days of Sumner, Garrison, and Phillips." *The Crisis* summed it up as "one of the most significant meetings ever held in defense of the rights of Colored Americans, and the greatest of our annual conferences." W. E. B. Du Bois, editor of *The Crisis*, wrote a paean to the movement as he described the messages as well as the messengers over the next two days. He wrote: "The speeches reached a high level of earnestness and not a false note was struck. There was a spirit of broad kindliness with no touch of personal rancor, and yet we were not

given a lukewarm mess of flat platitudes." Du Bois's summary of the conference in *The Crisis* that showed friction still persisted among blacks as he mentioned all of the major contributors to the conference by name except Wells-Barnett. He even included Bentley although the latter did not speak.

91. Constitution of the Chicago Branch of the National Association for the Advancement of Colored People, April 10, 1913, NAACP MSS., Branch Files.

92. This pattern of sporadic program activities was evidenced in the spring of 1913, the summer of 1915, and the fall and winter of 1919–1920. Allen H. Spear's *Black Chicago,* which was published in 1967, focused on the branch's heightened activities around 1913 but missed those in 1915 and 1919. The assessment of the branch's activities made by the Chicago Commission on Race Relations in 1922 referred to activities occurring in the aftermath of the infamous race riot of 1919.

93. *The Crisis* (May 1913): 27–28.

94. Lewis to Bagnall, March 27, 1922, NAACP MSS., Branch Files. When Spingarn biographer and historian Barbara Joyce Ross wrote about the trials of the national organization during the first decade of the century, she observed that "an eight-year test of the Association's program, with its strong reliance upon the sympathetic response of the public conscience, had proved largely ineffective" (Spingarn, p. 48).

95. *Chicago Defender,* March 8, 1913, p. 2.

96. Those who lobbied included Charles T. Hallinan, editor of the *Chicago Evening Post,* a member of the legislative committee, and chairman of the press service represented the branch in Springfield; Ida B. Wells-Barnett, who traveled to the capital on behalf of the colored women's clubs of Chicago; and Robert S. Abbott, editor of the *Defender,* who felt a compelling need to personally speak for his newspaper. Meanwhile, the Appomattox Club sent several well-known, civic-minded persons, including its president, Frank Hamilton, rising politicians Adelbert Roberts and Louis B. Anderson, attorney S. A. T. Watson, and Major Franklin A. Dennison of the famed, all-black Eighth Illinois Regiment.

97. "Chicago Branch of the NAACP to Members of the 48th [Illinois] General Assembly," April 23, 1913, Blaine MSS., NAACP File. In Ohio, where progressives previously sponsored similar legislation, the damage was not apparent to black labor until after the fact.

98. *Chicago Defender,* July 5, 1913, p. 1. The issue was a sensitive one to blacks, whether or not they favored marrying across racial lines. They viewed the right to marry as an essential part of citizenship and resented the hypocrisy on the part of whites who conveniently overlooked the presence of four million mulattoes in the national population. The interest of certain Chicagoans in interracial marriages in 1900 led to the formation, by the Rev. Reverdy Ransom, of the Manasseh Society, an organization devoted to serving the special needs of racially mixed families. By 1912, more than 500 persons belonged to this interracial body (Spear, *Black Chicago,* p. 109).

99. *Chicago Defender,* June 21, 1913, p. 8, and November 4, 1916, p. 12. The

branch received its share of praise in *The Crisis* (May 1913): 38, 39; (July 1913): 144; (February 1914): 192. Even the Appomattox Club received its share of recognition in *Chicago Broad-Ax,* April 26, 1913, p. 1.

100. Some of these activities preceded the branch's efforts against the infamous *Birth of a Nation* by a full year. Even in 1915, while the branch was approaching newly elected mayor William "Big Bill" Thompson about the film, State Representative Jackson was introducing a bill before the General Assembly to prevent, by law, the showing of inflammatory racial films or the recreation of any lynching scene in motion pictures, plays, sketches, or lithographs. Later, when the branch's efforts against the film were faltering, with *Birth of a Nation* being shown throughout the city with regularity, Jackson persisted. By April 1917, his bill was enacted over formidable opposition.

101. Charles R. Branham, "Black Chicago: Accommodationist Politics before the Great Migration," in Melvin Holli and Peter d'A. Jones, eds., *The Ethnic Frontier* (Grand Rapids, MI: Wm. B. Eerdmans, 1977), pp. 223, 230.

102. This episode also occurred while she was still basking in the triumphant spotlight of the annual NAACP conference held several months previously. Responding to intense national criticism from whites and blacks nationally, Addams attempted to explain and justify her position at a meeting at Hull House. She disappointed many of her fellow neo-abolitionist racial egalitarians when she admitted that she accepted Roosevelt's program based on expediency rather than on principle. With the exception of Ida B. Wells-Barnett's husband, Ferdinand, everyone present repudiated her action. Her friends saw her behavior as a "backward step and in no manner in keeping with the ideals of a democracy." Addams fared no better in the pages of the *Defender* and the *Broad-Ax,* and in letters written by some black and white supporters.

Later Addams explained her action in *The Crisis,* writing: "When I asked myself most searchingly whether my Abolitionist father would have remained in any political convention in which colored men had been treated slightingly . . . [the lesson I was taught was] look the situation fairly in the face with the best light you have." In adhering to this advice, Addams saw the overall salvation of blacks politically resting in the election of Roosevelt, even at the expense of the political rights of southern blacks. Over the long run, her position on Roosevelt only mildly alienated her from some of the key white supporters of the NAACP among Chicagoans. Notable among her critics were the Revs. Woolley and Jones.

Perhaps more importantly, just as Roosevelt "turned away from his ranks most of the militant Negroes in the North," according to Arthur S. Link, Addams alienated black racial egalitarians both inside and outside the NAACP movement by her support for a man who considered the rights of blacks expendable. The growing black political organization in the South Side's Second Ward opposed Roosevelt and backed William Howard Taft. Arthur S. Link, "The Negro as a Factor in the Campaign of 1912," *Journal of Negro History* 32 (January 1947): 98–99.

103. *Chicago Defender,* January 27, 1917, p. 12.

104. *Chicago Defender,* July 7, 1917, p. 1.

105. Harold L. Ickes, *The Autobiography of a Curmudgeon* (New York: Regnal & Hitchcock, 1943), p. 172; Gosnell, *Negro Politicians,* pp. 49, 50. Thompson's father served with Admiral Farragut during the Civil War.

106. Harold F. Gosnell, *Machine Politics* (Chicago: University of Chicago Press, 1937; Phoenix Books, 1968), p. 221.

4. The "New Negro" in the Black Metropolis, 1917–1924

1. Du Bois responded to his critics editorially in *The Crisis:* "If we organize separately for anything—Jim Crow scream the Disconsolate; if we organize with white people—traitors! . . . yell the Suspicious; if unable to get a whole loaf we seize half to ward off starvation—Compromise! yell all the Scared. If we let half the loaf go and starve—why don't you do something? yell the same critics . . ." (June 1917): 61. Also, Ross, *Spingarn,* ch. 3, and Kellogg, *NAACP,* ch. 11.

2. *Chicago Defender,* April 7, 1917, p. 12; April 28, 1917, p. 1; May 26, 1917, p. 1.

3. Clifton O. Dummett, *Charles Edwin Bentley: A Model for All Times* (St. Paul, MN: North Central, 1982), pp. 184, 185.

4. Dummett, "Charles Edwin Bentley: A Genuine Emancipator," p. 134, and "Postscript," *The Crisis* (December 1929): 423.

5. Brown to Dawes, December 14, 1916, Rosenwald MSS., Chicago Urban League File.

6. Addams to Blaine, August 18, 1917, Addams MSS. which is a portion of the Blaine MSS.

7. W. C. [Graves] to Rosenwald, November 23, 1917, Rosenwald MSS., Chicago Urban League File.

8. Brown to Spingarn, January 10, 1917, Spingarn MSS., Brown File.

9. Ibid., July 14, 1917, p. 12, and February 2, 1918, p. 11. Also, Duster, *Crusade for Justice,* p. 392.

10. *Chicago Defender,* April 26, 1919, p. 24.

11. Ibid.

12. See William M. Tuttle, Jr., *Race Riot: Chicago in the Red Summer of 1919* (New York: Atheneum, 1972), for a full treatment of the riot and its underlying causes.

13. Arthur I. Waskow, *From Race Riot to Sit-in, 1919 and the 1960s: A Study in the Connections between Conflict and Violence* (Garden City, NY: Doubleday, 1966), p. 48.

14. *The Crisis* (January 1920): 129.

15. MacNeal to Aldis, November 25, 1919, Aldis MSS., Race Prejudice File.

16. "Joint Committee to Secure Justice for Colored Riot Defendants to Whom

It May Concern," November 10, 1919, attached to Addams to Blaine, Blaine MSS., NAACP File.

17. Bentley to Aldis, November 10, 1919, Aldis MSS., Race Prejudice File. Identical letters bearing the same date are to be found in the Rosenwald and Blaine MSS.

18. MacNeal to Graves, April 3, 1920, Rosenwald MSS., NAACP File.

19. See Chicago Commission on Race Relations, *The Negro in Chicago*, pp. xxiii–xxiv; Merriam, *Chicago*, pp. 144–147; and Lloyd Lewis and Henry Justin Smith, *Chicago: The History of Its Reputation* (New York: Harcourt, Brace, 1929), pp. 388–397.

20. Alain Locke, "The New Negro," in Alain Locke, ed., *The New Negro* (New York: Atheneum, 1992), pp. 3–4.

21. Frazier, "Chicago: A Cross-Section of Negro Life," 73.

22. *Chicago Defender,* January 3, 1920, p. 15.

23. Frederick H. H. Robb, ed. and comp., *The Negro in Chicago* (Chicago: Washington Intercollegian Wonder Book, 1927), p. 16.

24. Drake and Cayton, *Black Metropolis*, pp. 81–82.

25. Graves to Rosenwald, January 26, 1920, Rosenwald MSS., NAACP File.

26. Bagnall to Johnson, November 29, 1920, NAACP MSS., Spec. Corres.: Bagnall.

27. Bagnall to Ovington, July 20, 1920, NAACP MSS., Spec. Corres.: Bagnall.

28. Bagnall to Johnson, March 11, 1922, and October 18, 1922, both in NAACP MSS., Spec. Corres.: Bagnall.

29. Bagnall to Johnson, March 11, 1922, NAACP MSS., Spec. Corres.: Bagnall.

30. Ibid.

31. Bagnall to Johnson, October 18, 1922, NAACP MSS., Spec. Corres.: Bagnall.

32. Ickes to Addams, November 1, 1922, Ickes MSS., NAACP File.

33. Reed, "Civic Organization," p. 66.

34. Lewis to Bagnall, April 17, 1922, NAACP MSS., Branch Files.

35. Lewis to Bagnall, March 27, 1922, and October 9, 1922, both in NAACP MSS., Branch Files.

36. Bagnall to Williams, November 8, 1922, NAACP MSS., Branch Files.

37. Spear, *Black Chicago,* pp. 65, 66.

38. Bagnall to Ovington, October 26, 1922, NAACP MSS., Spec. Corres.: Bagnall.

39. William E. Leuchtenburg, *Franklin D. Roosevelt and the New Deal* (New York: Harper and Row, 1963), p. 71.

40. Lewis to Bagnall, March 15, 1923, NAACP MSS., Branch Files.

41. Eugene W. Levy, "James Weldon Johnson and the Development of the NAACP," in Franklin and Meier, eds., *Black Leaders of the Twentieth Century*, p. 228.

42. Ickes's preoccupation with politics is attested to in the following items: Lewis to Bagnall, March 15, 1923; Bagnall to Lewis, April 3, 1923; Lewis to Bagnall, December 8, 1923—all in NAACP MSS., Branch Files.

43. Lewis to Bagnall, November 21, 1924; Lewis to Johnson, December 11,

1924; Bagnall to Lewis, October 8, 1925; Lewis to Bagnall, October 10, 1925—all in NAACP MSS., Branch Files.

44. Weaver to White, September 26, 1932, and October 11, 1932, NAACP MSS., Branch Files.

45. Pickens's penchant for gossip and information from any source is seen in Pickens to White, November 28, 1932. See Weaver to Bagnall, December 26, 1930, and June 10, 1931, along with Weaver to White, October 11, 1932, to ascertain Weaver's close association with the national office. For other examples of the officious tone Weaver assumed in his correspondence: Weaver to White, September 26, 1932, and Weaver to National Office, July 31, 1933, all items in NAACP MSS., Branch Files.

46. Reed, "Civic Organization," pp. 66, 67, and Frazier, "Chicago: A Cross-Section of Negro Life," p. 73.

47. Lewis to Bagnall, January 15, 20, and 25, 1923, all in NAACP MSS., Branch Files.

48. Lewis to Johnson, November 25, 1923, NAACP MSS., Branch Files.

49. Johnson to Ickes, December 22, 1924, NAACP MSS., Branch Files.

50. Du Bois, "Postscript," *The Crisis* (December 1929): 423. See also Ovington's comments on Bentley's administrative inefficiency by the 1920s: Ovington to Addams, October 23, 1922, NAACP MSS., Branch Files.

51. Lewis to White, January 21, 1922, NAACP MSS., Branch Files. Also, *Chicago Defender,* February 7, 1920, p. 16; February 14, 1920, p. 16; and February 21, 1920, p. 12. Dr. Bentley was also a member.

52. Philpott, *Slum and Ghetto,* p. 228. Given the branch's failure to develop an efficiently run program, it was surprising to black Chicagoans to see a quarter-page *Defender* ad in 1922 giving ten reasons why they should join a supposedly active, program-oriented NAACP! Fighting to gain ground, however, publication of an especially insightful program brochure in 1923 at least gave the impression to black citizens that the branch was aware of their concerns. The program brochure even called for vigilance on the housing front to prevent residential segregation from developing through municipal legislation. This warning preceded by one year the U.S. Supreme Court's decision in *Corrigan vs. Buckley* which upheld the legality of restrictive covenants. Previously, *Buchanan v. Waring* had struck down local zoning laws that promoted segregation as unconstitutional. In the educational sphere, the branch acknowledged the existence of *de facto* segregation in the Chicago Public Schools as a recurring problem even though no formal definition of the problem was at hand. On a case by case basis, the branch took on the challenge. It also tackled another significant problem—that of encouraging greater parental involvement in elementary and secondary parent-teacher associations. See "The NAACP: Its History, Achievements," 1923, NAACP MSS., Branch Files.

53. *Chicago Defender,* March 24, 1924, p. 6. See also Lewis to Bagnall, March 30, 1923, NAACP MSS., Branch Files.

54. Lewis to Bagnall, April 3, 1923, NAACP MSS., Branch Files.

55. Drake and Cayton, *Black Metropolis,* p. 77.

56. Abram L. Harris, *The Negro as Capitalist: A Study of Banking and Business among American Negroes* (1936; Gloucester, MA: Peter Smith, repr. 1968), p. 163.

57. "Binga State Bank," *Messenger* (November 1923): 5.

58. Johnson, "These Colored United States," 926–929, 933; Frazier, "Chicago: A Cross-Section of Negro Life," 70–73. One observation that especially irritated black Chicagoans was their conclusion that the Black Metropolis lacked an intelligentsia.

59. *Chicago Defender,* January 22, 1920, p. 16.

60. His enthusiasm was exemplified in his denunciatory rhetoric in the Congress as he lambasted southern states rights advocates who "only prated of state power when it was sought, with federal aid, to make the South obey the law." The early success of the effort, once it passed in the lower house of the Congress, was thwarted later by its failure to pass in the Senate. Although this setback bequeathed action on this matter to a succeeding generation, one immediate benefit was a substantial reduction in the number of lynchings because of this sustained pressure. See Warren D. St. James, *Triumph of a Pressure Group, 1909–1980* (Smithtown, NY: Exposition Press, 2nd ed., 1980), p. 161. See Zangrando, *NAACP Crusade against Lynching,* for a full treatment of the NAACP's effort to end this terror.

61. Gosnell, *Negro Politicians,* p. 229. See also George F. Robinson, Jr., "The Negro in Politics in Chicago," *Journal of Negro History* 17 (April 1932): 190–191, and *Chicago Defender,* May 27, 1933, p. 15.

62. Barnett Hodes, Corporation Counsel, to Hon. W. J. Cowley, July 29, 1938, Adm. File, Subject File: 1910–1940, Segregation-Chicago, NAACP MSS.

63. *Chicago Defender,* October 21, 1939, p. 1.

64. A recent dissertation exploring the extent to which the machine rewarded its constituents has given fresh, detailed narrative and analysis on the nature of the civic-political relationship. Now Diane H. Pinderhughes, *Race and Ethnicity in Chicago Politics: A Re-examination of Pluralist Theory* (Urbana: University of Illinois Press, 1987), has established the failure of the political machine, despite near black autonomy, to deliver equitably to blacks what it did for other ethnic components.

65. Ralph J. Bunche, "The Thompson-Negro Alliance," *Opportunity* (March 1929), p. 78.

66. Stanley Coben, "The First Years of Modern America: 1918–1933," in William E. Leuchtenburg, ed., *The Unfinished Century: America since 1900* (Boston: Little, Brown, 1973), p. 301; Philpott, *Slum and Ghetto,* pp. 188–190.

67. Merriam, *Chicago,* p. 146.

68. *Chicago Defender,* January 16, 1926, pt. 1, p. 1.

69. Bentley to Bagnall, March 13, 1922, NAACP MSS., Branch Files.

70. *Chicago Tribune,* January 16, 1926, pt. 1, p. 1.

71. Chindblom to Aldis, June 24, 1920, Aldis MSS., Race Prejudice File.

72. *Chicago Defender,* October 21, 1922, p. 2. and November 4, 1922, p. 2. See Zangrando, *NAACP Crusade against Lynching,* pp. 72–80. Despite the possibility

that some northern branches might be able to effectively mount concerted campaigns against senators who voted against the Dyer bill, the likelihood of such an effort ever being initiated given the strength of the Chicago Republican submachine under the leadership of Edward Wright was unlikely. The convening of the Non-Partisan National Association of Colored Voters in Chicago during late summer had no effect on the political situation in Chicago where party interests often overrode the interests of race betterment.

73. Lewis to Bagnall, September 9, 1922, NAACP MSS., Branch Files.

5. The Black Patriarchy, 1925–1932

1. Lewis to Bagnall, April 20, 1923, NAACP MSS., Branch Files.

2. *Chicago Defender,* February 22, 1930, p. 16.

3. Johnson, "These Colored United States," 933. Frazier, "Chicago: A Cross-Section of Negro Life," p. 70.

4. Bagnall to Lewis, October 8, 1925, NAACP MSS., Branch Files. It is significant that in the supercharged world of American color caste prejudice, tensions mounted during the twenties among African Americans of different hues. The anxieties were fueled partially during this century by the utterances of Marcus Garvey, who, on one occasion, referred to W. E. B. Du Bois as the "pale shame." Du Bois's retort had been to describe Garvey as a "short, squat, dark, ugly man." But most importantly, representing the vestiges of deep-seated experiences, these tensions were equally pronounced among the racial egalitarians themselves. J. Max Barber, who was brown-skinned, said of Walter White, who possessed blue eyes, blond hair, and a skin tone light enough for him to be regularly mistaken for a Caucasian: "I never did trust Walter White. . . . Somehow I never warmed up to him—never quite trusted a half-white or near white Negro. He is under a diversity of complexes which do not help his soul. . . . Mulattoes have split souls. . . . Those split loyalties make them shifting men, unreliable, treacherous." One wonders how Barber felt about Du Bois, with whom he supposedly had good relations. This quote is taken from Barber to Pickens, 18 June 1930, Box 1, William Pickens Papers, Schomburg Center for research in Black culture, Harlem, New York City. For his part, Pickens, who was very dark, referred to Garvey as a "squat, energetic, gorilla-jawed black man." Pickens's biographer, Sheldon Avery, described his subject as "quite black, with a high forehead, protruding brow, flat nose, and thick lips" (see Avery, *Up from Washington,* p. 204, note 19). Pickens was described by Roy Wilkins as "homely as a mud hen" in a basically complimentary note (see Wilkins, *Standing Fast* [New York: Viking Press, 1981], p. 98).

5. Michael Homel, *Down from Equality: Black Chicagoans and the Public Schools, 1920–1941* (Urbana: University of Illinois Press, 1984), pp. 155–157, details the NAACP's most extensive involvement, which occurred in the Far South Side Morgan Park community.

6. *Chicago Defender,* November 23, 1930, p. 5.

7. The role of women within the branch was limited to fund-raising activities, with no woman becoming a member of the Executive Committee until 1925 and no woman president until 1954.

8. Weaver to NAACP, February 27, 1926, NAACP MSS., Branch Files.

9. Annual Report for 1931, December 16, 1931, p. 9, NAACP MSS., Branch Files.

10. Duster, *Crusade for Justice*, pp. 346–348; *Chicago Defender*, February 28, 1914, pp. 1, 2.

11. Weaver to Bagnall, June 13, 1926, NAACP MSS., Branch Files.

12. *Chicago Defender*, November 22, 1930, p. 5. De Priest was even nominated for the Spingarn medal in 1930. See Weaver to National Office, May 19, 1930, NAACP MSS., Branch Files.

13. *Chicago Defender*, June 7, 1930, p. 8.

14. Ibid., May 17, 1930, p. 5; Strickland, *History of the Chicago Urban League*, pp. 74–79, 96–98; Stern to Rosenwald, October 15, 1929, Rosenwald MSS., Chicago Urban League File, along with Barnett to Stern, January 19, 1929, Claude A. Barnett MSS., Rosenwald Fund File, Chicago Historical Society.

15. Ovington to Ickes, June 18, 1925, Ickes MSS., NAACP File.

16. *Chicago Defender*, November 21, 1925, pt. 1, p. 3, and November 28, 1925, pt. 2, p. 10.

17. *The Crisis* (July 1926): 119.

18. Ibid. (May 1926): 24.

19. Bagnall to Weaver, July 12, 1926, NAACP MSS., Branch Files.

20. "To the NAACP Conference," June 22, 1927, NAACP MSS., Branch Files.

21. Haynes to White, January 12, 1925, and White to Proctor, January 14, 1925, NAACP MSS., Adm. Files: Theater Discrimination.

22. The Morgan Park community on the far southwestern fringe of the city represented one such hot spot. A long-residing black population composed of homeowners fought to repulse insult and official connivance involving school overcrowding, manipulative boundary changes, and bias at social gatherings. See "To the NAACP Conference," June 22, 1927, NAACP MSS., Branch Files. Also, Andrew to Turner, November xx, 1928, NAACP MSS., Branch Files; *Chicago Defender*, April 2, 1927, pt. 2, p. 2, and November 22, 1930, p. 5. For a complete history of a two-decade struggle for educational parity see Homel, *Down from Equality*.

23. *Chicago Defender*, March 2, 1914, p. 4, and Roi Ottley, *The Lonely Warrior: The Life and Times of Robert S. Abbott* (Chicago: Henry Regnery, 1955), pp. 124–132.

24. *The Crisis* (May 1913): 28.

25. Drake and Cayton, *Black Metropolis*, p. 752.

26. Tony Martin, *Race First: The Ideological and Organizational Struggle of Marcus Garvey and the Universal Negro Improvement Association* (Dover, MA: Majority Press, 1976), p. 279.

27. Lewis to Bagnall, October 13, 1923, NAACP MSS., Branch Files.

28. *Chicago Defender*, October 17, 1925, pt. 2, p. 12; October 31, 1925, pt. 1, p. 4; November 7, 1925, pt. 2, p. 10.

29. Ibid., July 7, 1928, pt. 2, p. 10, and March 5, 1927, pt. 1, p. 11. See also

Chicago Urban League Annual Reports for 1926 and 1928 in the Salmon O. Levinson MSS., Chicago Urban League File, Regenstein Library, the University of Chicago as well as for 1927, Rosenwald MSS., same named file.

30. Roger Biles, *Big City Boss in Depression and War* (De Kalb, IL: Northern Illinois University Press, 1982), pp. 21–23.

31. Eighteenth Annual Report of the Chicago Urban League, 1931–1932, p. 8, and Chicago Urban League Annual report: 1929–1941, bound copy.

32. Chicago City Council, *Journal of the Proceedings of the Chicago City Council,* October 22, 1930, pp. 3751–3752.

33. U.S., Congress, House, 71st Cong., 3rd. sess., January 30, 1931, 74: 3648.

34. Bagnall to Lampkin, November 28, 1930, and November 25, 1931; Bagnall to Weaver, November 28, 1932; Bagnall to Pickens, November 21, 1932; all in NAACP MSS., Branch Files.

35. Weaver to Bagnall, June 10, 1931, NAACP MSS., Branch Files.

36. Interview with Dr. Arthur G. Falls on March 10, 1978, in Chicago.

37. Annual Report of the Chicago NAACP, December 21, 1932, p. 11, NAACP MSS., Branch Files.

38. *Chicago Defender,* November 8, 1930, p. 5.

39. Telegram, Herbert A. Turner to Senator Charles S. Deneen, April 14, 1930, NAACP MSS., Branch Files.

40. Weaver to White, September 26, 1932, NAACP MSS., Branch Files.

41. Weaver to NAACP.

42. Bagnall to Turner, January 11, 1920, NAACP MSS., Branch Files.

43. *Chicago Defender,* December 6, 1930, p. 2.

44. Ethel R. Harris, "A Study of Voluntary Social Activity among the Professional Negroes of Chicago" (M.A. thesis, University of Chicago, 1937), p. 87.

45. Annual Report for the year December 1, 1931, to November 30, 1932, NAACP MSS., Branch Files.

46. White to Carl G. Roberts, April 25, 1930, NAACP MSS., Branch Files.

47. Bagnall to Daisy E. Lampkin, September 29, 1930, Adm. File, Spec. Corres.: Bagnall File; Archie L. Weaver to Bagnall, June 9, 1931, Branch Files; and *Chicago Sunday Bee,* November 23, 1930, in branch Files, all in NAACP MSS.

48. Weaver to Wilkins, June 17, 1932, NAACP MSS., Branch Files.

49. May 3, 1930, pt. 2, p. 16. Nelson, writing on the Philadelphia branch, found that its membership never exceeded 1,400 (*Philadelphia N.A.A.C.P.,* p. 38).

50. Kathryn M. Johnson to White, March 3, 1930, NAACP MSS., Branch Files.

51. Annual Report of the Chicago NAACP, December 16, 1931, p. 7, NAACP MSS., Branch Files.

52. *Chicago Defender,* May 17, 1930, p. 5. In comparison, the Philadelphia NAACP received very little support from black Philadelphia, or for that matter, any real interest in addressing the needs of the rank-and-file black Philadelphia population. By 1938, with a black population of 250,000, the branch had attracted 1,400 members and, with its middle-class orientation, had alienated a large portion of the citizenry. See Nelson, *Philadelphia N.A.A.C.P.,* pp. 1, 23–31.

53. Ottley, *The Lonely Warrior,* p. 126.

54. White to Lampkin, November 12, 1931, Adm. File, Spec. Corres.: White File, NAACP MSS. Also, Bagnall to Pickens, November 21, 1932, NAACP MSS., Branch Files.

55. Oliver Cromwell Cox, "The Origins of Direct-Action among Negroes in Chicago," p. 42 (MSS., 1932; rev. ed., c. 1965, microfiche copy at the Kent State University Libraries, Kent, Ohio.

56. Bagnall to Lampkin, October 28, 1930, NAACP MSS., Branch Files.

57. Robinson, "The Negro in Politics in Chicago," 228.

58. The political climate and the activities within it are covered in depth in Christopher Robert Reed, "Black Politics and Protest in Depression-decade Chicago" (Ph.D. diss., Kent State University, 1982), ch. 3.

59. August 6, 1931, p. 4.

60. Cox, "Origins of Direct-Action," p. 88.

61. Ibid., p. 92.

62. Interviews with Mrs. Lovelynn Evans on May 5, 1977, attorney Earl B. Dickerson on January 23, 1978, and Dr. Arthur G. Falls on March 10, 1978, all in Chicago.

63. Taped interview with Mr. Harry Haywood in Chicago in 1975, in the author's possession, and Gosnell, *Negro Politicians*, p. 323. It followed tactics which consisted "in putting forth concrete demands and slogans growing out of the every day economic or political life of the [locale] concerned. All workers, regardless of color, sex or age, [were] then called upon to unite for the securing of these demands." In particular, these demands revolved around those issues associated with the high level of economic deprivation being experienced during the early, pre–New Deal period. The Communist chapter shrewdly targeted unemployment, inadequate relief, and housing evictions. To structurally achieve its goals of alleviating the problems of the economically distressed, the Communist Party worked through several organizations, the activities of which often overlapped, to achieve its goals of alleviating the problems of the economically distressed. These were unlike Communist organizations that existed before 1930 in that before the Depression the personnel of all affiliated organizations were largely Communist, and in practice there was little separation from the general party line. Now, "cover" or "front" organizations were active that included Communists, Communist sympathizers, and non-Communist community activists. When properly controlled, the Communists hoped this arrangement would prove valuable in bringing about their desired "radicalization of the masses." The potentialities of the affiliated organizations seemed limitless, but there was often a large gap between theory and practice, and the Communists sometimes lost control of affiliated organizations. In Chicago, "the largest of five 'cover' [or affiliated] organizations of the depression period included the Unemployed Councils which had at least 80 locals [city-wide]." Founded in the fall of 1930, they were extremely active throughout the period and there were several locals on the South Side among blacks. The Unemployed Councils were active in Washington Park, a favorite ground of the dispossessed as well as the open-air, nationalist orators of

the day. It was from this municipal park facility, which stretched over a one-half square mile tract, that the crowds of men originated in late summer 1930 during the "street car riots." Then in 1931, the Councils assumed a high visibility in organizing blacks into groups that participated in the relief station protests and the eviction disturbances that culminated in the *cause célèbre* of the early thirties in Chicago—the eviction riot of August 3, 1931. Interestingly enough, due to strong, uncontrollable, non-Communist community leadership in some locals, there was no clear-cut course of action always followed in street demonstrations in 1930 and 1931. Protests, initially organized to deal with the problem of unemployment, often and unexpectedly branched off into what the party considered provincial, neighborhood concerns. They diverted beyond Communist control, much to the chagrin of party leaders. One such unit, led by Jesse "Pop" Helton, a black man, concentrated more on community problems than it did on any adherence to Marxist-Leninist doctrine. Helton maintained that he utilized the methods and finances of the Communists without accepting their ideology. Locals within the Unemployed Councils were broadly inclusive; among their members were jobless men, but also women and children. Dues for membership, reflective of the level of deprivation, were set at the minimum rate of two cents per week.

Perhaps the next most effective front organization employed by the party in its program aimed at winning support in the black community between 1929 and 1934 was the International Labor Defense (ILD). Although active programmatically before the Depression, it did not enjoy name recognition until the Scottsboro trial in 1931. Included in its ranks were many liberals and nonpolitical trade unionists. By November 1931, 49 branches in the city and suburbs contained a membership of 1,905. Closely affiliated with the ILD in its work was the creation of the League of Struggle for Negro Rights (LSNR), which took shape in November 1930. It sought to develop a wider-based race advancement movement than was already present as represented through the efforts of the Chicago NAACP and Chicago Urban League, and to bring a greater spectrum of blacks under party direction. When the Scottsboro incident occurred, it was the LSNR that "carried" the burden of the propaganda regarding the case in Chicago although the ILD was the legal arm nationally. The Trades Union Unity League (TUUL), which had been founded in the twenties, sought to build militant, racially integrated workers organizations in the steel and textile industries in Chicago. Its most notable affiliate in the city was the Needles Trades Workers Industrial Union. In March 1931, the TUUL presented Mayor Thompson with a petition that claimed to speak for 500,000 workers, demanding that $75 million be raised for unemployment relief; that evictions be stopped; that free gas, electricity, and food be provided to the jobless; that the school-age children of the unemployed be given hot lunches in school; and that blacks be given an equal opportunity to obtain work. Timely and fitting as these workers' demands appeared, there is no record of any governmental action taken by the Thompson administration to fulfill them. Internal problems accompanied encounters with the government, because less than a year from this energetic beginning, the TUUL was being criticized within the party hierarchy because it "was isolated from the masses, employed poor strike strategy, displayed a tendency toward formalism, and exhibited weakness in boring from within the old-line unions." Lastly, the Communists organized youths into the Young Communist League (YCL) which comprised college and pre-college students. It had support at the University of Chicago and was active in the black community in the period before 1932, but its most active period came later in the decade. See Gosnell, *Negro Politicians,* pp. 323, 339; Laswell and Blumenstock, *World Revolutionary Propaganda,* pp. 72, 78, and 323; interview with Jesse "Pop" Helton, May 16, 1972, Chicago.

64. *Chicago Defender,* November 5, 1932, p. 1.

65. Representative of these marches was the one of October 31, 1931, which metaphorically called on thousands to speak through their marching feet. In April 1932, the *Defender* reported that "two thousand men and women of mixed races and nationalities, representing the Unemployed Council and the Communist Party, marched to the Union Stockyards Tuesday afternoon and for a time it was feared the horde would storm the gates." Despite the high level of apprehension on the part of the governmental and police leaderships, conflict was avoided and interracial cooperation flowered. During 1931 and 1932, the Communist Party and its front organizations also organized another series of dramatic street incidents which took place in front of welfare stations. The actual exhaustion of relief funds in Chicago and Cook County occurred in February 1932 and, as a consequence, the Illinois General Assembly approved the appropriation of millions of dollars to meet the needs of the deprived. With this action, the harsh conditions under which Chicagoans had bravely suffered began to ease substantially. The total amount of money spent from both private and public sources for the year, $34 million, would be ten times as much as that spent in 1930 and nearly three times as much as the total for 1931. With this huge financial investment to relieve suffering, the Communists lost one of the key issues from which they could generate protest. *Chicago Defender,* October 31, 1931, p. 1, and April 23, 1932, p. 13; also Lasswell and Blumenstock, *World Revolutionary Propaganda,* p. 368.

66. Gosnell, *Negro Politicians,* pp. 320–321.

67. Ibid., p. 337.

68. Gosnell, *Negro Politicians,* p. 352, and Drake and Cayton, *Black Metropolis,* p. 738n and pp. 738f.

69. Drake, "Churches and Voluntary Associations in the Chicago Negro Community," p. 257. See also Ralph J. Bunche's Carnegie memorandum from the 1940s, published as *The Political Status of the Negro in the Age of FDR* (Chicago: University of Chicago Press, 1972), p. 578. Black members were usually young men and women in their twenties and thirties, unemployed, educated above the community level, and disillusioned with Christianity. By 1931, the Scottsboro case had attracted some very well-educated black persons, including some lawyers and poets, into the party's ranks. To a significant degree, the Communist genius in assembling and preaching to, but not necessarily converting, the masses accounted for the impression that developed that thousands actively belonged to

the "comrade's party." See Samuel M. Strong, "Social Types in the Negro Community of Chicago" (Ph.D. diss., University of Chicago, 1940), pp. 261, 262, and Gosnell, *Negro Politicians,* p. 348.

70. Wilson Record, *Race and Radicalism: The NAACP and the Communist Party in Conflict* (Ithaca: Cornell University Press, 1964), pp. viii, x.

71. Pickens to Weaver, June 20, 1931, NAACP MSS., Branch Files.

72. Telegram, Turner to White, August 5, 1931, NAACP MSS., Branch Files.

73. Mann to Press Service, NAACP, December 5, 1931, NAACP MSS., Branch Files.

74. Weaver to National Office, January 28, 1930, NAACP MSS., Branch Files.

75. *Chicago Defender,* January 31, 1931, p. 2.

76. Theophilus Mann to Press Service, December 30, 1931, NAACP MSS., Branch Files.

77. The police killing of a black man, Walter Collins, in his own home shook black Chicagoans to attention in 1930. As the twelfth in a series of South Side killings by police officers in a relatively short span of time, it attracted the attention of the national office (after an expression of concern from the Detroit NAACP in the matter). Once alerted, the Chicago branch began a probe of the shooting "with a doggedness and determination without parallel" and with a promise from Dr. Herbert Turner to carry the case to its just conclusion. Particularly disturbing to Turner was the fact that the killing of black men somehow apparently resulted in police department promotions. In the seeming absence of a follow-up report by the Legal Redress Committee, presumably the case was either dropped or lost in the courts. In 1931, the Legal Redress Committee continued its activities, investigating one case that involved the pistol-whipping of a black shopkeeper, Ernest T. Draine. Draine ran afoul of some overzealous law enforcement officials while attempting to keep a pledge to a neighboring businessman to protect his property while the man was away for an extended period. An altercation with police officers at the neighbor's property left Draine beaten, humiliated, and arrested, subsequently, on charges of drunkenness and resisting arrest. Immediately following the arrest, a trial judge at the Forty-Eighth Street Police Station refused to prosecute Draine because of the ludicrous nature of the charges. Then the original trial judge tried to get him and Attorney Earl B. Dickerson and his colleagues to drop the charges before the Civil Service Commission. A crusade led by the branch and including the *Chicago Defender* and the all-black Cook County Bar Association ensued. At a civil service commission hearing two months later, the officers were exonerated because of "political influence." White to Turner, March 3, 1930, NAACP MSS., Branch Files. See also *Chicago Defender,* March 8, 1930, p. 16, October 31, 1931, p. 1, and November 5, 1932, p. 1.

78. Press Release, December 27, 1933, and June 6, 1933, both in NAACP MSS., Branch Files, and interview with Earl B. Dickerson of January 23, 1978, in Chicago.

79. Spear, *Black Chicago,* p. 22.

80. White to [Marcus] Hirsch, October 16, 1930, and Bagnall to Weaver, October 16, 1930, both in NAACP MSS., Branch Files.

81. Frederick Burgess Lindstrom, "The Negro Invasion of the Washington Park Subdivision" (M.A. thesis, University of Chicago, 1941), p. 6.

82. Bagnall to Weaver, October 16, 1930, NAACP MSS., Branch Files.

83. Herman H. Long and Charles S. Johnson, *People vs. Property* (Nashville: Fisk University Press, 1947), p. 13.

84. Wilkins to Turner, October 31, 1932, NAACP MSS., Branch Files.

85. *Chicago Defender,* May 24, 1930, p. 5. For supportive views on the decisive role of African American lobbying, both political and civic, in bringing about Parker's defeat, see Goings, *The NAACP Comes of Age;* Walter White, *A Man Called White* (New York: Viking Press, 1948), pp. 104–115; and Wilkins, *Standing Fast,* pp. 91–92; 98. For a dissenting view, see Sitkoff, *A New Deal for Blacks,* p. 85. The latter maintains that pro-active labor and apathetic Southern Democratic influence, rather than activist racial activities, doomed the nomination.

86. White to Turner, January 26, 1932, NAACP MSS., Branch Files.

87. *Chicago Defender,* November 12, 1932, p. 5.

88. Pickens to Bagnall, December 3, 1932, NAACP MSS., Branch Files. In another letter, this time to Walter White, he responded: "In reply to your inquiry as to whether it is best to keep silent or to attempt to answer some of the critics, I agree with what is evidently your own opinion: that it would do more harm to publicly answer some of them, than it would to ignore them. In Chicago here, I have very well taken care of the situation in a casual way by the addresses which I have delivered and by showing the colored people how foolish it is for them to fall out over white people's politics." Pickens to Bagnall, November 17, 1932, NAACP MSS., Branch Files. At a meeting on November 13, 1932, Pickens had been called on by Chicagoans to explain the heavy involvement of the national office in national politics. See *Chicago Defender,* November 19, 1932, p. 22.

89. Pickens to Bagnall, November 17, 1932, NAACP MSS., Branch Files.

90. Bagnall to Lampkin, June 20, 1932, NAACP MSS., Branch Files.

91. Weaver to Pickens, Oct. 21, 1932, NAACP MSS., Branch Files.

6. A. C. MacNeal and the "Whole Loaf or None at All," 1933–1937

1. Williams to White, October 11, 1932, NAACP MSS., Branch Files.

2. Pickens to White, November 28, 1932; Pickens to Bagnall, November 30, 1932; "Dean" [Pickens] to White and Bagnall, December 3, 1932—all in NAACP MSS., Branch Files.

3. Interview with Mrs. Lovelynn Evans, May 5, 1977, in Chicago.

4. In Bronzeville, skin color and personality development were also interwoven as explored in Lloyd Warner et al., *Color and Human Nature: Negro Personality Development in a Northern City* (Washington, DC: American Council on Education, 1941), pp. 1, 20, 160–161, 167–168, and 190. Lewis's recent *W. E. B. Du Bois* further explores how the major architect of NAACP thinking among African Americans

channeled his ambitions and frustrations into an ideological and organiztional good. Moreover, the "Chicago School" of the Department of Sociology at the University of Chicago pioneered in the study of racial marginality. Major studies on this subject are Everett V. Stonequist, *The Marginal Man: A Study in Personality and Culture Conflict* (New York: Charles Scribners Sons, 1937), pp. 107, 110, 111; E. Franklin Frazier, *The Negro Family in Chicago* (Chicago: University of Chicago Press, 1932), note 3 on pp. 103, 104; and Edward Byron Reuter, *Race Mixture: Studies in Intermarriage and Miscegenation* (New York: McGraw, Hill, Brown, 1931), pp. 207f. and note 43, p. 171.

5. Kersey to Mitchell, August 3, 1935, Mitchell MSS.

6. Wilkins to MacNeal, March 26, 1936, NAACP MSS., Branch Files.

7. MacNeal to Goings, May 5, 1933; MacNeal to Hoffman, May 6, 1933; MacNeal to Horner, May 6, 1933; MacNeal to White, May 13, 1933—all in NAACP MSS., Branch Files. See also Press Release, May 27, 1922, NAACP MSS., Branch Files, and *Chicago Defender*, July 8, 1933, p. 4.

8. Press Release, July 8, 1933, p. 4. During this period, the Philadelphia NAACP continued its programmatic stagnancy, standing in stark contrast to the aggressive effort underway in Chicago. See Nelson, *Philadelphia N.A.A.C.P.*, pp. 23–31 (as well as n. 75 on p. 51, which seems to contradict the author's position).

9. "Notes and Proposals of the Executive Committee," February 1933, NAACP MSS., Branch Files.

10. Ibid.

11. Ibid.

12. Memorandum, New York Office, July 23, 1933, NAACP MSS., Branch Files.

13. In retaliation, Turner started a rumor that the new president lacked sufficient finances to administer his duties. Turner next turned his wrath on those members on the Executive Committee who voted at the end of his term to accept responsibility for holding the 1933 annual NAACP conference. Turner knew all too well that it was his personal financial commitment of money, name, and reputation as collateral that kept the branch operating. Now the leadership assumed that it could do what it had failed to do in his eight years in office—finance a successful and very expensive national conference. Even though Archie L. Weaver, in branch correspondence, described the presidential succession as having been conducted smoothly, the transfer of power from Turner to MacNeal was just as tempestuous beneath the surface as the succession from Roberts to Turner had been in 1925. See Weaver to Pickens, January 8, 1933, and Memo, New York Office, July 23, 1933, NAACP MSS., Branch Files.

14. Hansberry to Jackson, April 7, 1936, NAACP MSS., Branch Files.

15. MacNeal to White, April 3, 1937, NAACP MSS., Branch Files.

16. "Proposal for the Immediate Establishment of a Regional Office . . ." attached to Hansberry to Board of Directors, April 29, 1936, NAACP MSS., Branch Files.

17. Interview with Edwin Marciniak on January 19, 1988, Chicago.

18. Press Release, July 5, 1933, NAACP MSS., Branch Files.

19. MacNeal to Wilkins, April 4, 1936, NAACP MSS., Branch Files. Ovington was still as staunch an egalitarian as she had been in 1909, which made MacNeal's assessment of her inappropriate. In 1934 she delivered a speech before some of the NAACP faithful in which she criticized blacks within the Association who excluded whites from participation. See undated draft of speech in 1934 NAACP MSS., Branch Files.

20. MacNeal to Breckenridge, March 20, 1933, and March 27, 1933, both in Breckenridge MSS., Correspondence—NAACP.

21. Chicago NAACP Resolution On Segregation to the National Board of Directors, April–May 1934, NAACP MSS., Branch Files. The "whole loaf or none" approach abounded with inconsistencies, flaws, and deficits in logic. At the root of these flaws stood the immediate needs of black Chicagoans in contrast to a great ideal. Writing in the *Chicago Defender* on February 16, 1935, MacNeal lambasted "foundations and interested persons who benefit by salary who foisted a system of Jim Crow which will finally operate throughout the north and prevent Race medical students from entering the best schools for their training in medicine. The Jim Crow system has had the active support of some of the Race physicians who had stood all the insults of the white heads of Provident Hospital and the University of Chicago in order to pose and be 'big Negroes,' no matter how it hurts the coming generation of Race men in the profession." In addition to Provident as a target, the foundation referred to was the Rosenwald Foundation, a constant foil of MacNeal's.

22. MacNeal to White, March 23, 1933; MacNeal to the Organized Jewry of America, March 23, 1933; White to MacNeal, March 29, 1933—all in NAACP MSS., Branch Files.

23. Pickens to White, June 6, 1933, NAACP MSS., Branch Files.

24. Pickens to Wilkins, June 12, 1934, NAACP MSS., Branch Files.

25. Pickens to Bagnall, November 30, 1932, NAACP MSS., Branch Files.

26. MacNeal to White, May 27, 1933, NAACP MSS., Branch Files.

27. Annual Report for 1933, found in Memo to Wilkins and Pickens, January 31, 1934, NAACP MSS., Branch Files. In contrast, the Detroit branch during the thirties reached membership levels of 1,800 in 1935, 2,400 in 1937, 3,300 in 1938, and 6,000 in 1939 (Meier and Rudwick, *Black Detroit and the Rise of the UAW*, p. 79).

28. Press Release, July 8, 1933, p. 5, NAACP MSS., Branch Files.

29. MacNeal to Wilkins, March 14, 1936, NAACP MSS., Branch Files.

30. Press Release, June 12, 1933, NAACP MSS., Branch Files.

31. Drake and Cayton, *Black Metropolis*, p. 101.

32. Notes from Charles V. Hamilton's lecture on "The Dual Agenda: Social Policies of Civil Rights Groups from the New Deal to the Present," delivered on March 29, 1990, at Roosevelt University, Chicago.

33. Lampkin to White, December 5, 1936, NAACP MSS., Branch Files.

34. White to Lampkin, November 27, 1936, NAACP MSS., Branch Files.

35. The racial composition of this committee—a legal corps that was predomi-

nantly black—was a matter of pride to African Americans in Chicago. The nature of the change nationally within NAACP ranks from a white to a black legal corps is contained in Meier and Rudwick, "Attorneys Black and White: A Case Study of Race Relations within the NAACP," in Meier and Rudwick, eds., *Along the Color Line*, pp. 128–173. This essay mentions that while in Chicago in politically charged November 1932, William Pickens was criticized as a representative of the NAACP for the organization's near sole reliance on white lawyers (p. 148 and n. 110).

36. Press Release, July 10, 1933, NAACP MSS., Branch Files. Also see Press Release, June 5, 1933, and MacNeal to Williams, June 3, 1935, in the same archival source.

37. Telephone interview with Earl B. Dickerson in Chicago on December 16, 1982.

38. However, by the summer of 1933, MacNeal complained that the branch was losing the momentum it had generated earlier. Just as MacNeal had predicted, inactivity on the branch's part (while the problem persisted and received widespread, public attention), led one national black women's group to begin its own, independent campaign against Sears. By the fall, the most overt forms of discrimination stopped at Sears but the conflict had placed Walter White and the national office in a compromising situation with an activist Chicago branch.

39. Christopher Robert Reed, "A Reinterpretation of Black Strategies for Change at the Chicago World's Fair of 1933–1934," *Illinois Historical Journal* 81 (Spring 1988): 2–12.

40. *Chicago Defender,* June 10, 1933, p. 4; June 17, 1933, p. 4; October 28, 1933, p. 13; November 11, 1933, p. 17.

41. *Pittsburgh Courier,* August 12, 1933, sec. 1, p. 5, and *Chicago Defender,* August 26, 1933, p. 1. Also, List of Delegates [to the meeting of July 27, 1933], July 1933, NAACP MSS., Branch Files.

42. NAACP MSS., Branch Files.

43. *Chicago Defender,* February 18, 1939, p. 1.

44. The branch supported the legal defense of the boys and young men but questioned the national office's timidity in dealing with the Communist-related International Labor Defense (ILD) as well as the timing of New York's initiating activities. MacNeal was a frequent critic of what he perceived to be a cowardly approach toward the Left even before the Communists softened their attitude toward mainstream civil rights organizations in the mid-thirties. One successful meeting on the Scottsboro defense brought a nervous, unsure Association Counsel, Charles H. Houston, to Chicago in 1937 in the role of featured speaker for the national campaign. More effective on the rostrum than he imagined, he articulately convinced the assemblage of the continued need for the Association's actions in behalf of southern blacks. However, this campaign started at the same time the branch was raising money for its local defense fund drive against the restrictive covenant. The latter was an issue which was very popular to Chicagoans and one expected to bring greater support for the branch's program overall. Even though Chicagoans were sympathetic with the Scottsboro victims, instances

involving the color line were just as real to them since there was always the possibility that some of them might stray across a racial boundary and be attacked in Chicago, or suffer police harassment and possible brutality. The anti-lynching crusade initiated by the national office occupied a similar position as Scottsboro did in the hearts of black Chicagoans. Black Chicagoans were continually made aware of conditions in the South by the *Chicago Defender* and correspondence from relatives; therefore, interest remained current. During the time that the branch supported the anti-lynching crusade, it successfully stopped several attempts at extradition and the potential lynching of black men who had reached the safety of the city.

45. Meier and Rudwick, *Black Detroit and the Rise of the UAW*, p. 56.

46. Press Release, August 1, 1933, NAACP MSS., Branch Files.

47. Program Brochure, September 1933, NAACP MSS., Branch Files.

48. MacNeal to White, May 27, 1933, NAACP MSS., Branch Files.

49. MacNeal to Johnson, July 27, 1933, and MacNeal to Ickes, July 27, 1933, both in NAACP MSS., Branch Files. Also see the Annual Report of the Department of Branches, February 10, 1936, NAACP MSS., Branch Files.

50. *Chicago Defender*, July 8, 1933, p. 12.

51. Eugene W. Levy, *James Weldon Johnson: Black Leader, Black Voice* (Chicago: University of Chicago Press, 1973), p. 227.

52. MacNeal to White, April 28, 1934, NAACP MSS., Branch Files.

53. MacNeal to White, April 24, 1936, NAACP MSS., Branch Files.

54. MacNeal to White, October 20, 1933, NAACP MSS., Branch Files. Also, *Chicago Defender*, March 31, 1934, p. 24 and April 14, 1934, p. 10.

55. W. E. B. Du Bois, *Dusk of Dawn* (New York: Schocken Books, 1970), pp. 197f.

56. MacNeal to White, October 20, 1933, and April 28, 1934, as well as MacNeal to Mary White Ovington, May 12, 1934, all in NAACP MSS., Branch Files.

57. Wilkins to MacNeal, May 2, 1934, NAACP MSS., Branch Files.

58. Pickens to White, June 8, 1934, NAACP MSS., Branch Files.

59. Weaver to Pickens, October 26, 1934, NAACP MSS., Branch Files.

60. See Christopher R. Reed, "Black Chicago Political Realignment during the Great Depression and New Deal," *Illinois Historical Journal* 78 (Winter 1985): 232–246.

61. One major breach to local political neutrality occurred in 1936 when Association president Joel E. Spingarn came to Chicago to speak at the Democratic national convention on behalf of Franklin D. Roosevelt. According to Spingarn's biographer, he "chose to judge the Roosevelt Administration almost solely in terms of its efforts on behalf of black uplift." The impact of Spingarn's action extended further than would ordinarily be imagined. It caused a rift within the branch and threatened a much wider split within the Republican Black Metropolis as the Association now was liable to charges of partisanism. Following Spingarn's Chicago speech, Irvin C. Mollison, A. C. MacNeal, Carl A. Hansberry, and Spingarn argued on the advisability of the latter's using the speech for political endorsement. Mollison, surprisingly, came out for Spingarn's right to a personal

preference in political matters, and evidently was able to convince MacNeal and Hansberry of the legitimacy of his argument, since the dialogue ended on a peaceful note. Ross, *Spingarn,* p. 155, and White to Lampkin, October 30, 1936, NAACP MSS., Branch Files. Also, more exploratory than practical, the suggestion made by MacNeal to Walter White in 1935 to run a biracial duo for president and vice president has to be considered one of the most creative of the branch's political ideas. He justified this suggestion as follows: "The publicity attendant to such a move would certainly operate in such a manner to draw attention to the presently unstressed possibility that a Negro COULD be elected President. . . . It will at least give the Negro children of today a feeling that possibly their destiny in America 'might' include the White House." See MacNeal to White, May 27, 1935, NAACP MSS., Branch Files.

62. Wilkins to White, August 5, 1936, NAACP MSS., Spec. Corres.: White. For his part, Mitchell prided himself on how well he avoided confrontational situations with whites, just like Booker T. Washington. Oscar De Priest did it neither in the North nor in the Congress. See Reed, "Black Politics and Protest," pp. 88–92.

63. Weiss, in *Farewell to the Party of Lincoln,* pp. 87–89, explains Mitchell's victory in terms of the district electorate's acceptance of the New Deal policies. For an examination on how in black Chicago racial ideology withstood the political and economic incentives of New Deal democracy, see Reed, "Black Chicago Political Realignment during the Depression and New Deal," 242–256.

64. *Chicago Defender,* August 3, 1935, p. 1.

65. Mitchell to MacNeal, June 27, 1935, Mitchell MSS.

66. Resolution of the Chicago Branch, July 17, 1935, NAACP MSS., Branch Files.

67. Mitchell to Greene, August 6, 1935, Mitchell MSS.

68. Kersey to Mitchell, August 3, 1935, and Mitchell to Jones, August 13, 1935, both in Mitchell MSS. Also, Memo to White from Williams, August 7, 1935, NAACP MSS., Branch Files.

69. Mitchell to MacNeal, June 27, 1935, Mitchell MSS.

70. Hansberry to White, May 2, 1936, to NAACP MSS., Branch Files.

71. MacNeal to White, May 8, 1936, and attached telegram, NAACP MSS., Branch Files.

72. Mitchell to Sabath, March 5, 1935, Mitchell MSS. See Zangrando, *NAACP Crusade against Lynching,* pp. 141–142.

73. Attachment to Schuetz to MacNeal, January 20, 1936, Mitchell MSS.

74. Mitchell to MacNeal, June 27, 1935, Mitchell MSS.

75. White to Lampkin, April 20, 1936, NAACP MSS., Branch Files.

76. White to MacNeal, March 15, 1937, NAACP MSS., Branch Files.

77. MacNeal to White, March 17, 1937, NAACP MSS., Branch Files.

78. Wilkins to MacNeal, January 21, 1936, NAACP MSS., Branch Files. According to Naison, *Communists in Harlem,* pp. 177–184, the Association's caution was justified as the Communist Party decided to manipulate the opening conference in Chicago while maintaining a low profile, deliberately submerging them-

selves into nameless organizational work to make the conference a success, hoping that the small seeds they planted would bear fruit later.

79. Mollison to White, January 28, 1936, NAACP MSS., Branch Files.

80. MacNeal to Wilkins, March 14, 1936, NAACP MSS., Branch Files.

81. White to Spingarn, October 9, 1936, NAACP MSS., Branch Files.

7. Crises of Charter and War, 1938–1945

1. *Chicago Defender,* January 15, 1938, p. 3.

2. Press Release, January 8, 1939, NAACP MSS., Branch Files.

3. President's Report for 1938, Chicago NAACP, NAACP MSS., Branch Files.

4. "The Iron Ring of Housing," *The Crisis* (July 1940): 205.

5. Williams to White, September 28, 1939, NAACP MSS., Branch Files.

6. Morrow to National Office, November 14, 1939, NAACP MSS., Branch Files.

7. Walter [White] to Fred [Morrow], November 16, 1939, and Fred [Morrow] to Walter [White], November 22, 1939, both in NAACP MSS., Branch Files.

8. Ibid., December 23, 1939, p. 1. Also, White to Lampkin, January 16, 1940, and Lampkin to Ovington, January 18, 1940, both in NAACP MSS., Branch Files.

9. Memo of E. Frederic Morrow, December 20, 1939, NAACP MSS., Branch Files.

10. Morrow to White, November 14, 1939, NAACP MSS., Branch Files.

11. Memo, Lampkin to Executive Staff, December 21, 1939, NAACP MSS., Branch Files.

12. Memo, Marshall to White, October 11, 1939, NAACP MSS., Branch Files.

13. Pickens to Morrow, December 16, 1939, NAACP MSS., Branch Files.

14. Barnett to Dean [Pickens], December 14, 1939, NAACP MSS., Branch Files.

15. Wilkins to Lampkin, December 14, 1939, NAACP MSS., Branch Files.

16. White to Morrow, November 16, 1939, NAACP MSS., Branch Files.

17. White to Crump, October 6, 1941, NAACP MSS., Branch Files. See also Pickens to Williams, January 17, 1941, NAACP MSS., Branch Files.

18. Pickens to Williams, January 17, 1941, NAACP MSS., Branch Files.

19. Pickens to Williams, January 17, 1941, and Chicago NAACP Final Report, October 31, 1941, both in NAACP MSS., Branch Files.

20. Lampkin to Black, September 3, 1942, NAACP MSS., Branch Files.

21. Oscar C. Brown, Sr., *By a Thread* (New York: Vantage Press, 1983), pp. 4–20.

22. Ibid., pp. 30–32.

23. Ibid, pp. 55, 56, and *49th State Compass,* March 1936 (copy in possession of author).

24. Interviews with Oscar C. Brown, Sr., in Chicago, on August 18, 1984, and March 16, 1987.

25. McGee to White, July 15, 1946, and McGee to Current, November 11, 1946,

both in NAACP MSS., Branch Files. In addition, interview with Mrs. Rachel B. Shands in Chicago on January 8, 1988, by telephone. See also Drake and Cayton, *Black Metropolis*, pp. 390–395, on the role of the "Race Man" in Bronzeville.

26. Baker to McCray, May 28, 1945, NAACP MSS., Branch Files.

27. Wilkins to Harrison, October 28, 1949, NAACP MSS., Branch Files.

28. Press Release, October 26, 1944, NAACP MSS., Branch Files.

29. Press Release, October 30, 1942, NAACP MSS., Branch Files.

30. Chicago NAACP Brochure for 1943, NAACP MSS., Branch Files. Preliminary figures of 17,000 appear in Daisy [Lampkin] to White, November 2, 1945, and near final ones in Wilkins to Oscar [Brown], December 17, 1945, both in NAACP MSS., Branch Files.

31. Lampkin to Brown, June 16, 1943, NAACP MSS., Branch Files.

32. Shands to Young, March 9, 1945, NAACP MSS., Branch Files.

33. *Chicago Bee*, January 30, 1944, p. 1. in Mitchell MSS.

34. Shands to Young, March 3, 1945, and Young to Shands, March 20, 1945, both in NAACP MSS., Branch Files.

35. Flyer, Spring 1945, found in NAACP MSS., Branch Files.

36. Messrs. Jenkins et al., House Bill 353, 64th Illinois General Assembly, March 27, 1945.

37. News Release, NAPE, Chicago Chapter, March 25, 1945, McGee MSS.

38. Shands to Honorable Sirs [Illinois Congressional delegation], March 20, 1945, McGee MSS.

39. Ashby to Dawson, March 20, 1945, McGee MSS.

40. Chicago Branch, A Statement on Rising Prices, October 1947, p. 2, NAACP MSS., Branch Files.

41. Ibid., p. 1.

42. "The Iron Ring of Housing," *The Crisis* (July 1940): 205, 210.

43. *Chicago Defender* reprint of August 2, 1947, NAACP MSS., Branch Files.

44. Ibid., November 16, 1940, pp. 1, 2, 6. The influence of the Hansberry decision on future housing cases was significant. By 1983 "it had been cited in 665 other cases as shown in Shepard's Citator," a major legal reference. The source of this information is Weyand to Blakely, January 22, 1984, a part of Earl B. Dickerson's correspondence (a copy of which is in the author's possession). Other major cases to be consulted in the restrictive covenant struggle are *Corrigan v. Buckley* (1926), *Hurd v. Hodge* (1948), and *Shelley v. Kraemer* (1948).

45. *Chicago Defender*, November 16, 1940, p.1.

46. Ibid., November 30, 1940, p. 6.

47. Ibid., February 15, 1941, p. 2.

48. Interview with Oscar C. Brown, Sr., August 18, 1984, in Chicago.

49. President's Annual Report, December 12, 1947, p. 4, NAACP MSS., Branch Files.

50. Brown to White, February 26, 1945, NAACP MSS., Branch Files.

51. Brochure, "Keep Up the Good Fight," 1943, NAACP MSS., Branch Files.

52. NAACP Bulletin, May 26, 1942, NAACP MSS., Branch Files.

53. Brochure, "Join [the] N.A.A.C.P. Today," 1947, NAACP MSS., Branch Files and "We Say 'No' to Jim Crow," 1945, NAACP MSS., Gen. Office File: CORE.

54. Roy [Wilkins] to Oscar [Brown], July 1, 1944, and Oscar [Brown] to Walter [White], May 17, 1944, NAACP MSS., Gen. Office File: 1944 Annual Conference.

55. Huff to Mitchell, July 26, 1943, and Huff to Mitchell, December 26, 1944, Mitchell MSS. See also William Henry Huff, "Across the Table: The Chicago NAACP," *Chicago World*, December 11, 1943, n.p., in the NAACP MSS., Branch Files.

56. Abernathy to White, December 17, 1943, NAACP MSS., Branch Files.

57. Brown to [NAACP] Board of Directors, May 16, 1943, NAACP MSS., Branch Files.

58. Harry Wesley Morris, "The Chicago Negro and the Major Political Parties, 1940–1948" (M.A. thesis, University of Chicago, 1950), pp. 18, 24, 28f. As the party deserted the New Deal experiment in the late 1930s, jobs with the WPA and other alphabet agencies disappeared. Because of Roosevelt's reliance on his southern white bloc in Congress, civil rights never appeared on his agenda. The gloomy prospect of war was doubly disturbing to blacks because of the segregated nature of the armed services and war industries. Concomitantly, the Republicans pushed the strongest plank they had written on civil rights as part of their supposedly winning platform. The Democrats, not to be outdone, promoted a Negro plank as part of their convention platform for the first time in the party's history. With their work cut out for them, Chicago Democrats resorted to *ad hominem* attacks on the Republican candidate, Wendell Willkie, whose Indiana home town was a recognized hotbed of Negrophobia. The election results showed a Democratic party that was hard pressed to convince black voters of its sincerity and concern for their civil rights. Despite these faults, black Democrats, Alderman Earl B. Dickerson, Second Ward Committeeman William L. Dawson, Congressman Arthur W. Mitchell, and Third Ward Committeeman Michael Sneed, managed to produce a 55.9 percent winning margin for the president. This margin of victory was less than the city's average and clearly indicative of black dissatisfaction with the president and his party. Congressman Mitchell's winning total scraped along at 51.8 percent of the total votes cast in the First Congressional District.

59. For a thorough examination of Eleanor Roosevelt's influence and role, especially nationally, see Weiss, *Farewell to the Party of Lincoln*, ch. 6, as well as Carl T. Rowan, *Dream Makers, Dream Breakers: The World of Justice Thurgood Marshall* (Boston: Little, Brown, 1993), pp. 130–133.

60. Kirk H. Porter and Donald Bruce Johnson, comps., *National Party Platforms, 1840–1960* (Urbana: University of Illinois Press, 1961), p. 412.

61. Ibid.

62. *Chicago Defender*, October 31, 1942, p. 32.

63. Lucas et al., to Lampkin, October 31, 1942, NAACP MSS., Branch Files.

64. Lampkin to White, November 3, 1942, NAACP MSS., Branch Files.

65. Brown to White, November 3, 1942, NAACP MSS., Branch Files.

66. *Chicago Defender,* November 7, 1942, p. 3.

67. *Chicago Defender,* October 31, 1942, p. 32.

8. Democracy at Work, 1946–1953

1. Steele to White, July 15, 1946, and White to Oscar [Brown], July 17, 1946, both in the NAACP MSS., Branch Files.

2. "The National Association for the Advancement of Colored People," *Chicago World,* 3 July 6, 1946, n.p., attached to Occomy to White, July 9, 1946, NAACP MSS., Branch Files.

3. Brown to White, August 14, 1946, NAACP MSS., Branch Files.

4. Interview with Oscar O. Brown, Sr. in Chicago on August 14, 1984.

5. McGee to White, July 15, 1946, and McGee to Current, November 11, 1946, both in the NAACP MSS., Branch Files.

6. Interviews with Henry W. McGee in Chicago on August 18, 1986, and October 31, 1986.

7. Carter to Lucas, March 10, 1945, and Ashby [Carter] to Dawson, March 10, 1945, both in McGee MSS.

8. Baker to McGee, April 10, 1945, and Perry to McGee, May 22, 1945, both in McGee MSS.

9. "Report of the Committee on Permanent FEPC," May 6, 1945, McGee MSS.

10. Interviews with McGee.

11. President's Annual Report, December 12, 1947, NAACP MSS., Branch Files.

12. Henry [McGee] to Thurgood [Marshall], September 2, 1947, NAACP MSS., Branch Files.

13. President's Annual Report, December 12, 1947, p. 3, NAACP MSS., Branch Files, and interviews with McGee.

14. Strickland, *History of the Chicago Urban League,* pp. 163, 172–174. See also Sidney E. Williams, Jr., "Response to Berry Interview," *The [Hyde Park] Herald,* April 17, 1974, p. 10, and "Militant Feels He Has Honored His Ancestors," *Chicago Sun-Times,* March 8, 1982, p. 7.

15. League fund-raising suffered as a result of Williams's militancy. See Strickland, *Chicago Urban League,* pp. 174f.

16. Williams to Brown, March 10, 1947, Chicago Urban League MSS. in the University Libraries, the University of Illinois at Chicago (hereafter referred to as CUL MSS.).

17. President's Annual Report, December 12, 1947, NAACP MSS., Branch Files.

18. Memorandum to Mr. White from Mr. Current, May 7, 1948, NAACP MSS., Branch Files.

19. White to Sherard, July 7, 1948, NAACP MSS., Branch Files.

20. Memo, Smith to Current, November 3, 1948, NAACP MSS., Branch Files.

21. Morris to [Whomsoever], November 17, 1948, NAACP MSS., Branch Files.

22. Memo, Current to White, May 7, 1948, NAACP MSS., Branch Files.

23. Burgess-Robertson to Current, December 4, 1948, NAACP MSS., Branch Files.

24. Current to Branch Officers, December 6, 1948, NAACP MSS., Branch Files.

25. "Counterattack," November 28, 1947, NAACP MSS., Gen. Office File: Counterattack, 1947–1949.

26. Memorandum, Walter White to Branches, January 6, 1948, NAACP MSS., Gen. Office File: Counterattack, 1947–1949. See also White, *A Man Called White*, pp. 345–347.

27. Wilson Record, *The Negro and the Communist Party* (New York: Atheneum / Chapel Hill: University of North Carolina Press, 1951), p. 252. See also comments in *Chicago Defender*, February 22, 1947, p. 2.

28. Minutes of the Special Session, December 30, 1948, p. 5., NAACP MSS., Branch Files.

29. Hill to Kemp, November 30, 1949, NAACP MSS., Branch Files.

30. Birchman to Wilkins, November 28, 1949, and Latimer to Roy [Wilkins], March 21, 1950, both in NAACP MSS., Branch Files.

31. Nelson C. Jackson, *An Evaluation of the Chicago Urban League* (New York: Community Services, National Urban League, May 1955), pp. 53, 54. See also Strickland, *Chicago Urban League*, pp. 179, 180.

32. Douglas to Willis, July 5, 1950, NAACP MSS., Branch Files.

33. Current to Willis, December 28, 1950, NAACP MSS., Branch Files.

34. Riley to Current, March 3, 1950, NAACP MSS., Branch Files.

35. Riley to Wilkins, February 24, 1950, and Riley to Current, March 3, 1950, both in NAACP MSS., Branch Files. See also Current to Dickerson, April 21, 1950, NAACP MSS., Branch Files.

36. "George N. Leighton: A Biographical Sketch" (in the author's possession) and interview with the Hon. George N. Leighton in Chicago on August 25, 1986.

37. Griswold to White, September 10, 1951, NAACP MSS., Gen. Office File: Housing.

38. Roland to Black, December 3, 1951, NAACP MSS., Branch Files. See Willis to Current, November 19, 1951, NAACP MSS., Branch Files, for information on the machinations of Roland's supporters.

39. E. Franklin Frazier, *Black Bourgeoisie* (Glencoe, IL: Free Press, 1957), p. 171. See also the reference to Joseph Robichaux, who was hired by the Schultz Bakery, and whose presence helped increase the sale of Butternut bread throughout the South Side at a time when Butternut sales were down elsewhere in the city, in Quarterly Report, Industrial Department, n.p., January–February–March 1953, CUL MSS., as well as 2nd Quarterly Report of 1953, which detailed extensive employment of 200 persons in sales positions in dairy, whiskey, beer, cigarette, soft drink, and tobacco companies.

40. Frayser T. Lane, "Some Aspects of the Negro Population of Chicago," November 1948, Carey MSS.

41. William Julius Wilson, *The Declining Significance of Race: Blacks and Changing American Institutions* (Chicago: University of Chicago Press, 1974; 2nd ed., 1980), pp. 127–129. See also University of Chicago, Chicago Community Inventory, "Chicago's Negro Population: Characteristics and Trends" (June 1956, mimeographed report), pp. 28–37.

42. Bank Project Brochure, April 4, 1952, Industrial Department Report, CUL MSS.

43. Reports of the Industrial Department for September 1950 and Mid-year 1951, CUL MSS.

44. Bank Project Brochure, April 4, 1952, Industrial Department Report, CUL MSS.

45. Bell to Executive Committee, April 15, 1952, NAACP MSS., Branch Files.

46. Telegram, Bell to White, October 12, 1952, NAACP MSS., Branch Files.

47. *Chicago Defender,* January 17, 1953, p. 1.

48. Rich to White, January 15, 1953, NAACP MSS., Branch Files.

49. *Chicago Defender,* January 17, 1953, pp. 1, 2. See also Johnson to White, January 17, 1953, NAACP MSS., Branch Files.

50. Weaver to Abner, December 17, 1955, NAACP MSS., Branch Files.

51. Leighton to Current, June 12, 1953, NAACP MSS., Branch Files.

52. Bell to White, December 17, 1952, and Willis to Current, February 18, 1953, both in NAACP MSS., Branch Files.

53. Foster to Current, November 16, 1953, NAACP MSS., Branch Files.

54. Birchman to Current, December 29, 1954, NAACP MSS., Branch Files.

55. Huff to Foster, December 11, 1953, NAACP MSS., Branch Files.

56. See, as an example, Duncan to NAACP, February 11, 1945, NAACP MSS., Branch Files.

57. News Release, October 11, 1949, NAACP MSS., Branch Files.

58. Memo, Current to White, May 7, 1948, NAACP MSS., Branch Files.

59. Albright to Current, November 29, 1952, NAACP MSS., Branch Files.

60. *The NAACP Call,* October 23, 1952, NAACP MSS., Branch Files. See also Dempsey J. Travis, *An Autobiography of Black Politics* (Chicago: Urban Research Institute, 1987), p. 131.

61. Henry [McGee] to Gloster [Current], March 21, 1948, NAACP MSS., Branch Files.

62. Memo, Smith to Current, November 3, 1948 (attached to covering letter, "To Officers and Members of the Chicago Branch NAACP," dated December 22, 1948), NAACP MSS., Branch Files.

63. Ming to Leighton et al., February 27, 1952; Memo, Marshall to White and Wilkins, March 28, 1952; and Leighton to White, June 5, 1952, all in NAACP MSS., Branch Files. It appears to have first been the "Operation Civil Rights" banquet; see Program, July 2, 1952, NAACP MSS., Branch Files.

64. Memorandum from Weaver to Chicago Branch, August 22, 1953, NAACP MSS., Branch Files.

65. Treasurer's Report, October 13, 1953, NAACP MSS., Branch Files.

66. Treasurer's Report, October 27, 1953, NAACP MSS., Branch Files.

67. President's Annual Report, December 12, 1947, NAACP MSS., Branch Files.

68. August Meier and Elliott Rudwick, *CORE: A Study in the Civil Rights Movement, 1942–1968* (New York: Oxford University Press, 1973), p. 59.

69. Brown to White, April 24, 1946, NAACP MSS., Branch Files.

70. Ibid.

71. Henry [McGee] to Roy [Wilkins], September 2, 1947, NAACP MSS., Branch Files.

72. Henry W. McGee, President's Report, Annual Report of the Chicago NAACP for 1947, NAACP MSS., Branch Files.

73. "High Prices in Chicago," *The Crisis,* November 1947: 341, 349.

74. Henry W. McGee, President's Report, Annual Report of the Chicago NAACP for 1947, NAACP MSS., Branch Files.

75. *Chicago Defender,* April 5, 1947, p. 1.

76. Memorandum, Smith to Current, November 11, 1948, NAACP MSS., Branch Files.

77. Minutes of the Executive Committee, December 30, 1948, p. 6, NAACP MSS., Branch Files.

78. Martin Meyerson and Edward C. Banfield, *Politics, Planning and the Public Interest: The Case in Chicago* (Glencoe, IL: Free Press, 1955), p. 125.

79. Monthly Report of the Executive Director, Committee on Human Relations, August 1948, CUL MSS. See also *Chicago Defender,* February 22, 1947, p. 1.

80. McGee to Jones, August 12, 1946, NAACP MSS., Branch Files.

81. Reprint from the *Chicago Defender,* August 2, 1947, n.p., in NAACP MSS., Branch Files.

82. Memoranda, White to Marshall and Marshall to White, on February 25, 1946, NAACP MSS., Branch Files.

83. *Chicago Defender,* September 27, 1947, in NAACP MSS., Branch Files.

84. *Chicago Defender,* October 18, 1947, in NAACP MSS., Branch Files.

85. "Alderman Carey's Views on the Non-Discrimination Ordinance for Publicly Aided Housing," 1948, Carey MSS.

86. Meyerson and Banfield, *Politics, Planning,* p. 137.

87. Harold Mayer and Richard C. Wade, *Chicago: Growth of a Metropolis* (Chicago: University of Chicago Press, 1969), p. 376, and Strickland, *Chicago Urban League,* p. 157.

88. Ibid., in both sources.

89. *Chicago Tribune,* July 13, 1951, pt. 1, p. 4.

90. Charles Abrams, *Forbidden Neighbors* (New York: Harper & Bros., 1955), p. 104; "Ugly Nights in Cicero," *Time,* July 23, 1951, p. 10; and "Terror in Cicero," *Newsweek,* July 23, 1951, p. 17.

91. Press Release, from Walter White, September 27, 1951, NAACP MSS., Gen. Office File: Housing, and Abrams, *Forbidden Neighbors,* p. 105.

92. Ibid.

93. Bailey et al. to Executive Committee, July 24, 1951, NAACP MSS., Branch Files.

94. Walter [White] to Walter [P. Offutt], September 6, 1951, NAACP MSS., Branch Files.

95. Meyerson and Banfield, *Politics, Planning,* p. 101.

96. Chicago Commission on Human Relations, "The Trumbull Park Home Disturbances," Report Number 1, August 1953–May 1954, NAACP MSS., General Office File: Housing.

97. Ibid.

98. Ibid.

99. Ibid.

100. Hickman Defense Committee flyer, September 1947, NAACP MSS., Branch Files.

101. Telegram, McGee to Current, October 23, 1947, NAACP MSS., Branch Files.

102. Hickman Defense Committee flyer, September 1947, NAACP MSS., Branch Files.

103. Jackson, *Evaluation of the Chicago Urban League,* p. 60. From the sidelines, Williams also managed to sign a joint communiqué to President Eisenhower with the militant Chicago NAACP condemning a port-of-call visit by the *U.S.S. Midway* to Capetown, South Africa. The stop subjected 400 black naval personnel to the segregation laws of South Africa.

104. Strickland, *Chicago Urban League,* p. 168.

105. Meier and Rudwick, *CORE,* p. 61.

106. Report on Textbooks, Education Subcommittee, Chicago Branch NAACP, Faith Rich Papers, donated to the Chicago Public Library. See also Minutes, Chicago Branch NAACP Executive Committee, December 30, 1948, p. 6, NAACP MSS., Branch Files.

107. John Hope Franklin and John Moss, *From Slavery to Freedom* (New York: Knopf, 1987), p. 412; and Harvard Sitkoff, "Harry S Truman and the Election of 1948: The Coming of Age of Civil Rights in American Politics," *Journal of Southern History* 37 (November 1971): 614, 615.

108. Morris, "The Chicago Negro," p. 91.

109. For an examination of how white politicians handled the politics of race in a setting where black empowerment was a force to be reckoned with and neutralized, see Biles, *Kelly,* as well as Arnold R. Hirsch, "The Cook County Democratic Organization and the Dilemma of Race, 1931–1987," in Richard M. Bernard, ed., *Snowbelt Cities: Metropolitan Politics in the Northeast and Midwest since World War II* (Bloomington: Indiana University Press, 1990), pp. 67–70. See also Green and Holli, *Mayors,* p. 124.

110. *Chicago Defender,* February 13, 1943, p. 14.

111. Ethridge to Early, December 29, 1941; Mac [McIntyre] to Mark [Ethridge],

January 6, 1942; Ethridge to Mac [McIntyre], January 10, 1942; all in Franklin D. Roosevelt Papers, Box 3, Commission on Fair Employment Practices, Hyde Park, New York.

112. Carey to Bishop, January 24, 1947, Carey MSS.

9. At the Apex of Militant Activism, 1954–1957

1. Interview with the Hon. Willie Whiting in Chicago on September 16, 1989. See also "In Support of the reelection of Willoughby Abner . . . ," n.d. [c. December 1957], NAACP MSS., Branch Files.

2. Gruenberg, "Dawson of Illinois: What Price Moderation?" p. 198.

3. Banfield and Wilson, *City Politics,* p. 309.

4. Wilson, *Negro Politics,* p. 126.

5. Interview with Mrs. Beatrice Hughes Steele, September 21, 1989, in Chicago.

6. Weaver to National Office, May 4, 1954, NAACP MSS., Branch Files.

7. Weaver to Gloster [Current], August (no date), 1954, NAACP MSS., Branch Files.

8. Weaver to Moore, December 1, 1955, and Weaver to Current, December 1, 1955, both in NAACP MSS., Branch Files.

9. Report of the Executive Secretary to the Executive Committee, March 12, 1957, NAACP MSS., Branch Files.

10. Press Release, April 8, 1954, and Patton to Willis, June 30, 1954, both in NAACP MSS., Branch Files.

11. Strickland, *History of the Chicago Urban League,* p. 197. See Charles Davis, "Bill Berry: He Did It His Way," *Chicago Sun-Times,* February 16, 1986, pp. 8, 9.

12. Meier and Rudwick, *CORE,* p. 73. By 1958, the Chicago chapter was disaffiliated from its national structure; see p. 83.

13. Interview with Joffre Stewart in Chicago at Roosevelt University on April 15, 1993.

14. Pinderhughes, *Race and Ethnicity in Chicago Politics,* ch. 5, especially pp. 119–126, and pp. 91 and 138 elsewhere. Pinderhughes presents a most substantive treatment to the complex concept of status versus welfare needs in the African American community.

15. Newsletter, Chicago Branch NAACP, February 1954, p. 2, NAACP MSS., Branch Files.

16. Ibid.

17. *Freedom's Call,* April 1954, p. 2, and July 1954, p. 2, both in NAACP MSS., Branch Files.

18. Robert Frederick Burk, *The Eisenhower Administration and Black Civil Rights* (Knoxville: University of Tennessee Press, 1984), p. 112.

19. Press Release, January 25, 1954, NAACP MSS., Branch Files.

20. Press Release, March 9, 1954, NAACP MSS., Branch Files.

21. C. A. D. News, Council against Discrimination, March 1954, p. 2, NAACP MSS., General Office File: Housing.

22. Press Release, March 23, 1954, NAACP MSS., Branch Files.

23. Press Release, April 17, 1954, NAACP MSS., Branch Files.

24. Press Release, April 8, 1954, NAACP MSS., Branch Files.

25. Press Release, May 14, 1954, NAACP MSS., Branch Files.

26. *Freedom's Call,* July 1954, p. 1, NAACP MSS., Branch Files.

27. Press Release, August 2, 1954, NAACP MSS., Branch Files.

28. Press Release, April 26, 1958, NAACP MSS., Branch Files.

29. Press Release, April 26, 1955, NAACP MSS., Branch Files.

30. *Chicago Tribune,* October 26, 1955, p. 21 and Press Release, October 10, 1955, NAACP MSS., Branch Files.

31. Press Release, October 10, 1955, NAACP MSS., Branch Files.

32. Facts Concerning CHA Tenant Selection, 1954, NAACP MSS., General Office File: Housing.

33. "Chicago: Where Whites and Negroes Battle Again," *U.S. News & World Report* 43 (August 7, 1957), pp. 31–33.

34. Statement of Willoughby Abner . . . In re: Calumet Park, September 1, 1957, NAACP MSS., Branch Files.

35. "Equality of Races Means This . . . ," *U.S. News & World Report,* May 28, 1954, p. 25.

36. Report of June 30, 1954, of the Education Committee, Chicago NAACP, NAACP MSS., Branch Files.

37. *Freedom's Call,* January 1955, p. 4, NAACP MSS., Branch Files.

38. Abner to "Dear Friend," August 12, 1957, NAACP MSS., Branch File.

39. Interview with Mrs. Myrtle Brooks on August 1, 1989, in Chicago.

40. "De Facto Segregation in the Chicago Public Schools," September 25, 1957, p. 6, NAACP MSS., Gen. Off. File: Schools.

41. "NAACP on Local Schools: Segregation Is Increasing," *U.S. News & World Report* 43 (December 13, 1957), pp. 88, 89. A relatively recent article in the *Chicago Sun-Times* incorrectly credits Edwin "Bill" Berry with the results accomplished by the Chicago NAACP—February 16, 1986, "Bill Berry: He Did It His Way," pp. 8, 9.

42. Press Release, January 25, 1954, NAACP MSS., Branch Files.

43. "Statement of [the] NAACP on Defense of Equal Job Opportunity," July 2, 1959, NAACP MSS., Branch Files.

44. Press Release, July 2, 1959, NAACP MSS., Branch Files.

45. Edward C. Banfield, *Political Influence* (Glencoe, IL: Free Press, 1961), p. 38.

46. Banfield, *Political Influence,* pp. 18, 41.

47. Gertrude Gorman to Wilkins, August 29, 1957, NAACP MSS., Branch Files.

48. Press Release, October 10, 1955, NAACP MSS., Branch Files.

49. Travis, *Autobiography of Black Politics,* p. 270.

50. *The Crisis* (August–September, 1957): 417.

51. Campaign Letter from Thompson et al. to Dear NAACP Member, "In Support of the Re-election of Willoughby Abner as President...," December 1957, NAACP MSS., Branch Files.

52. See Hirsch, "The Cook County Democratic Organization and the Dilemma of Race," in *Sunbelt Cities*, pp. 75, 76.

53. Memo, Moon to Current, June 6, 1958, NAACP MSS., Branch Files.

54. Leighton to White, April 2, 1952, NAACP MSS., Branch Files.

55. Bernard [Brown] to Lucille [Black], November 26, 1952, NAACP MSS., Branch Files.

56. Gorman to Current, November 11, 1956, NAACP MSS., Branch Files.

57. Flyer, attached to Wilkins to Abner, February 14, 1957 and Abner to Wilkins, January 13, 1957, NAACP MSS., Branch Files.

58. Hanes Walton, Jr., *Black Politics: A Theoretical and Structural Analysis* (Philadelphia: J. B. Lippincott, 1972), pp. 147f., and *Invisible Politics: Black Political Behavior* (Albany: State University of New York Press, 1985), presents a totally new approach to understanding African American political behavior in its many complex, subtle, and misinterpreted forms. NAACP branch activities that were civic were, however, distinguished from those that were in fact political by all definitions. Lobbying and pressure group activities were political. Ira Katznelson's *Black Men, White Cities: Race, Politics, and Migration in the United States, 1900–30, and Britain, 1948–68* (London: Oxford University Press, 1973), pp. 55–61, depicts the NAACP as political as early as its lobbying for the Dyer Anti-lynching Bill in 1922 and assumes this posture was typical when in reality it was atypical.

59. Press Release, January 31, 1955, NAACP MSS., Branch Files.

60. Press Release, March 28, 1956, NAACP MSS., Branch Files.

61. Travis, *Autobiography of Black Politics*, p. 270.

62. Banfield and Wilson, *City Politics*, p. 305.

63. Edward T. Clayton, *The Negro Politician: His Success and Failure* (Chicago: Johnson Publishing, 1964), pp. 77, 78. Also, Dawson was well aware of the limits of his power, according to historian Paul Kleppner, *Chicago Divided: The Making of a Black Mayor* (De Kalb, IL: Northern Illinois University Press, 1985), p. 72.

64. Clayton, *The Negro Politician*, p. 78. Also, Wilson, *Negro Politics*, p. 83.

65. Most representative of this new wave of Chicago political revisionism is William J. Grimshaw, *Bitter Fruit: Black Politics and the Chicago Machine, 1931–1991* (Chicago: University of Chicago Press, 1992), especially chs. 4 and 5.

66. William J. Grimshaw, *Negro Politics in Chicago: The Quest for Leadership, 1939–1979* (Chicago: Loyola University Center for Urban Policy, 1980), pp. 12–14. See also Hirsch, "The Cook County Democratic Organization and the Dilemma of Race," in *Snowbelt Cities*, pp. 79–80.

67. [Charles Sumner] Chuck Stone [II], *Black Political Power in America* (Indianapolis: Bobbs-Merrill, 1968), p. 173.

68. Gruenberg, "Dawson of Illinois: What Price Moderation?" p. 197.

69. John Madigan, Radio Obituary for William L. Dawson, WBBM AM Radio, November 9, 10, 1970.

70. Clayton, *The Negro Politician,* p. 78.

71. Ibid., p. 85.

72. Charles V. Hamilton, *Adam Clayton Powell, Jr.: The Political Biography of an American Dilemma* (New York: Atheneum, 1991), pp. 230–235.

73. Wilson, *Negro Politics,* p. 84. According to August Meier, who has recently written on the views of Charles S. Johnson, another moderate on race, who had both old Chicago ties and a penchant for Booker T. Washington's approach to racial progress, "it was of a type that would have left him totally unprepared for what happened in the 1960s." Thus it was with Dawson, who encountered the winds of change in the 1950s and proved to be a reactionary (in the eyes of his detractors) until his death in 1970. See August Meier, *A White Scholar and the Black Community, 1945–1965* (Amherst: University of Massachusetts Press, 1992), pp. 16, 17, and Wilson, *Negro Politics,* p. 69.

74. Gruenberg, "Dawson of Illinois: What Price Moderation?" p. 198. Also see Travis, *Autobiography of Black Politics,* pp. 270, 271, for an unusual defense of Dawson. Claude A. Barnett wrote of a younger Dawson, "He is a fighter, but level-headed. . . . [Also,] Dawson is popular with the masses." Barnett to Hamilton, May 12, 1938, Barnett Papers, Chicago Historical Society.

75. See Stone, *Black Political Power in America,* pp. 173–178; Stokely Carmichael and Charles V. Hamilton, *Black Political Power in America: The Politics of Liberation* (New York: Random House, 1967), pp. 10–12; Charles E. Silberman, *Crisis in Black and White* (New York: Random House, 1964), pp. 204–207; Wilson, *Negro Politics,* p. 276.

76. Hamilton, *Powell,* chs. 11, 13, 16, and 17.

77. Gorman to Current, September 19, 1957, NAACP MSS., Branch Files.

78. Ibid.

79. Wesley South, "NAACP Foes Answered," n.p., *Chicago American,* November 26, 1957, in NAACP MSS., Branch Files.

80. Interview with Theodore A. Jones on September 23, 1986, in Chicago.

81. Weaver to Current, December 28, 1957, NAACP MSS., Branch Files.

82. Travis, *Autobiography of Black Politics,* pp. 261–264.

83. Nelson C. Jackson, "An Evaluation of the Chicago Urban League (New York: Community Services, National Urban League, May 1955), p. i.

84. Travis, *Autobiography of Black Politics,* p. 264.

85. Wilson, *Negro Politics,* p. 64.

86. Travis, *Autobiography of Black Politics,* p. 270.

10. Epilogue: The Era of the "Civil Rights Revolution," 1958–1966

1. Jones to Wilkins, December 30, 1959, NAACP MSS., Branch Files.

2. Interview with Carter D. Jones, Jr., on August 22, 1989, in Chicago. See also Arnold R. Hirsch, *Making the Second Ghetto: Race and Housing in Chicago, 1940–1960*

(Cambridge: Cambridge University Press, 1983), pp. 193, 194.

3. Hirsch, *Making the Second Ghetto,* ch. 5.

4. Van Goor to Geyer, February 26, 1957, NAACP MSS., Branch Files.

5. Statement of Willoughby Abner . . . in re: Calumet Park, September 1, 1957, NAACP MSS., Branch Files.

6. Archer to Jones, February 11, 1957, p. 8, NAACP MSS., Gen. Off. File: Housing.

7. Hirsch, *Making the Second Ghetto,* pp. 137–139 of ch. 5; the entire chapter covers the Hyde Park situation in detail.

8. Grimshaw, *Black Politics in Chicago,* p. 13.

9. William Braden, "How Daley Handled Racial Issues," *Chicago Sun-Times,* December 11, 1986, pp. 77–79.

10. Press Release, late August 1958, NAACP MSS., Branch Files.

11. Ibid.

12. Tobias to Archer-Lofton, September 18, 1958, NAACP MSS., Branch Files.

13. Travis, *Autobiography of Black Politics,* pp. 261, 262.

14. McAlpin to Current, December 17, 1958, NAACP MSS., Branch Files.

15. *The Crisis* (October 1959): 495.

16. Louis Lomax, *The Negro Revolt* (New York: Harper and Row, 1962), ch. 9, offers an illuminating, detailed account of how far behind the times the highly centralized NAACP had become as direct protest, democratic participation, and economic advocacy grew in the midst of the modern Civil Rights Revolution.

17. "A Statement of the Membership of the Chicago Branch," November 12, 1959, NAACP MSS., Branch Files.

18. Wilkins to Burleigh, December 10, 1959, NAACP MSS., Branch Files.

19. In the preface of the Harper Torchbook edition (1962) of *Black Metropolis,* vol. 2, p. xiii, Drake and Cayton refer to the middle and upper classes as having become complacent by this period. These are the groups which comprised the growing Black Establishment which helped oust Abner in December 1957 and which would only support Dr. King's 1966 Chicago sojourn with lukewarm enthusiasm. In contrast, in the same revised edition, Everett C. Hughes observed in the Torchbook Introduction, vol. 1, pp. xxxviii–xl, that the consumer-oriented middle class was nonviolently militant in pursuit of the American Dream.

20. Charles A. Davis, "In Memory of Edwin C. Berry," *Chicago Defender,* May 30, 1987, p. 18.

21. Travis, *Autobiography of Black Politics,* p. 303.

22. Interview with Dempsey Travis on September 27, 1989, in Chicago.

23. Brown et al. to Fuqua, July 17, 1963, NAACP MSS., Branch Files.

24. See Anderson and Pickens, *Confronting the Color Line,* pp. 105–126.

25. Travis, *Autobiography of Black Politics,* p. 319.

26. Ibid., p. 325.

27. Alvin Pitcher, "The Chicago Freedom Movement: What Is It?" in David J. Garrow, ed., *Martin Luther King, Jr. and the Civil Rights Movement: Chicago, 1966—*

Open Housing Marches, Summit Negotiations and Operation Breadbasket (Brooklyn: Carlson Publishing, 1989), p. 174.

28. Drake and Cayton, *Black Metropolis,* p. 267.

29. Ralph David Abernathy, *And the Walls Came Tumbling Down: An Autobiography* (New York: Harper and Row, 1989), pp. 367, 386, 395, and 399; Travis, *Autobiography of Black Politics,* p. 389; Mary Lou Finley, "The Open Housing Marches: Chicago '66," pp. 18, 34–38 in *Chicago 1966: Open Housing Marches, Summit Negotiations, and Operation Breadbasket;* Mike Royko, *Boss: Richard J. Daley of Chicago* (New York: E. P. Dutton, 1975), p. 154; Len O'Connor, *Clout: Mayor Daley and His City* (Chicago: Henry Regnery, 1975), 191; David L. Lewis, *King: A Critical Biography* (New York: Praeger, 1970), p. 351; and John A. Williams, *The King God Didn't Save* (New York: Coward-McCann, 1970), pp. 97, 98.

30. In 1962, Drake and Cayton (*Black Metropolis,* vol. 2 [New York: Harper Torchbook, 1962]), Preface, pp. xii, xiii, wrote about this generational element, which demonstrated attitudinal and behavioral differences to those persons supporting the Civil Rights Revolution: "The activities of non-violent Freedom Riders must not obscure the fact that among Negro teenagers patterns of violence are prevalent and that embedded in the character of the Negro masses lies a deep vein of suppressed hostility [toward whites and the many manifestations of white racism]."

INDEX

Abbott, Edith, 203n.2
Abbott, Robert S., 16, 32, 41, 45, 54, 59, 73, 80–81, 213n.96
Abernathy, Rev. Ralph David, 180, 245n.29
Abner, Willoughby: as chairman of Chicago NAACP Executive Committee, 6; and Benjamin Bell, Jr., 139; and Labor Committee of Chicago NAACP, 143; and militant activism of Chicago NAACP in 1950s, 161–63, 164–65, 166, 168–69, 177, 180, 183, 184–87, 189–90; and controlled protest policy of Theodore Jones as president of Chicago NAACP, 192
Abolitionism: and neo-abolitionism in early twentieth century, 2; and ideology of racial equality, 5. *See also* Neo-abolitionism
Abrams, Charles, 238n.90–91
Acker, Alberta, 194
Adamowski, Benjamin S., 172
Addams, Jane: influence of on Chicago NAACP, xii, 20–21, 32; and race relations in Progressive-era Chicago, 8, 9, 17, 34, 42; criticisms of position on racial equality, 20, 29, 95, 214n.102; on new Southern migrants to Chicago, 46; lack of civil rights activity in 1930s, 78; citations of, 206n.7, 208n.11, 211n.73
AFL/CIO, 96, 101, 140, 142, 200
African-Americans: historiography of urban history of black Chicago, ix–xii. *See also* NAACP; specific topics
Albright, Joseph F., 142–43
Aldis, Arthur, 27, 30, 31, 47, 64
Allinson, Thomas W., 23, 35
Ambassador Club, 80
Amenia conference (1933), 100
American Civil Liberties Union (ACLU), 85, 178
American Council on Race Relations, 122
American Giants (black professional baseball team), 110
American Jewish Council, 177
American Negro Labor Movement, 74

Anderson, Alan B., 203n.3
Anderson, Louis B., 64, 213n.96, 244n.24
Anti-Defamation League, 141
A & P and National Tea food chains, 101
Appomattox Club, 13, 38, 40, 41, 80, 213n.96
Aptheker, Herbert, 207n.2–3, 208n.6
Armstrong, Louis, 61
Arthur, George, 23, 31, 35
Arts: and culture of Black Metropolis in 1920s, 61
Associated Business Clubs (ABC), 59
Austin, Rev. Arthur, 193–94
Avendorph, Julius, 54
Avery, Sheldon, 203n.4, 219n.4

Bagnall, Robert W., 44, 51, 56, 66, 67, 72, 88–89
Baha'u'llah, Abdul, 39
Bandung Conference (1954), 187
Banfield, Edward C., 163, 178, 184, 205n.5, 238n.78, 86, 239n.95, 240n.3, 241n.45–46, 242n.62
Bankhead, Tallulah, 155
Banks: black-owned in Chicago during 1920s, 59–60; closures of during Great Depression, 75–76
Barber, J. Max, 18, 219n.4
Barnett, Claude A., 112, 172, 243n.74
Barnett, Ferdinand, 19
Bell, Benjamin, Jr., 139–40
Bentley, Dr. Charles E.: and class structure of black Chicago society, x, 29–30, 31; and patriarchal leadership style of Chicago NAACP in Progressive era, 3, 132; on racial antagonism in Progressive-era Chicago, 9; and DuBois, 19; and Julius Rosenwald, 25; and neo-abolitionism, 28; and establishment of Chicago NAACP, 32; and ideology of racial equality, 33; and grievance committee of Chicago NAACP, 35; on segregation of military during World War I, 45; and 1919 reorganization of

Christopher Robert Reed is Professor of History at Roosevelt University. He is also Director of the St. Clair Drake Center for African and African American Studies at Roosevelt and has published on black Chicago history in the *Illinois Historical Journal, Journal of Ethnic Studies, Michigan Historical Review,* and *Journal of Black Studies.*